DENISE LARI
AND JOHN T

ROMAN CATHOLICISM

An Introduction

MACMILLAN PUBLISHING COMPANY

NEW YORK

Collier Macmillan Publishers

LONDON

For Anna M. Carmody

Editor: Helen McInnis
Production Supervisor: George Carr
Production Manager: Nick Sklitsis
Text Designer: Sheree Goodman
Cover Designer: Sheree Goodman

This book was set in Electra by Digitype, printed by Hamilton, and bound by Hamilton. The cover was printed by Phoenix.

Macmillan Publishing Company
866 Third Avenue, New York, New York 10022

Collier Macmillan Canada, Inc.

Library of Congress Cataloging-in-Publication Data

Carmody, Denise Lardner, 1935 –
  Roman Catholicism.
  Bibliography: p.
  Includes index.
  1. Catholic Church — History. 2. Catholic Church —
Doctrines. I. Carmody, John, 1939 – . II. Title.
BX945.2.C37 1990   282'.09   88 – 37289
ISBN 0-02-319390-5

Printing: 1 2 3 4 5 6 7   Year: 0 1 2 3 4 5 6

Preface

This book is an introduction to Roman Catholicism for college undergraduates. Its hallmark is comprehensiveness. By treating Catholic history, worldview, ritual and ethics, and contemporary trends, we hope to suggest the overall shape of the Catholic tradition. Further readings, courses, and private study might sharpen the details, add necessary nuance, and even challenge the contours we have presented. In our view, however, one best begins by intimating the whole, offering an impression of the totality.

The style and viewpoint we have sought reflect the characteristic of Catholicism itself. In style we have sometimes striven for academic detachment, objectivity, and effort to convey information dispassionately — the qualities one associates with "religious studies," wherein one approaches religious phenomena as one would approach phenomena germane to political science or art history. At other times we have suggested the more engaged style of the theologian, whose work traditionally has depended on personal faith and so has borne some of the passion of the lover. This decision about style reflects our own background, which includes both training in religious studies and intense personal involvement with the Catholic tradition.

Concerning viewpoint, we have not concealed our preference for representatives of Catholicism who have been progressive and concerned to translate faith convictions into experiential terms, so that any person of good will might glimpse their rationale. Indeed, in two chapters (13 and 17) we ourselves have attempted such a translation. On the other hand, we have tried to present the good reasons behind traditional and conservative Catholic positions, in part by drawing on our own love for a spiritual tradition that has many spots but few peers.

Our thanks to Helen McInnis, executive editor of Macmillan Publishing Company, for sponsoring the book, and to the students with whom we have discussed Roman Catholicism through the years.

D.L.C.
J.T.C.

CONTENTS

CHAPTER 1

Introduction

On Catholicism
An Orientation to This Book
Glossary, Discussion Questions, Notes

On Catholicism

"Then you did what transcends our understanding—on this night he was resurrected from the dead, on this night he disarmed and conquered death."[1]

Central to Roman Catholicism, as it is to all the other branches of Christianity, is the mystery of Easter, the celebration (remembrance, representation) of Christ's Resurrection. Certainly the life, teaching, works, and death of Jesus of Nazareth might have won him admission to history's roll of spiritual heroes. Certainly the Sermon on the Mount (Mt 5–7), the parables of the Good Samaritan (Lk 10) and the Prodigal Son (Lk 15), and such signs as the raising of Lazarus (Jn 11) never fail to impress people looking for God. But what made Jesus the Christ, the anointed Messiah, and convinced his followers of his divinity was God's turning the defeat of his death into an astonishing victory, God's raising him from the dead and taking him to heaven.

There will be time to discuss the symbolism of these and many other central Christian beliefs. There will be time to suggest some of the different nuances the various Christian churches have placed on them. But it is important to begin our study of Roman Catholicism with the heart of the matter, the crux that no church can deny without forfeiting the name Christian. Ecumenism and "Catholicism" both suggest beginning with this crux.

1

One may hear in the term "Roman Catholicism" something separatist or partial. On the whole, it is not a term Catholics themselves prefer. The "Roman" part is not something Catholics would deny, and certainly some Catholics would go out of their way to stress it. But "Roman Catholicism" carries overtones of polemics between Catholics and Protestants (and, to a lesser extent, between Catholics and Eastern Orthodox). This is especially so when Protestants drop the "Catholic" part and simply speak of "Romans."

Such polemics, of course, cut several ways. Catholics sometimes have become triumphal about their ties to Rome. Catholics have sometimes implied, or said outright, that Protestants had no claim to the word "Catholic" because Protestants had willfully tried to fracture the wholeness, as well as the unity, of the Church. Fortunately, however, polemics among the different Christian churches have lessened in the past half-century. Since the Protestant ecumenical movement that culminated in the creation of the World Council of Churches in 1948, and the Catholic renewal accomplished during the Second Vatican Council of 1962–65, the shamefulness, indeed the sinfulness, of the separation and squabbling among the churches has become clear to most Christian groups and lessened their enthusiasm for polemics.

Ecumenism, which may be understood as the movement to bring the separated churches back to all the union their consciences will allow, has focused on what Christians hold in common. At its best, ecumenism has stressed how Catholics, Orthodox, and Protestants all have sinned, fallen short of God's glory, and failed to realize they owe everything good in themselves to the graciousness of God that is most powerfully manifest in Christ's Resurrection.

A second reason for attending at the outset to the **paschal** victory of Jesus, his passover from death to life, relates to the import of the word "Catholic" itself. Most commentators derive this word from two Greek words, *kata* and *holos*. *Kata* means "according to" or "referring to." *Holos* means "the whole." So "Catholic" doctrine is that held by, and so pertaining to, the whole of the Christian assembly. The Church is "Catholic" because in all places and at all times a constant reality has given the Church its essential identity: the life made available by the resurrection of Christ. Traditionally, "Catholicity" has been considered to be one of the four distinctive marks of the Church. When classical theologians thought about the true Church (in contrast to groups formed by heretics or **schismatics**), they agreed that the Church was one, holy, catholic, and **apostolic**.

Taken as such an essential mark, Catholicism or Catholicity has thus been appealing to all Christians. Eastern Christians — Greeks, Russians, Syrians, and others — all have thought of themselves as catholic. Protestants, especially such giants as Luther, Calvin, Zwingli, and Wesley, all thought their work was purifying the common faith, restoring the original sense of Christ that had existed always and everywhere in the early Church. The Catholicity of the Church, as Avery Dulles's recent D'Arcy lectures have shown, implies something central to all Christians' self-conception.[2] When Roman Catholics claim this term, they should realize that the Jesus of John 17, making his plea for Christian unity, would take no delight in their making it a cause of division.

The focus in this book shifts between the broad denotation of Catholicism, which orients one to the common faith, the mainstream beliefs and practices that have prevailed throughout the two thousand years of Christian history, and the narrow denotation, which calls to mind only those Christians in communion with the bishop of Rome (the pope). Some of what is expressed here will be acceptable to virtually all Christians, because it is grounded in the New Testament, the ecumenical councils, and the general sense of the faithful that furnish all Christians their basic patrimony. But the lens through which we will look, the form of Christian faith and practice in which we are most interested, will usually be that of Roman Catholicism.

Roman Catholicism alone amounts to a vast community and corporate empire. The 1988 *Britannica Book of the Year*, in which statistics on membership in the world's religious traditions tend to be conservative, lists the number of Roman Catholics at over 925 million and finds them living in 242 of the 254 countries of the world. If the total number of Christians overall is about 1,644 million, or nearly 33 percent of the world's population, Roman Catholics make up about 18.5 percent of the world's population. That means that more than one out of two Christians is a Roman Catholic, and more than one out of every six people now living claims the Roman Catholic faith.

To give some basis for comparison, Protestants now number about 332 million (not counting the roughly 70 million Anglicans), whereas Eastern Orthodox number about 160 million. There are more Roman Catholics than there are Muslims (860 million), Hindus (656 million), and Buddhists (310 million). There are even more Roman Catholics in the world than there are people who call themselves nonreligious (836 million) or atheists (225 million). Christians who wonder at the intensity of Jewish fears about anti-Semitism in the New Testament, or the historic policies of the major churches such as the Roman Catholic against the Jews, need to recall not only the history of Christian persecution of Jews but also the small size of the worldwide Jewish community: slightly more than 18 million. That means that for every Jew there are more than 50 Roman Catholics, to say nothing of all the other Christians.[3]

Whereas these figures arguably may carry several different implications, they suggest the inherent difficulty of any work on Roman Catholicism that attempts to be both brief and comprehensive. "Roman Catholicism" is a gigantic entity, vast in its population, geographical spread, and extension through time. There have been many different Roman Catholicisms, as Italians have differed from

Americans, and Latins have differed from Poles. The Medievals have thought and prayed differently than either Christians of the earliest centuries or moderns. This work therefore can only be a beginning, a sketch, an invitation to the diligent to move on and learn much more.

An Orientation to This Book

Our discussion of modest expectations provides an initial orientation to this book. What we propose is an overview — one interpretation of the Roman Catholic whole. Referring to our discussion of the overtones of the word "Catholic," we could say we hope to be catholic in our treatment of Romanism — to capture the whole, the essence, the crux. Ideally, we will also suggest enough of the differences among various groups of Roman Catholics, enough of the historical, ethnic, and sexual shadings, to remind both ourselves and our readers that the whole always has been filtered through partial appropriations. For example, Hispanic Christianity has been Catholic differently than Polish Christianity has been.

Still, we remain convinced that the best results of a text such as this occur when the writers try to give their students a solid overview, a mock-up of the big picture. Then students can gain the context, the framework, in which to place any further information they acquire, any further pondering of the main Catholic convictions. In the beginning, we believe, one should take first things first. The first things necessary for understanding Roman Catholicism are the fundamentals, the basic patterns, of such dimensions as its history, its worldview, its practical side (ritual and ethics), and its current features, interests, and trends.

These, then, are the four parts of our treatment. We begin with a capsule of the history of Roman Catholic Christianity. All periodizations of history are liable to criticism, but for our purposes a standard division into biblical, patristic/ medieval, Reformation, and modern periods seems wise and easily defended. The biblical period gives the earliest foundations: the Jewish and Hellenistic background, the person of Jesus himself, the earliest understandings of Christian faith, and the rise of features that later history would think of as distinctly Catholic. In the second historical period, in which patristic and medieval features are joined, Catholic Christianity becomes well established in the Greco-Roman world and then takes on such medieval features as the papacy, scholasticism, a well-developed monasticism, and alienation from Eastern Orthodoxy.

In dealing with the period between medieval Christianity and modern Catholicism, we focus on reform, both that of the Protestants who bitterly attacked Roman corruptions and that of the Catholics who regrouped to carry out the changes legislated at the Council of Trent. For the modern period we stress such factors as science, the Enlightenment, revolutionary socialism, and industrialization, which collectively created a new, in many ways post-Christian culture that put Catholicism on the defensive. We also consider the development of American Catholicism.

As a way of trying to concretize the spirit of Catholicism in each of these historical periods, we devote a section to what one might call a "representative personality." Just as other authors legitimately might structure their historical presentation of Catholicism into different periods than those we have chosen, so other authors legitimately might bring forward different people to represent a given era. The people we have chosen — Paul and John for the New Testament era, Augustine for the patristic/medieval period, Ignatius Loyola for the period of Catholic reform, and Pope John XXIII for the modern period — are not typical in the sense of average. None is an everyman. But reflecting on each of these men should humanize the discussion of what was happening in the historical era to which he belonged.

Our second angle onto the Catholic whole takes us to considerations of the Catholic worldview — the Catholic sense of reality, of how nature, society, the self, and divinity are configured. The four topics we have chosen to expose the Catholic worldview carry names from traditional Catholic theology: creation, incarnation, redemption, and eschatology. Creation, which bears on where the physical world and its inhabitants came from and how they arose, lays down a fundamental thesis, the influence of which would be hard to overestimate in Catholic Christian faith: we are not our own, God has more to say about ourselves and our world than we do. So whether it be the biblical account of creation one finds in Genesis 1–3, or such related topics as the Catholic senses of revelation, ecology, and history, the stress remains the implications of being a creature, one sprung from nothingness by the fiat of God's love.

Catholic Christianity, above all, is incarnational, probably deriving its distinctive stress on sacramentality and the goodness of this-worldly existence from its profound sense that if the Word has taken flesh, nothing human is to be despised. The **Christology** characteristic of typical Catholic theologians has owed more to John than to Paul (in contrast to typical Protestant theology, where Paul has had the greater influence), whereas the Catholic sense of the biblical God has stressed both God's trinitarian nature and the graciousness of God in making divine favor abound over all human sin. Thus the main song of the traditional Easter liturgy has called Adam's sin a "happy fault" (*felix culpa*), because it merited such a redeemer as Christ. The distinctively Catholic emphases in ecclesiology and sacramental theology finally have appealed to a similar sense of God's embrace of the totality of human existence through the incarnation.

In dealing with redemption, we illustrate Catholic views of human finitude, sin, and death to illumine such typical attitudes as the medieval master Thomas à Kempis' counsel *memento mori*: always remember you are soon to die. Balancing this has been the memory of the Resurrection, which Catholics have seen as the concrete, personal pledge of God not only that God the Father vindicated what Jesus had preached and been but also that all who share Christ's life, through membership in his Body the Church, can look forward to a similar complete vindication.

The last topic we study in probing the Catholic worldview deals with teleology: the end of life, as Catholic Christians have conceived it, the last things (eschatology). Thus we discuss the notion that life is a pilgrimage, if not simply a valley of tears, and ought to be held lightly, in view of the eternal destiny God has laid before all human beings. We also discuss the Catholic sensibility regarding Judgment by God, heaven, and hell.

As in our dealing with Catholic history, we illustrate each of these four aspects of the traditional Catholic worldview by considering a concrete yet representative personage: Julian of Norwich for creation, Thomas Aquinas for incarnation, Francis of Assisi for redemption, and Dante Alighieri for eschatology.

Our third treatment of the Catholic essentials takes us to ritual and ethics. First, we consider communal worship or liturgy, discussing the liturgical year, baptism, the Mass, and the **sacramentals** that have flavored Catholic piety. To personify the implications of Catholic ritual, we describe the liturgical life of Kurt Reinhardt, an aged Catholic we came to know and treasure as a living embodiment of a millennial tradition. Second, we deal with private prayer, discussing the contemplative life that Catholicism has always treasured, the characteristic features of Catholic mysticism, and such traditionally important foci of private devotion as the Rosary prayed to the Virgin Mary and the cult of the saints. Saint Teresa of Avila, an officially recognized authority on the mystical life, is our exemplary figure.

In dealing with Catholic ethics, we discuss such aspects of social ethics as biblical views, the doctrine of natural law, questions about the just war, and questions about human rights, striving for a blend of past and recent characteristics. Mother Teresa of Calcutta serves as our window onto the personal implications that Catholic social ethics might carry. To suggest what Catholics have been taught about personal, individual ethics, we explain the concepts of mortal sin and venial sin, Catholic views in the vexed area of sexuality, and the virtues of poverty and obedience that have been hallmarks of Catholic **religious life**. Bernard Lonergan, an influential, contemporary Catholic theologian, is our representative figure in this chapter.

History, worldview, and considerations of Catholic ritual and ethics might suffice to suggest what Catholicism has been, but all healthy Christians think of their faith as something alive, a matter of the present, so we have felt obliged to indicate major trends in present-day Roman Catholicism. No doubt, one would have to update this part every five years, but at the present time discussions of Catholic thought about peace and justice, Catholic feminism, the rapidly developing internationalism of the Catholic community, and political tensions within the Catholic community seem to us to create a good range of topics for suggesting recent developments. Issues of peace and justice take us to the teachings of Vatican II on the role of the Church in the modern world, to liberation theology, to the encyclical teaching of Pope John Paul II, and to the pastoral letters of the American Catholic bishops on nuclear arms and the U.S. economy. Mary Harren, a Catholic political activist we know, is our representative figure.

In dealing with feminism, we review the misogynism in the Catholic tradition, discuss recent Catholic debates about the ordination of women and abortion, and describe the emphases of an emergent Catholic women's spirituality. Rosemary Haughton, one of the most gifted present-day spiritual writers, is our representative figure.

To suggest the significance of internationalism, we explain the demographics of Catholic Christianity in the Third World, describe recent Catholic interest in an increasing dialogue with non-Christian religions, examine Catholic interests in such areas of conflict as Central America, Ireland, and the Middle East, and consider Catholic relief efforts aimed at alleviating world hunger. Karl Rahner, a very influential contemporary Catholic theologian, is our representative figure, largely because of the internationalist view of the Church he developed toward the end of his life.

Our last contemporary topic, political tensions in the Church, deals with Catholics who have fallen away from official Church membership, Roman attempts to tighten discipline regarding both faith and morals, the clamor of women and people of color to receive a better hearing, and recent Catholic attitudes toward ecumenism. Throughout we witness a deep tension between liberals and conservatives, and Edward Schillebeeckx, a leading theologian and critic of Roman authority, is our representative figure.

The Conclusion, as brief as this Introduction, discusses what we find to be the heart of Catholic Christianity and what we think this tradition must do if it is to prosper in the future.

Glossary

Apostolic: pertaining to the twelve apostles (and Paul) who were the primary companions of Jesus and formed the council that guided the decisions of the Christian community immediately after Jesus' death.

The Church soon came to think that a direct link ("apostolic succession") with these privileged witnesses was important to its authority and doctrinal purity, and so apostolicity became one of the marks of what orthodox Christians considered the true Church.

Christology: study and teaching concerned with explaining the nature and functions of Jesus Christ. Classical Catholic Christology has taken its lead from the councils of Nicaea (325) and Chalcedon (451), which developed what they took to be biblical teaching and long-standing tradition into articles of faith about the divinity and humanity of Jesus the Christ. Summarily, he has been held to be one person (an integral whole) with two natures (human and divine), although the key terms in this summary, "person" and "natures," require sophisticated handling if one is to maintain the balance Catholicism has thought ideal.

Paschal: concerning the Easter mysteries, from Holy Thursday to Christ's Ascension and sending of the Spirit at Pentecost. The word comes from the Jewish term for passover (*pesach*) and reminds us that the New Testament authors self-consciously assimilated the sufferings, death, and resurrection of Jesus to the primary Jewish feast of his (and our) day, the commemoration of the Hebrews' liberation from Egypt under the leadership of Moses. For the New Testament that liberation, the Exodus, was a type (prefiguring) of the spiritual liberation — freeing all humankind from sin — accomplished through Jesus' death and resurrection.

Religious life: the official, consecrated way of life embraced by Catholic men (priests and brothers) and women (nuns) who take public vows of poverty, chastity, and obedience, usually according to a "Rule" of a founding figure, such as Benedict of Nursia or Francis of Assisi, and in the context of a communal life shared with others living under the same vows and rule. "Religious," as Catholics often have called such people, have made gigantic contributions to the preaching, teaching, medical, and other public works of the Church, and they have been considered great sources of grace through their regular prayers.

Sacramentals: objects that Catholics traditionally have used in their devotional lives, such as holy water, palm branches blessed on Palm Sunday, and ashes signed on their foreheads at the beginning of Lent (the period of penance forty days prior to Easter). One may distinguish between such objects and the seven sacraments accredited in Catholic doctrine and liturgical life: baptism, confirmation, the Eucharist, penance, last anointing, matrimony, and holy orders. The sacramentals share with the sacraments the property of being material signs for God's communication of grace (divine life, divine favor).

Schismatics: those who separate themselves from the institutional authority and political unity of the Church. In contrast to heretics, who separate over questions of doctrine, schismatics separate over questions of institutional authority. Heresy and schism may be intertwined and at some point "institutional authority" becomes a doctrinal matter. But traditional Catholic theology found it useful to separate the two different sources of disunion, implying that both an overly independent mind and an unsubmissive will could be sources of unrest and fragmentation.

Discussion Questions

1. Why would Protestant and Eastern Orthodox Christians on occasion proclaim their churches catholic?
2. What does the size, geographical spread, and historical duration of Roman Catholicism suggest about its complexity?
3. What might a more comprehensive treatment of Roman Catholicism add to our considerations of Catholic history, worldview, ritual and ethics, and contemporary trends?
4. What is the function of the representative figures we intend to describe and what do they suggest about how Catholicism has functioned as a living religious tradition?

Notes

[1] Huub Oosterhuis, *Your Word Is Near* (New York: Newman Press, 1968), p. 93.
[2] Avery Dulles, *The Catholicity of the Church* (Oxford: Clarendon Press, 1985 [pb 1987]).
[3] *1988 Britannica Book of the Year* (Chicago: Encyclopaedia Britannica, 1988), p. 303. It bears noting that these statistics say nothing about the depth of the religious allegiance of the people enumerated. Many may be only nominal Catholics, as many may be only nominal Protestants, Orthodox, Muslims, Hindus, Buddhists, or Jews.

PART I

Catholic History

CHAPTER 2

The Biblical Period

The Jewish Heritage
The Greek Heritage
Jesus of Nazareth
The Synoptic Theologies
Early Catholicism
Representative Personalities: Paul and John
Conclusion: The Allure of Jesus
Glossary, Discussion Questions, Notes

The history of Catholicism officially is not separable from the history of Christianity at large until 1054, when the Western and Eastern parts of Christendom **anathematized** one another. Both parts continued to think of themselves as possessing Catholic or holistic faith, and, apart from a few relatively minor doctrinal and disciplinary differences, each was prone to admit the Catholicity of the faith of the other. Still, linguistic, political, and other cultural variances had long conspired to make the Christianity of the two realms perceptibly different. The Latin of the West produced a theology and worldview that did not completely coincide with the theology and worldview produced by the Greek of the East. The Western tension between pope and emperor had no exact counterpart in the East, where the emperor's self-conception included rule in the Church. Although both wings of Christendom had gorgeous liturgies and influential monastic institutions, the East was more interested in grace as the divine life spread through the world to work **divinization**, whereas the West concentrated more on how grace helps people overcome their sinfulness.

Nonetheless, both areas of Christendom traced their history back to the New Testament and to the era when the followers of Jesus were a small, sometimes persecuted group within the Roman Empire, considered by imperial officials as merely a Jewish sect. If the East seemed more clearly in continuity with the Hellenistic culture that prevailed throughout most of the Roman Empire, the West had thoroughly absorbed both the Hellenistic thought forms and the Christian theology that the early Church fathers, the apologists and conciliar theologians, had fashioned by reflecting on their New Testament faith in Greek philosophical categories. What is said in this first chapter, therefore, generally applies as much to Eastern Orthodoxy as to Roman Catholicism. Still, there are seeds of what later became distinctively Roman Catholic themes and attitudes even in the biblical foundations, as we shall indicate.

The Jewish Heritage

The Jewish heritage that shaped Jesus, the apostles, and the writers of the New Testament was nearly eighteen hundred years old. Abraham, who is usually accounted the father of Jewish faith, was nearly as distant in time from Jesus as Jesus is from ourselves. To the Jews of Jesus' day, Abraham had begun the special relationship (covenant) with God that came to full flowering with Moses and the giving of the Torah (Law, Guidance) on Mount Sinai. The distinctive mark of Abrahamic religion was its call to faith, an attitude of complete trust in God. From the flesh of Abraham and Sarah came Isaac and Jacob, the patriarchs who continued to wrestle with the promises of the strange god YHWH.

The Exodus from Egypt that YHWH accomplished through Moses, the giving of the Torah on Mount Sinai, the wandering in the desert for a generation, and the consummation of YHWH's promises by the entry into the promised land under Joshua constitute the next great phase of Jewish history. The Exodus may be placed around 1250 B.C.E. It has stood throughout subsequent Jewish history as the central paradigm of God's power and intent to liberate the chosen people from slavery (of all sorts). The Exodus provided the great impetus to solidify a monotheistic faith, making it clear that YHWH was not just one of the gods but the sole God, while the giving of the Torah provided Israel (as the people descended from the twelve offspring of Jacob, whose name was changed to Israel, was called) with a constitution spelling out the implications of its covenant with God. The Covenant Law has proliferated throughout Jewish history, but even in Jesus' day it was a comprehensive set of instructions for how to sanctify all aspects of life.

Set in the promised land, Israel went through a period when rule was in the hands of charismatic leaders called Judges and then, under Saul, David, and Solomon, enjoyed a time of monarchical consolidation. Later Jewish faith idealized David as the sacral representative (anointed King) to whom God had sworn an everlasting covenant, and it made Jerusalem, the city of David, the center of God's universe. After Solomon the kingdom split apart, and the regular refrain of the biblical historians is that the reason for the troubles of both Israel (the North) and Judah (the South) was infidelity — not keeping the laws of the covenant, especially the injunctions to pure cult (no idolatrous worship of foreign gods) and social justice. The prophets who complemented the biblical historians and sometimes overlapped with them saw the fall of Israel to Assyria in 721 as just reward for its immoralities, and they read out the same message to Judah when it fell to Babylon in 586.

Still, the experience of nearly fifty years of exile in Babylon caused some of the greatest prophets — Jeremiah, Ezekiel, Second Isaiah (Chapters 40 – 55) — to rethink their covenantal theology. All became convinced that God somehow would restore the chosen people, by giving at least a remnant a new covenant written in their hearts, or by giving their dry bones flesh, or by sending them an anointed king (a messiah). When the Persians freed the Jews to return to Judea in 539, these convictions seemed vindicated. It is hard to overestimate the influence of the prophets on Jesus, who took their concern for the poor and their trust in God's providence completely to heart.

The five hundred years between the return from exile and the coming of Jesus were dominated by such events as the rebuilding of the Temple (the center of worship in Jerusalem that the Babylonians had destroyed), the purification of the people from foreign influences (largely through a prohibition on intermarriage with non-Jews), the renewal of the cultic and ethical prescriptions of the Mosaic Torah, and various struggles to preserve Jewish identity while living as part of a foreign empire. The Wisdom literature prominent in the third part of **Tanak** reflects Jewish efforts to appropriate viable aspects of foreign culture and to integrate them with the faith laid out in the Torah and the Prophets. For the New Testament writers, Jesus embodied divine Wisdom.

When the Greeks, under Alexander the Great, conquered Palestine in 333 B.C.E., the Jews had to adapt to new political and cultural influences. The crisis latent in this adaptation came to boil during the rule of Antiochus IV Epiphanes (175 – 164 B.C.E.), who tried to paganize Jewish worship. The revolt led by the Maccabees gave the Jews a period of self-rule, but by 63 B.C.E. the Romans had established themselves as the controlling power in Palestine.

Along with the changes in Jewish sensibility worked by interactions with the Persian and Greek cultures, Jewish rabbis had been interested in continuing to develop the indigenous heritage left them in the Mosaic Law. The experience of exile had somewhat shifted the center of Jewish life from the worship carried out in the Jerusalem Temple to study of the Torah and effort to make the Torah penetrate all of daily life. Jewish groups varied in the way they understood the Torah, as they varied in their opinion of how much Judaism ought to borrow from Gentile cultures or how closely Jews ought to collaborate with foreign masters, but by the time of Jesus the rabbinic emphasis on studying the Torah (which was to become the backbone of Judaism throughout the Common Era [A.D.]) was well established. In Jesus' day the Pharisees were the party most committed to making observance of the Torah all-important, and the Pharisaic interpretation of Jewish religion serves the New Testament as the main foil for Jesus' innovative teachings.

If we step back to ask about the radical impact of this Jewish heritage on Catholic Christians, several features stand out. First, the Jewish instinct that culture and religion ought to marry or suffuse one another mutually appears in the Catholic desire to make a Christendom, a realm where a Catholic brand of convenanted life might flourish. Second, Jewish Torah, as well as Roman law, led to the Roman Catholic desire to regulate moral and doctrinal life rather strictly. Third, the Jewish priesthood, dedicated to the cult that centered in the Jerusalem Temple, shaped the Catholic priesthood, giving it many of its ideas about sacrifice and the purity required of priests. The New Testament's Epistle to the Hebrews, for example, which interprets the work of Christ against the background of the Jewish priesthood, helped to make the sacrifice of the Mass the center of Catholic piety.[1]

The Greek Heritage

Whereas the worldview of Jesus, the apostles, and many of the New Testament writers was mainly Jewish, the influence of Hellenistic (post-classical Greek) culture was significant, as was the influence of Roman military rule. Greek was the most important language throughout the Mediterranean world, and the Greek views of nature, family life, and religion all pressed upon the writers of the New Testament, who either wrote their gospels and epistles in Greek or soon saw them translated, edited, and circulated in Greek.

The dream of Alexander the Great (356–323 B.C.E.) had been to establish an ecumenical, worldwide empire that would unite various ethnic groups. Alexander had thought that reason, shared by all human beings, might be developed in all his imperial subjects sufficiently to establish a common mind (*koinonia*). And whereas the epoch-making era of the classical Greek dramatists (Aeschylus, Sophocles, Euripides) and philosophers (Socrates, Plato, Aristotle) had passed, the influence of such later developments as Neoplatonic thought, the thought of the Stoics, and the thought of the Epicureans was strong on such cultured Jews of the first century as Paul of Tarsus.

Jesus himself shows few signs of having studied Greek thought, but the Hellenistic dimension in the writings of Paul, John, Luke, and others makes it impossible to consider the New Testament a purely Jewish work. Indeed, Catholic Christianity received a Jesus Christ interpreted through Greek as well as Jewish categories. If for Matthew, Jesus was the new Moses, the Messiah, and the one who fulfilled Jewish prophecy, for John, Jesus was the Logos (Word, Speech, Expression) of God incarnate. If for Mark, Jesus was a suffering savior, in combat with Satan and possessed of the authority from God to reinterpret Torah, for Luke, the Church had expanded from Jerusalem to Rome, the capital of the Gentile world, and Gentiles formed in Hellenistic culture were the Church's future.

The overall impact of both the Hellenism predominating in the Mediterranean world and the Gentile character of much of the Church by the end of the first century c.e. quickly took Catholic Christianity apart from its Jewish matrix. Paul had struck the first blow toward severing the umbilical cord by opening the covenant to the Gentiles without requiring them to become circumcised (undergo the Jewish rite of entry into the covenant) or to assume the burdens (many Jews might have said the privileges) of the Torah. Paul worked out his principal theological categories in dialectic with Jewish ideas about election, the covenant, sin, and grace, but the Pauline school (followers a generation after Paul) responsible for such epistles as Colossians and Ephesians were as interested in Hellenistic notions of the fullness of divinity and the spread of divinity throughout the natural world as they were in specifically Jewish ideas about redemption. As in the gospel of John the Word is an eternal principle existing in heaven with God before the foundation of the physical world, so in the great Pauline epistles the Word or Son is the one in whom all of creation holds together, as well as the one whose cross reconciled all humanity to God.

Greek speculation about the law running throughout nature (including human nature) helped the early Christians to think about what God required of them, and it gave Catholic Christianity a confidence it has never lost in both the powers of God-given reason and the intelligibility of creation, enabling Catholics to withstand the Protestant Reformers' attacks on reason. Greek patriarchalism combined with Jewish patriarchalism to give all Christian women a heritage in which they were supposed to be submissive to men, as one can see from the household codes of Colossians 3:18–4:1, 1 Peter 2:11–3:12, and Ephesians 5:212–33.[2]

The mystery religions active in the Hellenistic world pressured early Christianity to explain how its faith might generate a passage into immortality and how its mysteries were sources of spiritual illumination. Greek pedagogy suggested that Christian maturation in faith should be a disciplined submission not only to the Spirit of Christ but also to the precepts of the Church. Key moments in the Christian liturgy were designated by Greek terms that carried rich overtones: the anamnesis (memorial) brought Christ's saving person and action into the present, the anaphora (eucharist prayer) offered the eucharistic elements (bread and wine) to God, and the words used to designate the liturgical assembly of the faithful (*synaxis*) as well as the Church generally (*ekklesia* — those called forth) were redolent of the usage of Hellenized Jews.

Perhaps the principal difference between the Greek heritage assumed by early Christianity and the Jewish heritage lay in the Greek contrast between spirit and body. Jewish religion had kept spirit and body together, eventually speaking not of an immortality for the soul but of a resurrection for the whole body-spirit composite. Greek thought was more dualistic, being fascinated by the mind and deeply impressed by the mortality of the flesh. Plato and Aristotle had charted the dynamic movements of the mind, realizing that divinity itself, the "beyond" that gives the mind its sense of limit and proper proportion, is what lures the mind forward into the light. Plato finally spoke of the human vocation as striving to become as much like God as possible, whereas Aristotle made contemplation of the deity that is the prime mover of all things in existence the personality's highest vocation. Although these theses of classical Greek thought did not directly impinge on the New Testament, they were revived in later Christian periods, Neoplatonism influencing both many of the Greek fathers and Augustine, and Aristotelianism becoming a powerful force among the medieval scholastics.

In the biblical period, Greek dualism sat awkwardly astride Jewish holism, leaving many New Testament discussions of the relations between flesh and spirit open to several interpretations. Both systems tended to downplay the flesh, but whereas Jewish thought made "flesh" the downward, world-enmeshed experience of the entire person bereft of God's grace, Hellenistic thought made flesh or matter something separable from spirit (mind, will, soul erotic for God) and so potentially despicable. Thus Pauline theology recognized that whereas the crucifixion of Christ was a stumbling block for the Jews, who thought that anyone hung from a tree was cursed by God, for Greeks it was foolishness: divinity would never be so ensnared in matter as to suffer pain and indignity. The Gnostics, whom Christianity had to battle in the second and third centuries, perpetuated this Greek line of thought. To their mind the problem that any savior had to solve was humanity's imprisonment in matter, so those Gnostics who called themselves Christians interpreted Jesus as the bringer of a secret knowledge that could liberate the spiritual (divine) sparks in the human being from their material prison.

In reaction to the Greek protest against the notion that God literally had taken flesh, being born, suffering, dying, and resurrecting, New Testament writers such as the author of I John went out of their way to stress Jesus' complete enfleshment or humanity: "Something which has existed from the beginning, that we have heard, and we have seen with our own eyes; that we have watched and touched with our hands: the Word, who is life — that is our subject. That life was made visible: we saw it and we are giving our testimony, telling you of the eternal life which was with the Father and has been made visible to us" (1 Jn 1:1–2).[3]

The Roman Catholic insistence on the validity of using matter to worship God derives from early Christian convictions such as that laid down at the beginning of 1 John. When this incarnational principle came under attack in Eastern Christianity, during the controversy about the use of icons, the response was the same: the iconoclasts were finally denounced as heretics. Judaism, Islam, and many Protestant traditions have never been comfortable with this incarnational response to the problem set by Christianity's Greek heritage. For them any representation of God or of things divine is an invitation to idolatry. But Catholics and Orthodox have pointed to the Incarnation as warrant for disagreement. If divinity itself had taken flesh and made flesh the prime means of its self-revelation, Christians ought to look upon all of God's creation as matter that the Spirit could make into means of grace.

Jesus of Nazareth

All discussions of the person, teaching, and activities of Jesus of Nazareth are bedeviled by what historians and New Testament scholars call "critical" questions. The present consensus among scholars is that there is no simply historical Jesus — no figure treated as an ordinary man by the records from which historians try to reconstruct figures from the past. The New Testament documents, which are the primary historical sources, assume throughout a faith in Jesus, believing that he was God's anointed messenger and servant, God's "Christ." Thus, contemporary scholars tend to avoid efforts to write biographies of Jesus, or even studies of what Jesus himself taught (prior to the reworking of his parables and explanations by those who fashioned the New Testament). Any simple opposition of the Jesus of history to the Christ of faith seems doomed to failure on critical grounds — i.e., by the nature of the sources one must use. All the portraits of Jesus that have come down to us interpret him in light of his Resurrection. The end of his story has shaped how the authors present his beginnings — for example, the narratives about his infancy. In trying to summarize Catholic Christological themes rooted in the New Testament, we therefore have stressed what one finds in the gospels, not venturing very far into the tangled matter of what Jesus himself thought about his work and his status.

The Catholic approach to Jesus of Nazareth has not been monolithic. Because the different writers of the New Testament, to say nothing of the Church fathers, had stressed various aspects of Jesus' person, teaching, and work, Catholic Christianity began with a sense that one could never compress the wealth of Jesus' import into a narrow band of images or doctrinal theses. Indeed, throughout later Catholic history leading saints appealed to different aspects of the New Testament portrait of Jesus to emphasize varying features of Jesus. Thus Francis of Assisi was drawn to the child Jesus, whereas Ignatius of Loyola thought of Jesus as the leader of a band of companions fighting for the advance of the gospel. Julian of Norwich was but one of several important spiritual writers who spoke of Jesus in feminine imagery, stressing how he nursed the devout soul, whereas the followers of Saint Dominic drew inspiration for their preaching ministry from Jesus the itinerant preacher. Overall, however, it seems fair to say that Western Christianity in general, including Roman Catholicism, has concentrated on Jesus the savior — the forgiver of sins, the one who died to free wretched sinners from the thrall of Satan or from the wrath of God threatening them with hellfire.

It is not difficult to configure much of the New Testament material around the saving work of Jesus. One may interpret the recent school called liberation theology, which numbers many Roman Catholics writing in third world contexts, as an updating of the long-standing Western concentration on salvation or redemption. When Jesus first appeared on the Palestinian scene, as Mark tells us, his theme was the good news that God's kingdom was dawning, to which the fitting response was repentance and faith: "After John had been arrested, Jesus went into Galilee. There he proclaimed the Good News from God. 'The time has come,' he said, 'and the kingdom of God is close at hand. Repent, and believe in the Good News'" (Mk 1:14–15).

The Kingdom of God at the center of the preaching of the synoptic Jesus was the time or the state of affairs when the power of God would be righting relationships presently distorted and out of kilter. Foremost among these relationships was that between God and human beings and that among human neighbors. One might add that Jesus' preaching about the Kingdom also implied a new relationship of the self to the self and a new relationship between the human being and the natural world. If one calls the disordered state of affairs in these relationships taken collectively the legacy of original sin, as Catholic Christianity has tended to do, then Jesus' preaching, miracles, parables, death, and Resurrection all combined to overthrow the regime of flawed Adam, the human condition dominated by original sin. The grace of God, the favor and divine life manifested in Jesus, were proclaimed as more powerful than original sin. In giving such grace, God was taking the initiative to restore relations between human beings and himself. Jesus' own way of relating to God, his confidence and intimacy, his addressing God as a beloved Father, all symbolized what the new possibilities were.

Similarly, Jesus' way of relating to other human beings symbolized the revolution in human relations that grace made possible. Not only did Jesus call for loving one's neighbors as oneself, he expanded the import of "neighbor" so that it included strangers. These included people one had been taught to consider alien or unclean, the women and children one was likely to ignore as insignificant, and even sinners who violated the going social mores. The love in Jesus abolished class distinctions, and sought to override barriers and alienations of every kind. This love was so powerful in Jesus' heart that it rendered both the laws of nature and the prescriptions of the Torah secondary. Thus Jesus was able to cure the chronically sick, cast out demons from the mentally ill, and raise the dead back to life. Thus he subordinated the laws forbidding work on the Sabbath to the good of the sick and suffering, freely working cures and calling those who stuck by the letter of the Law hypocrites.

Jesus the savior from sin, who plays such a prominent role in Catholicism, is an eminently powerful and eminently free figure. His power may take the form of gentleness and willingness to suffer, but he goes his way in complete self-possession. His freedom shows in his willingness to consort with sinners and with people his contemporaries considered unclean, as well as in his controversies with the Pharisees over his interpretations of the Torah. It is perhaps an irony of Roman Catholic history that Jesus the free spirit has been prized in a church which is often authoritarian, priest-ridden, and legalistic. Indeed, the Catholic tradition has been quick to quote the Jesus who assured his followers that the Torah remained in force:

> Do not imagine that I have come to abolish the Law or the Prophets. I have come not to abolish but to complete them. I tell you solemnly, till heaven and earth disappear, not one dot, not one little stroke, shall disappear from the Law until its purpose is achieved. Therefore, the man who infringes even one of the least of these commandments and teaches others to do the same will be considered the least in the Kingdom of heaven; but the man who keeps them and teaches them will be considered great in the kingdom of heaven (Mt 5:17–19).

Matthew probably has been the favorite Catholic gospel, or at least the gospel most cited by the Catholic authorities, because of its efforts to retain order, structure, and a disciplined community life.

Because the Protestant Reformers made so much of faith as the way to achieve salvation and opposed faith to works (good deeds), the Catholic reading of Jesus during the Counter-Reformation period stressed the good deeds Jesus had worked and the indications that Jesus had expected repentance, conversion, and the other moments of faith to flower in practical effects. Thus Jesus was remembered to have told the man he cured by the pool (Jn 5:1–18) to be sure not to sin again, and to have told his disciples that one could discern true prophets from false by their fruits (Mt 7:16). He was remembered to have worked on the Sabbath, when the mercy of God required it, and to have imitated his Father in working always (Jn 5:17). The greatest of Jesus' works was his obedience to his Father's will, which issued in his dying on the cross. The center of much Catholic piety has been Jesus crucified, whose redemptive work is remembered at each Mass.

It is probably fair to say that the humanity of Christ so vividly displayed in the pages of the gospels meant more to Catholic Christians down the ages than the Pauline stress on the Christ who was a living Spirit in the midst of the early Church. Catholic Christianity, however, did not deny this Pauline emphasis, as it did not deny the Johannine emphasis on the Logos. Indeed, there were periods of Catholic history in which the man Jesus was interpreted with more stress on his divinity than on his likeness to other human beings in all things save sin. But this interpretation seldom came across to the ordinary Roman Catholic as emphasizing the Logos or Christ who was a living Spirit (somewhat confused in Paul's mind with the Holy Spirit). Rather Catholic piety took to heart the Johannine sense, most richly expressed in the first half of John's gospel, that all of Jesus' words and actions had been sacramental signs — expressions of his divine Sonship. The danger in this reading of Jesus of Nazareth was that limitations consequent on his humanity — limitations in knowledge and culture, limitations following on his male sex and short life span — got short shrift. He had to be perfect, because he was divine, and so the fullness of his humanity could be blurred. Those who knelt before the infant Jesus or before Jesus hanging on the cross pondered the wonders and horrors of his full humanity, but Catholic faith, like all other species of faith, was never so logical as to realize that overstressing the divinity of Jesus could undermine such devotion.[4]

The Synoptic Theologies

With regard to the particular interpretations of the synoptic authors, the following characteristics come to mind. Mark, whom most commentators consider the oldest gospel (although a few propose Matthew as the oldest), stresses Jesus' sufferings, his power, the enigmatic character of his Messiahship, and the necessity for his disciples to be countercultural. Mark probably stressed Jesus' sufferings for several reasons: Jewish denial that a genuine Messiah would have ended up a crucified criminal, sufferings forced on the Christian community to which Mark belonged, rumination about the Suffering Servant portrayed by Second Isaiah (whose lineaments seemed to fit Jesus with eerie exactness), and the sense that God's way of dealing with the depths of human evil might have been to overturn human values completely and make suffering, which all of us instinctively abhor, the means of grace.

One notices rather quickly that although the Markan Jesus is the servant suffering for humanity's salvation, he retains a remarkable authority and power. There is no question of his being cowed spiritually, and his many miracles — acts of healing power, in the main — bear witness to the fullness of the Spirit guiding him. Mark's Jesus is in combat with Satan from before his ministry, since immediately after his baptism by John, the Spirit drives Jesus into the wilderness for a forty-day trial (reminiscent of Israel's forty-year trek between the Exodus and gaining the promised land) and testing by Satan (Mk 1:12–13). His authority and power therefore are those befitting God's warrior against the Evil One, and if he accepts suffering as the way to crush Satan's spine, suffering must be more than worldlings make it to be; it must be capable of being transformed by God into redemptive love. Since all human beings must suffer and die, that possibility becomes enormously encouraging: what none of us can avoid may turn out to be God's way of purifying us and taking us to the divine bosom.

The Markan stress on the enigmatic or mysterious character of Jesus' messianic identity intrigued scholars early in this century, when historical and literary criticism first began to be applied to the New Testament. The *Messiasgeheimnis* (Messianic Secret), much bruited about in German scholarship, took seriously Jesus' many warnings to the disciples not to speak about his miracles and his seeming reluctance to disclose just who he was. A sinful, faithless world was likely to abuse the most precious revelations, and in Mark's view the audience that Jesus regularly encountered was more interested in the spectacular side of miraculous displays of power than in their more important call for faith. Where the Markan Jesus called himself the Son of Man (fully human), the crowds wanted more. The irony is that he was much more, though only clearly so after his death and Resurrection.

This relates to the last characteristic of Mark's theology we discuss here, its countercultural thrust. The typical crowd was sufficiently unbelieving and sensual to distort Jesus' actual message and to abhor the demands of the gospel he was preaching. Why should the disciples of Jesus expect any different treatment? Mark almost brutally forces the early Christians in his community to face the fact that if they are faithful to their Lord they will suffer as he did. Mark's apocalyptic side, which leads him to expect the return of Jesus relatively soon, plays into this counterculturalism. If one expects the end of the world to come quickly, one has no need to assume responsibility for the cultural institutions that keep people going generation after generation.

Because Catholic Christianity largely did assume this responsibility, owing to both its own acceptance of Johannine incarnationalism (which itself owed much to the delay of Jesus' return) and the historical accident that it became part of imperial Roman culture, Markan theology has served Catholic Christianity mainly as an astringent reminder that it should never get overly mired in the world. Markan theology also teaches that when Catholic Christianity distances itself from its suffering savior it has lost the salt without which there is no true gospel. Medieval Christianity often needed to hear this message, as the many apocalyptic movements, dissents, and monastic reforms of the medieval period suggest, and early modern Catholicism got a stinging rebuke along Markan lines from the Protestant Reformation.

The Matthean Christ is less countercultural than the Markan, if only because Matthew is so bent on showing Jesus to have fulfilled Jewish prophecy, hope, and expectation. The Matthean Jesus is God's newly authorized Teacher, the successor and supplanter of Moses, and some commentators think that the easy division of Matthew into five discourses set off by the words, "when Jesus had finished" (7:28, 11:1, 13:53, 19:1, and 26:1), shows a deliberate effort to recall the five books of the Mosaic Torah that Matthew thinks was completed by Jesus' teaching. The theology of Matthew deals with the Christian community as the new Israel, Chapter 18 sketching how to deal with such community problems as pride, bad example, defection, brotherly or sisterly correction, common prayer, forgiveness of injuries, and the sense of gratitude all Christians ought to feel for God's remission of their sins. Throughout, the effort is to suggest the spirit worthy of a new Israel.

Of special significance in light of later Catholic history are Matthew 18:18 ("I tell you solemnly, whatever you bind on earth will be considered bound in heaven; whatever you loose on earth shall be considered loosed in heaven"), which served the Roman Catholic authorities as a scriptural justification for their claims to the power of the "keys" — the power to forgive sins, to admit people to Church membership, and to excommunicate the faithless or immoral, and Matthew 16:18 ("So now I say to you: You are Peter and on this rock I will build my Church"), which the successors to Peter as bishops of Rome claimed as a warrant for their papal primacy, if not indeed for their jurisdiction over the entire Church.

Luke, like Matthew, probably had available to him not only Mark but also a source scholars call "Q" that collected the (generally rather apocalyptic) sayings of Jesus. Again like Matthew, Luke also had available traditions about Jesus and Christian faith that were peculiar to the community for which he was writing. Most scholars insist on linking the gospel of Luke with the Acts of the Apostles, making Luke the author of a two-volume theology of early Christian history, from the conception of Jesus to the spread of Christianity to Rome, the center of the imperial world. The key to Luke's theological interpretation of history is the spread of Christianity to the Gentiles. Luke is thus at pains both to explain Jewish customs to his Gentile readers and to balance off the claims of both Jews and Gentiles to an important place in God's plan of salvation. Whereas the genealogy that Matthew gives in the context of Jesus' birth places Jesus in the line of David and Abraham, Luke takes Jesus back to Adam, as though to stress his more than Jewish import. For Luke everything that happened to Jesus transpired according to a divine plan and so had a certain necessity. Thus, after the Resurrection the Lukan Jesus tells the disciples he meets on the road to Emmaus:

> "This is what I meant when I said, while I was still with you, that everything written about me in the Law of Moses, in the Prophets and in the Psalms, has to be fulfilled." He then opened their minds to understand the scriptures, and he said to them, "So you see how it is written that the Christ would suffer and on the third day rise from the dead, and that, in his name, repentance for the forgiveness of sins would be preached to all the nations, beginning from Jerusalem" (24:44–47).

The Lukan Jesus is gentle and peaceful, somewhat in contrast to the Markan Jesus. It is in Luke that we find the most famous and artful of Jesus' parables, including those about the Good Samaritan and the Prodigal Son. The Lukan Jesus considers the lilies of the field, how they grow, and tells the disciples not to worry, because the God who cares for the flowers and the birds cares far more for them, numbering each hair of their heads. Roman Catholic piety loved these stories and poetic images, just as it loved the Lukan Jesus' interest in women, children, and prayer.

The theology of Luke-Acts served Catholic Christianity well in its missionary outreach to the Gentiles, helping to make "Catholic" coextensive with "ecumenical" (concerned about the entire inhabited world). When they had ears to hear, Catholics could find in the Lukan logia about poverty and detachment another warning against overabsorption in the world—one less bitter than that of Mark, but no less sobering. Throughout the ages Catholic concern to contemplate Jesus and to translate what he meant into many different cultural contexts was well served by Luke's pioneering effort to render the Jewish Jesus for Gentiles.[5]

Early Catholicism

We postpone our treatment of Paul and John to the end of this chapter, when we regard them as representative personalities (as well as enormously influential theologians). We turn now to the somewhat discrete materials at the end of the New Testament canon, where many scholars find the early Church settling down for a long stay in history.

The Pastoral Epistles (I and II Timothy and Titus) are the best sources on this question. Traditionally attributed to the apostle Paul, they now tend to be attributed to other, unknown authors who, under the cover of Paul's authority (perhaps they were members of the Pauline school), wanted to write about Church discipline. Protestant scholars dubbed this concern with Church discipline "Early Catholicism," somewhat unkindly linking the Pastorals' worries about preserving the authority of Church leaders with Roman interests in keeping the faithful in line.

The classical Reformation controversies, as structured by the Protestants, pitted the freedom that Luther and Calvin had found in the gospel against the constraints and abuses of the Law. They tried to associate the Reformers with Jesus the bringer of evangelical freedom and the Roman authorities with the Pharisees who upheld the minutiae of the Torah. There was a basis for this contrast, in that Roman claims to authority had swollen, become oppressive, and factored in the proliferation of practices, such as the granting of indulgences, that were easily abused. But when the two sides froze into postures that opposed Scripture (seen by the Protestants as the sole source of revelatory guidance) and Tradition (seen by the Catholics as a long-standing and unavoidable complementary source), both came out the losers. Catholics in fact, if not in theory, felt discouraged from reading the Bible, as though private interpretation of Scripture were the root of all evils, whereas Protestants were encouraged to think of the Bible as something unhistorical, detached from the realities of time, community life, and the other anchors necessary to keep it a human book.

One passage from the Epistle to Titus illustrates the concern with authority, organization, and discipline in both doctrine and morals that characterize "Early Catholicism." How one evaluates a passage such as this depends on what one assumes about the letter's background. For example, if one has Titus presupposing the rich Pauline theology of how disciples live with the risen Christ, its disciplinary emphasis may seem perfectly acceptable — a strong set of measures calculated to preserve such living.

Here is the passage:

The reason I left you behind in Crete was for you to get everything organised there and appoint elders in every town, in the way that I told you: that is, each of them must be a man of irreproachable character; he must not have been married more than once, and his children must be believers and not uncontrollable or liable to be charged with disorderly conduct. Since, as president, he will be God's representative, he must be irreproachable: never an arrogant or hot-tempered man, nor a heavy drinker or violent, nor out to make money; but a man who is hospitable and a friend of all that is good; sensible, moral, devout and self-controlled;

and he must have a firm grasp of the unchanging message of the tradition, so that he can be counted on for both expounding the sound doctrine and refuting those who argue against it. And in fact you have there a great many people who need to be disciplined, who talk nonsense and try to make others believe it, particularly among those of the Circumcision. They have got to be silenced: men of this kind ruin whole families, by teaching things that they ought not to. . . . So you will have to be severe in correcting them, and make them sound in the faith . . . (Titus 1:5–14).

Contemporary mainstream Protestant theologians and Catholic theologians tend to agree that both historically and theologically Scripture and Tradition are inextricably bound. Scripture arose from Tradition, in the sense that the experience of the early Church was the matrix from which the New Testament arose, and Scripture shaped all subsequent Tradition, being regarded as the standard against which any generation could judge the quality of its faith. One could say that both Catholics and Protestants have gained from this recent ecumenical agreement, because the Bible has entered more fully into Catholic piety and mainstream Protestants have inserted themselves more deeply into the two-thousand-year stream of Christian faith, moving apart from the fundamentalists who treat the Bible as though it had been delivered from heaven in a space capsule.

On the precise question of New Testament indications that by the end of the first century the Church had developed hierarchical structures and taken a defensive posture designed to safeguard the deposit of faith, ecumenism also has brought considerable consensus. The evidence is plain that bishops or presbyters had arisen to claim a preeminence in teaching, developing and applying Church discipline, and guiding Christians toward a good citizenship that would make them relatively unobjectionable to their pagan neighbors in the Greco-Roman world. Individual theologians continue to have different opinions about the desirability of this move, but their opinions often cross confessional lines. Some Catholics lament the rise of a mentality they see grown oppressive in Roman authority and some Protestants allow that the history of their own tradition, so replete with splinterings and subsplinterings of church after church, shows the wisdom of trying to establish central authorities that might preserve Church unity.

Nonetheless, the overall weight of Catholic theology tends to fall on the side of a both/and that accepts the structures and disciplines that grew from the Pastorals into the Roman Curia, whereas the overall weight of Protestant theology tends to fall on the side of an either/or that is quick to demand that all human authority submit itself to the authority of God's Scriptural Word.

We find a good example of the rather constrained, moralistic tone that

Church authority appears to have developed toward the end of the New Testament era in the following passage from I Timothy. The bias against women in this passage proved to be enormously influential in later history as a major reason that Christianity — Catholic, Orthodox, and Protestant alike — treated women as second-class Church members:

> Similarly, I direct that women are to wear suitable clothes and to be dressed quietly and modestly, without braided hair or gold and jewellery or expensive clothes; their adornment is to do the sort of good works that are proper for women who profess to be religious. During instruction, a woman should be quiet and respectful. I am not giving permission for a woman to teach or to tell a man what to do. A woman ought not to speak, because Adam was formed first and Eve afterwards, and it was not Adam who was led astray but the woman who was led astray and fell into sin. Nevertheless, she will be saved by childbearing, provided she lives a modest life and is constant in faith and love and holiness (2:9 – 15).

I Timothy goes on to talk about how church leaders, widows, and other categories of believers ought to comport themselves, filling out the reader's impression that the author is a rather sober-sided, moralistic type. In his (it is likely, though not certain, that all the New Testament authors were men) defense one might say that discipline had come to the fore because the Church then was facing threats from groups, such as the Gnostics, who taught untraditional faith or morals. Still, the overall impression given by the Pastorals is that because of them "faith" was in danger of shrinking to "doctrine," whereas the freedom of the children of God to live by Jesus' twofold commandment of love was in danger of shrinking to "morals."

Something of this shrinkage comes through in I Timothy 6:

> All slaves "under the yoke" must have unqualified respect for their masters, so that the name of God and our teaching are not brought into disrepute. Slaves whose masters are believers are not to think any less of them because they are brothers; on the contrary, they should serve them all the better, since those who have the benefit of their services are believers and dear to God. This is what you are to teach them to believe and persuade them to do. Anyone who teaches anything different, and does not keep to the sound teaching which is that of our Lord Jesus Christ, the doctrine which is in accordance with true religion, is simply ignorant and must be full of self-conceit, with a craze for questioning everything and arguing about words. All that can come of this is jealousy, contention, abuse and wicked mistrust of one another; and unending disputes by

people who are neither rational nor informed and imagine that religion is a way of making a profit (6:1–6).

Regarding slavery, one can only say that the Pastorals, like Paul himself, were more accepting of social circumstances (in Paul's case, perhaps because of an expectation that Jesus would soon return) than later Christian instinct came to be. Regarding the rest of the quotation, perhaps one can admit the unfortunate truth of the possibility that false teaching would turn into self-serving and community discord while still regretting that the vistas of liberation opened by Jesus seem so shut down.[6]

Representative Personalities: Paul and John

The Pauline and Johannine materials of the New Testament both constitute crucially important blocks that complement the synoptic materials and have been more significant than the materials in which Early Catholicism predominates. Paul is a clearer personality than "John," in terms of historical sources, and the first thing to note about Paul is that he did not know Jesus in the flesh but was converted to belief in the living Lord by a mystical experience:

Meanwhile Saul was still breathing threats to slaughter the Lord's disciples. He had gone to the high priest and asked for letters addressed to the synagogues in Damascus, that would authorise him to arrest and take to Jerusalem any followers of the Way, men or women, that he could find.

Suddenly, while he was traveling to Damascus and just before he reached the city, there came a light from heaven all round him. He fell to the ground, and then he heard a voice saying, "Saul, Saul, why are you persecuting me?" "Who are you, Lord?" he asked, and the voice answered, "I am Jesus, and you are persecuting me. Get up now and go into the city, and you will be told what you have to do." The men traveling with Saul stood there speechless, for though they heard the voice they could see no one. Saul got up from the ground, but even with his eyes wide open he could see nothing at all, and they had to lead him into Damascus by hand. For three days he was without his sight, and took neither food nor drink (Acts 9:1–9).

The significant point in this vision is the identification between Jesus and the Church. Ever after, Paul thought of Jesus as the living head of the Christian community, present in all its members. After he had learned the rudiments of Christian faith, Paul began to think through the problem that his own biography as a previously zealous Jew put to him: How did Jesus relate to the Torah? Paul's conclusion was that the death and resurrection of Jesus had brought a new period of salvation history, in which God's offer of covenanted relationship and shared life was now extended beyond Israel to all people. This conclusion impelled Paul upon a life of missionary activity and made him the preeminent apostle of Christianity to the Gentiles. All later Catholic missionaries — those trying to bring Northern Europe to the faith, and then those laboring in the New World, India, Asia, and Africa — had the work of Paul before them as a model.

The early letters of Paul, including Thessalonians and Galatians, struggle with what Christian life ought to be in the presumably brief interval before the Lord's return, and with the relation between the Torah and the Christian good news. By the time of I and II Corinthians (55 or 56 C.E.), Paul has had considerable experience with fledgling churches and is enmeshed in trying to explain the implications that possessing the life of Christ bears for personal morality and community concord. Romans is the masterpiece from Paul's own hand, and there one finds a mature version of the Pauline dialectic between sin and grace. For the mature Paul, Christ is the Second Adam, giving the entire human race a new start. If the sin of Adam has abounded throughout the world, sealing people off from the love of God, the grace of Christ has abounded the more. Catholic Christianity took seriously the Pauline assurances of the Spirit of Christ pouring love into believers' hearts (Rom 5:5). The image of Spirit making the believer's prayer with sighs too deep for words (Rom 8:26–27) gladdened many contemplatives suffering through dark nights. Paul believed that all people have in the works of creation sufficient evidence to convince them of God's existence (Rom 1:20). The unbelief, immorality, and idolatries of pagans therefore betoken minds darkened by sin and wills weakened by lack of faith. This buttressed the characteristically Catholic view of reason and will (human nature), according to which grace perfects nature and faith perfects reason (rather than destroying or simply contesting it).

The Pauline focus on the death and resurrection of Christ as the radical axis of both Christian faith and human existence entered deeply into the marrow of all the Christian churches. As a stimulus to make Easter the center of the liturgical year and the Mass the hub of Catholic devotional life, the Pauline riveting onto the passover of Christ has kept Catholic faith dialectical. Death and life, dying and rising, readily became the basic rhythm of the spiritual life, as one passed through purgative and illuminative stages, as one had to be stripped of worldly securities and self-love before experiencing God's nuptial embrace.

The later Pauline epistles, Colossians and Ephesians, by consensus are thought not to have been written by Paul himself. They have served Catholic Christianity as an incentive to understand the Church as the Body of Christ, to establish an ordered, patriarchal family life, and to assimilate the relationship between wife and husband to that between the Church and Christ, making the husband the "head" of the wife. Colossians also has given Catholics food for reflecting on how the Logos is the infrastructure of creation, making it intelligible (Col 1:15–20), whereas Ephesians speaks so lyrically of the height, depth, length, and breadth of Christ's love (3:16–19), and of the reconciliation of sinners to God worked by Christ, that when Catholics have wanted symbols of the cosmic outreach of redemption and the radical depths of atonement they instinctively have thought of Ephesians.

The Johannine literature of the New Testament, which some consider to include the Book of Revelation as well as the gospel and the epistles, is the most incarnational block. The gospel focuses on how the Incarnate Word went about revealing the nature of the Father and the way of salvation, culminating in the victory of Christ on the cross. For John, salvation begins with the moment of the Incarnation, since at that moment the world receives the divinity that is its consummation. The Johannine Jesus is presented ironically, people of "flesh" failing to understand either his words or his person. To understand Jesus, and realize that one who sees Jesus sees the Father (Jn 14:9), one must be filled with the divine Spirit, as Jesus was. Throughout the first half of the gospel, Jesus works seven signs that convince those with eyes to see that divinity has come into the world in his person. The second half of the gospel portrays Jesus on the verge of returning to the glory of the Father from which he came. In the discourses of the Book of Glory, as the second half of John often is called, one finds the primary New Testament evidences for the doctrine of the Trinity. The relations among Jesus, the Father, and the Spirit are presented as a mutual indwelling, and believers are assured that this communal divine life becomes their own, when they are united to Jesus in faith. Thus the basic Johannine image for the Church is the union of branches with the vine that gives them life, whereas the main injunction of Jesus is that his disciples abide in his love.

Love predominates in both the gospel of John and in the Johannine epistles, becoming the believer's best index of what God is like: "My dear people, let us love one another, since love comes from God, and everyone who loves is begotten by God and knows God. Anyone who fails to love can never have known God, because God is love" (I Jn 4:7–8). Catholic moralists were quick to point to other Johannine texts showing that such love had to be disciplined and sinless, but the radical implications of the Johannine message never were completely lost. When Augustine said, "Love and do what you will," he suggested that the Johannine understanding of God and the Christian life was alive and well in Africa more than three hundred years after John's death.

This brings us to the question of the author of John, that is, the question of who "John" was. The best suggestion is probably that the Johannine community was formed by the beloved disciple who lay on Jesus' breast (Jn 13:26), in the sense that either he gathered the kernel of what later became the Johannine church, or that he was one of its main inspirations. All of the New Testament literature sought a connection with an apostolic eyewitness of Jesus, and John the son of Zebedee, who may have been the beloved disciple, appealed to the Johannine church.

Whatever the historical source, the view of Jesus laid out in the Johannine gospel and epistles is remarkable for its incarnational, sacramental character. The Johannine school so fuses the complete humanity of Jesus with his complete divinity that it makes all of Jesus' actions and words revelations of what the eternal self-expression of the unbegotten Father was like—how flesh bore divine self-communication. This Jesus is the Bread of Life, the Good Shepherd, the Light of the World, the living water of eternal life. His own flesh becomes Christians' spiritual food and drink. His Spirit comes, after the death and resurrection, to continue his work, serving as a second Paraclete (advocate, helper). The Spirit anoints believers from within, giving them sure knowledge of God's ways.

The Spirit, like Jesus, is in conflict with the world, the flesh, and the Devil. Collectively, one of their most characteristic traits is to deny that Jesus was fully human (which means to deny that the Word actually did take flesh and work salvation by taking humanity definitively into the divine embrace). The Church figures rather marginally in the Johannine materials, but the likelihood is that the Johannine community reached a compromise with such other early communities as the Petrine, which thought that structure and authority were very important, in part because the Johannine Christians found themselves unable to defeat the unorthodox in their midst by mere appeals to experience, tradition, and inner anointing.

The Book of Revelation historically has been linked with John, but the self-proclaimed author, John of Patmos, is involved in such a different literary project that probably he was not a member of the Johannine community. Revelation, like all apocalyptic literature, is based on the conviction that God is soon to come to vindicate his suffering people. It therefore purports to be visions of how such vindication will occur. What John of Patmos lays out is a dazzling series of images, brilliant in their manipulation of Old Testament symbols, designed to shore Christians up in their resistance to the depradations of the Roman Empire, which the author stigmatizes as the Great Beast and Whore of Babylon. Catholic Christians have most loved the coruscant figures for the risen Christ and the scenes of the heavenly Jerusalem, where God would wipe away every tear from their eyes (Rev 21:4). Revelation confirms the Johannine instinct that Father, Son, and Spirit form a trinitarian divinity, and it makes holding steadfast in faith the great virtue. Medieval Christians, often looking at an early death, correlated this hortative teaching with their sense that they had on earth no lasting city and only were wise if they kept the last things well in mind.

Conclusion: The Allure of Jesus

After one has noted the various ingredients of New Testament Christian faith, there remains a whole more powerful than its discrete parts. In searching to understand this whole, one finds what can only be called the allure of Jesus himself. Behind the gospels stands the personality of the man from Nazareth who riveted people by his teaching, took their breath away with his miracles, and seared his being into their souls by his death and resurrection. Those who accepted him as the Messiah and Son of God thought that no one had ever spoken with such power and beauty, that only he had the words of eternal life. Those who did not meet him in the flesh but were drawn to his community learned to use the stories about him, and his presence in the liturgy, to create a passionate personal relation. The wit and beauty of Jesus, his compassion and healing power, the freedom with which he strode the roads of Nazareth, and his mysterious relationship to God combined to make him fascinating, challenging, a stimulus to rethink the foundations of one's existence. He was a sign that God might be better, more powerful and loving, than one had dared imagine. So it is Jesus himself who explains why the early Christian movement got under way and grew like wildfire, just as it is Jesus himself, resurrected and present in his Church, to whom Christians have pointed down the ages when they wanted to summarize their faith.

Glossary

Anathematized: declared abhorrent and excommunicate. In effect, the formula "Anathema sit" ("Let it be abhorrent") is a curse, laid on people or teachings that deviate from orthodox faith and so are like snakes in the bosom of the Church. This practice has been abused in

Christian history, not the least by Roman Catholic authorities. It is always dangerous, all the more so when it is linked with a crabbed, fearful, and ungenerous view of Christian faith. On the other hand, it testifies to the seriousness with which Catholic Christianity traditionally has taken faith (in both its doctrinal and moral forms), because it has considered faith the pearl of great price — the sole treasure on which one's heart should be set. The psychological, political, and theological problem is to find a generosity and tolerance that will not eviscerate the profound significance of faith but rather will flow from a confident sense that faith is so beautiful it is its own best advocate and persuasion.

Divinization: the process of being made a partaker of the divine nature (2 Pet 1:4). Whereas Eastern Orthodoxy has spotlighted divinization (*theosis*) more than Roman Catholicism, the essentials of the notion were communicated in the Catholic teaching about sanctifying grace. There believers learned that at baptism they became children of God, entering upon a life that would flower in eternity (heaven). Sin was the loss of this divine life — the worst failure one could imagine. God gave grace (help) to withstand temptations to sin, and the theological virtues (faith, hope, and charity) were the main powers through which the divine life expressed itself. Sophisticated Catholics linked sanctifying grace with the presence and work of the Spirit, or with Christ living within them (built up by each reception of the Eucharist, each "holy Communion"), or even with the presence of the Trinity on the model of the Johannine figure of abiding. But few of the ordinary faithful made the concept of being divinized — immortalized, sanctified, mysteriously made into God (without ceasing to be a creature and so not God, so rather something formed by a finitude or nothingness not found in divinity) — the center of their spiritual lives.

Tanak: the preferred Jewish term for the Hebrew Bible. Tanak is an anagram composed from the first Hebrew letters for each of the three principal parts of the Bible: Torah (Pentateuch), Nevi'im (Prophets), Ketuvim (Writings). Many Jews find Tanak preferable to either "The Old Testament," which can imply a Christian usage according to which this part of the Bible has been superseded (by Christ and the New Testament), or "The Hebrew Bible," which raises questions about the Septuagint, the Greek version of Jewish Scripture composed for the many Jews in the diaspora (scattering outside Israel) who did not understand Hebrew.

Discussion Questions

1. How did the Torah given to Moses relate to the covenant God made through Moses?
2. What did the experience of the Exile create in the faith of the major Prophets?
3. How did Jews and Greeks tend to differ regarding the human matter-spirit composite?
4. Why did many Greeks find the early Christian preaching about Christ to be foolishness?
5. How did Jesus' conception of the Kingdom lead him to reconceive of people's relations to God and to one another?
6. Why was Jesus so free to flout the conventions of his time, curing on the Sabbath and associating with sinners?
7. Why is the Markan Jesus so secretive?
8. How might the Matthean stress on Jesus' fulfillment of Jewish prophecy occasion anti-Semitism?
9. How legitimate or inevitable was the Church's institutionalization and switch to conservative views of doctrine and morality?
10. What spiritual rights does one have when official authorities such as the author of I Timothy teach about women, slavery, and other issues in ways that seem at least oppressive and perhaps sinful?
11. How did Paul contrast the living Christ experienced in his conversion with the Torah he had served as a Jew?
12. What are the advantages, and the dangers, in the Johannine equation of divinity and love?

Notes

[1] See Edward Schillebeeckx, *The Church with a Human Face: A New and Expanded Theology of Ministry* (New York: Crossroad, 1985); Shaye J. D. Cohen, *From the Maccabees to the Mishnah* (Philadelphia: Westminster, 1987); John Tully Carmody, Denise Lardner Carmody, and Robert L. Cohn, *Exploring the Hebrew Bible* (Englewood Cliffs, N.J.: Prentice-Hall, 1988).

[2] See Elisabeth Schüssler Fiorenza, *In Memory of Her: A Feminist Theological Reconstruction of Christian Origins* (New York: Crossroad, 1983).

[3] Throughout, New Testament quotations are from the Jerusalem Bible (Garden City, N.Y.: Doubleday, 1966), perhaps the most praised Catholic translation.

[4] As recent popular studies of Jesus by Catholic scholars, see Lucas Grollenberg, *Jesus*

(Philadelphia: Westminster, 1978); Monika Hellwig, *Jesus: The Compassion of God* (Wilmington, Del.: Michael Glazier, 1983); Gerard Sloyan, *Jesus in Focus* (Mystic, Conn.: Twenty-third Publications, 1983); Denise Lardner Carmody and John Tully Carmody, *Jesus: An Introduction* (Belmont, Calif.: Wadsworth, 1987). The outstanding scholarly work continues to be Edward Schillebeeckx's two volumes, *Jesus* and *Christ* (New York: Seabury, 1979, 1980). On ecclesiastical matters, see Raymond Brown, *The Churches the Apostles Left Behind* (New York: Paulist, 1984).

5 See John Tully Carmody, Denise Lardner Carmody, and Gregory A. Robbins, *Exploring the New Testament* (Englewood Cliffs, N.J.: Prentice-Hall, 1986).

6 See James Cone, "Black Worship," in *The Study of Spirituality*, ed. Cheslyn Jones, Geoffrey Wainwright, and Edward Yarnold, S.J. (New York: Oxford University Press, 1986), pp. 481–490.

CHAPTER 3

The Patristic and Medieval Periods

Martyrdom, Monasticism, and Establishment
The Ecumenical Councils
The Papacy
Scholasticism and Mysticism
Representative Personality: Augustine
Glossary, Discussion Questions, Notes

In this chapter we deal with well over a thousand years of Church history. Necessarily, therefore, our treatment is selective and thematic. To begin, we deal with three aspects of the change that Christianity underwent during the first 250 years or so of the post–New Testament era (approximately 100–350 C.E.). Martyrdom, monasticism, and the establishment of Christianity as the favored religion in the Roman empire were not the whole of Christian faith in those centuries, but studying them offers a sense of what the first great shifts and movements were. In dealing with the ecumenical councils that clarified doctrinal matters, we imply that the next 450 years or so found the Church involved with many controversies over how best to understand its central convictions about God and Christ. In tracing the history of the papacy, we suggest the political shape that Catholicism assumed after the fall of Rome and during the alienation of the Western and Eastern wings of the Empire. Focusing on scholasticism and mysticism allows us to suggest how the life of the mind and heart developed in the West during the medieval period. Finally, in taking Augustine as our representative personality, we imply that much of what Western Christianity had become by the time of the Protestant Reformation had been present in seed over a thousand years earlier, in the mind of the first great Christian genius.

Martyrdom, Monasticism, and Establishment

As the Book of Revelation suggests, by the end of the New Testament era a sufficient number of Christians were suffering persecution from Roman authorities to make dying for the faith a stark possibility. The "number of a man, the number 666" (Rev 13: 18), is usually associated with the emperor Nero (37–68 C.E.), because according to the Greek number system of the day (*gematria*) "Neron Caesar" had the value 666. The Roman historian Tacitus reports that Nero tried to blame the Christians at Rome for the fire that destroyed large parts of the city in 64 (a fire many suspect Nero himself caused), punishing many Christians as both arsonists and haters of the human race (because, like Jews, they would not agree to the live-and-let-live attitude of most cultured pagans regarding divinity and morality). Nero may have been responsible for the martyrdom of both Peter and Paul in Rome, and the Book of Revelation (probably written around 95) associated him with the Roman Beast (Rev 13), in part because of a popular myth that Nero would return to life.

The imperial rules of Decius (249–251 C.E.) and Diocletian (284–305 C.E.) were other times when Christians were slaughtered as apostates from the civil religion of the Empire, but until the Edict of Milan (313), which gave the Church legal status, Christians always had to walk softly, even though persecution was only sporadic. The example of Jesus, who gave his life in witness to the truth of his Father's commission, and the example of such apostles as Peter and Paul, who were killed for their profession of faith in Jesus, stood before the early Christians in hard times. Revelation assured them that those who persevered to the end would win a heavenly crown, joining the white-robed choirs of the saints who ceaselessly praised the beauty of God, whereas the courage of those who did give their lives without abjuring the faith became the stuff of pious legend.

Thus a "martyrology" recording the stories of the eminent early witnesses developed, and martyrs became the most praised of all the Church's saints. Christians came to speak of martyrdom as "baptism by blood," and to say that the blood of the martyrs had been the seed from which the Church later grew to be so populous. The liturgical tradition developed of remembering the "birthday" on which the martyr had died and entered heaven, whereas the tombs of the greatest martyrs became shrines, even pilgrimage centers. The doctrine of the **communion of saints** provided a context for seeing the martyrs as powerful intercessors in heaven — members of the Church triumphant who could help members of the earthly Church still on pilgrimage. Martyrdom was thought to have wiped away all sins, and the relics of the martyrs were prized possessions. Indeed, each consecrated Roman Catholic altar is supposed to contain a relic of a martyr.

Monasticism bore some connections to martyrdom, in that eminent monks and virgins were considered to be living a life of "white martyrdom," sacrificing many of their sensual appetites, if not their blood. Monastic life looked back to the example of Jesus, who apparently did not marry because of the all-absorbing character of his work, and who had praised those making themselves eunuchs for the sake of the Kingdom of Heaven (Mt 19: 12). Paul had praised celibacy as preferable to marriage (I Cor 7: 32–35), in view of the short time before the return of Christ, adding another authoritative reason for the pious to consider a life of consecrated virginity.

Thus the practice developed of remaining unmarried, to have greater freedom for prayer, austerities, and service of either the gospel (preaching, missionary work) or the poor. The clergy, including the bishops, did not have to be celibate, as evidenced by the example of many of the apostles (preeminently, Peter) and such New Testament writings as I Timothy. Chastity and living a poor life, in imitation of the Jesus who had no place to lay his head (Mt 8: 20) and who bade his disciples travel light (Luke 9: 3), had a growing appeal, all the more so because the Hellenistic environment was replete with teachings to the effect that bodily things were an encumbrance, if not outright evils.

Even prior to the legal recognition of the Christian community early in the fourth century, and then its establishment by Constantine as the official or privileged Roman religion (which Constantine hoped would unify his empire), people seeking a life of intense prayer and spiritual freedom could be seen withdrawing from secular life, either remaining in their homes most of the time or going into the countryside, or even into the desert. Those who tried to gain union with God in solitude soon became aware that isolation had its perils, so even prior to the Church's "establishment" as the official Roman religion small communities had grown up around anchorites who had gained a reputation for holiness and wisdom. St. Antony of Egypt, made famous by the biography written by the bishop of Alexandria, Athanasius, became the archetype of such figures, but a whole collection of early "desert fathers" furnished guidance to serious seekers.[1]

In the East, Pachomius and Basil wrote rules to organize a communal (coenobitic) religious life, whereas in the West, the rule of Benedict of Nursia (480–543) became the most influential. However, there was considerable cross-fertilization among those who were interested in pursuing union with God single-mindedly, and considerable agreement that chastity, poverty, obedience to a spiritual leader (abbot-father), prayer, fasting, silence, and austerities were all helpful. As monastic communities became relatively common and well organized, communal prayer grew to be important. The opus Dei (work of God) was to consecrate the whole day through a round of "hours" (times of vocal prayer, recited or sung, that mainly used psalms, readings from Scripture, and readings from eminent Church fathers). Such prayer was offered in constant praise of God and on behalf of the whole Church, indeed of the whole world.

Monks later became missionaries, teachers, and even prelates, and throughout the centuries when culture dimmed they were custodians of both classical and Christian traditions. To this day they and their female counterparts have furnished the Church with many of its saints, theologians, and witnesses to the value of a contemplative life focused on God that takes one apart from the world. The Protestant Reformers criticized monasticism as unbiblical, and in lands (such as England) where monastic holdings were large the monks often lost their estates during the Reformation and sometimes were pressured to return to lay life. Nonetheless, both Eastern Orthodoxy and Roman Catholicism have continued to praise monasticism and regard it as a splendid Christian vocation (as long as it is lived fervently).

When it was established by Constantine as the favored imperial religion, Catholic Christianity settled in for what has proved to be a long immersion in worldly affairs. Such immersion was a major stimulus for many of the early monks and nuns to flee into a consecrated life, and in both the eastern and western portions of the Empire it has had its negative impacts, sometimes leading to a wealth, power, and worldliness that ill-befit followers of the Markan Jesus. On the other hand, Christianity centers in the Incarnation, and Catholic faith has always felt that matter, the body, and even the world are more good than evil. Without underestimating the power of sin, one was not to call anything that came from God evil.

So the ideal developed of making a Christian society and a Christian culture, in which human aspirations would proceed with the blessings of grace. One could even speak of a Christian humanism, meaning an encouragement from faith in Jesus to make the whole world a place fit to live in. Science, art, politics, economics, wine, sex, athletics—to the pure nothing was impure. Anything decent could become a manifestation of God and an instrument of God's service. Established Christianity therefore took to heart Paul's own encouragement of the Philippians: "Finally, brothers, fill your minds with everything that is true, everything that is noble, everything that is good and pure, everything that we love and honour, and everything that can be thought virtuous or worthy of praise" (Phil 4: 8).

The Ecumenical Councils

Whereas martyrdom, monasticism, and establishment suggest some of the personal and political developments during the patristic era, the teachings of the apologists who defended Christian claims against Jewish and pagan detractors, of the bishops who instructed their flocks in the meaning of Christian life and the dangers of heretical sects such as the Gnostics, and of the Church councils that formalized certain features of Christian faith suggest some of the doctrinal developments. The New Testament, for all its riches, had not settled every question of faith. Indeed, there was no "New Testament" until perhaps the fourth century, because it took the Church some time to see the need for a canonical listing and to determine which early writings ought to be on it. In their day, such now noncanonical writings as the Didache, Pastor Hermas, the Epistle to Diognetus, the Epistle of Barnabas, and the Epistles of Clement and Ignatius could be as influential as Revelation, to say nothing of 2 and 3 John, Jude, and James. The Gnostics were circulating gospels attributed to apostles such as Thomas and Peter that had a significant vogue, whereas second-century dissidents such as Marcion were rejecting large portions of what later became the Christian Bible (in Marcion's view, the Old Testament had nothing in common with Jesus, and only Paul and Luke had gotten right Jesus' gospel of love).

Sources of authoritative teaching that would distinguish the wheat of orthodoxy from the chaff of heresy were at a premium, so the early Church magnified the office of the bishops, making them the authoritative teachers charged with preserving sound doctrine. The Church gradually created for itself an authoritative Scripture that would have privileged status as *the* word of God.

But certain problems cut across the geographical jurisdictions of individual bishops and seemed to call for concerted action. Some of these problems were disciplinary, concerned with such matters as liturgical practices, monastic rules, regulations for the clergy, and stipulations about Church (canon) law. Others were doctrinal, and it is these that made the first seven councils of the Church (the ones Catholics and Orthodox largely agree were ecumenical: authoritative for the whole Church) so important.

The first ecumenical council was held at Nicaea in Bythinia (Asia Minor) in 325 under some pressure from the Emperor Constantine. A crisis had arisen over how the relation between the Logos and the Father ought to be understood. Arius, a priest from Alexandria in Egypt, had proposed that "there was a time when he [the logos] was not." In other words, the Logos was not divine as the Father was. By implication, he was a creature. This grated on the ears of other Alexandrines, who were competitors of the theologians from Antioch in Syria for theological leadership in the patristic Church. Athanasius of Alexandria became the champion of the "orthodox" Alexandrine party, countering Arius with the position that the Logos and the Father were of the same substance— were equally divine. The Arians, as they came to be known, would agree that the Logos and the Father were similar in substance, but they would not agree to sameness. In Greek the difference was a single letter (*homoousios* for "same substance" and *homoiousios* for "similar substance"), but Athanasius saw that it had enormous implications.

If the Logos were not divine, Jesus had been no full revealer or savior. Only the entry of divinity itself into the human condition, as the prologue of the Gospel of John had definitively pictured it, could do justice to traditional faith about the Incarnation, salvation, and divinization. If divinity had not assumed the fullness of humanity, humanity was not fully saved. If the Arians were correct, one could not believe, as Christians traditionally had, that the Logos became human so that human beings might become divine.

The assembly of bishops at Nicaea agreed with Athanasius and stigmatized the Arian position as untraditional and so unacceptable. This did not settle the matter, because politics joined with theological convictions to harden the two parties into power blocs within the eastern empire. But Catholic Christianity, East and West, has always looked to Nicaea as the fountainhead of its official teaching about the most important mysteries: the Trinity, the Incarnation, and Grace.

The First Council of Constantinople (381) was convened to try to end the division between Arians and Orthodox. It ratified the work of Nicaea and condemned the teachings of Apollinaris, bishop of Laodicea, that seemed to threaten the full humanity of Christ. Constantinople I also officially declared the full divinity of the Holy Spirit, making it clear that the Spirit, too, is consubstantial with the Father (and with the Logos or Son).

The Council of Ephesus (431) dealt with the problem posed by Nestorianism, which taught that there were two persons in Christ, one human and one divine. Because of this teaching, the Nestorians had rejected the notion of the *theotokos*: Mary the Mother of Christ being regarded as the "Godbearer." But this notion was ancient and venerable, pointing to what the orthodox considered the traditional teaching that there was only one person (one bearer of the act of existence) in the God-Man Jesus Christ: the Logos.

In each of these conciliar cases, political and terminological problems abounded. Doctrinal history, like other kinds of history, tends to be written by the winners, and what later eras called orthodoxy was never easily identifiable as such at the time. Moreover, few groups or positions that found themselves condemned simply capitulated or crawled away. Most kept to their positions, as the Arians had with considerable success. Thus, to this day there are Nestorian Christians, convinced that Ephesus misunderstood their champion and that his was the more correct interpretation of biblical and traditional faith.

The Council of Chalcedon (451), ranks with Nicaea at the forefront of the official decisions that determined the infrastructure of Catholic theology. Convened by the Emperor Marcian to deal with the views of Eutyches (who so vehemently opposed Nestorianism that he went to the opposite extreme of denying the consubstantiality of Christ's humanity with that of all other human beings), Chalcedon both reaffirmed the *theotokos* doctrine and produced the key formula that shaped subsequent Catholic Christology: one (divine) person in two natures (divine and human). This formula came from Pope Leo, marking a significant intervention of the bishop of Rome in an Eastern (though ecumenical or church-wide) controversy, and it too was nowhere near so obvious or clear as later historiography often presented it. Nonetheless, the formula captured the essentials most pithily: Jesus Christ was fully human and fully divine, one subject of existence (one integral being) with two levels of being.

Constantinople II (553) was convened to deal with the controversy following on the publication of three "chapters" (by the Emperor Justinian in 543–544) that condemned the position of several leading theologians as verging on Nestorianism. Justinian wanted to conciliate the "monophysites"—those who opposed Nestorianism by stressing the singleness of personhood (or nature: a key problem was the confusion of the capital terms "person" and "nature," which different authors used with different overtones. Sometimes what one group was trying to indicate by "person" another was trying to indicate by "nature"). Pope Virgilius was involved in this council from afar, and many political pressures attended it. The council condemned various propositions of Theodore of Mopsuetia, one of those condemned by Justinian's three chapters, and so strengthened the official Church stand against Nestorianism and for the position developed at Chalcedon.

Constantinople III (680–681), convened at the demand of the Emperor Constantine IV, condemned monothelitism, the notion that Christ had only one will. Rather, it said, Christ has both a human and a divine will, physically distinct (however united morally because in complete accord).

The last of the seven councils generally considered ecumenical was Nicaea II (787), convened by the Empress Irene to end the controversy over icons. It vindicated the position of those who held reverence for icons traditional and warranted by the Incarnation, denouncing the position of the iconoclasts who condemned the use of icons as idolatrous.

This bare-bones listing of the councils cannot suggest either the complexity of the theological issues at stake or the intrigue created by the intervention of emperors, church parties, and others seeking power or influence. The councils were very human affairs, displaying both the positive and the negative effects of the Catholic Christian decision to embrace a leading role in the Roman Empire. Seen from a distance, perhaps their greatest significance (in addition to the specific clarifications of Trinitarian and Christological faith they developed) lay in their assumption that the Church is competent to go beyond the simple words of Scripture and declare, in response to new questions put by later ages, what the faith laid out in Scripture (but kept alive in the Church as a fully historical, developing entity through the guidance of the Holy Spirit) entailed. This assumption has become the distinctively Catholic position, leading to such stands as the defense of tradition articulated at Trent in opposition to the Protestant Reformers' notion of *sola Scriptura* (by Scripture alone). It correlates

44 CATHOLIC HISTORY

not only with the Catholic view of the powers given the Church (and most
clearly embodied in its episcopal leadership [under the pope]) but also with the
Catholic trust in reason and human nature, which trust stands apart from the
classical Protestant distrust of a reason often pitted against faith, or called a
whore, and a human nature considered depraved.

The Papacy

The office of the bishop of Rome has been central in Roman Catholicism, being
seen as the unfolding of the Petrine ministry conferred by Jesus. In this view,
Peter became the head of the "college" of the apostles, in part because of his
ardent confession of faith:

> When Jesus came to the region of Caesarea Philippi he put this question
> to his disciples, "Who do people say the Son of Man is?" And they said,
> "Some say he is John the Baptist, some Elijah, and others Jeremiah or one
> of the prophets." "But you," he said, "who do you say I am?" Then
> Simon Peter spoke up, "You are the Christ," he said, "the Son of the
> living God." Jesus replied, "Simon, son of Jonah, you are a happy man!
> Because it was not flesh and blood that revealed this to you but my Father
> in heaven. So I now say to you: You are Peter and on this rock I will build
> my Church. And the gates of the underworld can never hold out against it.
> I will give you the keys of the kingdom of heaven: whatever you bind on
> earth shall be considered bound in heaven; whatever you loose on earth
> shall be considered loosed in heaven" (Mt 16:13–20).

Tradition held that Peter had gone from Jerusalem, leaving that community
in charge of James, and taken control of the Christian community in Rome, the
center of the imperial world that gave the followers of Jesus their sense of the
spread of humanity. The Christian faith that Peter possessed probably was more
Jewish in its instincts than something transformed by contact with Gentiles,
although Acts 10 shows Peter being stretched beyond his Jewish sense of
cleanness and opened to God's action among the Gentiles.[2] Acts also shows
Peter at the head of the nascent Christian community gathered together in
Jerusalem after the Ascension of Jesus. Once the Spirit had descended at
Pentecost, Peter became a great preacher of the saving tale of Jesus, interpreting
Jesus' life as the fulfillment of messianic prophecies and Jesus' death as the act
that opened the treasuries of God's salvation.

Irenaeus, bishop of Lyons, writing in his *Against Heresies* about 180 c.e., speaks of the successors of the apostles Peter and Paul in Rome. First there was Linus, whom Paul mentions in his letters to Timothy. Then came Anacletus and Clement (the latter the author of influential epistles that suggest that the faith of the Roman church continued for some time to be dominated by Jewish ideas). Insofar as Clement wrote a letter to quell the tumult of the Corinthian church, his bishopric implies that from very early the Roman see assumed an influence, if not an outright authority, over other dioceses. Irenaeus goes on with his list of the bishops of Rome: Evaristus, Alexander, Sixtus, the martyr Telesphorus, and many others, down to the twelfth successor to Peter (who had been the head of the twelve apostles, who in turn had been the successors of the twelve tribes of Israel). Most of the bishops of Rome Irenaeus mentions now are simply names without biographical data.

Other listings of the bishops of Rome that take the sequence to the middle of the third century are unreliable, but they do paint a picture of the bishop of Rome as the personified center of the widespread Christian Church and as a major reference point for its unity. Gradually this primacy of the bishop of Rome clarified, although in the third and fourth century any preeminence of the successors of Peter emerged only in extraordinary cases, when an appeal was made from other church areas for a decision. Ordinarily, Church business proceeded by what Catholic theology came to call "the principle of subsidarity," according to which local authorities care for local problems whenever possible. In addition to Rome, Jerusalem, Antioch, Alexandria, and Constantinople were what might be called area-centers, each of their leading church officials (patriarchs) having influence on the churches clustered around, and each guiding the development of the liturgy and theology growing up in its orbit.

When Constantine transferred the residence of the emperor to the East, making the new capital at Constantinople, the bishops of Rome filled much of the political vacuum left in the West. They took the lead in supervising social welfare and in dealing with the effects of the barbarian invasions throughout Italy. Still, the residence of the emperor in the East inevitably elevated the importance of the patriarch of Constantinople, making him a rival of the pope. In the fourth century, then, the Church was tense with the competing dignities of Rome and Constantinople.

Able bishops of Rome at the turn of the fifth century brought Rome great prestige, so much so that Leo the Great (ruled 440–461), could have a determining say in the proceedings of the Council of Chalcedon. Toward the end of the fifth century, Pope Gelasius I explained to the Emperor Anastasius I that of the two great powers by which (under God's decree) the world was to be ruled, the sacred power of bishops was superior to the royal power of emperors. This view had a great impact during the early middle ages, because it was embodied in such forged documents as the False Decretals and the Donation of

Constantine to propose a definitive solution to the tensions between popes and emperors — a solution favoring the popes.

When the Frankish King Clovis I was baptized a Catholic Christian in 496, the Latin-German West began a movement away from the Greek East. Most of the Germanic tribes were Arians and set up national churches apart from union with Rome, whereas the locus of official imperial power in the East meant a denigration of things Latin. In the sixth century the popes Hormisdas and Agapetus I sought closer ties with Constantinople, but this only led to the Roman church's becoming subjugated to the imperial church system worked out by the Emperor Justinian (ruled 527–565). The main representative of the emperor in the West was the exarch of Ravenna, whereas the bishop of Rome was treated as just another patriarch.

The pope who turned things around and set the papacy at the forefront of the Western move from antiquity into the Middle Ages was Gregory I (ruled 590–604). Under his energetic leadership the bishop of Rome became the leading power in the West, Eastern claims to priority in the Church were rejected, and the papacy became the spearhead of a pastoral regime that sought to bring to the whole Church bishops who would care for the entirety of what would become the feudal system of medieval Europe. The successors of Gregory were instrumental in extending Catholic Christianity to the Germanic tribes, and they played a role as well in the conversion of the Slavs. Papal authority expanded, keeping close ties with the temporal authority of the Western emperors.

Benedictine monks had considerable missionary success among the Western tribes, and the Western ruler Charlemagne, crowned Roman emperor in 800 by the pope, ordered his entire kingdom to adopt the Roman liturgy and canon law. Although Charlemagne considered himself the spiritual as well as the temporal head of his kingdom, during the Carolingian age the Church was well patronized. With the advent of the Dark Ages, however, the popes were at the mercy of various marauders and despots, until the German king Otto I came to the rescue. From the crowning of Otto as emperor by Pope John XII in Rome in 962 to the end of the Roman Empire in 1806, the German kings retained the title holy Roman emperor and ties to the papacy.

The main preoccupation of Eastern Christianity during the early medieval period was the controversy over icons, which, as noted, came to a conciliar conclusion in 787. Whereas the West essentially supported the position of those who favored the use of icons, the popes were not much involved in the fights — a sign that the religious interests of West and East had already begun to separate. This is not to say that West and East did not continue to hold the same central affirmations of faith and many behavioral patterns. It is simply to suggest that the schism of 1054 that divided the two realms (each blaming the other for the division) expressed a long-standing cultural separation.

For example, the Sixth Ecumenical Council (Constantinople III, 680) had removed tensions between the Byzantine Empire and Rome, but the claims of the popes to jurisdiction over the whole Church, East as well as West, remained a bone of contention. As early as 691, a council summoned by Emperor Justinian II in Constantinople passed laws (for example, prohibiting fasting on Saturdays and permitting priests to marry) that contravened Roman practice. Pope Sergius rejected these laws as well as claims that the patriarch of Constantinople was the equal of the pope. Pope Leo III offended the Byzantines in 800 by crowning Charlemagne emperor. At midcentury Pope Nicholas (858–867) gave further offense by nullifying the appointment of Photius, the Eastern emperor's choice, as patriarch of Constantinople. This produced the "Photian Schism," and among other things led to the Eastern denunciation of the *filioque* (the Western addition of the words "and from the Son" to the Nicene Creed's treatment of the procession of the Holy Spirit). The Synod of Siponto, assembled by Pope Leo IX in 1050, promoted Western reforms that overturned Eastern usages and caused the Eastern Patriarch, Michael Cerularius, to order all Latin churches in Constantinople to adopt the Greek liturgical rite. All of this history, and much more, boiled over in the mutual excommunications of 1054. Alienation became fixed when the pope forced a Latin patriarch on Antioch at the end of the eleventh century, when the citizens of Constantinople revolted against Latin crusaders in 1182, and when in 1204 the crusaders sacked Constantinople brutally. After 1204, one had to speak of real hatred of East for West.

Popes of the eleventh century instituted some notable reforms, further advancing the claims of the papacy to be the central authority of the universal Church. What soon became the papal curia developed, featuring the college of cardinals (originally a liturgical group) as a political force. The Gregorian Reform of Pope Gregory VII (ruled 1073–1085) sought fuller freedom of the papacy from imperial influence, eventually resulting in the Investiture Controversy over who had the power to install bishops, the pope or the emperor. Gregory VII formulated the doctrine that the bishop of Rome had the power to excommunicate even the most eminent rulers of Western Christendom, should they egregiously offend against Christian faith. The strong-mindedness of Gregory VII shaped the papacy throughout the rest of its history, explaining much of its expectation to dominate the liturgical and legal structures of Western Christendom (the East being in schism). The successors of Gregory contended for secular power and were the movers of such events as the Crusades which tried to recover the Holy Lands. Popes and secular rulers frequently became involved in bitter clashes, the popes sometimes resorting to excommunications and the kings or emperors treating the papacy like a lesser national power they could easily crush by military force.

Until nationalistic tendencies started to split medieval Western Christendom, the papacy remained the center of Western life. Roman Catholicism drew from this heady though ambiguous experience the expectation that its head would always be accounted by other world leaders a political personage of moment, an expectation that continues to be fulfilled today. Roman law and authority came to stamp Western Catholicism, and while Christians outside Italy often chafed under what they considered Italian ecclesiastical hegemony, they frequently treasured the papacy as a source of order and unity, both prior to the Protestant Reformation and after it.

The history of the papacy in the patristic and medieval periods should disabuse one of the wisdom of any purely theological approach to the Church. The popes often gouged and scratched for power with the most savage of imperial infighters, certainly in the name of what they took to be the authority necessary to rule the Church well, but rather clearly also as people often carried along by what philosopher Friedrich Nietzsche would later call the will-to-power. The late medieval popes have become synonymous with decadence and disorder, especially those of the fourteenth century "Babylonian Captivity," when the papacy moved from Rome to Avignon in France, offering the disedifying spectacle of as many as three different prelates claiming the office of Peter.

One result of all this turmoil and political murkiness associated with the papacy has been that Catholics descended from European nations long involved with the popes (Italians, Germans, French) have tended to carry a rather minimalist, if not cynical view of Roman rule. At times this has served their faith badly, leading to agnosticism and anticlericalism. At other times, however, it has prodded them to clarify the distance of God and Christ from their earthly representatives, and so take the papal claims with a salutary grain of salt. Some students of the twentieth-century papacy (which has been morally superior to its medieval and renaissance predecessors) have been amused to see the papacy continuing to assert sweeping theological (seldom temporal) claims, in the style of the medievals, and so have been stimulated as many of their forebears in Catholic faith had been to relativize all things Roman in light of the much greater significance of Christ, the Trinity, the divine life of grace, the basic Christian law of love, the experiences of prayer, and the call of ministries such as preaching, administering the sacraments, missionizing the faithless, and serving the poor.

Scholasticism and Mysticism

If the papacy was the predominant external, political institution of medieval Catholicism, such intellectual and devotional trends as scholasticism and mysticism provided balancing fare for Catholics' interior lives. Scholasticism was the educational tradition of the Middle Ages, developed in cathedral schools, monasteries, and then in the medieval universities. Applied to philosophy and theology, it continued the work begun at the Church councils, where the door opened to developing biblical faith in virtue of challenges and needs arising in postbiblical times and categories.

The guiding motto of the scholastic theologians was "faith seeking understanding." As expressed and exemplified by giants such as Anselm, the effort was to assume faith and to probe for what illumination reason, guided by revelation and grace, might attain. The great scholastics never tried to supplant faith and never expected or desired to remove or avoid the mysteriousness of God. But they were confident that human reason could come to trustworthy conclusions about theological matters (as about things in the natural world), as they were confident that God, the source of human reason, expected people to use their heads. Such influences as the Neoplatonic speculations of Augustine, the philosophical works of Boethius, and then, as Arab translators made them available, the logical works of Aristotle, combined to make medieval scholasticism formidably rational. Powerful minds such as Peter Abelard tussled with powerful hearts such as Bernard of Clairvaux, battling about what shape theology ought to have. Eventually the partisans of Augustine and Neoplatonism were set against the partisans of Thomas Aquinas and Aristotle, but on the road to this denouement many different combinations of head and heart passed review.

What was developing among the scholastics was a sophisticated sense of the complex yet potentially mutually supportive relations between faith and reason, which relations led a thirteenth-century genius such as Aquinas to make the most important theological reasoning analogical. One could build bridges from the material sensations in which human knowledge began to the strictly theological matters rooted in the mysterious God. Because of divine revelation, realities such as the Trinity and the realm of grace had come into human ken, not as something human beings could ever master but as wonders that human probing could sufficiently illumine in people's minds and hearts that they might embrace faith with enthusiasm.

The scholastic method was to assemble on a given question opinions traditionally considered authoritative, see how they correlated, try to remove any discordances, and through such exercises bring into view the speculative or systematic crux of the matter. One could distinguish between the "way of discovery," which sought a judgment of fact about what traditional, authoritative Church teaching had been on a particular question, and the "way of teaching," which sought a (hypothetical) understanding of how the elements of such a question fell into explanation. The scholastics became both great citers of texts and sharp dialecticians, pursuing the *quaestio* that had stirred their minds to the limits of argumentative reasoning. At that point, the best of them counseled returning to a contemplative, prayerful attitude that would appreciate the mystery involved, using any light gained in the dialectical process to further the delight faith might experience in the beauty of God.

This love of sharp analysis and argument passed into the Catholic theological style, at high points making for a most intelligent display of reasoning about the foundations and implications of faith, while at low points becoming arid logic-chopping. From the advent of modernity in the seventeenth century, philosophical critics have had an easy time showing the deficiencies of scholasticism, as the sixteenth-century Reformers had had an easy time showing the effective superiority of their return to biblical concreteness. Indeed, later moderns clarified the scholastic drawbacks as a lack of historical consciousness and a lack of what we might call existential personalism: appreciation for all the ways that the individual is more than just a mind, and for the influence this "more" ought to have in theology and philosophy.

Medieval Catholicism also was rich in mystics, some of them scholastics but others simpler souls. One of the medieval mystical currents that present-day theologians find most appealing was a positive view of creation. Two female writers, Hildegard of Bingen (1098–1179) and Mechtilde of Magdeburg (1210–1280), recast Benedictine views to depict creation as a great display of God's gifts. Creation carried an original blessing from God, deep in its constitution, that no sin of human beings had ever destroyed. Similarly, these women viewed the human body as a great blessing, nothing of which to be ashamed. The Fall (sin of Adam and Eve) might have made things more difficult for human beings, but the proper response to earthly life continued to be great gratitude to God, along with great enjoyment of the beauty of God unfurled throughout creation.

Like many other medievals, Hildegard and Mechtilde contemplated the human person as a microcosm — a miniature of God's creative work. Spanning from lowest matter to flights of spiritual ecstasy, the human person synthesized several orders of being and so could be contemplated as a composite or epitome of divine blessings. The God who had made the human being and cared for its salvation was like a mother in wanting to nurture its best capacities. In imitation of this maternal deity, Hildegard and Mechtilde counseled supportive, nurturing attitudes toward one's fellow creatures, animals as well as other human beings.[3]

German mystics such as Meister Eckhart, Johannes Tauler, and Henry Suso offered the fourteenth century a profound metaphysical appreciation of creation to complement the stress of Hildegard and Mechtilde on the original blessing. Eckhart is generally accounted as both the deepest and the most controversial, because his insights into the presence of divinity in each creature verged on pantheism — making everything God. Many commentators think that Eckhart rather was teaching what one might call panentheism — the presence of God in everything and the repose of everything in God. However this debate ought to be resolved, the positive upshot of the writings of the German mystics was a most encouraging emphasis on God's nearness.

Augustine had spoken of divinity as "more intimate to me than I am to myself." Eckhart and his followers meditated on this truth (which could seem to have affinities with the Johannine counsels about "abiding") in light of the teaching of Thomas Aquinas (a fellow member of the Order of Preachers) about existence. Aquinas had taken much from Aristotle concerning how to think about the essences or natures of things, but he had added (to some extent from Neoplatonic sources) a fresh stress on the act of existence — the "to be" (*esse*) that makes any essence real. God, in fact, could be thought of as *esse subsistens*: a pure act of existence, such that God's essence (what God is) would be simply to be (is!). If so, then each actually existing being could be looked at as a presence of God. Without the immanent grant of existence that God, the fontal source of being, alone could give, no human being or other creature would ever come to be or remain in existence.

The Germans went on to discuss what the Christian East called divinization, concluding that by several titles human beings involved with God could think they were being brought into the divine substance or were finding themselves to be actualizations of divinity. None of this discussion, however, remained speculative or academic, because all of it focused on the experience of divinity in prayer. As Thomas à Kempis, a fifteenth-century spiritual master from the Netherlands, later would say, the point was not to know the definition of compunction but to feel it in one's heart. The German mystics got involved with the mysteries of the divine presence in people's souls because that was where their mystical feeling for God had taken them.

As such wonderful medieval writers as Chaucer and Dante suggest, metaphysics and concern with the original blessing of creation were not the only interests of Catholic piety. Later we see something of the spirituality of Francis of Assisi, the most beloved saint of the era, but we may mention here his love of the infant Christ and his reception of the stigmata — reproductions of the wounds caused by Christ's nailing to the cross. Chaucer's pilgrims and Dante's personnel populating the circles of hell and purgatory were more ordinary and sinful Catholic Christians than Francis, but the medieval concern with order and death seems regularly to have formed people such as they toward a balanced view of the human condition.

Thus, pilgrims setting out for Canterbury, Rome, or Compostela in Spain usually had in mind a good work that might mitigate the penalties their sins merited. They would believe that pilgrimage sites were holy places, suffused with grace, and that God would hear the intercessory prayers of the saints the sites honored. For these pilgrims, the Virgin Mary was the greatest of saints, so her intercessions were the most powerful, and thinking of the Virgin nearly inevitably called to mind the child who made her the Madonna. Mother and child were the favorite subjects of much medieval art, and the tender sense of God's love they evoked, along with the reminders that both Jesus and Mary had suffered terribly at the cross because of human beings' sins, fed the **mystagogy** of medieval Catholicism.

Representative Personality: Augustine

There is little dispute that Augustine of Hippo (354–430 C.E.) was the most important figure in the patristic West, nor that his influence greatly shaped both medieval and Reformation thought. The story of his lengthy delay in embracing Christian faith is familiar to many Westerners, if only because Augustine's years of concubinage have been much sensationalized. Suffice it to say that Augustine's having been mired in the flesh, as well as trapped in Manichean categories that set matter and spirit in opposition, made his conversion to Catholic Christianity spectacular.

In the *Confessions* that narrate Augustine's passage to continence and Catholic faith, one finds profound reflections on God's ways with the human soul expressed in elegant language. Augustine the pre-Christian teacher of rhetoric soon became Augustine the eloquent preacher and moving writer. Yet for all that the style bespoke the passionate man, and that Augustine's sins and his mother Monica's tears fascinated medieval Christians, the source of Augustine's great theological impact was the power of his meditations on sin and grace.

Joining his own experiences of bondage to sin with his reading of Scripture, Augustine took to heart both the account of the Fall in Genesis 3 and the Pauline discussions (above all in Romans) of the dialectic between sin and grace. His findings were complicated, and they provided much nuance, but the reading favored by such influential later interpreters as Martin Luther, John Calvin, and Cornelius Jansen seems justified. For them Augustine was pessimistic about human nature, thinking that only the grace of God could keep it from depravity. Still, one ought to read such sections of the *Confessions* as those where Augustine considers his childhood theft of pears and the greed of an infant at the breast in light of the bondage to sensuality he experienced in late adolescence and young adulthood. Escape from lust only came by movements of grace in his soul that Augustine felt came to him completely freely, apart from any merits of his own. Whereas Augustine dealt with the same scriptural texts about sin and grace that drew more optimistic medievals such as Aquinas, his sense of sin was darker and his sense of grace more prone to call it extraordinary. Augustine was not a man who looked at creation as Hildegard and Mechtilde did. He did not regard the divine being present to his own being as matter-of-factly as the German mystics did. His approach to God and Christ was more tortured and convoluted.

Augustine sometimes is referred to as the "Doctor of Grace," and from his controversial writings against the **Pelagians** both the patristic and the medieval worlds learned penetrating lessons about the gratuity of salvation. Augustine himself enjoyed a lifelong bedazzlement with the wonder of God's having saved him. His sense of God's goodness knew no bounds, so again and again he stressed that nothing in us human beings lures God to be gracious. God saves people from sin and grants them divine life purely because of God's own goodness, which makes grace secure. The Pelagians' stress on human freedom and responsibility fell on Augustine's ears as a denial or underappreciation of such goodness and security, so he attacked the Pelagians roundly.

In 529 the Second Council of Orange published several canons on grace directed against the lingering effects of the Pelagian heresy. The language of these canons came largely from the writings of Augustine, and it suggests what his successors had made of the theology of grace he had set forth:

If anyone says that the grace of God can be conferred by human invocation and that grace itself does not effect it, as it is invoked by us, he is contradicting the prophet Isaiah, or the Apostle who says the same: "I was found by them that did not seek me; I appeared openly to them that asked not after me" (Rom 10: 20, Is 65:1).

If anyone says that God waits upon our will to cleanse us from sins and does not confess that our desire to be cleansed comes about in us by the infusion and operation of the Holy Spirit, he opposes the Holy Spirit himself who, speaking through Solomon says: "The will shall be prepared by the Lord" (Prov 8: 35) and (denies) the salutary teaching of the Apostle: "For it is God who worketh in you, both to will and to accomplish, according to his good will" (Phil 2: 13).

If anyone says that, as the increase, so also the beginning of faith, indeed even the pious readiness to believe, whereby we believe what justifies the impious and attain to the regeneration of holy baptism, is not in us by a gift of grace, that is, by inspiration of the Holy Spirit changing our will from unbelief to belief, from impiety to piety, but occurs naturally, he shows himself to be an enemy of the apostolic teaching of St. Paul. . . .[4]

In addition to his massive influence on how later Western Christians thought about sin and grace, Augustine also shaped the historiography of the Western world by his work *The City of God* and set the main guidelines for trinitarian theology by his work *On the Trinity*. Both of these writings were sizable undertakings, the first mounting an extended defense of the Church against the charge that it had caused the decline of the Roman Empire, and the second producing a "psychological analogy" for the relations and movements of the trinitarian persons that drew on human memory, understanding, and will.

In Augustine's interpretation of history, divine forces of grace battled human forces of sin, and believers were never to expect on earth a comfortable city. In Augustine's interpretation of the life of the trinity, the Johannine texts became rich metaphors, stimulating an introspective genius to imagine the fathomless recesses of the memorial Father, from whom all things issued, including the dazzling light of the Logos and the wonderful love of the Spirit. The Neoplatonist in Augustine thought in terms of light descending from above to illumine human recipients, making them participants in what overflowed from a fontal divinity.

Until it found the Protestant interpretations of Paul and Augustine unacceptable, Catholic Christianity embraced the dialectic of sin and grace we have suggested. Under the pressure of Lutheran and Calvinist pessimism, however, it became leery of Augustine's views of original sin, which had alienation from God being transmitted through sexual intercourse, so that every new human being was an enemy of God. Catholicism also rejected some of Augustine's speculations about predestination, shying away from language that would present God as having from eternity consigned some people to heaven and some to hell. Without denying the errors of Pelagius, Catholic theologians came to the defense of both human nature and human freedom, believing that the operations of grace perfected a nature and freedom that needed help but were not vicious. God the Savior was not a repairman forced to redo a job God the Creator had botched. Where sin had abounded, grace from the beginning had abounded the more, preserving the original blessing.

Glossary

Communion of saints: the Catholic teaching that all members of the
Church, past and present, form a community across space and time, and
that the merits and needs of one may be related to the needs and
merits of others. The picture in the Book of Revelation of the saints
assembled in heaven contributed to this doctrine, as did the Pauline
theology of the Body of Christ. The doctrine of the Communion of
Saints had the consoling impact of making all Christians feel united in
faith and able to be helped by the saints, but it also had the dangerous

possibility of making the treasury of the saints' merits the foundation for an abusive policy about indulgences, as happened at the time of Luther.

Mystagogy: the exercise of mystical faculties, or the elaboration of the mystical dimension of a rite or teaching, that brings into focus the surplus of intelligibility divinity always carries, making it clear that a certain obscurity always attends the things of God. Mystagogy should both deepen people's appreciation of the bottomless depths in any dealing with God, encouraging their peace and joy, and humble them with the realization that their sins and finitude make them bound to experience God as one they can neither understand nor control.

Pelagians: those who followed the teachings of the Irish monk Pelagius, who was active around 400, to the effect that the burden of salvation lies in human beings' hands. Scholars are not completely certain what Pelagius actually taught, but popularly he was taken to have been a champion of asceticism, a strong will, and self-reliance. Augustine and the orthodox generally found Pelagius undervaluing the grace of God and the gratuity of salvation, as well as underestimating the effects of sin.

Discussion Questions

1. What is the significance of the Church's having called the days when the martyrs died their birthdays?
2. What were the main inspirations for the rise of Christian monasticism?
3. Why were the ecumenical councils so concerned about the status of the Logos?
4. What were the implications of denying the full humanity of Jesus?
5. What is the Petrine ministry claimed by the bishops of Rome?
6. What does the history of the popes' struggles with the imperial powers of Europe suggest about the Catholic sense of politics and history?
7. How was the scholastic understanding of theology an encouragement to strong dialectical reasoning?
8. Why did Hildegard and Mechtilde think of the Creator as a nurturing mother?
9. How correct was Augustine to make his own experience of bondage to lust a strong factor in his theological reflections?
10. How does the Augustinian stress on grace suggest one should think about God?

Notes

[1] See Philip Rousseau, "The Desert Fathers, Antony and Pachomius," in *The Study of Spirituality*, ed. Cheslyn Jones, Geoffrey Wainwright, and Edward Yarnold, S.J. (New York: Oxford University Press, 1986), pp. 119–130.

[2] See Raymond E. Brown and John P. Meier, *Antioch and Rome* (Ramsey, N.J.: Paulist Press, 1983).

[3] See Matthew Fox, "Creation-Centered Spirituality from Hildegard of Bingen to Julian of Norwich," in *Cry of the Envisionment*, ed. Philip Joranson and Ken Butigan (Sante Fe: Bear Publications, 1984), pp. 93–94.

[4] Joseph Neuner and Heinrich Roos, *The Teaching of the Catholic Church* (Staten Island: Alba House, 1967), pp. 378–379.

CHAPTER 4

The Period of Reform

Early Reform Movements
Protestantism
Trent
Foreign Missions
Representative Personality: Ignatius Loyola
Glossary, Discussion Questions, Notes

Early Reform Movements

Our sketch of the medieval papacy has suggested some of the motives for the reform movements that occurred throughout the Middle Ages. One might also note several significant monastic reforms that were aimed at returning monks to an austere practice of the Benedictine rule and at overcoming the too comfortable life that monastic wealth could create. One could consider the new religious orders founded by Francis and Dominic expressions of a desire for reform, although both were also directed at combatting heretical movements, such as **Albigensianism** (which gained some of its plausibility from its claim to be a purer faith). Still, it was the disarray of the Avignon papacy, and then the worldliness of the Renaissance Church, that sparked the conflagration of protests. In this section we consider reformers who worked prior to the early sixteenth century, whereas in the next section we consider such figures as Luther, Zwingli, and Calvin, who begot a Protestantism in schism from Catholicism.

Four early reformers who suggest the direction fourteenth- and fifteenth-century Catholicism might have taken are the Englishman John Wycliffe (about 1329–1384), the Italian Catherine of Siena (about 1333 to 1380), the Bohemian John Hus (about 1369–1415), and the Dutchman Desiderius Erasmus (about 1466–1536).

John Wycliffe was born into a wealthy English family, educated at Oxford, and established as a Master at Balliol College, Oxford, about 1360. He held various parish assignments in the 1360s and 1370s, while continuing his association with Oxford, and in 1374 he was one of several English envoys involved in negotiations with the papacy about matters of common interest in Bruges, Flanders. Wycliffe was known as a keen philosopher, much opposed to **nominalism.** His two works on the Lordship of Christ were notable for their claim that the sinful state of the Church rendered Christ's Lordship ineffectual. The remedy he proposed was to confiscate ecclesiastical properties and return the Church to a proper poverty, placing its wealth at the service of the common people. Wycliffe found grace implying that each individual has considerable liberty, a position that some scholars think helped stimulate a rebellion of English peasants in 1381. Whether he was responsible or not, the upper classes came to regard Wycliffe as dangerous.

The "Great Schism" between Papel Contenders that resulted from the Avignon papacy stimulated Wycliffe to more radical views of Church reform, based on such foundations as his finding no biblical basis for many papal claims and his conviction that the salvation of the pope was no more certain than the salvation of anyone else. Wycliffe became convinced that only conformity with the gospel justified any Church claims or practices. His language denouncing the Avignon popes, wealthy monks, and others he thought were abusing the Christian community became quite violent, and his views of the eucharist led him to oppose the medieval doctrine of **transubstantiation.** Because of his convictions about the primacy of Scripture, he began an English translation of the Bible.

These ideas won Wycliffe condemnation by a bull (document) published by Pope Gregory XI in 1377 and by a Council in London in 1382. Only after his death, however, was the totality of his views condemned, by the Council of Constance in 1415. In retrospect Wycliffe seems a clear precursor of the sixteenth-century Protestant Reformers, especially in his insistence that the Bible should regulate all of Christian life. He was a direct influence on John Hus and the source of the Lollards, followers who developed his views to establish a popular movement for radical social and ecclesiastical reforms in fifteenth-century England, thereby earning themselves considerable persecution.

Catherine of Siena was the daughter (the youngest of twenty children), of a Sienese merchant. She started receiving visions as a young girl and early entered upon a life of great austerity. Refusing to consider marriage, she joined the Third Order of Saint Dominic at the age of sixteen, giving herself over to contemplation and service of the poor and the sick. She quickly gained a reputation for great sanctity, drew numerous disciples, and later journeyed around Italy sponsoring good works. Toward the end of her life she became involved in Church politics. In 1376 Catherine traveled to Avignon to plead with Pope Gregory XI on behalf of Florence, which was at war with the papacy, and to persuade him to return to Rome, which he did. Although Catherine was illiterate, she dictated some significant spiritual writings, as well as many letters urging the popes and others to do something about the low morals and general corruption of the Church. When the Great Schism between different contenders for succession to Gregory rent the Church, Catherine supported Urban VI and worked diligently for his cause, all the while criticizing his harshness. Because of her labors, which wore her out and caused her death, she was popularly considered responsible for the eventual removal of papal claimants at Avignon and the reconsolidation of the papacy in Rome.

John Hus was born of a peasant family in Bohemia and became a master at Prague university in 1396. In 1401 he was made dean of the faculty of philosophy, and in 1409 he became the rector of the entire university. Ordained a priest in 1400, Hus soon established a reputation as a fine preacher. Through the marriage of Anne, sister of the Czech King Wenceslaus IV, to Richard II of England in 1398, Bohemia developed close ties with England and Hus learned of the writings of John Wycliffe. Hus was especially attracted to Wycliffe's advocacy of rejecting property rights and a hierarchical organization of society.

Although at first Hus received some official Church support, before long the violent tone of his sermons about the poor morals of the clergy led to his ideas being condemned, first at the university and then in Rome. Forbidden to preach, Hus next got involved in the dispute over papal succession. The university gained some independence from the machinations associated with this dispute, and for awhile Hus was riding high. However, in 1410 a papal bull ordered the burning of Hus's books, and in 1411 he was excommunicated.

Hus went into seclusion, writing a book on the Church that developed Wycliffe's ideas. He traveled to the Council of Constance to defend his views, thinking he had a guarantee of safe passage. In Constance, however, Hus was imprisoned and then in 1415, he was burned at the stake as a heretic. The University of Prague declared Hus a martyr and the Czech nation went into schism. His influence has continued throughout Czech history, which generally has considered him a martyr to the cause of Church reform and Czech freedom.

Desiderius Erasmus of Rotterdam probably was born illegitmate. He went to the Brothers of the Common Life for schooling, taking to heart much of their spirituality, which was associated with the "Devotio Moderna" most famously represented in *The Imitation of Christ* attributed to Thomas à Kempis. Somewhat reluctantly Erasmus became an Augustinian priest, but his great passion was the humanist movement then reaching Northern Europe from Italy. This movement led Erasmus back to the pagan classics and to the Church fathers. Erasmus traveled to France and England, making contact with leading humanists, solidifying his dislike of scholasticism and his love of the New Testament. At the accession of King Henry VIII in 1509 he went to England for an extended stay, living for a while with Thomas More and receiving honors at Oxford and Cambridge (where he was made Lady Margaret Professor of Greek and Theology).

Erasmus's reputation as a scholar, editor of the New Testament, and advocate of reform in education and Church affairs was such that he constantly received offers from royal courts and universities, but he generally preferred to devote himself to scholarship and the travel that kept him in touch with other humanist Reformers. He had mixed feelings about the Protestant Reformation, agreeing with many of its goals but not supporting all of its theology and feeling dismay at its division of the Church. Erasmus's main religious influence came through such writings as his *Manual of a Christian Soldier* (1504), which showed the utility of scholarship for Christian formation, his *Praise of Folly* (1509), which satirized monasticism and Church corruptions, and his new edition of the Greek New Testament text (1516). In 1524 he wrote against Luther's theology, arguing in his *Diatribe about Free Will* that people have more freedom and responsibility than Luther allowed. He also edited versions of many of the Church fathers.

Erasmus was the most famous man in the Europe of his day, admired for his wide learning. Whereas his attacks on corruption paved the way for the Protestant Reformation, he so abhorred strife that he could not join the Protestant movement. Thus he eventually became suspect to both reformers and Catholics. The University of Paris censured him in 1527 and after his death several popes forbade the reading of his writings.

If we generalize about the concerns and impact of these four forerunners of the sixteenth-century Protestant Reformers, it is clear that all four were sickened by the wealth the Catholic church had accumulated and the low estate of many of the clergy, who were ignorant and living in concubinage. The political upheavals, which came to a head in the Avignon papacy, argued for a full reform of the Church, in head as well as members. These four Reformers all lamented how the Church was failing Christ and not fulfilling its mission, which was to exemplify the gospel and so make Christian faith both persuasive and effective. If Wycliffe and Hus became intemperate in their attacks on the papacy and in some of their theological positions, one may say that they were pushed to extremes by the resistance of Church leaders to reform. Catherine of Siena and Desiderius Erasmus avoided such extremes, but their criticisms of the Church were nearly as biting. The fourteenth century was a low point in Church life, so all vital Christians were bound to feel anger and sadness.

Protestantism

Martin Luther (1483–1546) was the son of a miner. He studied at Erfurt University, Germany, where he concentrated on philosophy. In 1505 he joined the Augustinian hermits at Erfurt, fulfilling a vow he had previously made during a thunderstorm. Ordained a priest in 1507, Luther studied and lectured on moral philosophy at the newly founded University of Wittenberg. The Church abuses he witnessed during a visit to Rome in 1510 shocked him. In 1511 he became a doctor of theology and began lecturing on Scripture. From 1515 he held an important administrative position in the Augustinian order.

But all was not well with Luther's intellectual and spiritual life, as he found himself increasingly disaffected from Catholic tradition and worried about his personal salvation. Influenced by the **nominalism** at the contemporary universities, he rejected scholasticism. Accepting the pessimistic view of human nature held by the Augustinians, Luther developed such religious scruples that he gave up saying Mass. Between 1512 and 1515 he had an overwhelming experience that made him think the essence of the gospel was that faith alone justifies people, without regard for works. Studies in Augustine and such mystical writings as the works of Tauler and the *Theologica Germanica* convinced him that this view of justification had a traditional basis: human beings were nothing before God.

Soon Luther began to doubt the necessity of an ecclesiastical or priestly mediation of salvation. When he encountered the Dominican theologian Johann Tetzel's preaching of **indulgences** (ways to avoid punishment after death) in 1517, Luther wrote ninety-five theses expressing his demurrals. According to legend Luther affixed these theses to the door of the cathedral church at Wittenberg, throwing down the gauntlet to Rome. News of his defiance spread through Germany like wildfire, with many humanists embracing his position. Between 1517 and 1520 various disputes and attempts at mediation occurred, the result of which was to fortify Luther in his opposition to Roman views. His three writings of 1520 — an address to the German princes, a work on the Babylonian Captivity of the Church, and a work on the Freedom of Christians — completed his break with Rome.

Luther's main positions included the conviction that **justification** comes by faith or grace alone, that the Bible ought to be the sole authority in Christian life and that individuals have the right to interpret the Bible for themselves, that various abuses of the Mass (such as its being in a language most of the people did not understand) had separated the laity from proper nourishment, and that baptism and the Eucharist were the only genuine sacraments. A papal bull quickly branded these positions heretical and threatened Luther with excommunication. Luther burned the bull and was excommunicated early in 1521. Politics intervened and Luther came under the protection of the Elector of Saxony. During a period of seclusion he began his fine translation of the Bible into German. Under the influence of his ideas, which included attacks on celibacy and monasticism, many priests and nuns left their religious groups.

Luther himself married in 1525, and political conditions (the desire of many German princes to oppose Rome) favored the further spread of his ideas.

Liturgical hymns that he composed proved both popular and effective in promulgating his new religious emphases. In 1529, however, Luther and the Swiss German Reformer Ulrich Zwingli disagreed at the Colloquy of Marburg about the nature of the Eucharist, opening a major split in the Reformers' ranks. Luther approved the Augsburg Confession of 1530, which was largely the work of Philip Melanchthon, another major early Reformer, and which tried to bring the Lutheran and Roman positions into agreement. Little progress in reconciliation occurred after that, however, and in the Schmalkalden Articles of 1537 the two positions were set far apart.

More dissents among the Reformers inclined Luther increasingly to put disciplinary matters in the hands of the civil authorities. To the end of his life, though, he reserved his bitterest invective for the papacy. In his most extreme doctrinal statements Luther professed a complete pessimism about a depraved human nature and a useless reason, which led him all the more to stress the free grace of God and a salvation imputed to human beings because of Christ. On their own, human beings could do nothing but sin. Still, fortified by a strong faith in God's mercy, Luther enchanted many as a great preacher and robust champion of religious freedom.

Ulrich Zwingli (1484–1531), leader of the Swiss German Reformation centered in Zurich, was a great admirer of Erasmus. Disaffected by religious abuses he observed at the pilgrimage site of Einsiedeln in 1516, he came to focus his Christian faith in New Testament studies. Lectures he gave on the New Testament in Zurich in 1519 sparked the Reformation there, and soon Zwingli was giving sermons against **purgatory,** the cult of the saints, and monasticism, calling all corruptions of the original Christian faith. He seems to have developed his ideas apart from much influence from Luther.

Zwingli's congregation at Zurich successfully resisted the efforts of papal representatives to quell their movement, and Zwingli broadened his attacks to include all traditions he thought not rooted in the gospel, which included the papacy, the sacrifice of the Mass, fasting, and clerical celibacy. In 1524 Zwingli married, and in 1525 he suppressed the Mass and removed images from Zurich churches, convinced that the cult of the saints had taken people away from a proper worship of God. His Eucharistic doctrine became more radical, as he rejected any sort of presence of Christ in the Sacrament, a position that divided Zwinglianism from Lutheranism and other Protestant theologies. Reform spread to other Swiss cantons, but bitter resistance arose in the forest cantons, which remained Catholic. This led to Zwingli's death in a military skirmish in 1531.

John Calvin (1509–1564) was born in Picardy. Destined for an ecclesiastical career, he received the tonsure (the first step to ordination) at the age of twelve. He studied theology in Paris, and then law at Orleans and Bourges, where he first encountered Protestants. A religious experience in 1533 convinced Calvin he had a mission to purify the Church, precipitating his break with Catholicism. Fleeing to Basel to avoid possible persecution, he secluded himself for studies that resulted in the first version of his *Institutes*. In 1536 Calvin yielded to pleas of Genevans to help them organize the Reform there, beginning a very influential career.

Calvin's demands on the Genevan citizens were strict: if they would not profess Reformed faith they faced exile. However, when he tried to go beyond this to excommunicate some citizens, he himself was expelled. Working in Strasbourg, Calvin revised his *Institutes*, wrote a commentary on Paul's Epistle to the Romans, and engaged in controversy with Roman Catholic authorities. Having become friends with such other leading Reformers as Melanchthon and Martin Bucer, Calvin participated in various theological conferences, returning to Geneva in 1541 when his partisans regained the upper hand. Over the next fourteen years Calvin turned Geneva into a theocratic regime based on biblical principles. His regime included a sophisticated system for governing the church. It approved strict laws about moral behavior, with harsh punishments not only for religious offenses but for dancing and games. Several opponents of this new regime were tortured and executed.

By 1555 Calvin was in complete control of Geneva and an acknowledged Reform leader influential in other communities. Most of his study and writing went into voluminous biblical commentaries. There Calvin continued to contribute a systematic mind to the Reformed cause, expanding the impact of the *Institutes*, which became the most influential theological formulation of Protestantism. His personal austerity extended into his rule of Geneva, making it a city of the strictest morality. On the other hand, his vindictiveness and demand for complete power, including the right to decide what was true Christianity for all under his sway, alienated many. Overall, however, Calvin achieved a great reputation for learning and able administration that made him widely known and highly regarded throughout Protestant Europe. The churches formed by his theology have been among the most significant in the Protestant mainstream, including the United States, where Presbyterians and Congregationalists follow Calvinistic theology.

Trent

The attacks of Luther, Zwingli, Calvin, and other Protestant Reformers, along with the warm reception their programs received in many parts of Europe, put the Catholic camp, centered in Rome, on the defensive. At first, Roman officials tried to treat most of the new theology as a disciplinary matter, threatening punishments such as the removal of permission to preach or teach. By the time the Roman officials realized they had more than a series of petty revolts on their hands, the Protestant program was well established.

The fourteenth-century movements for reform and the positions of the sixteenth-century Protestants indicate that several emphases ruled throughout. Negatively, the Reformers wanted to purify the Church of its excessive wealth, landholding, and immersion in secular politics. The reformers also castigated the morals of the clergy, as well as their ignorance of solid doctrine, and thus their failure to pasture the flock of Christ as they ought to have done. Positively, the Reformers wanted a return to the relative simplicity, as well as the warmth and the depth, of the biblical portrait of Christianity. Scripture seemed capable of turning hearts aglow, moving people to generosity toward both God and neighbor. Scripture thus became the great rallying cry.

A combination of factors — the influence of Augustinian thought, the psychological aftermath of the Black Plague, and a sense of hopelessness when one realized the enormity of the Church reform that was needed — made the Reformers pessimistic about human nature. Their response was to exalt faith and grace as channels to salvation made available solely through the divine mercy. One could trust neither human reason nor human goodness. The other aspects of the Reformers' program — changes in Eucharistic theology and practice that might remove superstition and bring the sacrament deeper into the lives of the laity; pruning excesses in veneration of the saints and embellishment of worship; and lessening the distance between clergy and laity, by clarifying the priesthood of all believers — grew beyond this basic desire. When one added such factors as nationalism, the rise of a middle class, economic changes, and the development of printing, one sees why there was such turmoil.

The Catholic Counter-Reformation designed to meet the challenge of reform finally produced a compromise position. The Church ought to improve the education and moral standards of the clergy. Excesses in devotion to the saints and adornments of worship ought to be trimmed. The truth in the Pauline teaching about justification by faith and the Augustinian teaching about the constant priority of divine grace in all progress toward salvation ought to be acknowledged. On the other hand, the Catholic tradition forbade agreeing to the Reformers' dark view of human nature, as it forbade agreeing to their denial that the Mass represented the sacrifice of Christ on Calvary. Similarly, Catholics could not agree that there were only two authentic Sacraments, that laity and clergy were little different, that the Church was not an essential context and mediator of salvation, that reason was completely untrustworthy and good works were wholly worthless, or that Scripture ought not always to be complemented by tradition.

Unfortunately, the Catholics were so reluctant to deal with the Protestants as sincere Reformers, and so slow to get their own program of reform in place, that they lost the crucial generation when compromise might have meant not simply a set of conceptual readjustments but a political give and take that could have saved Church unity. Luther had posted his ninety-five theses about indulgences in 1517. The Council of Trent that institutionalized Catholic efforts at reform did not open until 1545, and it did not complete its work until 1563. The forty-six years between 1517 and 1563 were the life span of an average person in sixteenth-century Europe. By the time Trent had polished up the theology that was to shape Roman Catholicism until the middle of the twentieth century, the Protestants had launched their own founding age, heading off on a venture from which Rome could never call them back.

And whereas the schism between Catholics in the West and Orthodox in the East seemed mainly a tribute to cultural differences and the stubbornness of Church officials on both sides, because the two groups remained quite close in their sense of the traditional faith, the sundering of the Western Church at the Protestant Reformation shattered all pretense of Church unity, making the sinfulness of the division glaring. Both Catholics and Protestants were great losers, to say nothing of the peoples in the New World, Asia, and Africa whom they later strove to convert. Catholicism never took to heart the biblical warmth and institutional self-criticism the Reformers' might have provided it. The continuous further dividing of the Protestant groups into sects threatened to make Protestantism a caricature of willful disregard of the common good. As well, the unhinging of faith and reason in Protestant theology paved the way to the modern intellectuals' cultured despising of religion.

The Council of Trent was beset with policital machinations. Some of the Church leaders and secular princes involved wanted it to secure the return of the Protestants (by being conciliatory toward their demands) and others wanted the Council to denounce the Protestant positions and get the Catholic house in order as a private venture (in effect conceding the loss of the populations who had turned Protestant).

The main results from the first period of the Council (1545–1547) included reaffirming the Nicene-Constantinopolitan Creed as the formal basis of faith, asserting the equal validity of Scripture and tradition as sources of religious truth, asserting the sole right of the Church to interpret the Bible, and reaffirming the authority of the Vulgate (Latin translation) of the Bible. In decrees on original sin, **justification,** and merit, the Council attacked the Protestant positions, striving to uphold the place of human freedom, human responsibility, and the need to actualize the faith and grace given by God. Concerning the sacraments, the Council reaffirmed the validity of what it considered the traditional seven, rejecting the Reformers' assertion that only baptism and the Eucharist were authentic.

The second period of the Council (1551–1552) also dealt with sacramental theology, reaffirming transubstantiation and clarifying Catholic teaching about penance and extreme unction (last anointing). Protestant observers pressed to have bishops released from their oaths of allegiance to the papacy, and for an assertion of the supremacy of Church councils over the pope, but without avail. The papacy considered the Reformers' attacks on the authority of the popes a threat to both tradition and Church unity.

The third Tridentine period (1562–1563) came after a ten-year delay caused by political infighting and the bias of the strongly anti-Protestant Pope Paul IV (ruled 1555–1559). By the time Trent had resumed, the possibility of reconciling the Protestants seemed long gone. Struggles between the papacy and various nationalist groups of bishops hindered positive work on radical ecclesiastical reform, whereas most of the doctrinal decrees continued to focus on the sacraments, reasserting the sacrificial character of the Mass and clarifying the theology of orders and matrimony. Practical reforms for the seminaries and concerning the residence of bishops (their staying home to serve the area to which they were assigned) did emerge and have considerable good effect in subsequent decades.

After Trent, work begun on revising the Index of forbidden books and developing updated catechisms and creeds that would take into account the declarations of the council concluded, along with a revision of the Vulgate and of the breviary (prayerbook) used by priests. Overall, there were enough fruits from the council to allow Catholic Reformers to rejoice and feel they had a mandate. But Western Christianity was no longer the Church Catholic, living "according to the whole" of its tradition, despite all claims of Catholics or Protestants to have preserved or retrieved the faith that had been handed down long before. Thereafter the Church was battered and abused, manifestly divided in mind, heart, and community. In heaven no doubt it remained the bride of Christ, but on earth it was divorced and struggling.

Foreign Missions

From its founding the Church Catholic had considered outreach, preaching the good news about Christ, part of its constitution. The decision in the first generation to open Church membership to the Gentiles had settled in principle the question of who would be eligible to join the Body of Christ: anyone who came to faith. Christianity rapidly spread throughout the Greco-Roman world, and its support by Constantine in the fourth century was in good part a recognition of its de facto numerical significance. Missionaries evangelized the tribes of Northern Europe with increasing success, so that by the early Middle Ages many Germans, Franks, Celts, and British tribes had become Christian, which added considerable energy. Meanwhile Eastern Christians extended the faith in Asia Minor and Eastern Europe, finally winning the Bulgarians, Poles, Russians, and Magyars. Medieval missionaries then labored to convert the Scandinavian tribes, to establish missions among the Muslims (an effort wrecked by the Crusades), and to extend their field to the Tatars, Chinese, Indians, and Mongols.

The Reformation diverted the energies of the Protestant churches, but Catholic missionaries followed in the wake of the Spanish and Portuguese explorers of the New World. They established stations with mixed results in Florida, Puerto Rico, and what became the Southwest of the United States, and then later worked among the Indian tribes of Canada and the Northern United States. The Roman Catholic character of Mexico, Central America, and South America derives from the efforts of missionaries from the Iberian peninsula, who somewhat moderated the rapaciousness of the conquistadores.

Meanwhile Francis Xavier, one of the original companions of Ignatius Loyola in the founding of the Jesuits during the sixteenth century, did pioneering work in India and Japan, whereas Matteo Ricci later had considerable success among the Chinese. Ricci and his fellow Jesuit Roberto De Nobili, who worked in India, established the pattern of acculturating themselves as much as possible and translating Christian spirituality into a version of the indigenous people's sense of how the saint or the savant would live. In 1622 Pope Gregory XV founded the Congregation for the Propagation of the Faith to oversee the Church's growing expanse of missionary ventures. By 1645 the "Chinese Rites Controversy" had erupted, the eventual upshot of which was Rome's forbidding the sort of cultural accommodation that Ricci and de Nobili had advocated. Ostensibly the main issue was whether Chinese Catholics ought to be able to continue to venerate their ancestors, but implied were such further questions as whether to develop the liturgy and local church life in terms of the vernacular language and thought-forms. The party urging accommodation lost out to the party pushing for a uniformity throughout the Church such that Roman models would reign everywhere. Promising missions in China, Japan, and India failed, in some degree because of this policy.

A question raised in connection with missions to the New World was the dignity of tribal peoples such as the native Americans the Spanish missionaries met. The position of Pope Paul III, expressed in the bull *Sublimis Deus* of 1537, not only strengthened the hand of the missionaries who wanted to check the enslavement and degradation of the native peoples but also suggested how later missionaries to Africa ought to regard the peoples they were serving:

The sublime God so loved the human race that He created man in such wise that he might participate, not only in the good that other creatures enjoy, but endowed him with capacity to attain to the inaccessible and invisible Supreme Good and behold it face to face; and since man, according to the testimony of the sacred scriptures, has been created to enjoy eternal life and happiness, which none may obtain save through faith in our Lord Jesus Christ, it is necessary that he should possess the nature and faculties enabling him to receive that faith, and that whoever is thus endowed should be capable of receiving that same faith. Nor is it credible that any one should possess so little understanding as to desire faith and yet be destitute of the most necessary faculty to enable him to receive it. Hence Christ, who is the Truth itself, that has never failed and never can fail, said to the preachers of the faith whom He chose for that office "Go ye and teach all nations." He said all, without exception, for all are capable of receiving the doctrines of the faith.

The enemy of the human race, who opposes all good deeds in order to bring men to destruction, beholding and envying this, invented a means never before heard of, by which he might hinder the preaching of God's word of salvation to the people: he inspired his satellites who, to please him, have not hesitated to publish abroad that the Indians of the West and the South, and other people of whom We have recent knowledge should be treated as dumb brutes created for our service, pretending that they are incapable of receiving the Catholic faith.[1]

This statement expresses well some of the main assumptions of early sixteenth-century Catholic faith. One can easily imagine its application to the black slaves present in North America from 1619, although the majority of slaveholders were not Catholics. The principal assumption was that salvation — rescue from hell, preparation for heaven — only comes through overt, explicit faith in Jesus Christ. Indeed, most of the missionaries assumed that those who were not baptized continued to be in the power of Satan and be bent for hell. Certainly Francis Xavier, baptizing people until he got so weary others had to hold up his arm, thought in this way. The Catholic tradition had also spoken of the desire for baptism implicit in people who followed their consciences and lived good moral lives. God would provide for such people, in ways God alone knew. All people had sufficient grace for salvation. Nonetheless, the most secure route was to join oneself to the ark of salvation, the Church God had made the main and ordinary way to heaven.

As the quotation indicates, being human meant being a candidate for the good news — being capable of hearing the gospel and taking it to heart. The story of Christ and salvation knew no cultural or racial boundaries. It so appealed to all people's experience, and so served the plan of the one Creator from whom all people had issued, that the Church was bound to respect any tribe it met, seeing in even the apparently most primitive people potential children of God. Obviously Catholic missionaries did not always think this way, but that was the ideal.

The foreign missions that came into prominence through the explorations of the sixteenth century continued to have much vogue in later centuries, resulting in the vast numerical expansion of Catholic Christianity noted in the Introduction. Nowadays the numerical future of Catholic Christianity clearly lies in what once had been missionary territory—Latin America, Africa, India, and Asia. European culture has turned secularistic, with a consequent decline in Church membership and religious vocations, so some observers foresee missions from the third world to Europe in the near future.

Finally, it should be noted that the word "mission" has been expanded to cover projects such as work in inner-city slums, and to cover the institutional aims of religious works such as Catholic colleges. That is in keeping with the etymology of "mission" (a "sending"), but it can downplay the historic task of bringing the gospel into cultures where previously it was unknown or had not taken root.

Representative Personality: Ignatius Loyola

Ignatius Loyola (1491–1556) is the figure who is most often mentioned in any discussion of leaders of the Catholic Counter-Reformation. The Society of Jesus (Jesuits) that Loyola founded was a prominent source of missionaries to the New World, India, China, and Japan. Jesuit theologians staffed the later sessions of the Council of Trent, whereas Jesuit teachers and preachers made a great impact on counterreformational education and church life. Loyola's principal writings, *The Spiritual Exercises*, which sprang from his own conversion experience, and the *Constitutions*, which laid out the rules for the Society of Jesus, had a great impact on modern Catholic spirituality. Loyola envisioned the Jesuits as a highly mobile group, committed to laboring wherever the pope felt they were most needed, so he fashioned a spirituality that stressed the ability to contemplate God in the midst of ministerial works. *The Spiritual Exercises* became the foremost manual for retreats—periods of withdrawal from regular activities to renovate one's Christian faith—and the *Constitutions* became a model for other modern religious groups dedicated to an active life of ministerial works.

The crux of Loyola's spiritual genius came from a combination of personal circumstances and mystical gifts.[2] While recovering from battle wounds, Ignatius the soldier began to notice the different effects that secular and religious reading had in his soul. Gradually he realized that whereas romances and other works of distraction initially seemed appealing but eventually left him feeling impoverished, without peace and joy, reading about the saints or in the gospels regularly moved him from an initial reluctance to lasting feelings of peace and joy. From this perception came Loyola's views of how one might discern the different "spirits" moving in one's depths and so find the lurings of God.

Eventually Loyola became committed to placing his life in the service of the Christ he contemplated during a year of solitude and intense religious experience at Manresa in Spain. Transmuting his military upbringing, he dedicated himself to serving Christ under the banner of the cross. After a pilgrimage to Jerusalem, Loyola started trying to communicate his insights to others, to help their faith, but soon ran afoul of the **Inquisition,** which was highly suspicious of any talk about inner illumination.

Loyola realized he needed a better education, if he were to be an effective servant of Christ, so he studied at several Spanish universities and then at the University of Paris. In Paris he met fellow students who became the nucleus of the Society of Jesus, Francis Xavier among them. All were deeply impressed by Loyola's holiness, and the times made committing oneself to Christ for the defense and promulgation of the Catholic faith an attractive, adventurous vocation.

Ordained a priest in 1537, Loyola offered the services of his little group to the pope, an offer that was accepted in 1540 when Paul III authorized the Society of Jesus as a recognized religious order. Loyola himself served as the first general of the new order, guiding its development, and by the time of his death the Jesuits had already begun to distinguish themselves as perhaps the most effective agents of Catholic reform.

The major foci of the Jesuits during their first years say much about the diagnosis of Catholic needs that a shrewd saint was making at the time when it was becoming increasingly clear that the Protestant Reformation had come to stay. Loyola's personnel took the customary religious vows of poverty, chastity, and obedience, but he especially stressed an apostolic poverty—living simply and freely enough to go wherever the good of souls required—and a profound obedience. The Jesuits took a special vow of submission to the pope, offering themselves directly for whatever works the papacy favored, and Loyola wanted them to have the spiritual equivalent of military discipline. This was not to be harsh but informed by prayer and love, so that the individual would give up his personal will for the sake of whatever overall good his superiors saw his talents serving. The works that in fact predominated in the early Jesuit years were education, preaching and pastoral work that brought Catholics to more frequent use of the sacraments (especially of penance and the Eucharist), foreign missions, and controversy with Protestants (whom Loyola, like the pope, considered heretics) that might expose their theological errors, convert those open to Catholic truth, and safeguard the pious faithful vulnerable to Protestant influence.

This agenda expresses the temper of the Catholic Reformation. The controversial mood was shared by both sides, as seen, for instance, in the life of Luther, who instinctively thought of theses for a disputation as the natural mode for expressing his disagreements with Tetzel about indulgences. Jesuit theologians such as Robert Bellarmine, Peter Canisius, and James Lainez (who succeeded Loyola as head of the Jesuits) all were effective in theological polemics. Bellarmine became a cardinal, Canisius did much to save parts of Germany for the Catholic cause, and Lainez was a significant factor at the Council of Trent.

The Jesuit decision to focus on educating young men soon led to their running some of the most influential secondary schools (*colleges*) in Europe, from which emerged generations of leaders in government and business whom their teachers hoped would apply a strong Catholic faith to public life. Jesuit teachers helped to forward the humanistic reforms in education that had been sparked by Catholics such as Erasmus, although on the whole the Jesuits were not critical of the Roman establishment, monastic life, and other sources of corruption in Catholicism, as Erasmus had been. The Jesuits saw the great need of their generation to be rallying round the Catholic flag, lest Protestantism destroy the substance of the traditional faith.

Foreign missions obviously beckoned as fertile fields to men committed to serving Christ's cause under even the most adverse conditions. Several Jesuit missionaries to North American Indians were martyred, and the *Jesuit Relations* that reported on the French missionaries' experiences with the American Indians remain a prime historical source for the state of Indian affairs in the mid-seventeenth century.

The Jesuits' concern to bring Catholics to a more frequent use of the sacraments reflects a shift from late medieval piety, where reception of the Eucharist had become rare, because of a sense of unfitness. The Mass had become more a spectacle to be witnessed than a celebration in which one actively participated. Loyola was one of the first Catholic reformers to see the Eucharist, and the other sacraments, as a means toward spiritual progress, rather than as a reward for spiritual progress already attained. In this view he was returning to a more biblical attitude, and he could have drawn sympathy from some of the Lutheran Reformers. Loyola's *Spiritual Exercises* made following Christ the key, although the tone of such following was somewhat different from that of à Kempis's *Imitation of Christ*, which was more quietistic and less missionary minded.

Loyola took people who made the full course of the *Spiritual Exercises* through four weeks' worth of meditations. The first week was concerned with the basic condition of human beings as creatures and sinners, the second involved many contemplations of scenes from the ministry of Christ, the third focused on the passion of Christ, and the fourth was concerned with the Resurrection and life in the Spirit. The point to all the meditations was to help the exercitant find God's will, especially in the central matter of a life's work or vocation. The director was to help the exercitant interpret the different spiritual experiences that the meditations and contemplations generated, seeing where godly inspiration seemed to lead and how Satanic inspiration (as the imagination of the times pictured ungodly leadings) tried to thwart God's will. The result was a profound venture in what one might call reformation of character: changing imagination, will, and sensibility. Many exercitants emerged from the full course of the *Spiritual Exercises* committed to giving their lives to Christ in the active service of the Catholic Church and the cause of the Catholic Counter-Reformation.

Glossary

Albigensianism: a significant medieval heretical movement, named for the town of Albi, in southern France, where it arose in the eleventh century. In other parts of Europe the same heretics were called Cathari, from the Greek word for "pure" (whence the later English term "Puritan"). The Albigensians resurrected the Manicheanism that had entrapped the young Augustine, speaking of a dualistic battle between forces of evil and forces of good. The forces of evil focussed on bodily things, thereby suggesting that asceticism and contempt for material matters, distrust of the sacramental and institutional side of Catholicism, and a spiritualization or allegoricalization of the Scriptures and the person of Christ were ways to foster a purity that would allow the spiritual forces of good to bring one salvation.

Indulgences: remissions of temporal punishment (after death, in purgatory) merited because of one's sins. Indulgences could be gained for various good works, spiritual or temporal, and they depended on a theology in which the Church was the minister, if not the custodian, of both the ordinary means of salvation and the merits of the saints. The abuse of indulgences to which the Protestant Reformers vigorously objected included both giving the impression that one could buy one's way out of purgatory by contributing money to the Church and stressing purgatory itself, the cult of the saints, and the primacy of papal control over the spiritual treasury of the Church—doctrinal matters that the Reformers considered to be without scriptural foundation.

Inquisition: in reaction to the Cathari of the twelfth century, which they felt threatened both religion and the institutions necessary for ordinary life, Church officials sought the force of secular authorities to quell heretics. In the thirteenth century, Pope Gregory IX established an office of papal inquisition, in part to keep the secular authorities from gaining too much power over what he considered Church matters (doctrine, heresy). Dominicans and Franciscans frequently staffed the Inquisition, and usually those who recanted of their errors (after such errors had been established through quasi-legal proceedings) got away with a simple admonition. Those who remained obstinate could be imprisoned under harsh conditions, and in 1252 Pope Innocent IV sanctioned the use of torture. This Inquisition continued into the sixteenth century. In Spain the state established another Inquisition at the end of the fifteenth century that hunted down Muslims, Jews, and Protestants. The Grand Inquisitor at the head of this proceeding became a symbol of Church power wrongly applied. The Spanish Inquisition was in place until 1820 and burned perhaps two thousand people as heretics.

Justification: being made right or acceptable before God. The term is especially influential in the theological line that runs from Paul through Augustine to Luther. It carries legal or economic overtones, as though one had an account with God and could be punished if it were overdrawn. Realizing that no sinners could ever stand before God debtless, Paul, Augustine, and Luther all looked to faith and the merits of Christ to cover sinners' failings. Paul argued that fulfilling the Torah could not guarantee that one would please God, whereas Augustine stressed the complete gratuity of salvation. Luther said that only through Christ could one be justified, and that the salvation Christ had worked was merely imputed to sinners (did not become substantially their own, as the Catholic doctrine of grace and merit suggested).

Nominalism: a philosophical outlook that considers the names of things merely a matter of convenience or custom and not signs sprung from an expression of, or an insight into, the substance of such things. Nominalism has implications in both the epistemological (knowledge) and metaphysical (being) realms, but its main significance in Reformation times was its contribution to the Reformers' disgust with scholasticism in particular and all works of reason in general. Luther, for example, had been trained in nominalist philosophy. Such training seems to have contributed to his pessimistic view of human beings' rational and natural capacities, and so to his insistence that justification could come only by biblical faith.

Purgatory: a stage between earthly life and heaven, during or in which
people would be purified of their venial sins. The conception assumed
that mortal sins—serious offenses killing the divine life in the soul—
sent people to hell, whereas a saintly life or martyrdom allowed one to
pass directly to heaven. For the many who had been sinful yet still
possessed grace, faith, and love, purgatory would be a fitting experience.
The purification thought to be worked in purgatory would be painful,
but those suffering it would be sustained by the hope of eventually
gaining admittance to the beatific vision of God in heaven. Dante's
Purgatorio classically expressed the medieval belief in this middle state,
whereas the attacks of Luther and the other Reformers centered on the
weak or nonexistent biblical basis for the teaching. Eastern Orthodoxy
also has not been enthusiastic about the Catholic view of purgatory.

Transubstantiation: the teaching that in the Eucharist the material
elements of bread and wine change substance and become the flesh
and blood of Christ. This teaching was an effort to express the Catholic
commitment to the real presence of Christ in the Eucharist, in contrast
to any symbolic view (in the weak sense) that would make the
Sacrament merely a pledge or token. Catholics thus read the New
Testament texts concerning the institution of the Eucharist as having a
quite literal intent. Transubstantiation need not entail accepting the
Aristotelian understanding of substance and accident, but frequently
Catholic theologians have used this philosophical terminology. The
Reformers feared that transubstantiation undergirded the superstitious
or magical views of the Eucharist they found rampant in their time and
so strove to make the Eucharist something more symbolic. The more
radical of them, such as Zwingli, wanted to strip the Eucharist of any
intention toward a real presence, which the Catholics found both
unbiblical and contrary to tradition.

Discussion Questions

1. What does the life of Catherine of Siena suggest about the proper
   Catholic attitude toward the papacy?
2. Where did Erasmus fit into the Reform movements that preceded
   Martin Luther?
3. How did Luther's pessimistic view of human nature dovetail with his
   insistence that the Bible be the sole authority in Christian life?

4. Why did many Swiss find the strict moralism of Calvin attractive?
5. What does the protracted character of the Council of Trent suggest about the Catholic Counter-Reformation?
6. How did Trent sharpen the Catholic instinct for both/and?
7. Why did foreign missionaries such as Ricci and De Nobili take on the style of scholars or holy men?
8. What were the main implications of the teaching of Pope Paul III in *Sublimis Deus*?
9. Why did Loyola's stress on spiritual experience make him suspect to the Inquisition?
10. Why did the Jesuits make education one of their primary ministerial works?

Notes

[1] John Tracy Ellis, ed., *Documents of American Catholic History*, vol. 1 (Wilmington, Del.: Michael Glazier, 1987), pp. 7–8.

[2] See Antonio T. De Nicholas, *Powers of Imagining: Ignatius de Loyola* (Albany: State University of New York Press, 1986); Harvey D. Egan, S. J., *Ignatius Loyola the Mystic* (Wilmington, Del.: Michael Glazier, 1988).

The Modern Period

Modern Science

The Jesuit schoolmasters who played a key role in the Catholic Reformation numbered some significant mathematicians and astronomers, as the medieval monastic orders had numbered "natural philosophers" absorbed with the intricacies of plants, physical laws, and the stars. The Franciscan philosopher Roger Bacon (about 1220–1292), for example, included much experimental science in his various *opera*. Nonetheless, the Catholic tradition in what we now call science kept such work related to theology and philosophy. Consequently, the development of an autonomous body of knowledge about nature, and the related development of an empiricist view of human knowledge (one stressing sensory experience) brought traumatic shocks to Catholicism. The Church was used to claiming all knowledge as its province, inasmuch as it thought all knowledge ought to subserve theology, the queen of the sciences, and bear on people's eternal salvation.

Some of the way stations on the journey of natural science away from Church influence can be suggested by commenting briefly on the implications of such key figures as Francis Bacon, Galileo Galilei, Isaac Newton, Charles Darwin, and Sigmund Freud. Francis Bacon (1561 – 1626) was an English politician and philosopher who was loyal to the Church of England established through the English Reformation led by King Henry VIII and Archbishop Thomas Cranmer. Bacon's greatest influence came, however, through his works on induction and scientific method. Although he did not directly engage these with Catholic theology, they implied a body-blow to the traditional claims of theology to pass judgment on the findings of physical science. They also were at odds with the a priori, deductive approaches of scholastic metaphysics and deductive theology.

Bacon was proposing what became the characteristically modern view of reason as an empirical faculty interested in organizing the facts about nature, or any other field of inquiry, so as to dominate such a field both intellectually and practically. Virtually abolished was the medieval contemplatives' absorption in nature as an expression of God (a second source of revelation, alongside the Bible). Gone as well, at least in principle, was the sometimes enriching, sometimes confusing melding of the scientific and religious imaginations that late medieval and early modern thought (for example, Newton) still indulged. Now nature and divinity were separating. Bacon anticipated the Enlightenment philosophers in dealing with human reason as an autonomous entity, free of Church control, as he anticipated the industrialists in thinking of scientific findings as power: keys to the subjection of nature to human desire.

Galileo (1564 – 1642), Bacon's Italian contemporary, brought the potential conflict between the new science and the traditional theology of Rome to a head by advancing the astronomy of Copernicus (1473 – 1543), which advocated a heliocentric view of the planetary system. The Church still espoused the Ptolemaic view that the planets revolved around the earth. Influential Roman theologians viewed heliocentrism as a threat to the biblical depiction of creation, and also to the theological assumption that the history of salvation was the central drama structuring all reality and knowledge. In 1633 the Inquisition forced Galileo to recant his views, under threat of torture, and imprisoned him on suspicion of heresy. The case has come down through history as the classic instance of ecclesiastical bad faith, although on the churchmen's own grounds that was not necessarily so.

Still, the case of Galileo made plain the discrepancies between the older views of nature, which were directed by theological orthodoxies, and the new scientific views being developed on the basis of empirical experimentation and observation. The telescope, the microscope, and the other new equipment coming into scientists' possession gave them ranges of data that were not available to the classical theologians. The moral issue was personal integrity: fidelity to the honest findings of one's research, and this issue bore similarities to the Protestants' claims about the priority of individual conscience. As Protestant believers were following Luther in saying they could do no other than oppose a Roman faith in which they did not believe, so scientists could claim the need in conscience to stand by what their research had disclosed and seemed to imply. Church theology, in contrast, seemed dogmatic, in the pejorative sense of being imposed without regard to empirical facts or the moral imperatives generated in conscience by lived experience.

Isaac Newton (1642–1727) was the most eminent mathematician and physicist of his day. Among his principal achievements were formulating the law of gravity, discovering differential calculus, and fashioning the first correct analysis of white light. Newton still worked in a field called natural philosophy, but his own achievements helped further to differentiate physics from the philosophy of nature. His *Principia Mathematica* (1687) shows Newton to have been a naturalist in his approach to God: his faith rested on his perception of the admirable order of the universe. Although Newton remained in the Church of England, his faith was less a Christian orthodoxy derived from biblical revelation than a naturalist theology interested in the attributes of the divine Ruler of the physical world.

The main implication of Newton's work for traditional Catholic theology lay in its depiction of the universe as a realm of ordered relations that bespoke the mind of God but showed little signs of God's daily intervention. In contrast to the biblical and traditional views of God's relations with the physical world, the Newtonian vision distanced the Creator, paving the way for the Deistic teaching that God was like a clockmaker who had made the universe, set it ticking, but thereafter paid it little heed. It was unclear how miracles could function in the Newtonian universe. Human beings might have a singular dignity because of their souls, and one could speak of God's reign over those souls as paralleling God's reign in nature, but anthropocentrism (pivoting the universe around human beings) found little support in Newton's world. Like the shift from geocentrism to heliocentrism, the Newtonian revolution in physics seemed to dethrone humanity from the center of attention in creation and thereby to call into question humanity's special dignity.

By the time Charles Darwin (1809–1882) had launched the evolutionary view of the biological world, Newtonian physics had become the scientific orthodoxy, tied in the Church's mind to a revolt by the modern intellectuals from traditional faith. However, even the Church intellectuals who had accepted Newtonian physics took a blow when Darwinism became popular, because Darwinism threatened their effort to keep theology master of the realm of human nature. Darwin's theories seemed to imply that the human species was no special creation come directly from God and had no exemption from the chance governing selection and development in the plant and animal worlds. Thus Darwinism seemed another diminution of human dignity, popularly expressed in the idea that human beings had simply developed from apes. Most Church theologians fought this apparent godlessness, as they had fought prior encroachments upon the view of human destiny derived from faith, by rejecting Darwinism on the basis of theological judgments.

The psychoanalytic view of human nature developed from the writings of Sigmund Freud (1856–1939) raised similar reactions in Church authorities, as had the geological discoveries that seemed to threatened the biblical depiction of the origins of the earth. Freud's discussion of an unconscious realm, and his spotlighting sexuality, seemed to desacralize the realm of the psyche, much as Darwinism had desacralized the realm of the human body and Newtonism had desacralized the laws of physical movement. In popular imagination, again, Freudianism suggested a sick obsession with incestuous urges, buttressed by an analysis of religion as a grand neurosis.

Naturally, there were some Catholic intellectuals throughout the modern period who tried to give the new scientific theories a fair hearing. The Church had other business and theologians continued their labors in areas removed from the findings of empirical science. But overall Catholicism ceded the physical sciences to a modernity it considered areligious, or even atheistic. Overall the medieval confidence in the compatibility of reason and faith fell into crisis and the Church did a poor job at showing how nothing truthful, nothing proposed as the fruit of honest research, need threaten faith or detract from either the dignity of God or the dignity of the human beings redeemed by Christ's blood. Protestant and Orthodox Christians had similar problems, adding to the impression that modernity meant a steady separation of secular intelligence from Christian faith.

The Enlightenment

The philosophy that best expressed and forwarded the secularists' side of this rift came from the leading thinkers of the eighteenth-century Enlightenment. Their movement was imprecise, yet it found significant expressions in England, France, and, above all, Germany. Its leading exponents were deeply impressed by the new physical science (above all the work of Newton), which seemed the capital proof that humanity was far better off relying on its own powers of reason than on wisdom supposedly revealed by God through biblical texts and Church channels.

Part of the temper of the Enlightenment thinkers flowed in the channels dug by Francis Bacon, inasmuch as they wanted human enterprises to stick to empirical facts, proceed mainly by induction, and honor the character of the human mind as essentially a faculty for organizing sense perceptions. The British philosophers John Locke (1632–1704) and David Hume (1711–1776) expounded this epistemology with great success. In the Catholic camp René Descartes (1596–1650) took a different tack, but one ultimately just as challenging to traditional Catholic theology. Descartes was in search of an indubitable foundation from which he might build a philosophical system. He settled on the proposition, "I think, therefore I am," which alone seemed to stand up to the method of methodic doubt he had established. Cartesianism further stressed the split of the individual between a part that thought and a part possessing physical extension. The result was that modernity was given the perennial problem of explaining the unity of the human being. Cartesian doubt also cast a pall over the entire realm of faith, making faith seem much as Protestant theology said it should be: a thing of irrational leaps, based on either texts of Scripture or God's trustworthiness.

Immanuel Kant (1724–1804) was the leading German philosopher of the Enlightenment and perhaps its most representative and influential figure. Kant was shaped by both Newtonian physics and the empiricism of the Scottish philosopher David Hume, which together led him to inquire into the structures of human reason, both speculative and practical. The watchword that Kant developed was "criticism," implying that nothing heteronomous (imposed as a law from outside) ought to direct mature human beings. Only propositions that stood up to critical inquiry — judgments made on the basis of hard evidence and disciplined inferences — ought to be considered to have passed muster.

Kant's analysis of the conditions for human knowledge led him to conclude that speculative propositions about the intrinsic nature of reality so exceeded the evidence of the senses and so represented unverifiable outreaches of the human spirit that one had to be agnostic about their claims. Thus the existence of God, the immortality of the soul, and the existence of human freedom — all matters passing beyond the province of space and time, with which alone human reason was competent to deal — had to be judged uncertain. On the other hand, because human action and morality depended on accepting all three of these propositions, one found in the conditions for practical reason a basis for agreeing to the claims of traditional Christian faith.

For most of his life Kant qualified as an orthodox Lutheran, but the practical effect of his highly influential theory of knowledge was radically to challenge the claims of Christian doctrine. Faith virtually became reduced to ethics, whereas miracles, revelation, and an order of grace lying beyond nature all faded in significance, having been ruled ineligible for serious consideration.

Enlightenment thought had a more immediate influence in Protestant countries such as the United States than it did in Catholic areas such as southern Europe. Still, French *philosophes* such as Voltaire and Diderot shared the Enlightenment spirit and enjoyed waxing anticlerical. Religion came in for much scoffing and satire in their writings, for generally they presented religion as a realm of backwardness and superstition. The ideally educated man, as perhaps suggested by the American Thomas Jefferson, made much more of natural reason than he did of biblical faith. The educated man might retain a tinge of reverence for biblical language, and if he participated in public life he probably would agree that religion helped supply moral restraints upon the masses, who never would be led by critical reason. But the most such a man would applaud in the realm of theology proper would be a pale Deism, which endowed the Source of the physical and moral worlds with a patina of holiness or power that justified bowing one's head and offering some reverence.

The approach to Jesus stimulated by the Enlightenment took him as a moral teacher and tried to translate his precepts into ethical views that were proper to later times. Any claims that Jesus was truly divine, had worked astounding miracles, had been resurrected, and could be the source of a spiritual power tokening salvation from sins and unto eternal life fell on closed minds. Indeed, such claims made religion seem the province of the credulous. The most the typical intellectual formed by the Enlightenment would have likely accredited was the possibility of an immortality for the soul, and even then the basis for such a possibility was as likely to be the Platonic dialogues or the example of Socrates as it was the New Testament.

The mention of the pre-Christian Greek philosopher Plato should remind us that the moderns were the heirs not only of the Enlightenment and the Reformation but also of the Renaissance. Catholics had a much larger role in the Renaissance, if only because of its Italian beginnings, than they would later have in the Enlightenment. For some time an enthusiasm for the classics of Greece and Rome rode high even in the papacy. Michelangelo and St. Peter's in Rome stand as summary tributes to what this meant for Catholic faith. By the middle of the eighteenth century, however, it seemed clear that the hopes of Erasmus, Thomas More, and other early Catholic humanists that the revival of the classics would invigorate a renewal in Christian culture, education, and devotion were not going to be realized and probably had been misguided. Protestants might have said that they had indeed been misguided, because, adapting a dictum of one church father, Tertullian, Jerusalem (faith) ought to have nothing to do with Athens (paganism). Still, the Zwinglis and Calvins had owed a great deal to the humanist revival stimulated by the Renaissance, including their command of Greek and their consequent competence in studies of both the New Testament and the Church fathers.

The later moderns saw more conflict between the paganism of Greece and Rome and biblical Christianity than the early Christian humanists had. Lost to the later moderns was the medieval Catholic sense that faith could so harmonize reason and revelation that culture would emerge whole. Similarly, the Greek Orthodox instinct that Plato might be counted among the Church fathers would have seemed strange to such moderns, not because they did not honor Plato, but because the Church fathers seemed irrelevant.

The upshot of Enlightened thought, like the upshot of modern science, was thus a divorce between Catholic faith and the leading currents of modernity. In philosophy and matters of general worldview, as well as in matters bearing on the natural world, Catholic theology made few impressive statements and stimulated few impressive cultural constructs. Indeed, Catholicism developed a defensive mentality that went hand in hand with a solidified papal authoritarianism. Political movements also played an important role, as we see in the next section, but even in the domain of theology proper—faith seeking understanding—the modern period was difficult.

Political Developments

In this section we reflect on the impact of four modern political movements: the American Revolution, the French Revolution, the rise of Marxist thought, and the rise of Nazism. Each was bound to interest and worry Catholic authorities, because each was another unmistakable sign that Christendom was past.

The American Revolution rested on political convictions that owed much to the Enlightenment. As the Declaration of Independence made plain, beyond their grievances about taxation without representation the revolutionaries felt that their God-given rights had been abridged:

> When, in the Course of human events, it becomes necessary for one people to dissolve the political bands which have connected them with another, and to assume, among the Powers of the earth, the separate and equal station to which the Laws of Nature and of Nature's God entitle them, a decent respect to the opinions of mankind requires that they should declare the causes which impel them to the separation.
>
> We hold these truths to be self-evident, that all men are created equal, that they are endowed by their Creator with certain unalienable rights, that among these are Life, Liberty, and the pursuit of Happiness. That, to secure these rights, Governments are instituted among Men, deriving their just Powers from the consent to the governed.[1]

These lines suffice to indicate the differences between the emerging American view of politics and the traditional Catholic view. First, the God described in the Declaration is more the pale God of the Deists than the God of the Bible or Catholic theology. This deistic God bears some similarities to the divinity grounding the Catholic sense of natural law, but it is a far cry from the divinity and Christ that Catholic theologians were sure had established the Church as the basic mediator of salvation and so as the partner of the civil arm in all things bearing on human welfare.

Second, the unalienable rights described, though admirable, move into an area that Catholicism had little explored. Civil rights were a modern conception. Catholicism was more used to speaking of the duties consequent on each person's state. Catholicism was also more interested in the eternal goals people might contemplate, in comparison with which earthly entitlements greatly paled. The silence of the Declaration about the heavenly destiny of human beings would have rung ominously in contemporary Catholic ears, making theologians wonder about the trustworthiness of the American venture.

Third, the notion that governments derive their just powers from the consent of the governed implied a democratic view of social arrangements that was out of step with the traditional Catholic view of authority. In the traditional Catholic view, civil power, as well as ecclesiastical power, came from God. People ought to be treated fairly, and one could speak of unjust arrangements ill benefitting people's dignity as children of God, but to vest political power in the people themselves would have raised specters of anarchy or irreligious anthropocentrism.

As we see when treating American Catholicism, the Roman Church authorities long remained suspicious of the American experiment in democratic government and pluralistic culture. Roman ideas of authority continued to be monarchical, and any neglect of the rights and dignity of Catholic Christianity led Roman officials to lament the influence of godlessness. The French Revolution that followed shortly after the American Revolution struck Roman Catholic churchmen as the realization of their worst fears. The French revolutionaries trumpeted their slogan of liberty, equality, and fraternity with no regard for the divinity founding all human dignity. The terrors that came in the wake of the overthrow of the French monarchy concretized the bestial potential authoritarian Catholics had suspected lay in rule by the masses. Many of the revolutionary leaders hated the Church and were deeply anticlerical. Whatever one may say about the historical causes that made such an attitude understandable, the destructive **nihilism** of the Terror gave Catholic theologians all the evidence they needed that politicians who threw off docility to God and God's representatives opened themselves to a Satanic murderousness.

The Socialists, Marxists, and Communists who agitated in nineteenth-century Europe seemed but another chapter in the story of atheistic politics that were dramatized in the French Revolution. Most such political agitators associated the Church (on good grounds) with the wealthy and powerful they were trying to oust. The old order defended by Catholic instinct seemed to the new political radicals rife with corruption. The religious rationale associated with the old order became, in the Marxist view, merely an ideology: a self-serving intellectual justification that warped the empirical facts.

Whereas English Catholics might lament the rise of liberalism on the model of the thought of John Stuart Mill, continental Catholics had to deal with the deeper challenges of the French Socialists and the German Communists. The result was a reactionary response from the papacy, which in Italy was losing its temporal powers to a hostile government, and in its ruminations about global affairs feared that atheism would win out. The Russian Revolution based on Marxism-Leninism further confirmed this papal instinct, as once again blood ran in the streets and militant atheists attacked all things religious. Eventually Catholics witnessed similar scenarios played out in Communist China, Communist Vietnam, Eastern Europe, Latin America, and other areas where Marxist thought gained adherents.

At our distance from the political revolutions that started changing the Western world two hundred years ago, Church authorities had good reason for their fears. The wars and violence of the twentieth century indisputably are connected with the death of God foreseen by Nietzsche and feared by Catholic leaders. The religious tragedy, however, was the failure of Catholics and other people of faith to supply a creative alternative. The churches were so entangled with the powers that dominated European culture they could not carry out their biblical mandate to serve the poor and identify themselves with the needs of the marginal. So it was the political radicals who seemed more genuinely on the side of social justice and better reminders of the evangelical Christ:

> And he came to Nazareth, where he had been brought up; and he went to the synagogue, as his custom was, on the sabbath day. And he stood up to read; and there was given to him the book of the prophet Isaiah. He opened the book and found the place where it was written, "The Spirit of the Lord is upon me, because he has anointed me to preach good news to the poor. He has sent me to proclaim release to the captives and recovering of sight to the blind, to set at liberty those who are oppressed, to proclaim the acceptable year of the Lord." And he closed the book, and gave it back to the attendant, and sat down; and the eyes of all in the synagogue were fixed on him. And he began to say to them, "Today this scripture has been fulfilled in your hearing" (Ll 4: 16–21).

Certainly, one shouldn't try to leap directly from the model of Jesus to present-day political judgments, but when anti-Christians seem closer to Jesus' concern for the poor than Church leaders, Christianity is in serious trouble.

The rise of Nazism during the twentieth century was different from the rise of the other political movements we have described, in that it made little pretense of serving the poor and marginalized. Rather, it pretended to be the restoration of the dignity and manifest destiny of the pagan Aryan (noble) line. But Nazism was like many of the preceding movements in its militant atheism.

Jews suffered its worst assaults, becoming scapegoats essential to the Aryan myth of how the world had gotten away from its proper masters. Catholics also were Nazi targets, as were professing Protestants. (Catholics had their own history of anti-Semitism.) Indeed, any who believed in the living God and hated idolatry were bound to become enemies of Hitler, as were any who simply hated the brutalities and injustices of the Nazi butchers. The popes tried to minimize the hardships worked on both Catholics and Jews, and though some critics have claimed that the popes should have been more outspoken against the Nazis and the crimes against humanity, Rome faced a complicated situation and probably deserves more sympathy than American leaders such as President Roosevelt, who knew of the plight of the Jews in the Nazi concentration camps and yet kept silent.

Nazism was the final nail in the argument that modernity cut adrift from God would become a cauldron of unspeakable evils. Painfully enough, this argument vindicated the Catholic instinct that no culture can be whole without having the one God as its only treasure, just as it vindicated the Catholic instinct that God's incarnation in Jesus the Jew had put into the world a definitive stumbling block, over which would fall all people unwilling to bend their pride to God's chosen way of offering salvation.

In surveying the scientific, philosophical, and political movements that created "modernity," we perhaps inevitably have stressed ideas and shifts in outlook. Before focusing on industrialization, which dramatically changed the lives of the working classes, let us reflect on what modern ideas meant for the average Catholic layperson. First, there was the conflict that the well-educated faced between the trends that were carrying the day in cultured circles and the traditional views of Church leaders. Second, there was a tendency of Church leaders to stress their authority and so further separate the clerical class from the laity. The consolidation of Church authority in the papacy at the First Vatican Council (1869) is but the leading example of a general trend. On the whole, laity got the message that their main job in the Church was to provide financial support and carry out the teachings given them by their pope, bishops, and priests. Third, there was a temptation to separate the life of faith from workaday life and to make religion private, even nostalgic. Indeed, some interpreters see the apparitions of Mary and the upsurge of Marian piety in the late nineteenth and early twentieth centuries as a safety valve for average Catholics who felt out of step with the modern world. Such piety offered a haven from the apparent godlessness and cruelties of the times, just as fundamentalist movements did for Protestants. All in all, then, the effect of modern science, philosophy, and political theory was to leave many Catholics wondering how to reconcile their faith with modern culture. Among the poorly educated this effect may have been more felt (as a vague uneasiness) than clearly understood, but they too suffered a loss of confidence and an increase of anxiety.

Industrialization

Industrialization changed the face of European and American life during the nineteenth century. The patterns of family life, church life, work, and instinctive thought about God all shifted with the rise of the factories and urbanization. Traditional Catholic faith, as all traditional Christian faith, had long kept in view a peasant majority living close to the rhythms of nature. The early Christians had numbered many city dwellers, and Christian intellectuals who were responsible for forging the great theological visions, had clustered around the universities located in the cities. Still, pastoral theology traditionally had had to reckon with rural cultures that were very conservative. The feast days, the agricultural rhythms, the sense of the local church as the center of the village culture, and other features of peasant Catholicism all conspired to make faith seem an organic part of nature's way.

Similarly, rural family life centered in a home that was a place of work more than a haven from an outside world of buying and selling. Husband and wife, parents and children, usually worked together on the land. Together families prepared their food, produced their clothes, and cared for the practical education of the next generation. For millions of Europeans and Americans, industrialization changed such millennial patterns — so rapidly that disorientation was bound to ensue.

Of particular concern and interest to the churches were the harsh working conditions under which many factory employees had to labor, the poor housing they suffered, and the slashes at their faith caused by their new circumstances. Workdays were long in England, where the industrial revolution got its start and produced its first models. Workers often were on the job seven days a week, twelve to fifteen hours a day. Wages were as low as the factory owners and managers could keep them, working conditions often were unsafe, and women (to say nothing of children) got few exemptions. After a long, back-breaking day at the factory, workers often went home to miserable hovels, where their indebtedness to the company store or landlords only grew. It was a brutal existence, but one that most workers considered their only option. For most either there simply was no work on the farms, or by the time they had realized that the factories and cities were a dead end they could not escape.

The factory system raised the wrath of social reformers. The frequent (though far from absolute) silence of the churches about the evils of industrialization and the collusion of the churches with the factory owners fed the conviction of irreligious social reformers that religion was simply a tool of the oppressive capitalist classes. Certainly many churchpeople gave the lie to this conviction, laboring for the better lot of the workers and attacking the greed of the factory owners and those (politicians, churchmen) who conspired with them. But, overall, such churchpeople did not muster the clout to achieve effective reforms. The Catholic Church initially was cool to the labor movement, fearing possible ties to Communism, and too frequently it validated the social critics' attacks by prematurely consoling people with the thought that soon they would pass away to heaven.

From the cities and factories grew an increasing **secularization.** The sense of God that rural living had made relatively regular departed from the majority of even churchgoers, making them wonder whether religion was not largely a matter of social conditioning. The leisure, contemplation, and simplicity on which traditional faith had depended ceded to the bustle, noise, and dirt of the urban proletariat. The work that had been an outlet for personal creativity and had produced a sense of accomplishment ceded to the piecemeal production of the assembly line. Indeed, often industrial work so narrowed that it came to mean only the time spent in boredom or pain for the sake of a paycheck. Many factory owners only thought of their workers as economic entities, the cheaper the better, whereas many workers in turn only thought of themselves as cogs in an ugly machine, as much slaves as the biblical Hebrews had been in Egypt.

Slavery (of many sorts) was nothing new in human history. Peasant life often had been unromantic in the extreme, harsh and uncultured. But the encounter with mechanization forced upon millions of workers by the industrial revolution was a new thing in human experience. Never before had human artifacts so blotted out the forces of nature. Never before had people felt so deracinated — so torn from their roots in the earth, so distant from the earth's Creator. Such roots had sustained humanity since time out of mind. Within a few decades, though, the nineteenth century had changed all that. As one sees in much modern art, the psychic impact was enormous. People felt twisted out of shape, thinned to two dimensions, starved for beauty and meaning. They felt their aesthetic and religious senses atrophying from lack of exercise, cut off from the circumstances and experiences that once had stimulated them.

Once again Catholic theologians perceived the enemy clearly enough, as they had in the political revolutions, but they seemed powerless to do more than rail against errors and abuses. It is hard to know just what their positive programs should have been, although the ecological spirituality (the view of God's place in the delicate interconnection of nature) that has developed since the mid-twentieth century is suggestive.

The key battle should have centered on the status of money and financial profit, but this battle so obviously continues today that it is hard to fault the nineteenth-century theologians for not winning it. The Protestant proponents of the Social Gospel toward the end of the nineteenth century took to heart the problems of the factory workers and urban poor, using their plight to revive the message of the evangelical Christ about the primacy of the poor in the Kingdom of Heaven. The Catholic theologians of the early twentieth century who tried to revive the liturgy, vivify Catholic rural life, deepen the theology of marriage and family life, and defend the rights of labor to organize thought similarly. In researching the patristic tradition, they realized that private property rights had never been ultimate in the Christian tradition, and that dicta such as "no one has the right to luxuries as long as anyone lacks necessities" could claim a noble lineage. The social encyclicals of the popes, beginning with Leo XIII at the end of the nineteenth century, steadily moved in the direction of championing human rights, defending the poor, and pointing out the inadequacies of both socialist and capitalist views of society and economics.

Nonetheless, most of this response was too slow in coming, and carried too slight a punch, to dent the massive problems. So late modern (nineteenth- and early twentieth-century) culture organized much of its business around greed — no innovation in human history, but something now so established in the prevailing economics that the pulse of Western business beat completely counter to the corporate Christ, the Christian community understood as the branches all dependent on the vine for the best in them and so all called to love their neighbors as they loved themselves.

American Catholicism: Before the Civil War

The Catholic presence in the Americas preceded the Protestant presence, inasmuch as the first explorers and missionaries were Spaniards working in Central America, Florida, and Puerto Rico. Franciscans and Jesuits also were prominent missionaries in the Southwest and in Canada. In the British colonies, the Catholic presence was limited to Maryland, where Cecil Calvert, Lord Baltimore, had received the charter from King Charles I in 1632, the colony being named in honor of the King's French Catholic wife. Jay Dolan recently has characterized the colonial venture in Maryland as follows:

> Cecil Calvert converted to Roman Catholicism most likely when he was in his early or middle twenties, at about the same time that his father became Catholic. The conversion of both father and son to Roman Catholicism is important, because their allegiance to a minority religion would have a significant influence on the early history of Maryland. But it should be emphasized at the outset that the Maryland colony was not founded primarily as an asylum or refuge for Catholics. Maryland was established first and foremost as a commercial enterprise, with profit, not religion, the primary impulse. As one historian put it, "Religion was

important, but not too important. In stark contrast to Massachusetts, where a religious outlook predominated, in Maryland religion was not to get in the way of man's other pursuits."[2]

Economic priorities notwithstanding, Maryland offered Catholics a haven free of the explicit anti-Catholicism of other colonies, such as Virginia. In Virginia an Anglican establishment was explicitly and strongly anti-Catholic, articulating the fear of "popish" plots and imperialism that prevailed in most of the other colonies. In England, Catholics who refused to conform to the Church of England were known as "recusants" and were suspected of being politically disloyal. In this spirit an act of the colony of Virginia made it clear that any Catholic settlers were to be barred from both political office and proselytizing:

> It is enacted by the authority aforesaid, that according to a Statute made in the third year of the reign of our sovereign Lord King James, of blessed memory, no popist [sic] recusant shall at any time hereafter exercise the place or places of secretary, counsellor, register, commissioner, surveyor or sheriff, or any other public place, but be utterly disabled for the same. And further, be it enacted by the authority aforesaid, that none shall be admitted into any of the aforesaid offices or places before he or they have taken the oaths of supremacy and allegiance. . . . And it is enacted by the authority aforesaid that the statutes in force against popish recusants be duly executed in the government; and that it shall not be lawful, under the penalty aforesaid, for any popish priest that shall hereafter arrive here to remain above five days, after warning given for his departure by the governor or commander of that place where he or they shall be, if wind and weather not hinder his departure.[3]

The Catholics of Maryland invited Protestants to settle in their colony, guaranteeing them religious liberty in an Act of Toleration passed in 1649. Nonetheless, when Protestants later became the majority in Maryland they refused to grant similar guarantees to the Catholics and so Catholics came to suffer religious liabilities in the one colony they had launched.

The beginnings of Maryland in 1634 were accompanied by a Jesuit chaplaincy in the person of Andrew White, who describes the trip up the Chesapeake that brought the first colonizers to their land, and then describes with some emotion the first Mass celebrated there:

> Having arrived at the wished-for country, we allotted names according to circumstances. And indeed the Promontory, which is toward the south, we consecrated with the name of St. Gregory (now Smith Point), naming the

northern one (now Point Lookout) St. Michael's, in honor of all the angels. Never have I beheld a larger or more beautiful river. The Thames seems a mere rivulet in comparison with it. . . . On the day of the Annunciation of the Most Holy Virgin Mary in the year 1634, we celebrated mass for the first time, on this island. This had never been done before in this part of the world. After we had completed the sacrifice, we took upon our shoulders a great cross, which we had hewn out of a tree, and advancing in order to the appointed place, with the assistance of the Governor and his associates and the other Catholics, we erected a trophy to Christ the Saviour, humbly reciting, on our bended knees, the Litanies of the Sacred Cross, with great emotion.[4]

In the middle of the seventeenth century, Spanish missionaries were hard at work in what is now New Mexico, Texas, and Florida. In the early eighteenth century, missionary reports were streaming back to Europe from what is now Arizona and Florida. French missionaries were working with the Hurons, Iroquois, Illinois, and other Indian tribes of the Northeast and Midwest, some giving their lives. For although Juan Padilla, a Franciscan missionary murdered about 1542 by Plains Indians in what is now Kansas, is usually considered the protomartyr in the Americas, the "North American martyrs" (Isaac Jogues, Jean de Brebeuf, Jerome Lalamant, and other Jesuits working with the Hurons and Iroquois in the 1630s and 1640s) are more famous. French priests were pioneer explorers of the Midwest, Marquette and Hennepin bequeathing their names to schools and streets. Catholics moved up and down the Mississippi, founding stations in Louisiana and Alabama and making much of the North America that lay outside British control Catholic territory.

Prior to the American Revolution, Catholics continued to be in a tenuous position in most British colonies. Massachusetts had passed an antipriest law in 1647, Catholics had been disenfranchised in Maryland in 1656, and the grant of toleration in New York in 1683 had been an exception proving the general rule of anti-Catholic sentiment. In 1748 John Carroll of Baltimore was appointed by Rome as the first Superior of the Mission to the United States, and both prior to the Revolution and after it he led the fight to keep the Catholicism of the colonies an independent venture, free of interference from Roman authorities. In 1789 Carroll was elected the first bishop of the United States, chosen not by Rome but by his fellow clergymen.

The Carrolls were the leading American Catholic family (Charles Carroll signed the Declaration of Independence). In a debate carried out in 1773 he had responded angrily to an attack that would have discredited his political opinions and service on the basis of his Catholicism, entering his name on the lists in the long-playing American struggle to work out religious toleration.

Following the Revolutionary War, in which the United States received considerable help from Catholic France, the Constitutional Congress set about establishing a new law for the land. The First Amendment to this Constitution, declared in force in 1791, set the guidelines for all subsequent national treatments of religion: "Congress shall make no law respecting an establishment of religion, or prohibiting the free exercise thereof; or abridging the freedom of speech, or of press; or the right of the people peacefully to assemble, and to petition the Government for a redress of grievances."[5] This did not keep individual states from discriminatory practices, but gradually the states gave up their established churches. Catholics were still in the great minority, but they could shelter under the national policy of a government that would take no position against them. In fact America has continued to be a Protestant nation, but minority groups such as Catholics and Jews, as well as dissident Protestants and African-Americans, have long modified the culture of the majority.[6]

In the first half of the nineteenth century, Catholics began to emigrate to the United States in significant numbers, Irish and Germans being most prominent among the first waves of immigrants. This led to the Irish hegemony in the American Catholic hierarchy, who were associated with the eastern cities in which the Irish immigrants concentrated, and to the German character of much mid-western Catholicism. The Church hierarchy debated as an ongoing question how Catholicism ought to adapt to American culture. Most bishops wanted to help their people enter the mainstream of economic and political opportunity but feared a loss of Catholic identity if they did not retain some separation.

The issue of parochial schools focused much of this ambivalence, and, on the whole, the reluctance of the Protestant majority in the United States to offer Catholics financial help with their parochial schools buttressed the instinct of the majority of the Catholic hierarchy that Catholic children would do best being educated in separate Catholic schools. Still, such debates as that conducted by the archbishop of New York, John Hughes, and the Yankee convert to Catholicism Orestes Brownson in the 1850s showed that Catholic adaptation to America was a divisive issue. Brownson thought Catholicism was the wave of America's future, if only the bishops such as Hughes (who was Irish born) would get over their dislike of the independent American character and embrace their new country enthusiastically.

Among the Protestants, the influx of Catholics raised anew the fears of popery that were present from the colonial beginnings. By the 1850s a nativist movement known as the Know-Nothings had gained considerable political power and tried to curb the rights and influence of the new immigrants. The nativists feared the political influence of immigrants such as the Irish, sometimes feared their competition for jobs, and generally disliked the different traditions that the immigrants brought, such as not observing the sabbath with the solemnity favored by many Protestants and thinking that drinking, dancing, and other recreations were compatible with Christian faith.

In 1834 anti-Catholic sentiment had broken out in Charlestown, Massachusetts, where a mob burned down a convent and academy housing Ursuline nuns
and their students.

> This incident was inspired by misinformation circulated by Rebecca Reed,
> who had been dismissed from Mount St. Benedict [the convent] as
> unsuited to religious life after a six-month novitiate. (She later wrote the
> first of the anticonvent books, *Six Months in a Convent*, published in
> 1835.) A second nun, Elizabeth Harrison, had left briefly because of a
> breakdown caused by overwork, but then had petitioned to reenter. It was
> falsely rumored that she was being held by force. The mob looted the
> buildings and desecrated the chapel, even digging up the bodies of the
> sisters in the cemetery, before burning the convent and academy.[7]

American Catholicism: After the Civil War

Catholics had served in the Revolutionary Army and they served on both sides
during the Civil War. Indeed, the Civil War offered Catholics another opportunity to demonstrate their patriotism, a demonstration that would become even
more signifcant during World War I, when the many different immigrant
groups that had arrived in the United States since the last decades of the
nineteenth century rushed to prove their allegiance to their new country. In
fact, the major event of the second half of the nineteenth century for American
Catholics was the great increase that immigration brought in their population.
Although the Irish and Germans, as noted, already had arrived in large numbers,
they continued to grow after the Civil War. Between 1851 and 1920, over 3.3
million Irish settled in the United States. Similarly, during the great century of
immigration, 1820–1920, over 1.5 million German Catholics settled here.

The 1880s saw the beginning of a significant Italian immigrant population,
about a million arriving before the turn of the century and over 3 million
arriving by 1920. Between 1870 and 1920 about 2 million Poles entered the
United States, and by 1920 over 1 million Americans worshiped in French-
speaking parishes, many of them coming from French Canada. The Mexican-
American war (1846–1848) had gained the United States territories in the
Southwest with many Spanish-speaking people. By 1920 more than 550,000
American Catholics were worshiping in Spanish-speaking parishes. Eastern
Europeans comprised the great majority of the other Catholic emigrants to this

country by 1920. Perhaps 500,000 Slovaks immigrated, along with 350,000 Czechs, 300,000 Lithuanians, and 250,000 Ukranians. All of these people began to increase in number, as they married and raised children. So, for example, on the eve of World War II the Ukranian population in the United States (Ruthenian Catholics) had probably doubled to about 500,000.

This influx of newcomers to the Catholic community determined the character of the American Catholic church from 1850 to 1950. The first order of business was building the churches, schools, social agencies, and other organs that were necessary to help the immigrants adapt to their new land and preserve their faith. A reminiscence of a visit to a newly established Hungarian community, written by a Hungarian bishop in 1905, captures much of the flavor of the "problem" presented to the Church authorities by the large number of immigrants:

> The workmen and their families awaited me at the entrance of the building. For the greater part they were still dressed in their simple costume "from over the sea," and their whole demeanour showed they had not long since arrived in these parts. Set adrift in that great city [Chicago], without knowing the language, without friends or any one to advise them, these poor folks are at the mercy of chance. And, in addition to all the other difficulties and problems which the municipal authorities have to face, we can well understand that this question of dealing with the foreign population of inferior civilisation is one of the greatest and hardest to solve. They have not only to be fed, they have also to be protected and educated. The church and the school are their only safeguards. As long as the people will go to church and are willing to have their children brought up on religious principles there is nothing to fear. As long as they recognize their duty towards God they will also recognize and fulfill their duty towards their neighbor.[8]

Several of the tensions associated with ethnic American Catholicism lodge beneath the surface of this reminiscence. First, one can appreciate how loyal a newly arrived ethnic family would feel toward those who had helped it survive and establish itself in its new home. Often such helpers included the local Catholic parish, where the nuns were doing heroic work trying to educate the children of the newcomers, and where one was most likely to find aid in getting a job, learning about medical care, and obtaining a circle of friends. The ward politicians and labor leaders who also assisted with such problems understandably could beget a similar loyalty.

Second, one should note the clerical opinion that if the people would stick by their faith, all finally would be well. Allied to that was a strong desire to instruct the children of the newcomers in Catholic doctrine, as an assurance that they would grow up in the faith. The somewhat condescending tone of the Hungarian bishop, who brands his own people of inferior civilization, probably reflects the patrician character of the clergy of his country. Although one can appreciate his sympathies for the American civil authorities who were trying to cope with the influx of foreigners, and one can see that such a sympathy would go a long way toward making church people and civil authorities allies in the battle on the newcomers' behalf, it yet remains true that such a paternalistic attitude has characterized American Catholic leadership throughout its history. Generally, American bishops have feared lay autonomy (reversing the hopes of John Carroll in the prerevolutionary period) and looked down on those of their people not yet adapted to the American language and culture.

The polyglot character of the American Catholic church after the waves of immigration understandably led to tensions among the different linguistic and cultural groups. By virtue of their longer presence and greater facility in English, the Irish had taken control of the Church hierarchy, somewhat contested by the Germans. The Irish bishops tended to think that the American church should be relatively uniform, and so they tended to be reluctant to sponsor ethnic parishes. Many of the non-Irish fought bitterly to retain their native religious customs, to obtain schooling for their children in their native language, and generally to preserve the sense of Catholic faith they had brought with them.

Protestant actions and feelings against ethnic Catholics gradually faded from the American mainstream, although one still finds them in rural America and they were potent until the election of John F. Kennedy as president. The presidential candidacy of Alfred E. Smith in 1928 brought out much anti-Catholic sentiment, and Kennedy only defused the long-standing question of whether a Catholic could be a loyal American citizen by meeting with Protestant ministers in Houston. The program of the infamous Ku Klux Klan has long been targeted against Catholics, along with African-Americans and Jews, and it seems inevitable that the recently risen White Supremacist and Neo-Nazi groups will imitate the Klan.

Still, American Catholics have generally considered the United States a wonderful place in which to exercise their faith and achieve their overall potential. Despite the suspicion of Rome, most pointedly expressed in the condemnation of the so-called "Americanist heresy" by Pope Leo XIII's encyclical *Testem Benevolentiae* in 1899, American Catholics have argued that the religious liberty enshrined in the Constitution of their land is a model for all modern countries, and that religious liberty itself is a right the Catholic Church has been scandalously slow to recognize. (The standard Catholic position prior to Vatican II was that in Catholic countries Catholicism ought to be the established religion and religious minorities ought to have lesser rights.) The great victory for American Catholicism came when the views of the American Jesuit John Courtney Murray on religious liberty were incorporated into Vatican II's "Decree on Religious Liberty", making it standard teaching in Roman Catholicism thereafter that rights of conscience require that no one be compelled toward religious practice or suffer civil liabilities because of religious practice (or nonpractice).

The experience and decrees of Vatican II were like midwives bringing Catholics into the light of the postmodern world. The experience was exhilarating, as bishops from all over the world, along with non-Catholic observers and Catholics in supporting roles, met to fulfill Pope John XXIII's mandate of *aggiornamento:* bringing the Church up to date. Although the Vatican's first drafts of most of the proposed documents suggested few changes in traditional Church teaching, the bishops quickly called for more substantial changes. Thus the documents on such key topics as the Church itself and the operation of the Church in the modern world ended up showing considerably more openness to modern developments. The Council adopted a pastoral, rather than a strictly doctrinal outlook, seeking to facilitate the Church's ministry to precisely contemporary conditions. In addition, the bishops' experience of receiving from their colleagues an overall, global impression of how Christian faith was faring brought a new sense of the Church's place in the world. Many laity the world over read with great interest the reports, official and unofficial, about conciliar debates, and for many it was the first time that the humanity of Church leadership, its inevitable immersion in controversy and politics, became fully clear. Most documents ended up being products of compromise, trying to balance both past convictions about faith and the freedom to dialogue with the contemporary world. But on the whole the Council concluded with both Catholics and Protestants having high hopes that a new era had dawned, both for ecumenical cooperation and for the Church's dialogue with the outside world.

The death of Pope John XXIII in 1963 brought Pope Paul VI into the Council as the man elected to oversee the completion of its work. Paul proved good at the compromises that most of the final documents expressed, but in the matter of birth control he experienced great problems. The bishops had debated whether advances in science (mainly, the contraceptive pill) allowed a change in the traditional prohibition against using "artificial" methods of contraception. A commission of lay, medical, and theological advisers recommended changes and allowing the use of the pill, but the pope delayed action on its recommendations. Finally, in 1968, three years after the conclusion of Vatican II, Paul VI's encyclical on birth control, *Humanae Vitae,* officially settled the matter: there would be no change.

The majority in the American Church found this decision traumatic, as polls taken in 1968 and subsequently steadily have shown. Anywhere from two-thirds to three-fourths of the Catholics polled differed with the pope's stance, feeling that birth control was a matter for couples to decide according to their own consciences and family circumstances. Opinions vary as to how much Church authority suffered from the encyclical. The American sociologist Andrew Greeley has made the encyclical the major reason for a significant decline in Sunday church attendance in the United States and has found that it helped make many American Catholics selective in their allegiance to Church teachings.[9]

The combination of Vatican II and *Humanae Vitae* did spotlight the twin questions of how to update Catholic faith and how to square private conscience with official Church teaching, setting them at the center of postconciliar Catholicism. As the reforms stipulated by the Council swung into place, conservatives and liberals tended to become more sharply defined, if not indeed to be polarized. That polarization has continued to the present day, making the final years of the pontificate of Paul VI very difficult and shading the pontificate of Pope John Paul II. The end of such tension is not yet in sight, as we see in Chapter 18. Interestingly, John Paul II has shown himself to be a composite pope, liberal in matters of social justice and conservative in matters of church discipline.

Representative Personality: Pope John XXIII

As noted, the pope responsible for convening Vatican II, and thus for bringing the Roman Catholic Church fully into the modern world, was Angelo Roncalli (1881–1963), Pope John XXIII. The third child and eldest son among thirteen children of a poor family living near Bergamo, Italy, Angelo began his preparations for the priesthood when he was only eleven. The poverty of his beginnings taught him a lesson he retained throughout his life, with the result that at his death his personal fortune amounted to only enough to bequeath $20 to each surviving member of his family.

After beginning his theological studies in Rome in 1900, Roncalli was drafted for military service (he also served as a chaplain during World War I). Ordained a priest in 1904, he went on to receive a doctorate in canon law. At the request of Pope Pius X, Roncalli assisted at the consecration of the new bishop of Bergamo, so impressing this bishop that he was asked to serve as his secretary. This post gave the young priest considerable experience of the workings of a diocese, but for nine years he also taught at the local seminary. Since the bishop of Bergamo, Giacomo Radini-Tedeschi, was one of the most progressive prelates in Italy, Roncalli benefited from having a significant role model. Indeed, Roncalli wrote a biography of his superior, sent it to the new Pope Benedict XV, and after the war was assigned by Benedict to be director of the Italian agency concerned with foreign missions. This job put Roncalli in touch with Vatican officials, and some historical research he did at the time on St. Charles Borromeo, a leader in the implementation of the sixteenth-century reforms of the Council of Trent, brought him in contact with Achille Ratti, the Milanese prelate destined to become Pope Pius XI.

Pius XI drafted Roncalli into the Vatican's diplomatic corps, appointing him apostolic visitor (representative of the Vatican) to Bulgaria in 1925, a post that entailed Roncalli's being consecrated an archbishop. For the next ten years he served in the lonely Bulgarian post, protecting the interests of the small Catholic community. Roncalli's next assignment was to be apostolic delegate to Greece, as well as head of the Vatican mission to Turkey. Once again his main task was to deal with a non-Catholic (in Turkey, a Muslim) majority on behalf of a minority Catholic church. Roncalli lived in Istanbul, receiving little notice from either the Turks or the Vatican, but acquiring a reputation as an affable host and dinner companion.

Because he had served so long in backwaters, his appointment as papal nuncio to France in 1944 stunned Roncalli. He was sixty-three years old and this was his first significant posting. The former nuncio to France had been close to some French collaborators with the Germans, so Roncalli's main task was to soothe wounded feelings. He was successful enough in this task to merit Pope Pius XII's appointing him a Cardinal in 1953. With this promotion went an appointment to be patriarch of Venice, which most observers judged would probably be the seventy-one-year-old Roncalli's final position.

Remarkably, however, at the death of Pius XII in 1958 the College of Cardinals could not decide on a successor and so, on the twelfth ballot, chose Angelo Roncalli as a compromise candidate, probably elected mainly because he was nearly seventy-seven years old and would not have a long reign. Shortly after his election, though, Pope John XXIII got the idea of convening an ecumenical council, the first in nearly a century, to help bring the Church an *aggiormamento*. The Curia (Vatican bureaucracy) was cool to this idea, but the pope patiently overrode its opposition and opened the Second Vatican Council in the fall of 1962. The style of the Council was to be positive and pastoral, seeking a new outpouring of the Holy Spirit. It would open the Church to ecumenical cooperation with both Orthodox and Protestants, and to an ongoing dialogue with the modern world.

The personal style of Pope John XXIII exemplified his hopes for the Council and the Church. Warm and outgoing, he charmed outsiders as much as insiders, traveling freely and stressing the ancient notion that the pope ought to be "the servant of the servants of God." Typical of the dignitaries he met were representatives of Jews, the president of Italy, the Soviet Premier Nikita Khruschev, and the Archbishop of Canterbury. His encyclical *Pacem in Terris* of 1963, issued less than two months before his death from stomach cancer, became John XXIII's last will and testament. Along with Vatican II and his own sunny personality, it provided a model for how the Catholic tradition ought to approach the modern world.

Pacem in Terris was addressed not just to the Catholic Church but to the whole world, exemplifying the hopes John XXIII had that Catholicism would open windows it had long kept shut and begin an honest exchange with outsiders. The encyclical discussed human rights, the dignity of the individual person, and how the international community might be better ordered toward justice and peace. It urged an end to the arms race, denounced racism, and supported the idea of a strong world body endowed with the powers to solve worldwide problems. Although the style remained that of the traditional Catholic theory of **natural law,** *Pacem in Terris* was so international in outlook and so comprehensive in its care for human rights that it won much praise from the global community. It made room for dialogue with Marxists, by distinguishing between Marxist philosophy and Marxist political regimes. Throughout, it was in keeping with John's self-understanding as one called to reconcile enemies and make the Church an agent of international peace and understanding.

Several anecdotes suggest why John XXIII became so loved. In visiting inmates of a Roman prison he said, "Since you could not come to me, I came to you." When anticipating a visit from Mrs. John F. Kennedy, he rehearsed various titles (his English was poor): "Mrs. Kennedy. Madame Kennedy." When she appeared before him, however, he opened his arms wide and burst out, "Jacqueline!" Once he told a Communist diplomat, "I know you are an atheist, but won't you receive an old man's blessing?" Once he stopped and told a peasant woman reaching up to touch him as he walked past, "Come closer. Why shouldn't you get as close as the King of Jordan did?" So the short, fat pontiff became one of the most recognized figures in the world. Everything about him seemed to radiate a peasant warmth that conveyed Christ's gospel of love.

The remarkable pontificate of John XXIII, which has forever changed Roman Catholicism through the Second Vatican Council, seemed like a direct sign from God, although on the human level clearly the pope was simply putting into effect ideas about the needs of the modern Church that he had developed through his many years of service outside of Rome, which had let him know how the outside world regarded Catholicism. Ironically, the docility he showed during his years of progress up through the Church ranks, accepting whatever assignments he was given, made him seem a safe papal candidate and so put him in the position where he could explode a bombshell.

The successors of John XXIII, Popes Paul VI and John Paul II (John Paul I was short-lived) have struggled to control the forces set free at Vatican II. In reflecting on their trials, even the death of John XXIII that limited his pontificate to five years seems significant. It spared John the political tasks consequent on the Council and so rounded his life off as a nearly perfect parable — a lesson in how to let the spirit work, trusting that a gospel of love is its own persuasion.[10]

Glossary

Natural law: the view that God has encoded in all creatures, including human beings, basic patterns and obligations that reason can discern. For human beings, natural law theory suggests that by analyzing human nature one can infer much of the ethical life that human freedom ought to pursue. Natural law can be further illumined by revelation, but the view that grace perfects nature rather than supplanting it has led Catholic theorists to continue to reason about the implications of human rationality, freedom, sociability, desire for God, and so forth, thinking that all people might join in such inquiries, using natural law as a common ground all shared, despite their different religious, philosophical, and political allegiances.

Nihilism: the philosophical position that nothing finally matters, because human beings can know nothing definitive about their situation, or because what human beings can know suggests that the world has no ultimate order or destiny. One can understand nihilism as a fatigue, despair, or cynicism visited on spirits that have struggled to find light and found themselves still trapped in darkness. One can theorize that nihilism may be God's way of impressing the divine mystery on certain people. But taken on its own grounds, without such further perspectives that can ameliorate it, nihilism is the deadly enemy of human hope and creativity. Indeed, it is a logical and ethical contradiction, the moral equivalent of the skepticism that Aristotle counseled people to rebut by simply having skeptics assert their position (if skepticism were true, then something could be known and asserted, which meant that skepticism itself would be untrue). Any act that we undertake, even suicide, seems a movement toward something potentially good — a cessation of pain, a proper show of defiance, whatever. We human beings cannot act to pursue nothingness as such — peace, oblivion, forgetfulness, perhaps; nothingness, no.

Pastoral theology: faith seeking an understanding of how to communicate the truths of the gospel and Christian tradition to ordinary people, in ministerial situations, with an awareness of the symbols and language that might convert the ancient convictions into present-day assurances of hope. Ideally, pastoral theologians listen to the people with whom they want to communicate, learn about the situations in which such people live and the problems with which they struggle, and know how to "translate" the basic truths of the Christian message because they themselves have long meditated on them and so come to grasp their inner essence, the doctrinal substance capable of being applied differently according to different circumstances.

Secularization: the process by which the world comes to seem less and less sacral or filled with divine mysteries, and comes to seem more and more a realm both matter-of-fact and amenable to human investigation or manipulation. For the secular person, such words as "divinity," "sacraments," "grace," and "salvation" are irritatingly vague. They sit awkwardly in the marketplaces and recreational sites shaping the secular worldview. So secularism implies an atrophy of religious instinct and, if religious instinct is crucial to human beings' finding their true measure, a source of immaturity or retardation. On the other hand, secularization can remind religious people that their language ought to bear on the here and now world in which human beings are suffering, longing for God, struggling to find meaning and peace. Thus secularization can criticize faith that amounts to pie in the sky and encourage believers to be more incarnational, more concerned with following Jesus as a way to a profound humanization.

Discussion Questions

1. What was characteristically modern in the understanding of human reason expressed by Francis Bacon?
2. How did the physics of Isaac Newton distance God from daily life?
3. How did the Enlightenment's stress on human autonomy and a critical spirit jar with traditional Catholicism?
4. In what ways was the Jesus of Enlightenment thinkers but a ghost of the New Testament Christ?
5. Why was the God of the *Declaration of Independence* a far cry from the divinity of traditional Roman Catholicism?
6. How did the Soviet and Chinese Communisms verify long-standing Catholic fears?

7. What was the connection between industrialization and secularization?
8. How might insights of the Social Gospel movement and of present-day ecological sensibilities have aided the Catholic Church in responding to the pastoral crises sparked by industrialization?
9. Why were the American colonies so phobic about papists and priests?
10. What did the immigrant character of the American Catholic church mean for the agenda of its leaders?
11. Why did Roman authorities long suspect American Catholics of having been harmed by the pluralistic culture of the United States?
12. How did nativist movements contradict the American tradition about religion expressed in the First Amendment?
13. What are the lessons in the relatively undistinguished ecclesiastical career of Angelo Roncalli prior to his elevation to the papacy?
14. What are the implications of John XXIII's having thought of himself as primarily a reconciler?

Notes

[1] Richard B. Morris, ed., *Encyclopedia of American History* (New York: Harper & Row, 1976), p. 563.
[2] Jay P. Dolan, *The American Catholic Experience* (Garden City, N.Y.: Doubleday, 1985), p. 72.
[3] Edwin S. Gaustad, ed., *A Documentary History of Religion in America*, vol. 1 (Grand Rapids, Mich.: Eerdmans, 1982), pp. 96–97.
[4] John Tracy Ellis, ed., *Documents of American Catholic History*, vol. 1 (Wilmington, Del.: Michael Glazier, 1987), pp. 113–114.
[5] *Encyclopedia of American History*, p. 574.
[6] See R. Laurence Moore, *Religious Outsiders and the Making of Americans* (New York: Oxford University Press, 1986).
[7] Mary Ewens, O.P., "The Leadership of Nuns in Immigrant Catholicism," in *Women and Religion in America*, vol. 1, ed. Rosemary R. Ruether and Rosemary S. Keller (San Francisco: Harper & Row, 1981), p. 132. See also Barbara Welter, "From Maria Monk to Paul Blanshard: A Century of Protestant Anti-Catholicism," in *Uncivil Religion*, ed. Robert N. Bellah and Frederick E. Greenspan (New York: Crossroad, 1987), pp. 43–71.
[8] John Tracy Ellis, ed., *Documents of American Catholic History*, vol. 2 (Wilmington, Del.: Michael Glazier, 1987), p. 557.
[9] See Andrew M. Greeley, *American Catholics Since the Council* (Chicago: Thomas More, 1985).
[10] See "John (XXIII)," in *The New Encyclopaedia Britannica*, vol. 6 (Chicago: Encyclopaedia Britannica, 1987), pp. 574–576; also Peter Hebblethwaite, *Pope John XXIII* (Garden City, N.Y.: Doubleday Image Books, 1987).

The Catholic World View

Creation

Genesis 1 – 3

The key point in the Christian understanding of physical reality is that all of creation has come from God as an act of love that drew it forth from nothingness. This doctrine of creation from nothingness took some time to develop, drawing upon such books as Genesis, Isaiah, the Psalms, and Job from the Hebrew Bible. The New Testament writers assumed this Old Testament background and concentrated more on the role of the Logos in creation. Thus the prologue of John's gospel and Colossians 1:15–20 shaped the Christian imagination to think of the Word as the medium, the matrix, that in which physical reality took rise.

Tertullian probably was the first to use the term "creation from nothingness," and Augustine made a major contribution to conceptualizing evil as a nonbeing that did not threaten the Christian view that a good God could only make a good world. Only with the medieval scholastics, however, did an adequate conception of creation develop. This conception depended on the notion that being is proper only to God, so that whatever exists directly depends upon God. Only God by nature exists. For the world to be, God has had to keep communicating "isness," being. Thus the medieval mystics praised God for the original blessing of creation, which they sensed moving toward them from every fruiting branch and winging bird.

105

Nonetheless, the origins of the entire Catholic conviction about the goodness of creation arise in the first chapters of Genesis, which liturgical usage kept making contemporary for believers each year. Genesis 1 : 1, the very first line of biblical revelation, sounded the foundational theme: "In the beginning God created the heavens and the earth." Catholic theology was constrained by this verse to two significant conclusions. First, the world had a beginning, a definite originating point, and so was not as some Greek and Indian speculation had depicted it: eternal, revolving in an endless cyclical return. Did this biblical fact imply that the world also would have an end? Christian theologians had little doubt that the answer was yes, though their conviction tended to spring more from New Testament imagery about the **Parousia** (return) of Jesus, apocalyptically presented in passages such as Mark 13, than from either Old Testament figures or the scholastics' reflections on contingency (dependence in being), which at points brushed the modern notion of entropy (the notion that creation is running down, toward disorder and dissolution).

Second, the maker of the world was the One God, the only true divinity. The world had not come from a secondary god, as some of the Gnostics implied. It was not a field of forces presided over by various deities — gods of storm, sun, earth — who gave it its vitality. The One God alone had brought the world into being, alone supplied all its form and order, all its beauty and wonder. The Spirit of God moving over the face of the waters (Gen 1 : 2) was like a mother stirring and warming her brood.

The rest of Genesis 1 depicts the creation of various elements of the world: light, the firmament called heaven, the waters, the dry earth, the vegetation, the sun and the moon, the fishes and birds, the cattle and beasts of the earth. Finally, as the acme of creation, God made a being in the divine likeness to carry dominion over the rest of creation. Genesis 1 : 27 - 28 was enormously influential in the Catholic understanding of humanity's place in creation: "So God created man in his own image, in the image of God he created him; male and female he created them. And God blessed them, and God said to them, 'Be fruitful and multiply, and fill the earth and subdue it; and have dominion over the fish of the sea and over the birds of the air and over every living thing that moves upon the earth.'"[1]

The reflection of divinity in the human makeup, the relation between male and female, the command to be fruitful and subdue the earth have been master-ideas in Western history. These thoughts are so foundational one cannot separate them from Christian culture. Those seeking the source of the Western effort to endow humanity with a singular dignity, and ideally to honor such dignity in each individual, ought to linger over Genesis 1 : 27. Those upset at the patriarchy of Western culture, as well as those who are sure that men and women have been created as complementary parts of a human whole, can find much of their instinct sharpened by the same verse. Ecologists who are convinced that a biblical depreciation of physical nature lies in the background of our modern pollution of the waters, the earth, and the skies will hear ominous overtones in Genesis 1 : 28. In contrast, entrepreneurs and developers easily can read the same verse as God's will that all human beings be go-getters.

The account of creation we find in Genesis 1 comes from what biblical scholars call the priestly source. The account we find in Genesis 2 and 3 comes from a source called the Yahwist. It is more concerned with human nature, which it depicts as a composite of dust from the ground and spirit breathed in by God. For the Yahwist, original humanity was a solitary male enjoying a paradisal garden, not burdened by the knowledge of good and evil. But such solitude did not work, so from the male God made a female, so perfectly suitable that both the man and the editoral voice break out in appreciation: "Then the man said, 'This at last is bone of my bones and flesh of my flesh; she shall be called Woman, because she was taken out of Man.' Therefore a man leaves his father and his mother and cleaves to his wife, and they become one flesh. And the man and his wife were both naked, and were not ashamed" (Gen 2 : 23 – 24).

Chapter 3 concerns the disobedience of the first couple, which theologians tend to treat in connection with sin rather than creation. On the basis of the first two chapters, the Catholic tradition has argued that both physical nature and human nature are intrinsically good. The refrain of Genesis 1, "And God saw that it was good," coupled with the indications that human beings carry the divine image and breath, have weighed more heavily in the Catholic, Orthodox, and Jewish theological estimate than have the effects of the primal disobedience. When one added the gift of Christ, the new Adam, one could understand why Paul said that where sin had abounded grace abounded the more.

The debates at the time of the Protestant Reformation turned on the relative weight the two sides placed on Genesis 3. Lutherans and Calvinists, who argued that humanity had become so depraved that there was no health in it, took Genesis 3 as overbalancing both Genesis 1 – 2 and the effects of Christ's grace in the human substance. Catholics and Orthodox admitted a wounding, symbolized by Genesis 3, without giving up either the original affirmation of God that creation was good or the intrinsic holiness they thought came to the human substance in grace and warranted speaking of divinization (sharing divine life).

The imagery of Genesis 3 spells out a disobedience worked by a desire for both sensual and spiritual gains that beckon as goods. The fruit and knowledge that the serpent promotes to the woman and the woman promotes to the man stand for the full range of apparent goods that can lure people to disobey God. Similarly, the effects that their disobedience brings upon the couple afflict both their bodies and their spirits. They lose their innocence, feel ashamed of their naked (original) condition, try to shift responsibility onto others, for the first time fear God, and hear that the hardships of their existence, from physical toil to childbearing, stem from their having broken the harmony God intended.

All this is powerful myth: truth in a storied form that does justice to the psychic complexity of the human situation. We should note that the Bible never blames God, and that God clothes the couple before sending them from the garden. We should also note that there is no indication that their disobedience has rendered humanity incapable of obeying God or achieving a good life. Whatever women or men have to suffer, their memory of God's benefactions and punishments can suffice to show them the path of wisdom. Creation has not conspired against them. The divine image and breath in them, like their coordination to one another, remain. If they now know good and evil as they need not have, and so now stand outside of paradise, God may yet have a destiny for them, since their story is far from finished.

Revelation

Where have Catholics gotten their distinctive views of physical nature, human nature, and the rest of reality? Our use of Genesis 1 – 3 suggests the answer and, with the answer, the essentials of the Catholic view of revelation.

Genesis 1 – 3 assumes that readers have some experience of both physical nature and human nature. What people know about God comes through their senses and brains. If these apparatuses were not reliable, there would be no effective human enterprise, let alone literature, wisdom, and theology. So it is only common sense to grant reason, or humanity's natural faculties, a certain competence. With this grant comes a basis for both honoring all human beings and thinking that, in principle, all human beings ought to be able to communicate and cooperate.

Nonetheless, Catholics, like other Christians, have thought that certain information and symbols are privileged. Certainly Genesis 1 – 3, the rest of the Bible, and above all the figure of Christ, merit such a status. For the traditional Catholic, the Church merits a privileged status, both for its teaching and its sacramental activity. The designation given these privileged sources of knowledge is "revelation." Etymologically, the word brings to the imagination the removal of a veil or covering. More specifically, the word has conjured up divinity unveiling itself, making something of its awesome mystery known.

One cannot make a hard and fast distinction between the disclosures about ultimate reality that come through human experience, study, and reflection and the disclosures of God that one finds through the privileged channels of Revelation, because both employ the same human apparatus (sensation, imagination, understanding, judgment, will). But one can think, on the basis of what prophets and seers, saints and mystics, have reported, that in the formation of the privileged symbols divinity has taken a special initiative, making extraordinary disclosures.

Insofar as biblical and traditional imagery bear on the personal being of God and carry forth God's designs for human beings, one can even speak of revelation as "supernatural." In this traditional usage, revelation conveys information and perspectives that human beings would not have come to possess, had God not done something special. Revelation therefore adds to natural knowledge. More importantly, it lifts the human spirit to visions that nature — humanity apart from special disclosures and helps — would not have imagined. For example, the triuneness of God, the divine plan to overcome sin through the grace of Christ, and the vocation of human beings to become partakers of the divine nature, all exceed what men and women on their own could know.

What we have just described is the way that the Catholic tradition has generally thought about revelation. We are well aware that these are not a series of propositions that the modern mind, even the modern mind that is piously Catholic, is likely to accept without question or difficulty. Nature and supernature, revelation and ordinary reason, where intuitions about the Trinity and divinization come from — each can raise a dozen questions. The old assumption that God dictated the Torah to Moses, or that the writers of the New Testament composed their works virtually under dictation from the Holy Spirit, does not sit well today. So we probably better imagine inspiration as occurring at that mysterious point, familiar to all poets, where images and ideas seem to flow without one's deliberate choosing.

As the Spirit moved over the waters to make a world, and as God reknit human destiny to take account of the disobedience of the first couple, and as Christ worked within the constraints of a particular body, mind, and people, so biblical inspiration and the revelation occurring through the Church have developed within human consciousness, labor, and social circumstances. The best imagery for revelation is not one of light pouring down from a distant heaven, not one of agents unconditioned by space and time passing on static secrets. Revealed knowledge rather differs from ordinary knowledge by its depth, its accreditation in the community of believers, its consonance with our best human instincts and what we sense when we contemplate Christ. We need neither deprecate ideas traditionally considered to have been specially revealed, because now we see that they come with manifest signs of the mechanics of everyday human knowledge, nor puff up the human factor in the construction of the Bible or Church doctrine, least of all to the point that we deny revelation any privileged status and become as cynical about it as we can be about other human claims.

A proper docility takes us to the Bible, the teachings of the Church, the central imagery surrounding Jesus, and the like as people who give their tradition a vote of confidence, who realize that for thousands of years men and women at least as good as themselves have found it to be a way to a profound life. A proper maturity helps us realize that none of that docility removes the need for moments of criticism, personal estimate, decision about what the consequences of revelation seem to be here and now. Revelation has been abused by the too docile, who become credulous, and by the too skeptical, who become unbelievers—people closed to God.

Like all significant human achievements, gaining a proper purchase on revelation, taking it to heart in the ways that make for that fruitfulness so important to the Johannine Jesus (Jn 15:8), requires a delicate balance. Indeed, such is the delicacy required that at the times one can feel one is achieving it, the Spirit seems palpable—revealing itself then and there. Paul has given the classical description of the fruits of the Spirit: "But the fruit of the Spirit is love, joy, peace, patience, kindness, goodness, faithfulness, gentleness, self-control. . . ." (Gal 5:22-23). Any time that one experiences such fruits and correlates them with Christ, one has the substance of the Christian theology of revelation.

The Catholic accent in this whole matter has been to draw from revelation a sense that God has not left divinity without witness anywhere. Under the impress of faith, nature could become a manifold of testimonies to the divine intelligence, beauty, and power. The Bible brimmed with stories, images, and pithy expressions of wisdom attributable to the Holy Spirit. The greatest revelatory symbol, however, was the flesh of Jesus Christ, where the Word (which one might call the Father's eternal self-expression or revelation) became available to human senses, "pitching its tent in our midst." Everything that the Incarnate Word had said and done was revelatory. Better, Jesus himself was the *Ursymbol*, expressing as much of what God was like as human terms could.

The Church carried on for Jesus after his resurrection, serving as his Body and living under the guidance of the Paraclete he had sent to continue his mission of comfort, aid, and defense. The sacraments of the Church brought the life of God flowing through the Body into especially significant moments in the life cycle, when people entered on Church membership, repaired the relations that sin had broken, joined with another in the adventure of marriage, began a life of ecclesiastical service, or found themselves at the verge of death.

The reading of Scripture in solemn liturgical assemblies dramatized how God had disclosed the divine nature, will, and love in those privileged pages. Thus Moses and David, Deborah and Mary, Jesus and the Magdalene came before the mind's eye as paradigms of faith. The warmth the Spirit stirred now and then, as the liturgy rehearsed the story of God's love, and the tears of joy one could feel, put a seal of authenticity on the Bible. God remained mysterious. No book, no ceremony, no institution, not even the perfect flesh of Jesus could remove divinity's inalienable excess of light, its too-fullness of love. But enough had been revealed to vindicate the biblical promise that where two or three gathered in Jesus' name, they would feel his presence, would find his power disclosed.

Ecology

Although one can make a historical case that Christian revelation has stimulated some profound appreciations of nature, it remains true that the Christian instinct that nature is not divine led most ages to regard the land, the flora, and the animals as raw materials placed at the disposal of human beings for whatever use human beings desired.[2] The examples of Jesus loving the lilies of the field, of Augustine interrogating creation in search of God, of Francis of Assisi writing canticles to Brother Sun and Sister Moon, of John of the Cross letting his contemplative ardor be nourished by solitary converse with nature, and of Teilhard de Chardin brooding his way deep into the mystery of the cosmic Christ, who one day would make God all in all, suffice to indicate that nature has not been absent from high moments of Catholic spirituality. Similarly, the Catholic instinct to use bread and wine, water and oil, and wax and incense so that nature might both token God's coming and enter into the great song of praise that human beings were raising up approaches Eastern Orthodox wisdom in its understanding of the implications of the Incarnation.

Nonetheless, if we wish to speak of Catholic overtones to ecology, we have to move from the historical to the idealistic mode, more speculating about what help Catholic sensibility might offer the ecological crisis than bringing forward case studies of stirring models achieved in the past. The stewardship that Benedictine monks achieved on some of their landholdings may indeed suggest valuable lessons for future land use, but the Benedictines were not faced with toxic chemicals oozing from every water table or acid rain poisoning entire ecosystems of lakes and trees. Today we need something less amiable and more prophetic, something less tied to past anthropocentrism and more passionate about the divine presence in nature that renders pollution a form of deicide.

The foregoing suggests the proper theological form for the ecological question and then makes it a subquestion suitably fitted into our general inquiry into the Catholic understanding of creation. In a word, does the traditional view of creation so separate the material world from God that we not only may but should read Genesis 1:28 as conferring on human beings the right to use or abuse nature as they see fit? Has the secularization that began slowly in the early modern centuries and then came with a rush in the twentieth century a writ of emancipation stemming from the Bible? Was this permission to use the earth for human gain suggested in the debates of the Church fathers about the follies of pagan idolatry, solidified in the medieval appropriation of Aristotle's radically rational view of creation, and forwarded in the this-worldliness of the late medieval and Renaissance papacy? Is it folly to try to reinvest nature with an aura of holiness that might protect it from further rape?

The answer to all of these questions, of course, is no. Whatever the abuses of the doctrine of creation in the past, we may consider nature a sacred realm. It is a "body" of divinity worthy of respect and good treatment, because of perennial insights both inseparable from the Catholic Christian sense of creation and essential to human health in any age, at any place. The perennial insights include the imagery playing through the biblical account of creation and the reflective probings of the mystics, theologians, and philosophers that established the intimacy of divine being to whatever draws breath.

In the biblical account of creation, God is the primary cause. No string of secondary causes, on the order of the chain of influences familiar from modern physics or evolutionary biology, separates God from the firmament, the waters, the plants, and the creeping things. The biblical imagery shouts that nothing in existence is far from God's creative hand, interest, or care. Modern humans have to grapple with the prescientific character of this account. The mythological mind of the biblical authors is no rightful opponent of contemporary science. But the religious mentality without which Catholic Christianity would lose its identity insists that this mythology continues to read out to us from nature invaluable lessons. When we watch the waves crash at Bass Rocks in Massachusetts or enjoy the play of the otters off Point Lobos in California, our religious sensibility has not gone on holiday. The wonder we feel, the reknitting of our spirits and incitement to praise, escapes the confines of science. God is moving through the brilliant, or frightening, or simply incomprehensible landscape we are surveying, just as God is moving our spirits to turn what we are seeing and feeling into prayer.

The mystics who sensed the divine presence everywhere, like the theologians and philosophers who deduced that a genuine Creator would be the inmost reality of everything in existence, gave the aesthetic spirituality obvious in the biblical texts a solid rationale. Whether or not one thinks that panentheism (the mutual inherence of God and creation) is the best articulation of this rationale, the point remains that God is more intimate to any of us creatures than we are to ourselves, and that this applies to rocks and trees as well as to presidents and professors. As the scholastic theoreticians concluded, whatever is is one, true, good, and probably beautiful. Each of these qualities comes from the participation of whatever is in the fontal being of God. Just as nothing escapes the divine intentions for nature and history, with the result that there are no accidents from God's point of view, nothing stands apart from the divine source of existence, not even the sinner bubbling with hatred of God. In the fact of our material being, as well as the intentions of our rational spirits, we human beings point to a transhuman source. So do the cardinals decorating our trees, the tornadoes whirling up from the south, and the whales spicing their long migrations with songs of eerie beauty.

This is part of the long-standing Catholic speculative tradition, however much we authors have offered present-day examples. That tradition frolics in the writings of the medieval mystics we have cited, from Hildegard to Meister Eckhart. Thomas Aquinas was the great medieval existentialist, the one who brought *esse* (the act of existence that ties creatures directly to God) to the center of both metaphysics and Christology. Ignatius Loyola ended his *Spiritual Exercises* with a contemplation on the divine love streaming down from heaven and diffusing itself throughout creation. According to the Epistle of James, a writing that Catholics (for other reasons) defended against Luther's criticisms and his plan to remove it from the canon, "Make no mistake about this, my dear brothers: it is all that is good, everything that is perfect, which is given us from above; it comes down from the Father of all light; with him there is no such thing as alteration, no shadow of a change. By his own choice he made us his children by the message of the truth so that we should be a sort of first-fruits of all that he has created" (Js 1 : 17 – 18). Catholics can echo the Psalmist, then, and say that the Lord has sworn and will never repent: creation will always be a cornucopia of divine makings and presences.

If this is so, we have a theological, faith-inspired corroboration of the instinct one finds in virtually all cultures that harmony with nature, appreciation of natural beauty and care for nature's flourishing, is part of the profile of human health, maturity, and wisdom. This instinct is so strong in recent nonliterate cultures and (by inference from recent nonliterate cultures as well as from artifacts and artistic remains) in prehistoric cultures, that one could call it the overriding religious imperative of earliest humanity. It is nearly as impressive in East Asia, where Taoist and Shinto sensibilities most clearly carry it, but Confucian and Buddhist views are not far behind. As philosopher Eric Voegelin has argued, the basic worldview of humanity prior to the "leaps in being" expressed in Greek philosophy and Israelite revelation amounted to a cosmological myth that made human beings consubstantial (of one substance) with other creatures. Nature was an organic whole and human beings were more like than unlike the other beings that nature vivified or preserved in inanimate forms.[3]

The catholic, universal testimony of Christian faith and non-Christian wisdom thus heads in the direction of bowing before nature, offering reverence if not actual worship. Measured against such testimony, our recent treatment of nature brands us moderns as aberrant and probably pathological. What we do outside, to the forests and streams, mirrors destructions inside, deep in our psyches. The greed, forgetfulness, carelessness, insensitivity, and simple stupidity of our current way of life, our current defiance of the carrying capacity of nature and the needs of the biosphere, are like blow-ups of the mark of Cain (Genesis 4:15), or like technicolor, mixed-media projections of the disobedience still twisting us. Catholic theology should roundly condemn all of this disobedience, even as Catholic theology should continue to say that God has a more ultimate word.

History

The Word of God came into history, ever after shaping Christian faith as an enjoyment of space and time, as a sense that God is a spinner of tales, a Scheherazade limitless in her capacity to rework the elements of nature and humanity and keep a disastrous finale at bay. The Bible itself has the form of a story, an interpretation of Israelite and then Christian time. The famous meeting between Moses and God at the thornbush (Ex 3:14) leaves Moses with no God he can name or contain, with only the promise that God will reveal the divine nature through time, as Israel sojourns with Him. As the present-day Jewish writer Elie Wiesel has said, "God made man because he loves stories." The ambiguous "he" in the sentence, justifying the generic "man," summarizes the point. What God and humanity are engaged in, covenanted to, is a story dear to the hearts of both. Human beings would go mad had they no stories of hope by which to orient themselves.

￼he stories of the Bible are much less historical reports, concerned with fidelity to exactly what happened in the past, than they are dramatic paradigms. In the past God dealt with the ancestors faithfully. In the past people found they could make it, could pull through, if they tried to compose their spirits after the example of Abraham, Sarah, Jacob, Moses, Deborah, David, Ezra, and Nehemiah. Christians thought of the great cloud of witnesses (Hebrews 12:1) who had pulled through by placing their hopes in Christ. Their great paradigm was the birth, life, death, and Resurrection of Jesus, whom they believed God had made the first of many brothers and sisters. Then there were the stories of Peter and Paul, of the Beloved Disciple and John of Patmos, of the Virgin Mary and the Magdalene. Each of these evangelical figures, as each of the significant saints whom Catholic piety later revered, was a bit of history touched by divine grace. Each suggested that time, as much as space, could bring good things from God, need not be feared, and had the potential to become a congenial home.

Catholic Christianity naturally had to honor the tension, clear in the Bible, between now and then, between the incarnational present and the eschatological future. It had to honor the wisdom of both the Bible and human experience that we have on earth no lasting city. Qoheleth's lament (Ecclesiastes 1:2) that all is vanity was bound to strike a responsive cord. Thomas à Kempis calling all the wise to remember death, like the corps of monks and virgins trying to escape the temptation to shelter too comfortably in time by establishing themselves in the desert, testified that time was short and only God was long. As Isaiah had said long ago, "All flesh is but grass. The grass withers, the flowers fade. Only the Word of God endures" (Isaiah 40:6-8).

Catholic time has been a tense, complex, often conflicted entity. History has been a penultimate value, nothing the orthodox ever placed as the final treasure or confused with God. Yet the Incarnation of divinity in Jesus the Christ had baptized history, along with everything else fleshly, assuring history an eternal value. Christ raised to the right hand of the Father had brought flesh, and so history, into the divine existence itself. Indeed, God had assumed Mary, the bearer of divinity, the one who gave the Logos flesh, into heaven in further testimony to the significance of time. The Annunciation scene, where Mary said yes to God's intentions for time, fittingly came to a climax in Mary's enthronement as Queen of Heaven.

In a dozen ways, therefore, both formal Catholic faith and popular Catholic piety sought a balanced view of temporality. Human beings, who were images of God, could never escape history, which meant that history, the story carried by human time, had to be **ontologically** good. Nature gained a history through human beings' interactions with it, so much so that Teilhard de Chardin could speak of nature's developments as Christogenesis. And yet beyond history lay eternity. Beyond the shrouded divinity that time now and then revealed lay James' Father of lights. The beatific vision of the essence of God, of the whatness the mind sought whenever it probed the causality that might explain the world, would be an endless transcendence of history. Entering the limitless, unbegotten life, light, and love of God, the beatified would share not only the divine deathlessness but also the divine completion. If bungling theologians could not appreciate how heaven would not be boring, mystics who had felt the transports of divine love had little doubt. One could never exaggerate the vastness of God, whether one spoke about being or goodness. The parables of Jesus constantly warned people not to underestimate the divine goodness, not to think that God is limited as human beings are. The speculations of the best mystics and theologians moved to the same conclusion about God's beauty and intelligibility. There would always be more to know and love.

With such a description of the human destiny, history risked becoming a second-rate vocation. Indeed, at times Catholic Christianity seemed to devalue works on earth, but such a stance was usually neither long-lived nor subsequently approved. The ideal was a delicate balance, and the Catholic preference was for a full-bodied, if not indeed lusty, incarnationalism. That preference justified the difference between American Catholic immigrants and their non-Catholic fellow-citizens who feared drinking, dancing, and good times. It removed Catholicism from the Puritanism that ran strongly in rivulets of history, from the medieval heretics called Cathari to the murderous Oliver Cromwell.

Admittedly, Catholicism suffered pruderies, failures of nerve, and clericalisms that refused a full embrace of flesh and time. Admittedly, Catholic piety sometimes so contemplated a Jesus meek and humble of heart, a Jesus fated from the womb to hang from the cross, that its lust for life flickered low. In such low times the Virgin could be an enervating role model, just as in the best of times she could rouse women to their own **magnificats**. The saints could suggest quirky austerities, contempt for the world, and an eccentricity more suspect than admirable. But these failings were the aesthetic and spiritual equivalents of the doctrinal heresy expressed in **Jansenism**. They were missings of the mark that attentive readers of scripture and tradition, like attentive examiners of what went on at the table and in the bedroom of a happy Catholic home, knew in their bones were unwise.

For the love of God poured forth in believers' hearts by the Holy Spirit produced a peace and joy running more toward friskiness than gloom. The perfect love occasionally revealed in moments of peak religious experience cast out fear. If one asked God for bread, would God return a stone? If one asked for an egg, need one fear a scorpion? If human beings, evil as they could be, knew how to give their little ones good things, indeed would give their blood to keep the little ones whole, how much more must not God care for his children? Therefore, one ought not to care overmuch about the morrow, with its problems of food, drink, or what one was to wear. Only the heathen worried about that. If one was seeking the Kingdom of God, the rest would turn out fine. Following Paul, Catholics knew that to live was Christ and to die was gain. The majority certainly did not attain such a profound faith, but most suspected what Paul had meant. For most recalled that God numbered every hair of their heads. Surely, then, God wanted them to bless the time he had given them.

Representative Personality: Julian of Norwich

The most blessed time God gave Julian of Norwich was five hours of ecstasy on May 8, 1373. The revelations or "showings" she received then fortified her through the more than thirty years of her life that followed. Because she wrote descriptions of her experience, which later circulated into the mainstream of late medieval English piety, Julian now stands with the anonymous author of *The Cloud of Unknowing* and Walter Hilton as a giant of fourteenth-century mysticism. Her thought is sufficiently mature to merit several different sorts of studies, but for our purposes presenting her view of creation will suffice.

Most of Julian's visions focused on the suffering Christ, bloodied and hanging from the cross. Yet her profit from contemplating Christ's passion was much like that of Thomas Aquinas, who had counseled those feeling depression to take a warm bath and study the suffering Christ. Julian herself was sickly, burdened with bodily pains. The racked, lacerated body of Christ offered her a surprising consolation:

> And at the same time as I saw this corporeal sight, our Lord showed me a spiritual sight of his familiar love. I saw that he is to us everything which is good and comforting for our help. He is our clothing, for he is that love which wraps and enfolds us, embraces us and guides us, surrounds us for his love, which is so tender that he may never desert us. And so in this sight I saw truly that he is everything which is good, as I understand.
>
> And in this he showed me something small, no bigger than a hazelnut, lying in the palm of my hand, and I perceived that it was as round as any ball. I looked at it and thought: What can this be? And I was given this general answer: It is everything which is made. I was amazed that it could last, for I thought that it was so little that it could suddenly fall into nothing. And I was answered in my understanding. It lasts and always will, because God loves it; and thus everything that has being through the love of God.
>
> In this little thing I saw three properties. The first is that God made it, the second is that he loves it, the third is that God preserves it. But what is that to me? It is that God is the Creator and the lover and the protector. For until I am substantially united to him, I can never have love or rest or true happiness; until, that is, I am so attached to him that there can be no created thing between my God and me. And who will do this deed? Truly, he himself, by his mercy and his grace, for he has made me for this and has blessedly restored me.[4]

Being a mystic and truly holy woman, Julian is enraptured by God. Nothing matters, compared to God's love. And yet, God's love leads her to a love of creation. It is not an unmeasured or uncritical love. She remains different from the worldlings who plunge into sensual experience, trying to grab pleasure with right hand and left hand. Instructively, however, Julian is also different from those who hate the world, from the fastidious whose spiritual progress makes them think the world too messy to be borne. Christ on the cross was totally messy. He was bruised, split, uncomely. Julian on her bed of pain felt twisted and ugly. Yet the Spirit that exalted her spirit transformed in an instant what she felt, what she saw, what she thought. Lifted up to a God's-eye view, she thought of God's "familiar" love. God's love was near, comfortable, long-known. It was the sort of affection one might find in a close family. Indeed, it was everything good, comforting, helpful. So God was as proximate as the light that filtered through Julian's window, as the bed that gave her rest, as the table on which rested her few things. God's love was like the atmosphere or the inner pulse of creation. Whatever was, whatever looked or felt good, whatever helped tokened God's love and conveyed it.

The vision of the little nut is one of the most famous symbols in the *Showings*. One can take it as a deprecation of creation, showing how tiny the universe is compared to its source. Or one can take it as another figure of intimacy: God showing that creation is something human beings need not fear, something they can accept like a toy a parent gives a much-loved child.

The symbolic ball seems threatened with nothingness. Representing all creatures, it reminds Julian that only God is. Whatever is less than God strangely combines being and nonbeing. Only God is being without restriction, being that nothing limits. All else is God stopped, defined, bounded by nothingness. Somehow God overcomes this nothingness enough to make the creature be. In moments of clarity, however, the holy person realizes that everything utterly depends on God's grace. Because God loves the world, the world stays in being. Without the love of God, there would be no world, only nothingness.

The foolish pursue the void of nothingness when they have been made for the fullness of Existence. Until she is substantially united with God, either in a mystical marriage brought about by God or in heaven, Julian will know no full rest or happiness. Like Augustine, she has been made for God and her heart will be restless until it rests in God. When she does rest in God, however, she will see that nothing created comes between her and God. Then all creatures will stand forth as what they really are: expressions of God, gifts from God, results of God's love.

What is Catholic in this spirituality is the balance the love of God inculcates. Julian is so enamoured of God, so impressed by Christ's passion, so exalted to a heavenly perspective that she risks accounting the world, the realm of physical creation and human strivings, unimportant, even contemptible. Yet her very love and mystical experience prevent her from crossing the line. She stays on the right side of downplaying the world and avoids contempt because she realizes that "the world" is God's doing. God cannot despise what God has made. Neither should she. The better she appreciates the love of God, the more profoundly she realizes that this love is the ultimate explanation for the world, the more she is bound to find God in every decent creature, every sound experience. And then the natural elements, her body, the food she takes, the sleep that comes, the birds that sing her awake in the morning all reconfigure themselves. Then all become gifts from on high, signs that God's love enwraps her like a blanket.

It is important to realize that this view of creation as an outpouring and presence of God's love is not sentimental. Most of the time Julian focuses on the passion of Christ, contemplating the results of sin and the extremities to which her savior went on her behalf. She speaks more of her bodily pains than of her bodily pleasures. She is not a woman for whom fine sights and touches, let alone luxuries, have much appeal. And yet the fierce, nearly rude love of God displayed on the cross softens as she considers how God comes to her, how for those who love God all things conspire unto good. Even sin and the passion of Christ it necessitated stand transformed:

> He answered with these words, and said: Sin is necessary. In the word "sin," our Lord brought generally to my mind all which is not good: the shameful contempt and the complete denial of himself which he endured for us in this life and in his death, and all the pains and passions, spiritual and bodily, of all his creatures. For we are all in part denied, and we ought to be denied, following our master Jesus until we are fully purged, that is to say until we have completely denied our own mortal flesh and all our inward affections which are not good. And the beholding of this, with all the pains that ever were or ever will be—and of all this I understood Christ's Passion for the greatest and surpassing pain—was shown to me in an instant, and quickly turned into consolation. For our good Lord would not have the soul frightened by this ugly sight. But I did not see sin, for I believe that it has no kind of substance, no share in being, nor can it be recognized except by the pains which it causes. And it seems to me that this pain is something for a time, for it purges us and makes us know ourselves and ask for mercy; for the passion of our Lord is comfort to us against all this, and that is his blessed will for all who will be saved. He comforts readily and sweetly with his words, and says: But all will be well, and every kind of thing will be well.[5]

Glossary

Jansenism: a seventeenth-century Catholic heresy associated with Cornelius Jansen (1585–1638), bishop of Ypres. The propositions condemned in 1653 included the idea that without a special grace from God people cannot keep the commandments, and the idea that the operation of grace is irresistible. Thus Jansenism was understood to teach a determinism: either human beings were determined by nature to sin, or they were determined by grace to be obedient to God.

Jansen had developed his ideas through a long study of Augustine, and they bore obvious similarities to the ideas of Luther about the corruption of human nature and of Calvin about predestination. Many followers of Jansen claimed they did not recognize his or their views in the condemned propositions. Through the influence of Blaise Pascal and the Jansenist community at Port Royal, such ideas nonetheless had considerable vogue in France, whereas many Irish priests trained in French seminaries brought Jansenistic leanings to congregations in Ireland and the United States, fostering a rather pessimistic, gloomy piety.

Magnificats: songs, or prayerful expressions, in the spirit of Mary, the mother of Jesus, as described in Lk 1:46-55. The Magnificat builds on the prayer of Hannah (I Sam 2:1-10) and celebrates God's exaltation of the lowly and diminishment of the proud, the wealthy, and the powerful. It places God on the side of the poor and ponders the paradoxes of God's ways, which frequently contradict the ways of the world. Mary thus speaks for all people who feel unjustly shunted to the sidelines of history, and liberation theologians have taken up her Magnificat as a model of the spirituality they want to develop.

Ontologically: concerning the being or metaphysical status of something. Ontology ponders existence, trying to answer the basic philosophical question, Why is there something rather than nothing? Catholic ontology fills out the biblical descriptions of creation by concentrating on God's grant of existence, which keeps contingent creatures from falling back into nothingness. Ontology operates on a different level from the scientific investigations that mainly assume the existence of the phenomena with which they deal and ask about their histories, structures, and changes. Insofar as science does not concern itself with ontological matters, and such matters pose significant questions, and theology suggests significant answers without intruding upon the legitimacy of the different questions and answers of science, ontology can point to the proper relations between religion and science and so can help theologians minimize conflicts with scientists.

Parousia: the return of Jesus to consummate history. The term implies a fullness of power, proper to the one God raised from the dead and exalted at his right hand. It suggests a judgment on the powers currently ruling the world and a vindication of the faithful who are suffering from such powers. The early letters of Paul reveal his expectation of the Parousia and so his eschatological accents: the end is near, so stay clear of worldly attachments (including marriage).

Discussion Questions

1. What was the main impact of Genesis 1:1?
2. What is the tension implied between Genesis 1–2 and Genesis 3, and how has Catholic theology tended to handle it?
3. Why did Catholic theology consider the Trinity something revealed?
4. What does a balanced view suggest about the place of the human imagination in Christian revelation?
5. Why has Genesis 1:28 become significant in discussions of ecology?
6. What sort of divine presence in nature can one legitimately acknowledge and what behavioral consequences ought this acknowledgment to beget?
7. How ought one to qualify the statement, "History is the story of God's love"?
8. What are the implications of thinking that the Incarnation baptized history?
9. How does Julian of Norwich link the Passion of Christ and God's love for creation?
10. Why do mystics so regularly counsel detachment from all creatures, and what does this tend to do for their view of the world?

Notes

[1] For a Jewish view of the Torah, see H. Gunter Plaut, ed., *The Torah: A Modern Commentary* (New York: Union of American Hebrew Congregations, 1981). For Catholic commentary, see Raymond E. Brown, Joseph A. Fitzmyer, and Roland E. Murphy, eds., *The Jerome Biblical Commentary* (Englewood Cliffs, N.J.: Prentice-Hall, 1968). A new edition is promised for 1989. As a general introduction to the Hebrew Bible, see John Tully Carmody, Denise Lardner Carmody, and Robert L. Cohn, *Exploring the Hebrew Bible* (Englewood Cliffs, N.J.: Prentice-Hall, 1988).
[2] See H. Paul Santmire, *The Travail of Nature* (Philadelphia: Fortress, 1985); John Tully Carmody, *Ecology and Religion* (New York: Paulist, 1983).
[3] See Eric Voegelin, *Order and History* (Baton Rouge: Louisiana State University Press, 1956–1987); John Tully Carmody and Denise Lardner Carmody, *Interpreting the Religious Experience: A Worldview* (Englewood Cliffs, N.J.: Prentice-Hall, 1987), a work based on Voegelin's views.
[4] Julian of Norwich, *Showings* (New York: Paulist [Classics of Western Spirituality], 1978), pp. 130–131.
[5] Ibid., pp. 148–149.

CHAPTER 7

Incarnation

Christology
The Biblical God
Ecclesiology
Sacramentality
Representative Personality: Thomas Aquinas
Glossary, Discussion Questions, Notes

Christology

Christology is the study of Jesus Christ, the effort of faith to understand what it can of the God-man. Jesus obviously is the "cause" of Christianity, in the sense of being the reason it arose. Those who have accepted the Johannine interpretation of Jesus as the Logos incarnate have received a firm impulse to think of creation as centered in the Christ, and to think that faith everywhere ought to bless the matter God chose to make the basic sacrament of divine revelation: human flesh.

The Christology of the New Testament is both simple and complicated.[1] On the one hand, the gospels make it plain that Jesus was a full human being. He was born of Jewish parents at a specific time and place. He grew up before his neighbors, increasing in wisdom and grace. Baptized by John the Baptist, he preached, taught, healed, hungered, grew discouraged, was buoyed by those who showed him faith, went to parties, debated with Pharisees, felt the cold shudders that come from betrayal, was arrested, was beaten, and finally died on the cross like a common criminal. All of this shouted, whispered, in every way proclaimed that he was like all other human beings—vulnerable, needy, able to muster special strength for special occasions, grateful for friends and supporters, bedazzled by the mystery of God—save in one crucial respect. He did not sin. Nothing in the records about him shows him to have turned away from God or to have refused any neighbor his care. Sebastian Moore is the Catholic theologian who recently has pondered the implications of Jesus' sinlessness most profoundly, and his conclusions bear rumination.[2] He sees Jesus as freed by his sinlessness to let a dialectic of desire have full play in his life, and so freed to be passionately involved with both divinity and his brothers and sisters.

We all want to be wanted—that puts Moore's thesis into a terse, easily abused, but still accurate epitome. We take fire, come into our own, realize why we have been given breath and time when we want someone else and find our wanting (hoping, admiration, and the rest) returned. In such a return of desirous love, we find ourselves, perhaps for the first time, and are amazed at the possibilities: we might actually be people of worth. Christology suggests that God desires us in this way, that God has embarked upon a love affair with us, however improbable or even scandalous that may seem, especially if we are uneasy with desire. Can God desire us? Could any mortal flesh move God to want intimacy with it? Classical theology immediately would begin throwing up a dozen objections, most of them centered in the solid enough notion that God has no needs, is completely self-sufficient. But classical theology by no means has exhausted the wonders emanating from the flesh of Jesus. Neither has it exhausted what human beings think they learn from the experience of love and why the Johannine writings say that God is love. What God doesn't have to do, God could choose to do, for the play in it, the helpfulness in it, the heaven of it. In Jesus, God found a beloved, certainly known from time out of mind in the love life of the Trinity, but now touchingly enfleshed. The beloved, as the voice from the heavens called Jesus at his baptism, now had been small as a baby, vulnerable as a creature who had to eat, sleep, and hope that some few would take his words to heart and so justify his human existence.

In the Christology of Karl Rahner, certainly the most influential Catholic theologian of the past generation, what God accomplished in romancing Jesus of Nazareth is a peak, nonpareil instance of what God wants to do for all human beings. The communication of self that God achieved perfectly in Jesus God wants to accomplish in all of us. We all have a capacity, a potentiality, for receiving the divine self-understanding and love. We all can "incarnate" something of the divine mystery and give it a humble residence in a rushing world. Jesus is unlike us in his sinlessness, and in his strict divinity as the eternal Logos, but he is like us in being flesh that God can divinize, mind-heart-soul-strength that God can lure and fill.

The balance of the New Testament's descriptions of Jesus includes enough about his miracles, mysteriousness, unique intimacy with God, and Resurrection to set in counterpoint with his manifest humanity an indisputable divinity. For the New Testament writers, no honest witness of Jesus could have doubted his singular holiness, and when one pondered that holiness in the light of his death and Resurrection, as the fathers of the Church for example did, it was plain that he was divine. If the Council of Nicaea was the first occasion when bishops, formally assembled and faced with a clear challenge to the divinity of Jesus (as the Logos enfleshed), came forth with an unambiguous assertion of Jesus' divinity, the Council of Nicaea, according to the self-understanding of the orthodox, was merely declaring under duress what had always been implicitly believed and handed down. So, for example, Christians had from the beginning baptized newcomers to the Church "in the name of the Father, and of the Son, and of the Holy Spirit," treating the three as equally divine.

The history of Christology, from New Testament times, through the conciliar period, and continuing into the present has been structured by the twofoldness of Jesus' full humanity and full divinity. The further attributes of Jesus that the scholastics and moderns deduced from this central dogmatic affirmation probably are less interesting than is the mystery at their center. For the Jesus who possessed the two natures, human and divine, still was one integral being. The "personal" union of the two natures in the Logos did not remove the intrigue of his historical personality but enhanced it. The attraction that Jesus had for so many who heard and observed him was not because of God's having manipulated him like a puppet. Jesus showed that humanity becomes most profound, poetic, beautiful, holy, and worthy of complete loyalty when it is most intimately bonded to divinity. It was because of his love of the Father that Jesus had the words of eternal life and spoke as none before him. It was because his meat and drink were to do the Father's will that Martha, Mary, Lazarus, Peter, John, James, and the rest felt so privileged to be his friends.

Thus the best way to present the traditional Catholic instincts about Christology today may be to follow investigators such as Moore who want it to illumine what is most tender and ardent in them. Taking Jesus as the fully successful instance of God's desire to love humanity, we may read the intercourse between Jesus and the Father not as a pale or predetermined collection of pious chats but as the communication of two who could not take their eyes off one another, whose hearts were burning within them all the while that Jesus walked the earth.

Naturally it skews things somewhat to use romantic, even erotic imagery for the relation between Jesus and the Father that is at the heart of the mystery of the Incarnation. We would welcome the chance to take many pages to make the distinctions and suggestions for the future impact of Christology on Catholic faith that such imagery implies. But even in this limited treatment we cannot back away from the conviction that the Father was to Jesus like a parent so enthralled by a child that he or she could "eat the child up," like a friend so united in spirit to a friend that the friend became another self, like two lovers lost in one another, become one flesh, wanting only a single destiny. True enough, the New Testament itself does not use this diction. The Father remains properly

lordly, as required by the Jewish theology of the time. Yet Jesus did call God his
Abba, presuming to an intimacy with little precedent, and the Johannine Jesus
did tell the disciples that when they saw him they saw the Father, that abiding in
him would bring them communion with the Father, that whatever they asked of
him he would get the Father to grant them, and much more.

So Jesus is the Christ, the messiah so perfectly anointed as God's liberator for
human beings that he revealed himself to be of the same substance of G 1, a
Son of God in a capital sense, because of the love between the Father and nim.
On another occasion, we could investigate the role of the Spirit in this love, and
the relations between Jesus and the Spirit, to similarly rich effect.[3] Here it seems
enough to suggest that the upshot of the Catholic insistence on the **hypostatic**
(personal) **union** of the divinity and the humanity of Jesus Christ in the person
of the Logos was a bond of love so perfect that it included all the eros we lesser
human beings know is our best index of salvation.

The Biblical God

Using the foregoing reflections on the Incarnation as our guide, we can continue to think about Jesus, the Father, and the Spirit in terms of biblical imagery
and so approach the inner sanctum of Catholic theology, the mystery of the
Trinity. Two procedural notes come to mind at this point and it may be the path
of wisdom to acknowledge them explicitly. The first is that it is not difficult to
suggest what the biblical images that led to the doctrine of the Trinity were and
why they seemed natural to the early Christians. The second is that the
bafflement present-day Catholics, and others, seem to experience concerning
the Trinity is the sort of sad commentary on the state of present-day faith that
should rouse writers to their most effective efforts.

The biblical data one instinctively moves to cite as a rationale for the Trinity
begin with the imagery of the Hebrew Bible, where the Lord (YHWH), so holy
that one dare not utter his proper name (which is less a name than a call to
continue living with him in the ineffable mode called faith), strangely gets
"companions" in the divine mode of existence. Islam, striving to achieve a
radical monotheism, has fought strenuously against any "association" of others
with Allah. To this end, it has castigated the Christian doctrines of the Incarnation and Trinity as defilements of monotheism. Judaism, too, has wanted God to
be One, with the implication of singular, unique, perhaps pure and simple. Yet
the Hebrew Bible spoke so substantively about the Word of God and the Spirit
of God that Christian biblical theology was bound to think of God as a corporate

personality, a sort of primitive community or self that had the richest expression and vitality.

The Word was what seized the prophets. It was communication from the Lord ad extra, to the outside world. The Spirit was the quickening presence of the Lord, moving over the waters at creation, reknitting the dry bones, giving them flesh, and stirring them back to life. One should reckon with the anthropomorphism and metaphors involved in this biblical theology. One should also agree that those who created it were not offering conciliar definitions, let alone scholastic theses. But the fact remains, plain despite its symbolic richness, that the Lord was presented as richly communicative, full of vitalizing power he wished to send forth, and bent on persuading Israel by his love, as a spouse might try to persuade a spouse or a parent might try to persuade a child. The Book of Hosea by itself makes this case, and the other prophets only enrich it.

The New Testament drew on this background to show a Jesus who was the enfleshment of the divine self-expression, who was in constant communication with his Lord God (whom he called his Father), and who was led by the Spirit into the wilderness, anointed by the Spirit to bring good news to the poor, sustained by the Spirit in his sufferings, and raised by the Father to His "right hand." These were the bases for the Christian theological developments that led to the doctrine of the Trinity. The Trinity did not come as something arbitrary or artificial. It came from the most primitive Christian creeds and liturgical usages, as the New Testament literature and the literature of the first centuries captured them.

Theologians, such as the Greek father Athanasius, who wrote about the Incarnation and the Holy Spirit, were merely setting their good minds to the task of thinking through the rich traditional symbolism, to gain what understanding of their faith they could. They were not geometers trying to triangularize a circle. They had no desire to produce the conundrum of conundrums. They merely wanted to express the fullness of the imagery that past generations of believers had bequeathed to them. They merely wanted to be sure that none of what God so graciously had condescended to reveal about the divine nature would be lost.

This brings us to the situation of Catholic believers, and any others, who want to wrestle with the Trinity today. First, let us all admit that God, whether taken as One or taken as also Three, is strictly mysterious and so is never going to parse out as a tidy formula. Second, let us remind ourselves that "mystery," in this context, is not an admission of defeat or an easy way out but rather is a cipher for something richer, more precious, more primordially real than what we limited human beings can appreciate. The fault is not with God or traditional faith. The fault is with ourselves, our irremediable dullness. Just as "nature" can, with proper reservations, be termed a strict mystery, a realm of intelligibility so vast and full that no human mind is ever going to comprehend it, so "God" is incomparable, a reality so far beyond us that the proper response is adoration, worship, mute or boisterous praise. We can love God better than we can understand God, which is why love is more important to all orthodox Christianity than understanding.

This said, the doctrine of the Trinity is best understood as an elaboration of "God" that never removes the mysteriousness but does offer more for the mind to admire and the heart to love. The doctrine of the Trinity adds that we should understand the otherness of God on analogy with our own most profound capacities, which are to know and to love. We should think of God not as an inert or icy perfection but as blindingly beautiful light, as breathtakingly precious love. God throbs with vitality, understanding, warmth, and fulfillment. The simple "Is!" of God that the classical Greek ontologist Parmenides intuited comes out in Christian translation as "Is coruscant, brilliant understanding! Is perfectly ardent and peaceful love!" Some theologians like to speak of God as a perfect community, and then to skate interesting pirouettes that lead to a metaphysics in which plurality and communication become more primordial than unicity and self-possession. If that helps to get across the idea that God's essence, God's inmost being, is something shared without being diminished, something mutual and communal without requiring notes, communiqués, or meetings, let alone arguments and reconciliations, that is all to the good. The Father and Son differ only inasmuch as the relationship binding them has to denote some difference if it is to say anything significant. Similarly, the Father and Son differ from the Spirit only as the ones who breathe forth perfect, eternal love and the love so breathed. Everywhere the three suffuse, mutually inhere, *circumincess* (to reflect the technical Latin term). Everywhere all that the Father is is known and expressed in the Son, all that the Father and Son are is expressed and loved in the Spirit.

Take the most perfect friendship or sexual intercourse you can imagine. Think about how such love both individualizes the partners and unites them. Think about the humble yet real mystery of one and one making much more than two, of two both finding themselves in their oneness. The tiny, teasing movement of the numbers in this analogy only nudges rather feebly at the mysteriousness involved. This is all the more so with the names and numbers we mention when we talk about the Christian God. The point is not numerical dexterity, not a cabalistic mysticism of numerical signs. The point is a halting yet still utterly precious way of at least glancing toward the perfection of divinity. To be as perfect as the perfect humanity of Jesus suggested his God must be, the Father, the Word, and the Spirit had to make a community of splendid sharing. They had to be more etched in their particular identities and more suffused throughout one another, more exhaustively bonded and coordinated, than the best of what human beings could glimpse in ecstatic moments of earthly love. So the threeness of the Christian God ideally is dazzling, rather than puzzling, and so is alluring rather than discouraging. Because the threeness is our human own, because the grace of Christ takes us into God's inner being, the dazzle and allurement should be the joy of our lives. The faith of Catholic Christian believers, and others, is so audacious that it says Father-Son-Spirit abide in their hearts, taking their human knowing and loving up into the eternal processions of knowing and loving that make God God.

Ecclesiology

The basic Christian truths about Jesus, the trinitarian God, and the grace that makes both Jesus and the trinitarian God ingredients of the believer's deepest identity have been published, celebrated, handed down, and worked through in the *ecclesia*, the community of those called out of the darkness of unbelief and despair into the circle of God's love. As the flesh of Jesus manifested the Word of God given for salvation, so the flesh of the Church ought to shine with a sacramental luster. That the Word of God should take flesh from Mary was a marvelous condescension. Indeed, Paul called it a *kenosis*—a self-emptying, undertaken for love, and he proposed the attitude of the kenotic Christ as the model for the entire Christian community:

> In your minds you must be the same as Christ Jesus: His state was divine, yet he did not cling to his equality with God, but emptied himself to assume the condition of a slave, and became as men are; and being as all men are, he was humbler yet, even to accepting death, death on a cross. But God raised him high and gave him the name which is above all other names so that all beings in the heavens, on earth, and in the underworld, should bend the knee at the name of Jesus and that every tongue should acclaim Jesus Christ as Lord, to the glory of God the Father (Phil 1: 5-11).

The Church has been formed from the inside by the Spirit of Christ, poured forth at Pentecost in virtue of Christ's Resurrection. It has been formed from the outside by scriptures such as Philippians, in which it possessed a permanent, ever fecund standard against which to measure its mind and heart. It has also been formed through the sacraments, in which scriptural convictions and themes could take an active form, so inspiring material elements such as water and oil that they became credible carriers of God's healing touch, God's elevating invitation to share the trinitarian life.

Another external formation has been the hierarchical structure that the majority of Christians—all Catholics and Orthodox, many Protestants—have considered part of the Church's endowment from the beginning. From the beginning the twelve closest disciples served as leaders in the Church, and from New Testament times one spoke of presbyters, deacons, and others who specialized in particular tasks and gifts. The notion from the beginning was that the Spirit of God distributed various gifts (*charismata*) throughout the local churches (see I Cor 12), all of which ideally served to build up the corporate faith of the whole. Among these gifts were those of administration, official teaching in matters of faith and morals, and leadership at the weekly eucharist. *Acts* and the New Testament epistles make it clear that women shared many of these gifts in the early generations, even though by the end of the New Testament era the patriarchalism of both the Jewish and Hellenistic cultural traditions on which the early Christians drew was shaping (some would say was deforming) the Christian sense of community structure and authority, and so was marginalizing women. As the Church settled down for what has proved to be a long wait for the Parousia, it elaborated the institutional forms it thought necessary for both its internal operations and its missionary work in the outside world.

Richard P. McBrien, author of a well-regarded two-volume study of Catholicism, has expressed the distinctive ecclesiological accents and convictions of the Roman Catholic community as follows:

One must distinguish between what is *characteristic* of Roman Catholicism and what is *distinctive* about it. What is characteristic may also be found in different shape or form in other churches, but what is distinctive will be found in Roman Catholicism alone. What is *characteristically* Catholic? Its conviction that *grace* is finally triumphant over sin, not only as the declaration of God that we are just but through a real interior transformation by the power of the Holy Spirit. *Secondly*, its sense of *tradition, of doctrine*, and of the importance of maintaining *continuity* not only with the Church's origins but with its principal points of passage from its beginnings to the present. *Thirdly*, its sense of *peoplehood*, of *community*, and of *church*. *Fourthly*, and most significantly, its sense of *sacramentality* and its correlative sense of the importance of *mediation*. God is present to us through signs and symbols, and the presence of God is effective for us through these same visible signs and instruments.

What is *distinctively* Catholic? Here the answer given earlier by Hans Küng in his *Council and Reunion* still applies: The ecumenical question is the question of ecclesiastical office, and of the Petrine [papal] ministry in particular. It is true that Catholic ecclesiology posits a collegial understanding of the Church—i.e., that it is a communion of churches. But, so, too, does the Orthodox tradition. But Roman Catholicism alone insists on the role of the Petrine ministry, the pope, as the "perpetual and visible source and foundation of the unity of the bishops and of the multitude of the faithful" (*Dogmatic Constitution on the Church*, n. 23).

One may become, be, and/or remain a Catholic for any number of reasons which have something to do with what is characteristic about Roman Catholicism but nothing to do with what is distinctive about it. But that fact does not negate Catholicism's distinctive *ecclesiological* feature, namely, the importance it assigns to the place and function of the Petrine ministry exercised by the bishop of Rome.[4]

McBrien has summarized very well the characteristic features of Roman Catholicism, many of which we have already noted. One might further summarize such characteristics by stressing sacramentality. For the faith that God does effectively communicate salvation and divine life through our human embodiment explains the Catholic position on the relation between sin and grace, on the validity of past tradition, and on the Church's reason to be. Sacramentality itself, in the Catholic view, flows directly from the Incarnation, where God confected the primordial sacrament, the enfleshment of the Logos. So one might say that the Catholic understanding of Christianity, the understanding which traditionally and etymologically wants to preserve the whole, stands or falls with the Incarnation. If the whole of God's self-gift was communicated through the flesh assumed by the Word, Catholic Christianity makes great sense.

McBrien's description of what is distinctive about Roman Catholicism, like his addiction to italics, necessitates a more critical response. Although it is undoubtedly true that its understanding of the Petrine ministry separates Roman Catholicism from the other Christian communions, both historically and doctrinally, such a separation raises further questions and invites reactions of both praise and blame. An ecumenical era pressures all Christians to face such questions, and praise and blame as well, honestly and peacefully. Why, for example, have Orthodox and Protestant Christians not felt about the Petrine ministry as Roman Catholics have? Have the ties to the bishop of Rome that have given the generic term Catholicism its specific difference for hundreds of millions of Christians been more dubious than Roman theologians have liked to think? What ought the historic abuses of power by the popes to mean for an estimate of the Petrine ministry? What ought the Petrine ministry to entail in today's world, where many Christians long for visible symbols of Church unity and feel the pressure of their minority status in the global world as a call to minimize accidental differences among Christian communions and make agreement about core essentials the heart of the movement for ecumenical reunion.[5]

The Petrine ministry can be considered a gift to the Church, and one can point to historic services that show how that gift has been a benefaction. But shouldn't any distinguishing (and so separating) feature be examined in the context of what it does for the flourishing of the whole Christian Body? Hasn't the history of Christian division taught us that churches soon come to love their distinguishing features and so to define themselves over-against other communions in order to preserve their lusty rallying cries? If so, then "distinctive" features are not immediately badges of merit. The Church ecumenical ought to provide for everything positive that the histories of the separated communions have generated, but it should not grant the distinctions by which separatism has prospered a constitutional status. The wiser path by far would seem to be to make features that sizable portions of the Christian world have not considered essential matters about which there is some liberty. If Roman Catholicism can elaborate a rationale for the Petrine ministry (and, even more importantly, can elaborate an actual practice of that ministry) that wins widespread support according to the **sensus fidelium** of the whole (Catholic) Church, well and good. If it cannot win such a consensus, then perhaps it would offer a major ecumenical service by removing (its traditionally strict understanding of) the Petrine ministry from the list of nonnegotiable items it brings to ecumenical discussions and concentrating more on the major items listed in the historic creeds (none of which spotlight the Petrine ministry).

Fortunately, ecumenical exchanges among Catholic, Protestant, and Orthodox theologians since Vatican II have removed many of the previously long-standing conflicts about the Petrine ministry. Nowadays, there is a sufficiently solid theological consensus about the papacy among ecumenists that the burden of overcoming the churches' separation has shifted to church leaders. If church leaders can choose to act on the agreements about the Petrine ministry that the theologians have worked out, they may substantially unite churches that have been separated for hundreds of years. If they choose to delay, or to reject the theologians' consensus, one will have to fear for both ecumenism and Christians' fidelity to Christ's command that they be one (as the world's main sign of God's love: see John 17).

Sacramentality

We have discussed the principles of sacramentality sufficiently to warrant our dealing with this aspect of the Incarnation with some dispatch. If one accepts the Catholic understanding of the Incarnation, which many theologians describe as a **high Christology** come down especially from the Johannine communities, then the extension of the Incarnation—of Christ's being and work—in the Church makes eminent sense. Relatedly, if one accepts the Catholic understanding of the human being, according to which matter and spirit are ineluctably joined and shape one another mutually, then to use material things to convey spiritual meanings makes eminent sense. On both counts, sacramentality is what one gets when imagination, drama, song, art, poetry, sensuality, sex, sociability, and the other entailments of embodiedness receive their due.

When such due is granted, the aniconic tendency that many Jews and Muslims, and some Protestants, have read out of monotheism is quickly corralled, as it was during the iconoclast controversies of the eighth and ninth centuries. Admittedly, those who warn that God can never be adequately represented have grasped a profound truth. Admittedly, human beings do regularly, perhaps nearly inevitably, fashion idols for themselves and so pervert their faith. The affirmative (kataphatic) theology that thrives by virtue of the Incarnation always requires the balance of the negative (apophatic) theology highlighted in mystical experience. The passage to mature faith does require dark nights and clouds of unknowing, in which God teaches the human spirit the reality of the divine Spirit, which none can ever grasp or comprehend. God is Spirit, and those who want to worship God well must do so in spirit and truth.

On the other hand, for Christian faith it is God who has not made us angels but people of flesh, blood, and nerve. Indeed, it is God who has made us people of phlegm, excrement, and pus. God is the one who designed the plan of salvation and determined it would pass through the flesh the Logos took from Mary. God is the one who wanted a voice with which to tell us we are not servants but friends, who wanted hands with which to touch our suffering flesh and heal it, who wanted eyes to see the lilies of the field, the widow offering her mite, the crowds milling about like sheep without a shepherd. It was with a human voice, in the distinctive tongue called Aramaic, at a squalid corner of a petty provincial capital that God asked God to forgive those who were crucifying him because they did not know what they were doing. It was prophets called by God who created scripture, bringing their wonderful imaginations to bear on the task of rendering at least smidgens of the divine beauty and will. For Christians to propose a monotheism so radical that it swept aside these initiatives of God would be disobedient in the extreme. Certainly such a monotheism could never claim lineage from Jesus of Nazareth, that great speaker of parables and worker of signs. All with an instinct for the wholeness of Christian faith would have to brand it unacceptable—flunked by the tests of incarnationalism and sacramentality.

This is all rather easy to wax poetic about and lay out. It flows from the crux of Christian tradition and experience like a torrent. But the implications of sacramentality are so positive and immediate that the majority of Christians throughout history have hesitated to embrace them. Even when most Christians accepted the doctrines of the Incarnation and sacramentality, they were slow to look upon their own bodies as blessed gifts of God, upon their eating and drinking as acts in which God had to delight, upon their social gatherings as anticipations of the Messianic banquet, when the return of Jesus would launch a great party.

Through many centuries, Christians shied away from frequent reception of the Eucharist, the sacrament in which Christ gave himself as food, thinking themselves unworthy, in virtue of their sins of both flesh and spirit. Often this sense of unworthiness wandered from the specific sins they might have committed, the serious of which could in fact have separated them from communion with God, to focus on a generalized sense of human lowliness. Then they felt that God couldn't have meant his Incarnation, his sacramentality, and his forgiveness of sin to have extended to the likes of themselves. Those grand notions must have been just that: notions. They could never have been meant to serve as the coordinates of the human condition that actually was.

Nowhere was this disbelieving attitude, this sense that the patent message was too good to be true, more influential than in the realm of sexuality. Admittedly, all religions have had problems with sexuality, because of its power and the interest of religions in maximizing what they have taken to be spiritual freedom and pure worship. Jews, Muslims, Buddhists, and Confucians have all sponsored prudishness, puritanism, and practical treatments of sexuality that have shown they did not love their flesh, had not found their way to wisdom powerful enough to bless through and through passions that make for life. Thus fearful Christians have had much company. The special pathos in the Christian case, however, has stemmed from the Christian doctrine of the Incarnation. None of the other religions proposed that divinity had so fully accepted humanity into the divine embrace that one could say in strict, if paradoxical, orthodoxy that God died on the cross. None of the other religions had proposed as its core sacrament a meal so powerfully symbolic that it conveyed a real presence of divinity as the nourishment of human beings, body and soul. And none of the other religions had proposed as the heart of its doctrine of God, its deepest sense of the divine identity, that God is love and those who abide in love abide in God.

The sacramentality that Catholic Christianity seems desirous of embracing nowadays could profitably focus on sexuality, to the end of fully incorporating women into the Church as absolute equals of men, and to the end of making the sexual love blessed in the particular sacrament of marriage clearly publicized as the most ordinary and so significant of God's variegatedly extraordinary comings. What happens when two people are drawn to become one flesh and make new life is the utter axis of salvation history, just as what happens when the forces of sexual love misfire shows all the healing men and women require. Were the sacramental mindset of the Church to become effectively ministerial along this axis, reconciling body to spirit and sex to sex, the cause of the

Incarnate Word might make quantum leaps of progress. Many people might hear the word for which they most long ("God loves your desire and love"). Many people might feel more acceptable, more comfortable, at the core of their emotional lives, where most of their creativity and most of their hope lodge. If so, then sacramentality would be beautiful and powerful indeed. Then Catholicity would seem so obvious, so shining with the oil of gladness, that it would translate much as Paul wanted it to: "everything that is true, everything that is noble, everything that is good and pure, everything that we love and honour, and everything that can be thought virtuous or worthy of praise" (Phil 4:7-9).[6]

Representative Personality:
Thomas Aquinas

Thomas Aquinas (about 1225-1274), the most esteemed of the Roman Catholic theological authorities, was the youngest son of a Count of Aquino in Italy. His parents destined him for an ecclesiastical career and sent him to the neighboring Benedictine school at Monte Cassino when he was five. At the age of fifteen he went to Naples to finish his training in the liberal arts. Encountering the intellectual work of the Dominicans, he resolved to join that order. His parents were so opposed that they virtually imprisoned him at home for over a year, but finally they relented, letting him join the Dominicans in 1244. During studies at Paris from 1245 to 1248, Aquinas was much influenced by the teaching of Albertus Magnus, through whom he learned about Aristotle. After studying at Cologne, Aquinas returned to Paris as a lecturer in theology, becoming a master of theology in 1256. Throughout the 1260s he taught in various parts of Italy, returning to Paris in 1269. His final teaching occurred at Naples, where he labored to complete his *Summa Theologica*. He died while on the way to serve as a theologian at the Council of Lyons. Although shortly after his death some propositions attributed to him were condemned, Aquinas became the standard authority of the Dominicans in 1278 and was canonized in 1323.

Aquinas appears in this chapter not because he concentrated his theology on Christ and the Incarnation, but because the entire style of his thought reflects the trust in reason and experience that, in consequence of the Incarnation, Catholic Christianity has promoted. Aquinas willingly borrowed much of the philosophical substructure of his theology from Aristotle. His other great authorities were the scriptures and the Church fathers, especially Augustine. The method of his theological treatises, which are composed as an integrated series of questions, reasons for both negative and positive answers, resolutions of the key issues, and then responses to the authorities or reasons discarded, came from the scholastic format that was in vogue in his day. This method makes for rather dry reading, until one grasps the power of Thomas' vision and comes to share his passion for pure understanding.

Thomas sought to achieve a balanced relationship between reason and faith, nature and grace, the mediation of the Church and the sphere in which God deals with individuals according to their unique needs. To the essentialism of Aristotle, where the philosophical accent fell on the materialized forms of things that render them intelligible to the human mind, Thomas added a stress on existence: the act of being that relates the creature directly to God.

The upshot of Thomas' teaching was a certain Catholic congeniality with the world. Certainly his influence did not banish the Augustinian tendency to focus on human sin, and so to think of human existence as an exile or alienation. But it did establish the world as a sphere that human beings could confidently seek to understand and transform. Without deviating from the Western focus on redemption that had dominated Christology since Augustine (Thomas taught, for example, that had there been no human sin there probably would have been no Incarnation), Thomas made both the drive of the human being to know and love and the goodness of creation motives for accepting the human condition. Moreover, he applied such acceptance in his teachings about Christ.

So, for example, Thomas accepted the reality of sadness and fear in Christ's life:

> As sadness is caused by an awareness of evil that is at hand so fear is caused by awareness of evil to come. But if this anticipation of future evil is completely certain it does not give rise to fear. It is Aristotle who remarks that fear only arises when there is some hope of escape: for when there is no hope of escape, evil is seen as something already present, and so it causes sadness rather than fear.
>
> There are two things, therefore, to be considered about fear. Firstly, the sense appetite naturally reacts against what harms the body, by sorrow if it is presently happening, and by fear if it is about to happen. In this sense there was fear in Christ, as there was sorrow. But then there is the question of uncertainty about the future event, as when we fear a sound in the night, not knowing what it is. On this score there was no fear in Christ, as Damascene observes.
>
> Hence: 1. the just man is said to be without fear when by fear is meant a fully-indulged emotion, such as would turn a man away from the good dictated by reason. Christ did not have fear in this form, but only as a feeling. And that is why the text [Mk. 14: 33] says, "He began to be greatly distressed and troubled," which, as Jerome explains, suggests a kind of instinctive feeling.

2. Hilary excludes fear from Christ in the same way that he excludes sadness: he excludes the necessity of fear. However, to prove the genuineness of his human nature he voluntarily undertook fear, as he did sadness.

3. Although Christ could avoid future ills by the power of his divinity, they were inevitable, or at least not easily avoidable for him in the weakness of his flesh.[7]

We can see in this single example of Thomas' treatment of Christ his regular intellectual style, his acceptance of the humanity of Christ, his acceptance of the divinity of Christ, and some of both the strengths and the weaknesses that make him a mixed blessing nowadays. Concerning his style, we should note the crucial importance Thomas gives to scripture, the support he draws from the patristic tradition, and the orderly layout of reasons for his position. We have omitted from the quotation the preliminary lines of the question, where Thomas offers reasons for saying that Christ did not experience fear. Those reasons have served him as the first part of a dialectic. The second part lodges in the quotation from Mark. His job, then, is to justify the statement in Mark and then explain the light it sheds on the reasons for thinking Christ did not experience fear.

In his analysis, Thomas relies on Aristotle, inasmuch as fear is a common human experience and Aristotle is his master in the realm of reason where such common experience may be clarified. Thomas' justification for positing fear in Christ is that Christ had a full human nature and so a set of sense appetites that opened him to sadness, fear, and the other experiences consequent on sensation. Note that response 1 suggests that Christ never was controlled by his sense appetites to the point where reason ceased to prevail. In thinking of Christ as perfectly human, Thomas must have Christ's reason always prevail. This dovetails with Thomas' understanding of sin as an irrational act.

Further, Thomas cannot imagine Christ not knowing the future, so the fear that comes from uncertainty about the future was foreign to Christ. This judgment implies difficult questions about the relation between Christ's human knowledge and his divine knowledge that we fortunately can avoid right now. Later theologians have tried to downplay any reading of the knowledge Christ had as the Logos that would have detracted from his experience of a full humanity. Since a full humanity is finite, mortal, passible, and the rest, Christ must have experienced these and through them limitations on his feelings, knowledge, and love.

The analysis that Thomas makes of human nature offers admirable clarity on many points and so can enlighten present-day Christians struggling with what can seem fundamental confusions about human nature. On the other hand, Thomas' distinctions between sensation and reason, intellection and volition, and emotion and rationality strike many of our contemporaries as leading away from the actual experience of human beings. The holism of the existential personality suggests more interaction among its different aspects, more affect and confusion at the core of human existence. This relates to the historical and social conditioning of the individual, which have become much more prominent in our day than they were in Thomas'. Our natural world is much vaster and more complex than was the natural world of thirteenth-century Paris and Naples. The intentions of our God seem much more mysterious than Thomas found the intentions of his God to be. So wide canyons separate us from Thomas Aquinas, even when we may love the clarity of his worldview and greatly admire the penetration of his genius.

Glossary

High Christology: an interpretation of Jesus that stresses his divinity and takes him as the enfleshment of the eternal Logos. In contrast, a low Christology stresses the humanity of Jesus, sometimes to the neglect of his divinity. The dangers in a high Christology are that Jesus will emerge as less than fully human, which would be a heretical position, and that, even if one retains orthodoxy, the intrigue that brims in the gospels and clearly made Jesus a great success will fade away. The saints most honored in the Catholic tradition have loved Jesus as a brother, leader, or spouse. Without denying his divine origin and holiness, they have been most moved by the love he showed in his labor and death on human beings' behalf. A high Christology can enhance our appreciation of such love, making it clear that God's chosen way of healing us, divinizing us, and so doing us unimaginably great good was to assume flesh just like our own, to take our painful human condition to heart, and to transform it from within, as one who had experienced our pain, confusion, desolation, and hopes as a full member of our kind.

Hypostatic union: the integration of the human and divine natures of Christ in the person (*hypostasis*) of the Logos. The doctrine of the hypostatic union makes plain the trinitarian specification of the doctrine of the Incarnation: precisely the Logos took flesh. We can pass by the implications that this specification carries, derived from the attributes accorded the Logos in trinitarian theory (primarily: his being the expression of the Father), but we have to note that the hypostatic union entails making the mystery of Christ ultimately the fathomless light and sonship of the Word. Christ had what today we would call a full human personality, but the ultimate bearer of his act of existence, and so the ultimate source of his unity — what made his rendering of divinity into human terms so perfect, and what made his elevation of humanity into communion with divinity so perfect — was the divine personhood of the Logos.

Sensus fidelium: a Latin term for the sense or instinct of the mass of Christian believers. The notion depends on the conviction that all believers possess the Holy Spirit as their innermost teacher and guide. The Spirit comes with grace, and the operations of the Spirit include giving people an instinct for what coheres with Christ's teachings and being and what is discordant. This instinct has to be nurtured, and Christian education is well understood as precisely such a nurturing. Certainly the instinct has spiritual as well as intellectual aspects, so that one who had studied much but never prayed would probably be deficient. Yet ultimately it connotes a subtle intelligence sifting experience, learning, past feelings in peak experience, and the rest to discern whether a given teaching or course of action seems wise — seems to honor the full tradition, the anointing given by scripture and prayer, and the visage of Christ in one's favorite icon.

Discussion Questions

1. How does the love of God for Jesus align the main theses of traditional Catholic Christology?
2. How does the life of Jesus suggest that human creativity and freedom flourish in proximity to God?
3. How do the biblical images of the Word that came to the prophets and the Spirit that anointed Jesus factor in the Christian theology of the Trinity?
4. How could one justify the claim that grace makes human knowing and loving modes of the Son and the Spirit?
5. How does the Petrine ministry function to distinguish Roman Catholic ecclesiology?
6. What does making sacramentality characteristic of Catholic ecclesiology do for the link between the Church and the Incarnation?
7. What is the truth in iconoclasm?
8. Why have human beings found it so hard to believe God would make their flesh the prime locus of revelation?
9. Was Aquinas justified in using Aristotle?
10. What was your reaction to Aquinas' discussion of Christ's fear?

Notes

1 See James D. G. Dunn, *Unity and Diversity in the New Testament* (Philadelphia: Westminster, 1977).
2 See Sebastian Moore, *Let This Mind Be in You* (Minneapolis: Winston/Seabury, 1985).
3 See James D. G. Dunn, *Jesus and the Spirit* (Philadelphia: Westminster, 1975).
4 Richard P. McBrien, *Catholicism* (Minneapolis: Winston, 1980), vol. 2, pp. 722–723.
5 See Heinrich Fries and Karl Rahner, *Unity of the Churches: An Actual Possibility* (New York: Paulist, 1985).
6 See McBrien, *Catholicism*, vol. 2, pp. 731–816; also Bernard Cooke, *Ministry to Word and Sacraments* (Philadelphia: Fortress, 1976).
7 Thomas Aquinas, *Summa Theologica*, III, 15: 7 (New York: McGraw-Hill, 1974, vol. XLIX), p. 213.

CHAPTER 8

Redemption

Finitude
Sin
Death
Resurrection
Representative Personality: Francis of Assisi
Glossary, Discussion Question, Notes

Finitude

We are all bothered by the fact that bad things happen to good people. When a colleague comes down with cancer, or a young person dies in a car accident, or the son of a friend is arrested for selling drugs, our spirits sink and there seems a great tear in the goodness of God. We remember the friend's son as first we met him: red hair, freckles, a lopsided grin to steal your heart. We imagine the future of the young person killed in the car crash, what she might have made of her musical talent, the lives she might have brightened. And as we watch the colleague come to grips with the remorseless enemy in his gut, we hate the pathogens built into human biology, even though we are awed by his spiritual strength.

In all of these cases, the blow to our spirit, the clouding of our imagination, comes from encountering evil. The evil of cancer is statistical, though no less frightening or unacceptable for that reason. A certain fraction of us, a certain quotient of our cells, is going to be afflicted. It is the way of our world, the effect of our gene pool. Even though we admit the good effects of fiber and calculate how much better things would be in a world with fewer carcinogens, cancer remains a mysterious reality. To have the physical world we do, there has to be

140

the chance for accidents, mutations, dysfunctions. Why did God make such a world? God only knows, and we at best struggle to get glimmers of God's reason.

The car accident is also a statistic, shaped by traffic patterns, teenage exuberance, the figures on dope and drinking. Each party to an accident is concrete, specific, not reducible to numbers, but actuaries can come chillingly close to saying how many fatalities will happen each year. Why does God run a world in which brakes can fail and people unfit to drive can take the wheel; where familiarity breeds contempt for the lethal potential of our driving machines? Indeed, does God run this world, or is it just a system out of control, a megamachine no one is guiding?

In the case of the car accident, natural evils may mix with moral evils. The thunderstorm that made the street slick is natural, not even evil (disordered) on its own, simply a contributor to a bad set of physical arrangements. The drinking that led the driver of the other car to jump the center strip is a moral evil, a disorder traceable to human choices (though how free such choices are in the case of problem drinkers raises another series of questions).

The worst evil in our brief catalogue clearly is the drug pushing, because there the free choices are clearest and ugliest. There may indeed be mitigating circumstances, but we can be reluctant to hear them. The shock of learning that someone we know not only took hard drugs but pushed them on others takes away the sympathy that might make us amenable to excuses. We can only see the betrayal in the parent's eyes, can only imagine the damage done to the pusher's customers. Drug dealing is such a disregard of the love that ought to flow between people, the mutual care not to hurt, that it seems utterly cynical. Something of Dante's Satan, trapped in the ice of his own hate, wafts into our nostrils: the stench of lovelessness, the rank smell of the will to hurt.

Human beings are limited, we say. The spirit is willing but the flesh is weak. Even those who try hard for a while can get discouraged, give up, stop caring. Because our culture is spiritually illiterate, not knowing the things for its peace, we thrust many of our children out like sheep to the slaughterer. They hear so much about money and pleasure, about fashion and power, that they think these are great treasures. With so much buzz about them, they must be the things to acquire.

How often Christ would have gathered such children to his bosom, like a hen gathers her chicks, but they would not come. They would see no connection between the Christ of boring Sunday mornings or strange New Testament stories and the pressures of their schooling or the fast tracks spread before them at their jobs. No one had taught them, convinced them, that it profits nothing to gain the whole world and suffer the loss of one's soul. They did not listen, and few teachers or preachers were able to translate the arcane imagery, make it bear on the desires bubbling in their souls, the hopes ricocheting in their fantasies.

So they thought the loss of their souls was a faraway thing, postponed to when they would die and meet their Maker. Or they thought hell must be an anachronism, no rank Satan having made them blanch. They had not read the masters, ancient and modern, who show that we gain or lose our souls day by day. No one had schooled them in the ecstasies of understanding, the transports worked by beauty, the maturation that only comes by reflecting, coming to terms, taking responsibility for one's judgments and decisions.

All of these matters, our perceptions of the evils that score the human condition and our intuitions of the defense the Holy Spirit offers, bear on spirituality. The human beings who, having come fully alive, redound to God's glory anticipate the Christ transfigured before Peter, James, and John, the Christ raised to the Father's right hand and made a living spirit. The dormant, depressed, even bestial people who never come fully alive experience themselves, and so history and evolution, to be pointless. The real race is not for wealth and pleasure, fashion and power. The real race is for meaning, possibility, hope.

How can limited, twisted human beings defeat their so daunting condition? How can they find a way out of the prison that evolution seems to have set for them, find a way through the paradox of having been given desires nothing earthly can satisfy? To ask these questions is to ask about redemption. Is there a way of redoing the human condition? Can an individual buy out the wretched contract written by ignorance and weakness, bred into finite bones?

Catholic Christians are far from being the only ones who offer affirmative, hopeful responses. Buddhists speak of the therapies that flow when one puts the brakes on desire. Muslims speak of the transforming effects that come when one's psychology starts to match the ontological reality of the Lordship of Allah. For Jews, the paradigms of the covenant, as practically laid out in the Torah, mark a way to life, a way to avoid spiritual death. The Christian analogue is faith in Christ, imitation of Christ, experience of Christ as one's personal Lord and Savior.

The casual evangelistic use of the terms proposed in the last sentence has robbed them of their drama. As displayed in Abraham and Jesus, faith is neither mainly emotional nor mainly an acceptance of doctrinal formulas. It is a passionate response to a passionate God. It is an encounter with darkness, evil, all the burdens of not knowing and not being able that afflict finite creatures. But then faith passes beyond mere encounter, lets go, and thereby floats one over the abyss. That is why Abraham's faith could be ascribed to him as righteousness. That is why the faith of Jesus could move mountains and restore withered limbs. Abraham and Jesus confronted their situation, their selves, and did not flee from the awful mysteries of life. They abided with the nothingness seeping through the cracks in all creatures. They raised their voices and shook their fists. "This should not be," they said time and again. "Do something about this," they begged the Master of the Universe. And somehow he did. Whether in their circumstances or in their souls, God intervened to make a difference.

But how are people, young or old, to know about this crucial difference, if no missionaries are sent to them? How are they to be persuaded there is a history of salvation, a record of changes felt, if no one can speak with authority? Where are the witnesses to stand up and say, "It happened to me. I once was lost but now I'm found, was blind but now I see." Don't be fooled by the familiarity and simplicity of the hymn. Don't limit to alcohol and depression the range of images it conjures up. Take the words to the core of the human condition, where darkness and weakness can seem overwhelming. Make the tune match the moans that come when one agonizes not just over a feckless self but even more over a broken world.

Then maybe, just maybe, the infinite mercy of God will slip under the door. Then maybe the end of dead-ends, the opening of tombs, will glimmer. Could it be that our finitude, all our limitation and lack, is not the last word? Could it be that something, someone, not finite, not limited, without lack is offering help? All those double negatives make for a rocky road, something straight, narrow, and hard. Yet if one has tried the easy paths and found no joy, the no-thing-ness of God can feel a blessing. One can want something hard, if it truly is sure and stable. One can be famished for tough, nourishing fare. As deep calls to deep, so finite calls to infinite. Catholic Christian faith says that infinity has listened and answered: no eye has seen, no ear has heard, it has not entered the human heart to conceive how well.

Sin

In speaking of moral evil — disorders freely chosen — we have introduced sin. The disorders that play in the depths of finitude, introduced by ancient choices from time out of mind, suggest what theologians want the term "original sin" to convey. Original sin is the sin of the world, the tilt in the cosmic game, the warp of the entire social fabric. Each child is born into it, sure to suffer from it, virtually certain to reaffirm and forward it. It is the systemic poverty denying the majority of the world's people a fair chance. It is the corruption accepted in most political regimes along with death and taxes. It is the blindness, the torpor, the habitual, ingrained resistance to light and love.

Sometimes original sin glances off human finitude, seeming to arise as much from weariness as from deliberate initiative. Sometimes it seems the pathetic wail of people who do the evil they would not, who cannot do the good they would. And always it makes faith seem impossible, makes hope seem naive, makes love seem a chimera. It is the world, the flesh, and a good servant of the devil. Because the Bible summarized and personified it in fallen Adam, Christ had to be a Second Adam, making what Paul called a new creation, a completely fresh start.

Personal sin is less grandiose than original sin, more shabby, tawdry, and domestic. We know it the way we know the streaks in the bathroom mirror, the ragged edging of the cheap apartment rug, the smell of the garbage out back. Personal sin can seem exciting: the rush of insider trading, the flush of the short-lived affair. It deals in slinky fabrics, loyalties chipped away, the half-truths that try to cover greed or lust, lest they be embarrassingly naked. If you cheat on your exams, or your income tax, or your expense account, or your spouse, you know the effort to deceive yourself that most personal sin involves. If you want sex without love, or praise without performance, or easy money, you know the diminishments that personal sin carries. In most such sinning, we are simply all too human, too weak or bedazzled, too hungry or ignorant. We simply don't know the things for our peace, and sometimes, at least, we wish someone would show us a more excellent way.

The deeper impression of personal sin is the closure of spirit it threatens. Until we stop drawing breath the Spirit of God continues to lure us, but the more we turn aside to inordinate pleasures or gains, the less the Spirit succeeds. Where the Spirit would open infinite horizons, we grow comfortable with low roofs and blocked vistas. A little boost in the bank account, a little "action on the side" — so have our ambitions shrunk. We may tell ourselves that shrunken ambitions are the part of wisdom. We may say that humility is becoming. But as we do we hate the sound of our voice, are saddened by the defeat our words carry.

Sin is disorder. On the grand scale, it shows in the disorders of international injustice, of war, of wasteful nuclear arms, of ecological pollution. On the small, personal scale, it closes people's souls, blocks their experience of God, keeps them from loving their neighbors and themselves. An example is the problem drinker, of whatever degree of free will. When the thirst is upon him or her, the world shrinks to the bottle. Consider also the person in thrall to lust, wanting only the tingle of the nerves, the soft, sibilant pleasure, the violent orgasmic relief. Certainly, the lust may be love in sorry garb. Certainly, loneliness and insecurity may be crying. But the adulterer narrows to the moment, thrusting spouse, children, responsibilities at work toward oblivion. Life condenses to the scope of an afternoon soap opera, to soft core and sleaze. No passion for God carries the two away. They have nothing better to do.

Again and again the theologian studies the remedies, the legal approaches, that have been proposed to handle vice — drugs, prostitution, pornography, gambling — and winces. The campaign to just say no, however simplemindedly or self-servingly displayed, goes in a better direction. The only radical solution to most crime and vice is to give people something better to do. Many better things leap to mind: study, prayer, science, art, social service, enjoyment of nature. Certainly all require some preparation, and certainly all make some demands. Obviously, none of these alternatives makes up for wretched housing, unemployment, loveless homes, battered psyches. On the other hand, all are positively addictive. Like aerobic exercise, all fit human nature enough to become self-validating. In each case the physical entailments make it plain one must act in moderation, but in their spiritual outreach all the alternatives are limitless. One cannot exhaust the hunger for beauty, love, truth, or creativity. When the body can take no more sex or exercise, the spirit continues to ride the glow of good health or the joy of incarnate love like a magic carpet.

The difficulty in this analysis is the Catholic Christian claim that all people have a capacity, a hunger for God and the spiritual life that God incites, such that we can write no people off. Patient and realistic as dealing with concrete sinners will make us, faith continues to say that God's Spirit is always trying to stir people's souls, cleanse their hearts. Certainly faith says that all people are sinners, with the implication that only the naive, those little formed by theology, will be surprised by human abuse and wrongdoing. Certainly the demands of God can make people seem haters of everything noble and good. To face the self, as faith requires, can be so painful that people will do anything to avoid it. To deal with feelings of not being loved, even by God, many people will act cynical, detached, even cruel.

Nonetheless, Jesus consorted with such people: tax-gatherers, prostitutes, and sinners. The good people of Jesus' day despised them. The Pharisees wrote them off. Indeed, they thought themselves unclean and defiling, like the pariahs of India. Yet Jesus saw through their defenses, often very unattractive, as he saw through the judgments by which society tried to write them off. He spoke to them of new starts, of ways of being turned around, of judgments of God contrary to the judgments of society. Indeed, he spoke to them of forgiveness, not mitigating their sins or denying their culpability but making more of God's love.

When we were sinners, Paul says, Christ died for us. Before we were repentant, converted, and aware that things could be otherwise, God went out to meet us, like the father in the story of the prodigal son. That is why sin is only the penultimate word. That is why one can believe that God is always greater. Even when our hearts, owning up to the folly and hurt of our sins, condemn us, God is greater than our hearts. The only limit to our possibilities in the spiritual life is the limit of the love of God. Jesus said that seventy times seven (the number standing for wholeness multiplied by ten and then squared, to stand for "endlessly") would not exhaust the patience of God. If so, the sin so distressingly, fatiguingly familiar, on the street and in the mirror, is by no means the gridlock that the mass media suggest. If so, the depths of sin are hidden with Christ in God, sure to be revealed one day as both more malignant than we could ever appreciate and more puny compared to God's love.

The Catholic stress on finitude makes much of the human problematic something natural, the inevitable by-product of the evolutionary world God has chosen to create. The Catholic understanding of sin takes it seriously but will not let sin mottle the core of the human personality. Equally, it will not let sin override the intrinsic reconstitution of the personality that is possible through Christ's grace. Nonetheless, Catholics have a great deal to learn from the Protestant penetration of sin, which has long meditated on the ravages worked in both the psyches of individuals and the social patterns governing most cultures. The depressing facts reported every day in the major newspapers bear witness to the acuity of the Protestant wonder about whether there is any health in human beings. The loss of the contemplative spirit that opens the wounded personality to the healing of the Spirit has made modernity a case study in the problems of correctly estimating human nature. Reinhold Niebuhr can stand for the wisdoms of Protestant instinct about the need to confront the Hitlers and Stalins of the world. In Niebuhr's view, we are right to suspect not only our enemies but ourselves of regularly slanting things for personal or national gain. In the view of Paul Ricoeur, a most impressive philosopher who has blended Freudian and Reformed insights, we are right to employ a "hermeneutic of suspicion" in most cases, asking that our interpretation of people and events come to grips with the biases every honest examination of conscience reveals.

Death

Still, it would be the death of hope to let the hermeneutic of suspicion destroy the basic Pauline conviction (which we might call a hermeneutic of appreciation) that where sin abounded grace has abounded the more. It would be a distortion of the primordial Christian proclamation of Christ's paschal victory to let his death blot out his Resurrection. In the West the passion and death of Christ have shaped Christian piety more than the Resurrection has. One of the major gains from Western ecumenical dialogue with Eastern Christianity has been its help in redressing an imbalance. The concentration of the East on the Resurrection, the mission of the Spirit throughout the cosmos, the rule of Christ the Pantokrator (Master of All), and the energies of God working our divinization could be like a breath of fresh air renewing Western spirituality.

Consider, for example, the classical Western treatment of Christ's death.

Whereas the Church fathers concentrated on Christ the victor over Satan, the champion who had broken the bonds of sin and death, Anselm and much popular Catholic piety depicted Christ's redemptive death as a ransom paid to God, or even to Satan, to write off humanity's debts. The honor of God had required such a satisfaction, and even when the God whose honor was thought to have been affronted was not presented as a Lord of wrath, he certainly was not the Abba of Jesus of Nazareth, not the father of the prodigal son.

For earlier Christianity, the death of Christ was the death of death and so was a cause for great joy. The ancient song of the Easter liturgy took this stance in speaking of Adam's sin as a happy fault. The redeemer merited or occasioned by Adam's sin was so great a boon that, by comparison, the harm done through Adam's fault seemed secondary. God might have had the Logos take flesh apart from human sin, as (in contrast to Aquinas) some Franciscan theologians opined. Eastern Orthodox thought could furnish a rationale for thinking that from the beginning God's intentions for grace had focused more on divinization than on the repair of human fracture. (Even better, one could argue that divinization is the best way to explain the radical repair of human brokenness and need that God wished to bring about.) But in fact humanity has been burdened with the forces we haltingly try to name when we speak of original sin, so in fact the willingness of Christ to lay down his life for his friends has met a most pressing need.

Indeed, the death of Christ matches so exactly with the sufferings and mortality of the rest of us that one would want to toast God as a designing genius, when it came to structuring history, were such a notion not potentially offensive. Of course God has been a genius, and so much more, elaborating forms for the divine love that surpass our appreciation. God's foolishness, blazing from the cross, has been so much wiser than human wisdom that most of our pundits have never taken it seriously. It has been left to the artists, and the ordinary people not afraid to walk to the front of the church, to go on their knees and speak to the Crucified from the heart, to appreciate how exactly the death of Christ has met our human needs.

Take the alcoholic, racked with guilt, thinking himself, or herself, a pariah. Christ on the cross could stand for knowledge of such humiliation, such degradation, because Christ had been despised, rejected, a man of sorrows and acquainted with grief. Take the person who has terminal cancer, living with the certainty that death will come within the year. Christ on the cross is a God to whom one could go as to a fellow sufferer, one who was equally subject to the necessity that the Gospel of Luke, especially, saw shaping of all Christ's days. Was it not necessary that the Messiah should suffer and so enter his glory? Had it not been the plan from the beginning, suspected by the prophets who cast forth better images than they knew, virtually rehearsed in the Suffering Servant songs of Second Isaiah? If Christ could deal with the necessities God asked him to bear, perhaps a less innocent sufferer, a fellow human being with more for which to atone, could also manage to see things like cancer through.

In the influential theology of Karl Rahner, death offers the one chance for human beings to hand themselves over to God whole and entire. Because of human finitude, to say nothing of sin, prior to death we can never fully descry our selves or our consciences. By some theological equivalent of Heisenberg's principle of indeterminacy, our very efforts to reflect on our situation skew the reality. Thus Paul knew that no one could be certain of salvation. True, all orthodox Christians have realized that conscience is unfathomable and must throw itself on the mercy of God. God is the one who justifies us, which makes Jesus' portrait of God all the more marvelous. For God to be on our side, like a loving parent, a nursing mother who could never cast off the child of her bosom, is a mercy beyond compare. Being left in God's hands is the best fate that could befall us. Thus Jesus, commending his spirit unto God, could transmute the agony of the cross into a consummating peace.

Death, which Paul made the wages of sin, has been subjected to God's good intentions on our behalf. It now serves not only to make life serious but also as a passover, a way of going down with Christ to the depths of humanity, the places where we can no longer deny that God has always had all the priority. An activist time, especially, should be grateful to death for forcing it to see that the major reality in our lives is their passion. What we undergo is much more significant than what we do, despite the fact that we must do what we can, lest our faith show itself dead by having produced no good works. We undergo our heredity, our environment, and the mysterious dispensations of God's grace. We undergo past history, which presses upon us like an avalanche, and the darkness of the future, which stays locked in the counsels of God.

So as we reach the age of thirty, forty, fifty, we do well to reflect on our passions. The fires we have for beauty, which we rightly may hope are dim searches for God, are only the outer portion of our "passion." What we suffer in the opacity of our center, in our constant inability to gain God or self once and for all, places us with the pilgrim Christ. Despite his complete union with the Father and the Spirit, Christ had a mission to fulfill, a mandate to carry out, that only finished at Gethsemane and Golgotha. For our sakes, he made death the conduit to divine life. For our sakes, Christ took the sting from death, the poisonous possibility that death robbed life of all meaning. Ever since, all the starving children, the abused women, the people ravaged by natural disasters and disease, the insane, the lonely, the sick souls closed in on themselves have had a reason for thinking that their failures and sufferings subserved a greater passion. In the Body of Christ, for which they were destined despite all the protests from the superficial portions of themselves, not one of their pains or temptations to despair would be lost. In the mercy of God, they, we, have been carried into the tide of the passionate God, as Rosemary Haughton has so well called the deity set on our redemption, taking us, almost despite ourselves, toward the ocean where all manner of things will be well.[1]

Resurrection

The Resurrection of Christ served the early Christians many utilities. It was the news, nearly too good to be true, that God had not let Christ end or be defeated. It was a ratification of Christ's cause, the Father's stamp of approval. With the Resurrection came the surest proof of Jesus' divinity, as he moved in the disciples' midst with a glorified body. With the Resurrection came the upward swing of the paschal U, heading toward the consummating mysteries of the Ascension and Pentecost. The Spirit poured forth at Pentecost was the Spirit of the Resurrected Christ. The Johannine Christ rapt in prayer, speaking the unforgettable monologues of John 14–17, shone with a prefiguring of heavenly glory. Revelation drew on the resurrection when John of Patmos rendered his dazzling visions. Pauline theology, shaped in Romans by the Spirit so intimate it could make the believers' prayer, relied on the Resurrection to nail down its convictions about the conveyance of divine life and the surety that nothing can separate us from the love of God in Christ Jesus.

The mind naturally looks for analogues to the Resurrection, and certain faint ones readily appear. There are the seasons of the natural world, which make it fitting to celebrate Easter in the spring. There are the seasons of the spiritual life, famously celebrated by Qoheleth: for every time a purpose under heaven. Those who are serious about prayer learn that they must die to meditation, die to consolation, be stripped of their securities and childish images. When consolation returns, it is like sunshine after the storm, like sunrise after the long winter's night, like Lazarus being called forth after he had resigned himself to rotting. Personal relationships—marriages, friendships, connections between parents and children—have times of fallow and times of full. Creative work passes through deaths and rebirths, blocks and sudden openings. Even the body has its biorhythms, its fluctuations of energy, its hormonal highs and lows.

For faith, however, the mysteries of Christ more illumine ordinary human experience than they are illumined by human experience. Sacramentality, metaphor, and suggestion are richest when the light or inspiration comes from on high. The drama one sees when raised by the Spirit is much richer than the drama one can extrapolate from the history books or the psychiatrists' journals. Fine as such testimonies from below remain, it is the person born of water and the Spirit, as the Johannine Jesus told Nathaniel, who gets the fuller sense of what is going on. The wind blows where it will. Only those attuned to the wind, made sailors by the Spirit, tack to the divine ports of meaning.

In light of the Resurrection, the human drama becomes a divine comedy. Dante wrote the definitive artistic statement of this theme, but one can find it implied in the simple word "gospel." The good news of Jesus Christ was that God was doing everything humanity had ever longed for and more. The good news that Jesus preached was that God was coming to reign, as all righteous hearts wanted God to. The good news preached by the apostles after the death and Resurrection of Christ was that the heavens had opened, God had not called us servants but friends, humanity thenceforth had no lesser vocation than a sharing in the divine nature.

The divine nature is deathless. The Greek mind was especially impressed by that. For pagan Greece the great difference between the gods and human beings was the humans' mortality. Certainly such mortality gave human life an edge that the Olympian gods could never know, but it also made human existence pathetic. Socrates, Plato, and Aristotle concentrated on the spirituality of the human composite, hoping that the immateriality of the soul would render it immortal. Thus Plato conceived of the human vocation, as specified in the love of wisdom, as an effort to become as much like God as possible: as much focused on deathless, fully spiritual truths as one could manage to be. Thus Aristotle spoke of the action of the divine in reaching into the human spirit and luring it forward as an immortalizing language not lost on Greek Christianity.

Jewish Christianity rather favored Resurrection, a notion that had developed in Second Temple times. It could not be that God would allow his heroes to suffer annihilation. It had to be that God would restore them to vitality, so that they might gaze upon the divine visage, and such vitality had to be a blessing for the entire psychosomatic unity. Jesus resurrected completely fulfilled this typology. Although the language of the evangelists seems deliberately calculated to assert that Jesus rose physically and was sensibly perceptible in his new state — the holes into which Thomas was to put his fingers, the food Jesus ate by the seaside — there is no reason to deny that the evangelists wrote under the influence of the Jewish interest in Resurrection that had circulated for a century before them. Jesus returned showed vitality completely restored. Jesus returned was a complete demonstration of what the favor of God could do for human flesh. The anointing that had marked Jesus for death turned out to be a sealing for deathlessness. The great descent of Jesus to the realm of the souls of the just who had died before him, known to the medievals as the harrowing of hell, turned out to have a greater curve of ascent. Seated at the right hand of the Father, as the biblical imagery liked to depict Jesus' return to heavenly glory, the Christ was a personal pledge that those who clung to God, who stayed faithful to the end, would not be disappointed. As Revelation above all argued, the Christ would give crowns of victory and glory to all who persevered.

In Pauline terms, the Resurrection of Christ proved not only that there was a Resurrection (contrary to the **Sadducees** and doubting Greeks) but that members of Christ could look forward to their own resurrection. I Corinthians 15 is the classical text, known to all frequenters of Catholic funerals. A similar message has long been read out of the bread of life discourse in John 6. Those who ate the flesh of the Lord and drank his blood were nourished for immortality. The eucharist was not merely a memorial of Christ's passion and Resurrection, not merely an anticipation of the messianic banquet. It was also an immortalization, an event in which the dictum of Athanasius that the Son of God became human so that human beings might become divine gained effective form. In the twinkling of an eye, at the sound of the trumpet, the **general resurrection** of all who had taken the bread of life and lived under the immortalizing impetus of the Spirit would occur. The graves would open, in rich symbolism of the submission of death to the experience of Christ, and the dead would come to stand before God restored to bodily integrity. How would all this happen? What was the literal intent of the obviously symbolic imagery? None could say. What all had to say, however, if they were to be orthodox Christians, was that the victory of Christ embraced all of human nature, making death, which had seemed the last and worst enemy, a servant of God's undying love. As the Creed recited at most Sunday masses put it: "We believe in the Holy Ghost, the holy Catholic Church, the communion of saints, the forgiveness of sins, the resurrection of the body, and the life of the world to come."

Representative Personality: Francis of Assisi

Francis of Assisi (about 1181–1226) is the Catholic saint most admired for his ardent, seraphic love of Christ. He worked for his father, a rich cloth merchant, until he was twenty, living a carefree existence, but brief experiences of imprisonment (during a local war) and serious illness gave him pause. Determined to change his life, Francis went on pilgrimage to Rome, where the poverty of the beggars touched him deeply. Thereafter ministering to the poor and living a life of evangelical poverty and freedom consumed him.

Francis had such a glow about him that soon he drew followers wanting to share his simple way of life. In 1210 he secured papal approval for the rule he had written to direct his community. The commitment of Clare of Assisi, a local noblewoman, led to the formation of a women's group to parallel the Little Brothers (*Fratres Minores*), as Francis called his male followers. Thereafter

Francis traveled through France, Spain, and Eastern Europe, preaching and helping the poor.

Upon his return to Assisi, Francis realized that those who had governed his now large group of followers in his absence were better suited for administration than he, so he never resumed control of his order. He did, however, found a lay group, called Franciscan Tertiaries, for those who wanted to embrace his ideals but had commitments that kept them in the world. In 1227 Cardinal Ugolino, with whom Francis had become friendly, became the new pope, Gregory IX, and the fortunes of the Franciscans soared. By that time, however, Francis himself had died, after receiving in 1224 the stigmata — impressions in his body of the wounds Christ had suffered from being nailed to the cross. Gregory IX canonized Francis in 1228, less than two years after his death.

Francis impressed all who met him by his great joy, his ardent love of Christ, and his concern to associate himself with the poorest of the poor. Perhaps the most dramatic sign of his holiness, however, was the stigmata, which understandably aroused great wonder and awe. *The Little Flowers of St. Francis*, a collection of reminiscences and legends about the saint, conveys how the companions of Francis understood the stigmata to have been granted. Francis had been praying on Mount Alvernia, asking for the grace to be identified with the suffering Christ. In the passion of Christ he saw concentrated the tremendous love of God for human beings, as well as the effects of the sins that had made Christ's sufferings necessary. Francis wanted to enter into the mystery of redemption epitomized in the passion, and his followers understood the stigmata as the granting of his desire.

Thus the Franciscan tradition passed on that Christ had appeared to Francis on Mount Alvernia:

"Do you know what I have done?" said Christ. "I have given you these Stigmata which are the emblems of My Passion, so that you may be My standard-bearer. And as I descended into Limbo on the day when I died and took from there by virtue of these Stigmata of Mine all the souls that I found there, so I grant to you that every year on the day of your death you may go to Purgatory and by virtue of your Stigmata you may take from there and lead to Paradise all the souls of your Three Orders, that is, the Friars Minor, the Sisters, and the Continent, and also others who have been very devoted to you, whom you may find there, so that you may be conformed to Me in death as you are in life."

Now when, after a long time and a secret conversation, this wonderful vision disappeared, it left a most intense ardor and flame of divine love in the heart of St. Francis, and it left a marvelous imprint of the Passion of Christ in his flesh. For soon there began to appear in the hands and feet of St. Francis the marks of the nails such as he had just seen in the body of

Jesus Crucified, who had appeared to him in the form of a Seraph. For his hands and feet seemed to be pierced through the center with nails, the heads of which were in the palms of his hands and in the upper part of his feet outside the flesh, and their points extended through the back of the hands and the soles of the feet so far that they seemed to be bent and beaten back in such a way that underneath their bent and beaten-back point — all of which stood out from the flesh — it would have been easy to put the finger of one's hand as through a ring. And the heads of the nails were round and black. Likewise in his right side appeared the wound of a blow from a spear, which was open, red, and bloody, and from which blood often issued from the holy breast of St. Francis and stained his habit and breeches.[2]

The historical likelihood is that in fact Francis did receive such wounds, as other saints (Catherine of Siena, Catherine of Genoa) are reputed to have received them. One may conjecture that the stigmata flow from the intense identification of the saintly believer with the crucified Christ, as a bodily expression of the force of the person's love (psychic fusion with the Crucified). Whatever the explanation, Francis of Assisi became known as the purest exemplar of the evangelical Christ, replicating in medieval terms the most that an ordinary human being could of the freedom and love Jesus had demonstrated. Francis considered himself a great sinner, unworthy of the love Christ had shown him, but that did not make him depressed or lugubrious. Rather he radiated a joy that suggested how the highest angels (seraphs), granted the supreme privilege of constantly beholding the divine beauty and singing its praises, would appear.

One of the several prayers for which St. Francis is famous expresses the joy the saint found in creation. In his love of God, Francis saw all God's creatures as gifts of the divine goodness:

Oh most high, almighty, good Lord God, to Thee belong praise, glory, honour and all blessing. Praised be my Lord God with all his creatures, especially our brother the Sun, who brings us the day and who brings us the light; fair is he and shines with a great splendour; O Lord, he signifies to us Thee. Praised be my Lord for our sister the moon, and for the stars, the which he has set clear and lovely in the heaven. Praised be my Lord for our sister water, who is very serviceable unto us and humble and precious and clean. Praised be my Lord for our brother fire, through whom Thou givest us light in the darkness; and he is bright and pleasant and very mighty and strong. Praised be my Lord for our mother the earth, the which doth sustain us and keep us, and bringeth forth divers fruit, and flowers of many colours, and grass. Praised be my Lord for all those who pardon one another for his love's sake, and who endure weakness and tribulation; blessed are they who peaceably shall endure, for Thou, O most Highest, shall give them a crown. Praised be my Lord for our sister the death of the body. Blessed are they who are found walking by thy most holy will. Praise ye and bless ye the Lord, and give thanks unto him, and serve him with great humility.[3]

One sees why Francis has become the patron saint of ecology. To his innocent mind, everything that breathed bespoke the divine bounty and returned God praise. Equally, everything useful to human beings had come down as a gift from on high and ought to have moved human beings to constant gratitude. Francis therefore suggests the eccentricity that Christian sanctity develops. People deeply in love with God lose the egocentricity that characterizes ordinary human beings and so seem to be centered differently, oddly. To them God is obviously the most significant and beautiful "thing" life offers, so more and more their time becomes an offering of service and praise to God.

Glossary

General Resurrection: the notion that at the end of history God will call all the dead from their graves and raise them up bodily. This notion is related to the notion of a General Judgment, at which the sins and merits of all will be made known to all. How the resurrection of the dead is to occur, when it will take place, where it will take place, and other such questions have remained obscure. The only certainty faith has offered is that since Christ was raised, resurrection has become the destiny of all people, some to enjoy eternal blessedness with God, others perhaps to languish eternally apart from God in a hell of lovelessness. The tradition has been surer about the Resurrection of the just than that of the apparently unrepentant, but usually the doctrine of the General Judgment seemed to necessitate the raising of all the dead.

Sadducees: a religious and political party in the Israel of Jesus's day. The Sadducees were an upper-class group, associated with the priestly rulers of the Temple, who held that only the written Torah (Pentateuch) of Moses was binding. They also denied the (relatively new) doctrine of the Resurrection. They opposed the Pharisees, a lay group who held for an oral Torah alongside the written Pentateuch and supported the doctrine of the Resurrection.

Discussion Questions

1. How does a natural happening such as cancer epitomize human finitude?
2. What do intimations of an infinite God say about the finite human makeup?
3. How does original sin show in global poverty and starvation?
4. Why did Jesus consort with sinners?
5. What would be the implications of regarding death as human beings' first chance to make a complete response (yes or no) to God?
6. How does Christ crucified meet the needs of mortal humanity?
7. Why did God raise Jesus from the dead?
8. What New Testament evidence challenges the notion that the doctrine of the Resurrection is merely a projection from natural experiences of death and rebirth?
9. What does the attention given the stigmata of St. Francis suggest about medieval Christian piety?
10. What was your reaction to Francis's canticle to brother sun and sister moon?

Notes

[1] See Rosemary Haughton, *The Passionate God* (New York: Paulist, 1981).
[2] *The Little Flowers of St. Francis*, trans. Raphael Brown (Garden City, N.Y.: Doubleday Image, 1958), pp. 192–193.
[3] George Appleton, ed., *The Oxford Book of Prayer* (New York: Oxford University Press, 1985), p. 363.

Eschatology

Pilgrimage

From its New Testament beginnings, Christianity has housed a central tension between "now" and "not yet." In virtue of the Incarnation and Resurrection of Jesus Christ, Christians could say that salvation was available now, in the present. Jesus had brought the Kingdom of God. The union of the Logos with his flesh had already accomplished the divinization of humanity for which the transcendent human spirit longed. Jesus not only worked miracles, he forgave sins. He not only spoke of fulfillment to come, he established as the constitutional law of his community the love that would be the marrow of such fulfillment. When he was raised by the Father, the new age palpably dawned. The descent of the Spirit at Pentecost elaborated more of what the new age was to be like: people inspired to proclaim the way of the Crucified, people worshiping God and relating to one another in the joy and confidence of children of God.

On the other hand, it was equally clear that the fullness of the Kingdom had yet to arrive. The forces that had slain Jesus continued to dominate both Israel and the rest of the Greco-Roman world (which, for all practical purposes, gave the early Christians their sense of humanity). Injustice, disease, sin, and death all remained lethal powers. Manifestly people often did not love one another. Manifestly God was not revered in many zones of human existence, was not paramount in many people's consciences. Thus Revelation and other strata of the New Testament sent up to God a lament reminiscent of the more plaintive Psalms. When would God deliver his people once and for all? When would the Spirit establish the reign of Christ on earth so clearly that every knee would bow and every tongue confess that Jesus was Lord?

The "yet" of the phrase "not yet" soon became focused on the Parousia. When Jesus returned in full power and glory, things would be made aright, in keeping with what conversion and grace, salvation and triumph over Satan, implied. Still, the very fact that the Spirit had been given, along with the fact that Christ had been raised, suggested that in principle fulfillment already was at hand. The Spirit could be considered the first fruits of the Parousiac release of godly power. Faith could be considered the real beginning of a life that soon would unfold as full glory. If death continued to take people away as soon as they had reached their mysterious span, death no longer was the dismal victor it had been before Christ. Christ had defeated death. The disciples of Christ were not to fear those who could only bring them physical death. Their worse enemies were those who could slay their spirits, could bind them to the sinful world that was passing away. In Pauline terms, Christ had inaugurated a new creation. Those who were incorporated into Christ lived by a new principle that took them up into the divine deathlessness. Already they were partakers of the divine nature. Soon they would be fully joined to the beloved Lord, who would wipe away every tear from their eye.

To say that this tension between "now" and "not yet" made Christian life a pilgrimage is to import language that only became fully formative of the Christian imagination in the medieval period, but the term captures enough of the psychology of Catholic Christianity from the earliest times to warrant our applying it to the full Catholic history of eschatology. When the Epistle to the Hebrews (12: 2) spoke of Jesus as the pioneer of Christians' hope, it placed in the canonical scriptures the seed of the notion that all believers were following after their perfect scout, much as the Israelites had wandered in search of the promised land. The new promised land was the Kingdom of God, where Christ had been set at the Father's right hand. Compared to the treasures of this heavenly Jerusalem, the foremost of which would be the chance to thank Jesus, praise him and the Father, and enjoy communion with the divine three, earthly riches faded toward insignificance. All true believers were on a pilgrimage to what the eye had not seen, the ear had not heard, and it had not entered the human heart to conceive. All were bound for the good things God had in store for those who loved him.

The sense that with Jesus had come the definitive phase of history, the crucial irruption of God's saving love, and that present existence was a movement, a being en route, toward the full sway of Jesus implied by "heaven," has made eschatology basic to Christian existence. Through the centuries, Christian spirituality has not always appreciated the richness of the eschatology bequeathed it by the New Testament. Frequently Catholics have narrowed their sense of "the last things" to death, judgment, heaven, and hell, all conceived in rather individualistic terms. Thus a recent article on eschatology has argued for a return to the richer beginnings:

> Eschatology in the minds of many is understood to refer to the study of the last things (*Eschata*), namely death, judgment, heaven, hell and the second coming of Christ. Within this perception, eschatology appears as an appendix to the rest of theology. However, from a historical point of view this description of eschatology is derivative, coming from a broader and more biblical understanding of eschatology which is founded on the Christ-Event: the announcement of the coming reign of God, the public ministry of Jesus, the death and resurrection of Jesus, and the outpouring of the Spirit. In the first century of Christianity the "end of time" was understood to have been anticipated in the death and resurrection of Jesus; the "last days" have been inaugurated by the outpouring of the Holy Spirit. This primary meaning of eschatology should be the basis of any particular understanding of death, judgment, heaven, hell and the second coming of Christ.[1]

Let us agree that "pilgrimage" will connote not a Christian existence unhappy with present times and longing to get out of history but a Christian existence trying to promote the growth of seeds already present in time, so that they increasingly manifest the divine life that the Parousia will more fully reveal. When we do, we find ourselves facing one of the many delicate balances that Catholic Christianity traditionally has striven to maintain. For the implication of calling Christian existence a pilgrimage can be that by being under way toward something not built by human hands, toward a city of God more lasting than any human establishments, Christians can become the best lovers of time and space, history and culture, as Jesus in principle was.

The incarnate Logos, entering into such human events as wedding feasts and religious ceremonies, gave them new depth and resonance. The Body of Christ, at its best, has given art and intellectual inquiry a sacramental character. Humanists certainly have many grounds for saying that Church history calls into question whether the Church has more helped or hindered human justice and culture. Marxists have many grounds for arguing that Christian religion has kept people retarded with regard to their social consciences and their commitment to building the best possible earth. On the other hand, no institution has provided more profound reasons for loving the earth, for not letting death cast a pall over the entire human enterprise, and for sacrificing personal advantage for the common good and posterity than the Christian Church. No institution has offered a more riveting model of how to overcome sin and hatred with love, how to expect wonderful things from human nature without being naive about the depths of human twistedness.

So a pilgrim Church ought to be a sacramental Church, a gathering of people convinced that by God's grace they can make their "now" not only a time fit for images of God but an adumbration of what God will deliver in heaven.

Judgment

The New Testament Christ spoke of God's gathering people before him and rendering judgment on their lives. Matthew 25, for example, has a famous scene in which the Son of Man (Jesus), returned in Parousiac glory, separates the sheep (just) from the goats (unjust):

> When the Son of Man comes in his glory, escorted by all the angels, then he will take his seat on his throne of glory. All the nations will be assembled before him and he will separate men from one another as the shepherd separates sheep from goats. He will place the sheep on his right hand and the goats on his left. Then the King will say to those on his right hand, "Come, you whom my Father has blessed, take for your heritage the kingdom prepared for you since the foundation of the world. For I was hungry and you gave me food; I was thirsty and you gave me drink; I was a stranger and you made me welcome; naked and you clothed me, sick and you visited me, in prison and you came to see me." Then the virtuous will say to him in reply, "Lord, when did we see you hungry and feed you; or thirsty and give you drink? When did we see you a stranger and make you welcome; naked and clothe you; sick or in prison and go to see you?" And the King will answer, "I tell you solemnly, in so far as you did this to one of the least of these brothers of mine, you did it to me" (Mt 25: 31–40).

The text goes on to indict the goats for not having served Christ and the needy who crossed their path. The King then casts them into eternal punishment whereas the virtuous pass on to eternal life.

The impulse to imagine judgments after death that redress the injustices prevailing during life has brought many different religions to doctrines like that of Christianity. Zoroastrianism, for example, developed a colorful depiction of judgment that had considerable influence on Judaism (as did the Zoroastrian views of angels). Egyptian religion pictured the dead coming before Osiris in the underworld to learn what fate their earthly lives had won them, and the *Egyptian Book of the Dead* includes a famous "negative confession" in which the dead person composes a defense by listing the many evil things he or she did not do. Plato also taught that there would be a judgment on the immortal soul after death, to fix the scales of justice that human governments and courts so often tilt.

One can say, then, that human conscience naturally fashions the view that were there not to be an accounting after death human existence would be a moral absurdity, a realm over which any finely tuned awareness of what ought to be would have to despair. All the crimes that go unpunished, all the secret sins and hurts, have to be patent to God and remembered, if the human sense of what is fair, what befits a God of truth and power, is not to atrophy or commit suicide. What has Christianity done with this general impulse of the human spirit in light of the Christ-Event?

On the one hand, Christianity clearly has retained the impulse toward justice and supported it. In the New Testament Jesus proposes rewards and punishments, not because he thinks they are the noblest motives for human action, but because the thirst of the human spirit for justice requires them. The Church, following the teachings of the New Testament Jesus, has elaborated the notion of judgment so that both the individual person after death and the collectivity of human beings at some indeterminate time will pass before God's scrutiny.

On the other hand, the note of mercy in Jesus' message, along with his teaching about the divine creativity and the loftiness of God's sense of justice, considerably changed the notion of tit for tat or of a strict accounting that has tended to prevail in other faiths. Certainly one can speak of mercy, forgiveness, and a less than ruthless application of justice in devotional Hinduism and Buddhism, where faith and love can cover a multitude of sins. But the parable of Jesus about the master who hires workers at various hours and pays them all the same wage (Mt 20: 1–16), along with Jesus' consorting with sinners and pronouncing the forgiveness of sin for people of faith, gave the Christian sense of justice a new slant. Paul's theology of justification by faith deepened this sense of newness. For Paul no one could pass God's scrutiny on the basis of good deeds. The laws developed in pursuit of a covenantal perfection were bound to condemn all people as moral failures.

So Christian theology moved into more obscure areas of the heart, where the final issue became one's love. God would forgive much to those who loved much. God would look kindly on the sort of neighborly love illustrated by the Son of Man in Matthew 25, probably making it cover a multitude of sins. "Justice" no longer was something one could tally by the numbers. After Christ it had become a function of one's overall character, person, and being. What had one in fact treasured? Where had one's heart and desire rested? If they had rested on God, in a plausible obedience to the first commandment (to love God alone, with one's whole mind, heart, soul, and strength), then one could hope for God's understanding and mercy. If they had gone out to help one's needy neighbors, one could hope that Christ would account one's responses good deeds done to himself.

Neither Christian imagination nor Christian theology sorted out the strands of justice and mercy so that they became completely tidy. All of Christianity's eschatological teachings labored under a great cloud of mystery, for no one other than Jesus had ever seen God. So all of the imagery and teaching was wisest when it stayed minimal. Sufficient was the clear assertion that God would render a better justice than the world ever did, and that with God one could hope for mercy. Most important was the clear assertion, not always ringing in clerical quarters but on the whole well served, that love was the final measure.

The Catholic sense of the communion of saints, the solidarity of all believers in the Body of Christ, led to a belief that favorites of God could intercede for sinners and ease their trials at Judgment. Christ himself was the primary intercessor, who could claim before the Father that this was a soul for whom he had shed his blood. The Mother of Christ, the Virgin Mary, was a favorite intercessor, the popular hope being that a good Son would deny his mother nothing. The saints also could be approached for help, and we saw in the report about Francis' reception of the stigmata the gift Christ conferred on him of being able to free souls from purgatory (or **limbo**). Well into the twentieth century, Catholics frequented devotional meetings called **novenas** and **missions** to pray to the saints, refurbish their spiritual lives, receive indulgences, and gain a better chance of pleasing God at Judgment. And whereas petitions to the saints have always included requests for help with temporal matters — sickness, debt, family troubles, jobs — they have also stretched beyond the temporal horizon to include prayers for help with the greatest task, saving one's immortal soul.

As the quotation about biblical eschatology implied, the Catholic sense of the last things often has lost the positive note that the last age has already arrived with Christ and so a positive judgment by God has already commenced. To be sure, the Catholic teaching about sanctifying grace has included such a positive note in other terms, but frequently it has not been riveted to the evangelical Christ as ideally it would have been. For had Catholics been better readers of the Bible, they would have better noted that the burden of the New Testament Christ's preaching and ministry fell on calling sinners to a great opportunity.

Like the God of the Hebrew prophets, the Father of Jesus wanted mercy rather than sacrifice. He wanted this not only from the common people but from himself, in the sense that he much preferred to deal with people who came with contrite hearts than with people who were absorbed in their own righteousness. That is the stunning message of Jesus' parable about the Pharisee (by focus a man bent on fulfilling the letter of the Mosaic law) and the publican (a tax gatherer and so technically a sinner, one working in an unclean profession):

> Two men went up to the Temple to pray, one a Pharisee, the other a tax collector. The Pharisee stood there and said this prayer to himself, "I thank you, God, that I am not grasping, unjust, adulterous, like the rest of mankind, and particularly that I am not like this tax collector here. I fast twice a week; I pay tithes on all I get." The tax collector stood some distance away, not daring even to raise his eyes to heaven; but he beat his breast and said, "God, be merciful to me, a sinner." This man, I tell you, went home again at rights with God; the other did not. For everyone who exalts himself will be humbled, but the man who humbles himself will be exalted (Lk 18: 9–14).

Heaven

The upshot of any orthodox Christian understanding of God's Judgment is that heaven always is a mercy of God, based on God's perception that the person in question did want to do what was right and did respond to the great love God had shown. Heaven could never be something one earned, something one had to be granted because one had passed all the courses and gained all the credits. Without making salvation something only imputed to human beings, and so not transforming their inmost selves, the Catholic position on heaven has remained that heaven is always a wonder of God's grace.

When Catholic speculation was applied to the question of what heaven would be like, it drew from the imagery of the New Testament and its debts to Greek philosophy a concentration on divinity itself. God had to be the substance of heaven, because only God could satisfy the desires built into the human spirit. As Augustine had put it so memorably, "You have made us for yourself, O Lord, and our hearts are restless till they rest in you." The "rest" possible only in God, alluded to by Hebrews (cc. 3 and 4), meshed with the viatorian, pilgrim character of earthly existence. Were human beings never to find an understanding to quiet their anxious, noisy search for meaning, their minds properly could speak of an absurd situation, precisely as the French existentialist philosopher Albert Camus defined absurdity. To be made for (comprehensive) meaning and always to experience confusion, lack of meaning, would be to have been placed in an intrinsically contradictory and frustrating situation. The only sort of God to whom one could attribute such a situation would be a sadist, and the greater likelihood would be that there is no God at all, just a flux of happenstance. But in that case nothing finally would matter and suicide might seem the most rational or honorable course. At some point any people of integrity would stop pushing their stones up the hill and would simply revolt, ending such a demeaning existence.

One could make the same argument by analyzing the dynamics of human love. Unless people who were made to love without restriction could encounter a goodness without restriction matching their makeup, they would have been constituted as existential frustrations. The only sane, rational inference from the desires of the human heart was that we have been made for a goodness the world does not offer, for a love transcending what is available in space and time.

Thus the Catholic analysis of heaven as essentially the beatific vision of God and experience of God's absolute goodness depended on its reading of the human makeup. For the intellectuals most responsible for this analysis, the defining characteristics of *homo sapiens*, the capacities that make our species not just a vestige of God, like the inanimate and subhuman species, but a true image of God, is the spirit displayed in knowing and loving. The movement of this spirit, brilliantly analyzed by Plato and Aristotle, shows that divinity itself both defines the span of human awareness and is the prime mover of the humanity's *kinesis* toward goodness, being, and intelligibility as such.[2] As taken over by the Neoplatonic Augustinians and the Aristotelian Thomists, this classical Greek analysis led to a heavenly fulfillment in which the essence of God itself would become the preoccupation of the human mind, the goodness of God itself would fill the human will.

The biblical equivalents of this speculative analysis were less clear but more personal and emotionally satisfying. There was the explicitly Christian theme of being united with Christ, having one's abiding come to fruition by one day seeing the Lord face to face, knowing as one had long been known. In heaven faith and hope would pass away, for their object would be nigh. Charity, the greatest and most godlike of the virtues, would suffice, consuming the person's full potential.

More socially, Revelation imagined heaven as a great chorus, anchored by the one hundred forty-four thousand saints (a multiple of the twelve tribes, the whole people of God), endlessly enjoying and praising the divine goodness, justice, and beauty. The key idea seems to be that in heaven the saints (all the faithful who had persevered to the end and won the crown Jesus had promised) would find the saving plan of God, the entire divine economy of salvation, so replete with wonders that they would never cease being amazed. Like the seraphim and cherubim of the visions of Isaiah and Ezekiel that had meant so much to Jewish mysticism, the Christian images of the glory surrounding the divine throne blazed with light. All was so holy that fire, white linen, and burnished bronze came to mind. Jewels, gold, glass, and precious minerals adorned the heavenly Jerusalem. The saints would thrill to the exploits of the Word of God, riding out to avenge all injustice, and to the prominence of the Lamb of God, whose willingness to be slain had made him worthy to receive all power, honor, and glory. The Ancient of Days (the Father) presiding in heaven, He who is and who was and who is to come, who dominates all time, would be so awesome that the saints would only prostrate themselves in worship. The Spirit circulating in the seven lamp stands, filling all the churches with the holiness of heaven, was less prominent in early Christian apocalyptic, but the Johannine literature made it clear that abiding in Jesus and the Father meant abiding in and with the Spirit as well.

Still, perhaps the most winning or touching note was that in heaven God would wipe away every tear from the saints' eyes and death would be no more. All such former things would have passed away, finally giving human beings the existence for which they had been made. Where there had been injustice, now there would be utter fairness. Indeed, there would be such an abounding of grace that sinners would feel completely new, as though all the rents and tears they had experienced in life had been completely repaired, making them better than ever they had been, better even than reborn. New wineskins for new wine. The dispensation of Satan and death having vacated the scene, heaven would be the great peace, love, and joy presiding at the center of the riot of images thrown up by the hopeful Christian imagination. It would be a share in the divine nature so generous that the saints would spend an eternity loving with the divine love, knowing with the divine knowledge, enjoying the relations and processions that made God God.

In many periods of Church history, the popular Catholic imagination took these images rather literally. The New Testament texts, and the speculations of the theologians, set forth some awareness of the mysteriousness of heaven, some appreciation of the fact that God alone knew the specifics of the divine estate. But the common people were bound to love the images of Jesus, Mary, and the saints that tradition suggested, as they were bound to think fearfully about the parallel images of Satan and his minions accompanying their sense of hell. Thus one finds in the little church of San Toma in Toledo, Spain, a magnificent painting by El Greco depicting the burial of Count Orgaz and his translation to a heaven where the saints crowd forward to meet him. The Father, Jesus, and the Spirit are there. The Virgin Mary figures prominently, and one can distinguish such saints as Peter, Paul, and Augustine. The general idea is of a great homecoming, the saints welcoming one of their own. So the communion of saints, with all its possibilities for warmth and celebration, added grace notes to the chorus of images promising Catholic Christians that all would be well, would be much better than they had ever suspected. At last they would be fully in the hands of God, and that had to be the best of fortunes.

Hell

The worst of fortunes was hell, definitive separation from God. All of the analysis that went into making union with God in heaven the fulfillment of the human constitution was deployed negatively to make separation from God in hell the definitive human ruin. Some periods of Christian history imagined all too vividly Satan breathing forth his foul stench, laughing hideously, delighting in having brought human beings into his own terrible frustration and agony of self-hatred. Certainly the devils, minions of Satans, depicted torturing the souls of the wicked, devising fiendishly suitable punishments for particular sins, influenced the common people. The picture of the rich man who had refused the beggar Lazarus help and so was suffering agonies in hell (Lk 16) brought punishment to bear on injustice and lack of charity. The weeping and gnashing of teeth to be visited on those who had spurned Christ suggested the frustration that hell would entail, the anguish of knowing one could easily have gained eternal bliss but had been so stupid, so weak, that one had let beatitude slip away.

Nonetheless, more sober analysis of hell suggested key caveats. First, one had to say that all people had sufficient grace for salvation and that none could be lost except through personal choice, made with full knowledge and malice aforethought. There were no mistakes in hell. No one was there because of an inadvertent glance at a comely maid or a trifling peccadillo. Indeed, no one was there because of an eternal decree of God, a portion of a supposedly double predestination that consigned some to heaven and others to hell before ever they had drawn breath. Catholicism rejected as monstrous this logically possible interpretation of Pauline lines about God's plan and Augustinian ruminations about predestination. It befit neither the goodness of God nor the reality of human freedom.

Certainly God held all fates in his hands, but God was benevolent and just. Certainly nothing future was hidden from God, but God did not exist in time, did not grope among past, present, and future. For God to know something as actual was for that something to be actually existing. So it was bad theological imagination to picture God laying out people's lives before they had lived them, determining people's eternal destinies before they had consummated their dramas in death and entered upon their definitive estate.

Still, the question of what it profited a person to gain the whole world and suffer the loss of his or her immortal soul remained sobering. The man who planned on a long life, filling up his barns, giving himself over to the accumulation and enjoyment of riches, was a fool. Any given day or night his soul might be required of him. If he were not always ready to undergo the judgment of God, he was always in mortal peril. Even the simplest of souls had to know that life could end suddenly. Even the simplest of the faithful had to think that playing games with God, postponing repentance, was the utmost folly.

In recent theological reflection, hell has emerged as a real possibility, yet something never certain. One has to say, as an orthodox Catholic theologian, that people are free to say no to God and so to choose eternal separation from God. Free people truly can engineer their definitive ruin. But one cannot say that any particular person certainly has done so. One cannot pronounce Judas Iscariot, Hitler, Stalin, Genghis Khan, or any other apparently great sinner surely lost in the bowels of hell. Even though the Catholic church has always shied away from the doctrine of *apocatastasis*, according to which the love of God would triumph in all human hearts, assuring that none ever fell into hell, neither has it definitively ruled out the hope such a doctrine carries. One simply does not know whether any people are in hell. One believes that the saints are surely in heaven, and one trusts that the mercy of God abandons no person in life or death. But one has to leave all final fates to the mercy of God, most pertinently including one's own.

That is not to say that Catholic Christianity, like Protestant Christianity, has not known periods when popular preaching, writing, and teaching made it seem that the path to salvation was so narrow that the majority wouldn't follow it. At times the *massa damnata* of which Augustine spoke could be depicted as lemmings rushing to their destruction. Then it could seem that only heroic Christianity — flight to the monastery, a diet of bread and water, use of hair shirts, chains, and other austerities, constant weeping over one's sins — could let one avoid hellfire. Then one could accredit such Augustinian teaching as the notion that every human act was tainted by sin, especially the sexual acts made for love and the transmission of life.

To be sure, at such historical times the mercy of God might loom up as all the more important, though the stern justice of God was more likely to prevail. But eventually some people, perhaps many lay Christians possessed of common sense, would realize that all this pessimism was developing a terrible picture of God and was making God quite unlike the Abba whom Jesus had completely trusted, whom Jesus had said one could ask for bread in full confidence one would not receive back a stone. If human beings, for all their faults, loved their children and wanted to give them good things, how much more must the Father be on the side of his children, be always inclining them to the things that would bring them home to his rest.

But what would it be like to reject God utterly? How might such an abuse of the freedom God had given, so that human beings could love him without constraint, unfold? Perhaps such rejection would take the form of carelessness. Many people, clearly, got lost in the pleasures and pressures of the world. Many never rose above rather brutish passions for food, drink, sex, and power. Some were so perverted they loved to inflict pain. Scores of battered wives and children testified to their reality. Worse, some abused their children sexually, lacking the self-control, the decency, the love without which parent-child relations become a nightmare. Were these people candidates for hell? Could their drowning in sensuality, self-indulgence, and perversion finally render them deaf to the call of conscience, blind them to the signs God had strewn saying that they should serve only the Lord God?

Perhaps so. The typical sinner did indeed seem an amnesiac, one forgetful of the full sweep of God's plan, one unmindful of death and judgment, one careless about the command to love. On the other hand, the sins that Catholicism has stigmatized as most likely to mimic the Satanic rebellion that constituted hell were sins of the spirit. It was pride and lovelessness that the tradition associated with Lucifer. It was his "I will not serve" that brought his definitive alienation from God. Weakness of the flesh was nothing compared to fierce hatred of God. Terrible as the effects of brutish lust could be, they paled before the will to power of the great butchers of history, the madmen who inflicted pain and made blood run as easily as they opened the blinds in the morning. Perhaps their apparent madness would excuse them, but it raised profound questions about the destruction sin caused in the sinner.

Without neglecting the sufferings that great sin caused to others, Catholic tradition held that sinners punished themselves, so abusing their spiritual constitution that it was bound to give them pain, like a shoulder out of joint, a broken bone jutting out at an ugly angle. Hell would only be the ratification and prolongation of the inner division a great sinner had freely chosen. It would only be the allowance of "I will not serve" that God had to grant, if freedom were not to be an illusion. So the choices one made as one formed one's soul through a lifetime were deadly serious. Little by little vice could be taking away one's freedom to say yes to God, one's desire to be holy. Each time that one refused to feel compassion and act upon it, each time that one rode over the good of others in pursuit of one's own sensual or egotistical satisfaction, one sent out feelers toward hell. Like heaven, hell was a state of mind, a state of soul, a stance toward God. Everything was tilted in favor of helping one choose heaven. All justice, truth, beauty, goodness, and love called one to ascend toward the light. But one could prefer the sirens of dark pleasure and fierce pride that called from below. One could turn a deaf ear to God, even refuse to be moved by the sufferings of Christ, and so turn in on oneself in hellish isolation.

Representative Personality: Dante

Dante Alighieri (1265–1321) was the poet who put the Catholic triad of hell, purgatory, and heaven into unforgettable verse and made the definitive statement about the last possibilities for human beings. His parents died while he was a boy. He studied with the Dominicans, imbibing a lasting influence from the thought of Thomas Aquinas. As a youth Dante fell in love with Beatrice, probably a fellow Florentine, who died young and served him ever after as his literary muse. In 1301 political entanglements got Dante ostracized from Florence, the false charges souring his view of human nature ever after. Reduced to wandering from city to city in search of employment, usually as a tutor, Dante finally settled in Ravenna in 1315. His political experience convinced him of the necessity of separating the temporal and religious powers. (One of the reasons he was *persona non grata* in Florence was his opposition to papal interference in Florentine politics.) Although Dante wrote several other works meriting study, the project of the last decades of his life, *The Divine Comedy*, established his reputation as one of the greatest poets of Christian history, rivaling Shakespeare in depth and beauty.

At the depths of Dante's *Inferno*, in the ninth circle, called Cocytus, lies Satan, a most hideous manifestation of the rejection of God expressed in sin. During his passage through the different levels of hell, under the guidance of the Latin poet Virgil, the good pagan who knows the ins and outs of human nature, Dante has seen the effects of the various vices. They wrap steel bands around the soul and squeeze out its love. At the nadir of hell, however, lies a huge fallen angel, whose very disfigurement suggests the splendor he might have carried in heaven, when they called him the Lightbearer. Satan has three heads, beneath each of which beat two giant wings that make a great storm. The beating of Satan's wings causes Cocytus to freeze, creating the ice in which the creatures imprisoned there are bound. In one of his mouths Satan is devouring Judas Iscariot, the former disciple who betrayed Christ. The other two mouths work on Brutus and Cassius, betrayers of Caesar. The message is that betrayal, traitorship to the point of handing over one's Lord, is the foulest of sins. It is significant that Dante makes pagan betrayal of a political leader nearly the equivalent of Judas's betrayal of Christ. He is convinced that the secular and religious realms both come from God and carry a divinely sanctioned authority.

Dante and Virgil have literally to climb up the mountain of Satan if they are to escape from the *Inferno*. At the top of the climb they realize that Satan and the realm of hell are a complete inversion of the realms of purgatory and paradise. The gravities of the spiritual world above and the hellish world below meet at Satan. Having taken Satan's measure and risen above him, Dante and Virgil are free to explore the next of humanity's possible fates, purgatory.

The basic conception of purgatory has been that those who do not merit hell, because they died with some love of God and neighbor, and yet do not merit heaven, because their souls are still impure and so not fit for union with God, require a time and place of purification. In the sufferings that such purification would entail, such souls would be sustained by the hope that eventually they would gain union with God and so eternal bliss. The biblical grounds for purgatory are slim, and both Orthodox and Protestant Christians have not had much enthusiasm for the notion. Catholic theology has thought purgatory a logical inference from its analysis of how heaven and hell match the human constitution for God, so Catholic theology has proposed it (more strongly in ordinary catechetical teaching than in formal conciliar definitions). The councils of Lyons [1274] and Florence [1439] did affirm the existence of purgatory, but they avoided discussion of a material fire purifying the souls there, because of Greek objections. The official teaching thereafter has affirmed only the existence of purgatory and the value of prayer and good works performed on behalf of any who might linger there.

The lowest realms of Dante's purgatory, where those most in need of purification dwell, house the excommunicated and the indolent. Interestingly, at the top of purgatory Dante places the lustful, those who loved much but not wisely or purely. Passed beyond this top realm, Dante and Virgil encounter purer love, reminiscent of Venus coming out of the East, in the form of a maiden innocent and beautiful. She is Lethe (forgetfulness), who may make lust and the other vices requiring purification a thing of Dante's past. With their exit from purgatory to the earthly paradise free of vice, Virgil has reached the end of his competence. For guidance through the heavenly paradise Dante requires a Christian leader, none other than the Beatrice who has personified pure love in his own life.

Toward the heights of paradise, in a realm dominated by St. Peter, Dante hears the first bishop of Rome violently condemn papal corruption. He then moves through the sphere of the angels, who constitute a vast mystical rose. Beatrice hands him over to St. Bernard, who will take him to the vision of God. On the way he sees Mary, the Queen of Heaven, and then her Son, the divine one become a creature. At the consummation of his quest, the beatifying vision, Dante sees the eternal light and its radiance, finally realizing that divine love is the ultimate force in the universe, moving the sun and all the stars.

The so hierarchical, ordered and symbolic poetry of *The Divine Comedy* is a perfect translation of medieval Christianity. Dante's analyses of why different sinners are in their particular circles of hell and purgatory express acute psychological insights into how the different vices and virtues operate. Such ethical insight was one of the strengths of medieval scholasticism, developed through a close study of Aristotelian introspective ethics that examined the various strengths and weaknesses of the soul. Dante is saying, with poetic concreteness and genius, that the fates people finally receive are the products of their own choices, of the acts through which they have made themselves. Dante is constrained by the theological assumptions of his time, such as the impossibility of unbaptized people such as Virgil entering heaven, no matter how virtuous or noble their lives. Certainly the recent history of Florence and the papacy bulks large, populating hell and purgatory with a disproportionately large number of

Italians. But the beauty of Dante's language, and the depth of his Christian sense of reality, make us quickly forgive him these limitations. In his work one can see how profoundly eschatology had shaped the Catholic Christian spirit, and after Dante all Catholic literature, theological and artistic alike, regarded the *Commedia* as the classic statement on Christian existence, both its present forms and its forms to come.

Thus James Collins, commenting on Dante's life and work, explains:

> Dante is addressing his fellow human beings as such, but, more specifically, he is addressing his fellow Christian pilgrims. . . . All of us, then, especially those who share Dante's Christian faith and have experienced some of the sorrows and joys of this life, can identify with Dante's story because it is *our* story. Dante discovers that he is lost and tries to find himself. He sets out on a journey and invites us, the readers, to join him in this quest for self, which will simultaneously be a quest for God. . . . As a pilgrim, however, he is one of us: lost, incomplete, broken, in need of direction. Sinful, fearful, ignorant, and weak, he is, however, aware that deep down in the secret chambers of his heart he is being drawn by some unknown force: a love for all that is beautiful and good and true. But that is not all. This mysterious force turns out to be God Himself, the Lover who is drawing us all back to Himself.[3]

Glossary

Limbo: the term comes from the Latin word for the border or hem of a garment. It designates the state of those who have died without the baptism necessary for entrance into heaven but also without the mortal sin necessary for condemnation to hell. Tradition has distinguished the limbo where those who preceded Christ remained until his descent to them after his death from the limbo in which unbaptized infants dwelt. Although the Church has made no authoritative, conciliar statement about limbo, in many eras limbo was accepted as part of popular Catholic faith. Insofar as recent theology has suggested that death can be a moment of definitive choice for or against God, it has removed the necessity for limbo.

Missions: devotional sessions, more popular before Vatican II than since, during which many parishes sponsored preaching, prayers, exhortations to frequent the sacraments of penance (confession) and the Eucharist, and generally an amendment of life. One might consider such missions the Catholic equivalent of the revivals popular in many Protestant sects.

Novenas: nine-day devotional sessions, much like missions and usually focused on a particular saint or aspect of the Virgin Mary. The Novena of Grace, for example, focused on St. Francis Xavier and was popular in many Catholic areas during Lent. Sermons would deal with the fundamentals of Catholic faith, calling people to give up their backsliding into sin. Often the preachers would use the life of Xavier to illustrate the Christian virtues, whereas hymns and prayers would petition the saint's aid. The novena would end with the conferral of a plenary indulgence (remission of all temporal punishment [in purgatory or hell] because of sin), on the condition of one's having received the sacraments of penance and the eucharist.

Discussion Questions

1. What is the basic eschatological tension between "now" and "not yet"?
2. How did Jesus bring the end of time, and how does that bringing relate to his Parousia?
3. How valid is the perennial human depiction of a judgment after death at which divinity would render the justice earthly life does not provide?
4. How has Jesus' portrayal of the divine mercy colored the Christian sense of judgment?
5. What is the beatific vision and how does it relate to Catholic anthropology (understanding of human nature)?
6. How does the biblical imagery of heaven depict its social dimension?
7. Why has Catholic Christianity made more of sins of the spirit than sins of the flesh?
8. In what sense is hell merely making definitive the self fashioned through habitual choices against God?
9. Why has Dante depicted Satan as frozen in an ice of his own making?
10. How adequate a view is Dante's final notion that God is the love that moves the sun and the stars?

Notes

1 Dermot Lane, "Eschatology," in *The New Dictionary of Theology*, ed. Joseph A. Komonchak, Mary Collins, and Dermot Lane (Wilmington, Del.: Michael Glazier, 1987), p. 329.
2 See Eric Voegelin, *Anamnesis* (Notre Dame, Ind.: University of Notre Dame Press, 1978).
3 James Collins, *Pilgrim in Love: An Introduction to Dante and His Spirituality* (Chicago: Loyola University Press, 1984). p. 49.

PART III

Catholic Ritual and Ethics

CHAPTER 10

Communal Worship

The Liturgical Cycle
The Eucharist
Sacraments of Initiation
Sacraments of Reconciliation
Marriage and Orders
Representative Personality: Kurt Reinhardt
Glossary, Discussion Questions, Notes

The Liturgical Cycle

Space and time are the basic coordinates of human existence. The
Christian teachings about creation and incarnation have shaped the Catholic
sense of space, ideally producing an incarnational sensibility. According to such
a sensibility, the divine mystery has blessed the sweep of the land falling away to
the horizon, the sky above and the earth below. Indeed, the Son of God has
taken flesh, inserting himself into the tensions between heaven and earth. In the
liturgy that has called people to remember these blessings, to thank God for the
light of their eyes and the air they breathe, everything that God has made is
invited to be a co-conspirator. From the beasts of the deep to the bees that made
the wax spent to give light and warmth, all creation ideally sends up praise and
thanksgiving, in the spirit of Psalm 148. Wherever the Spirit of God has
breathed, people can feel space being sanctified. Space then has become the
potential for the city of God, a place where human beings might realize their
exalted vocation to be images of God and sharers of the divine nature.

Nonetheless, it seems fair to say that the liturgical cycle has been more
influenced by time, which the Christian doctrine of redemption has specified to
be a history of salvation. Integrating itself with the natural turn of the seasons,
the Christian liturgy has passed through seasons of anticipation and fulfillment,

175

of penance and rejoicing, of ordinary times and times considered special. The beginning is Advent, which comes late in the fall in the Northern hemispheres where the liturgy grew up. The days grow short. The air passes from the crispness of midautumn to the cold of winter, when it touches one's marrow. Once the leaves have fallen from the trees, a mood of melancholy tends to set in. The old year is dying. At the end of October, the Church celebrates the feast of All Saints, as though to wrap up what five-sixths of the year have been about. With the coming of November, thoughts turn to All Souls, the myriad departed who constitute the Church suffering and the Church triumphant, extending the Christian community into the past and the future, into its memory of exemplars and family members who have passed faith along and into its hopes for heavenly glory.

This remembrance fits the mood of November. Thanksgiving is not a European or native Catholic feast, so little has stood between All Souls and the beginning of the new liturgical year at Advent, four weeks before Christmas. People can let the old year wind down. They can enter into the melancholy of the mortality nature shows everywhere, into the analogies to the human span. Despite the biblical projection of three score years and ten as the human lifetime, in most periods of Christian history living to the age of fifty years was a considerable achievement. Indeed, following Aristotle, Aquinas and much of the tradition thought that reaching the age of fifty accredited one to start passing judgment on how human beings ought to live. At fifty experience was rich enough to set one up as an ethicist or sage, if one was so minded.

Advent brings to mind John the Baptist, the precursor of Christ, carrying the longing epitomized by late November around a corner, where it might pick up hope. John announced the need for repentance. Putting the axe to the roots of their sin, people might turn around, be converted, start to open themselves to the solution their painful appreciation of the human problematic implicitly carries. As Advent picks up speed, the liturgical antiphons play with the titles of messianic hope furnished in the Hebrew Bible. The one coming, the anointed savior, will turn the darkness of death into God's undying light. He will be a refining fire, a champion of justice, the fulfiller of the hopes of the poor, of the *anawim* whom God has long kept as the apple of his eye.

The mood of Advent mixes purification, sharper attention, and eager expectancy. When Christmas arrives, to celebrate the birth of the Messiah, what had been only the shortest day of the year, the nadir of humanity's distance from the Sun of Justice, becomes a pivotal point. As if to stress the paradoxes of God's redemptive ways, a baby appears in the dead of the year to establish apparent powerlessness as God's chosen mode of salvation. God blesses the poor, represented by Mary and Joseph, with visits from the powerful, the Magi. The shepherds keeping watch represent all decent humanity, on the lookout for God's help. In the person of Herod one can see the enemies of God, those who want darkness and brutal power to prevail. But as Jesus grows up full of wisdom and grace before God and his fellow human beings, one sees that darkness and brutal power hear their death knell. A new principle has come into the world, as intimate as people's own flesh. So Christian imagination turns the Mother and Child into regal icons. From the moment the Word takes flesh, pitching his tent in our midst, the angels of God shout for joy.

Between the peak of Christmas and the greater peak of Easter lie commemorations of other aspects of the incarnational mystery and then the forty days of Lent. Lent is like Advent in being a time of purification and preparation, but its mood is more somber. For Lent only anticipates Easter and the Resurrection by remembering Good Friday and the death of Christ. The sins of humankind responsible for Good Friday and the death of Christ make all honest Christians take stock. If they have contributed to the death of God, as they have, there is much in their histories, on their consciences, for which they should do penance and make amends. The fasting and abstinence from meat traditionally stipulated for Lent have been attempts to bring such penance and amendment home to the body. The call to spend more time in prayer, to meditate on one's sins, to renew one's expressions of gratitude to Christ on the cross, should bring an upturn of religious devotion.

Holy Week, from Thursday to Sunday, is the dramatic climax of Lent and the epitome of the entire liturgical year. Jesus giving himself to his followers under the figures of the bread and wine of his farewell meal and washing their feet reveals both the means he has fashioned to abide with them, as the nourishment of their souls, and the mentality he wants them to exhibit, which is one of selfless service. This modeling carries on through Good Friday, where the paradoxes of God gain a sharp edge. How can one call good the day on which all purity and goodness were brutalized, the day on which the enfleshment of God's love was done to death? Only by accepting the law of the cross that God has made statutory for redemption. Only by seeing in the way of the cross the undoing of the hatred and violence that have kept humanity at war and in tears since time out of mind. Christ is saying that love is stronger than hatred. He is saying that love can absorb hate and defang it. He triumphs over Satan by letting Satan do his worst and smothering that worst in a more creative, more powerful, more primordial reality: the love that moves the stars.

On Easter Sunday the full import of this love bursts forth. Love is stronger than death as well as hate. The love of God reaches down into the grave and snatches God's man away, for it could not be that God would desert his champion, his witness, his Son. So Christ resurrected blazes with supernal glory. So the disciples' weeping and lamentation turn to joy and human time becomes a comedy. The women at the tomb are the first to enter into this joy, as they had been the last to part from Christ in his sufferings on the cross. The word of the risen Jesus to Peter that Peter is to show his love for his Lord by feeding the

Lord's flock puts the institutional implications in a nutshell, as Paul realized when the Risen One told him that to persecute the Church was to persecute its living Lord.

The paschal mystery holds center stage for fifty days, rising to another climax at Ascension Thursday and Pentecost Sunday, when Jesus enters the domain of heaven once and for all and sends the Spirit in testimony to his Lordship. The ordinary time that stretches from Pentecost to the next Advent proceeds under the guidance of the Spirit, whom Jesus has given the disciples as a second Paraclete, one who will continue the encouragement and teaching he himself provided. Many weekdays during ordinary time celebrate the faith of outstanding saints — martyrs, virgins, confessors — who in their day extended the incarnation and showed what the whole Church might be. Their lives of intense prayer and self-sacrifice for their neighbors sum up Christ's twofold commandment of love. That is ordinary holiness: love under the Spirit. That is divinization, sanctification, and redemption in one. That is the germ, the crux, the climax of personal time. To become a lover of God, a saint, is the only calling, the only exegesis of personal time, that the liturgical cycle finds to matter in God's sight.

The Eucharist

The Eucharist to which Catholic Christians have been called each Sunday, as a matter of obligation as well as privilege, has been the weekly reminder and summary of the full liturgical cycle. There the redemption lavishly displayed over fifty weeks graciously condenses itself into a Sunday hour. The various parts of the Sunday Eucharist both cooperate to create that condensation and send out lines of connection to all the ramifications and roots of redemption that any serious Christian would want to investigate. So the scriptural readings featured in the first part of the Eucharistic ceremony (Mass) call to mind saints from the Old Testament and New Testament periods who witness to what faith entails. They, the various opening prayers, and the sermon ideally bring people to focus on their need for forgiveness and their privilege of praising God for his great acts of salvation and mercy.

Indeed, the *magnalia Dei* (great deeds of God) dominate the liturgical use of scripture. For the entire people assembled in church on Sunday, scripture should be what monks and other people of serious prayer have made of it each day: *lectio divina*. The "divine reading" of scripture proceeds slowly, addressing the heart even more than the mind. When done well in the Sunday church, it gives the entire assembly an object lesson in how to take God's word to heart and let it nourish one's soul, one's imagination, one's wellsprings. The result of a lifetime of faithful attendance at the liturgy is a treasury of images and stories reminding people of how Jesus spoke, worked miracles, asked for faith, rewarded faith, suffered from those opposed to the reign of God, and consistently enfleshed God's love.

Even the illiterate have taken home catchy phrases and stirring, riveting images. Even they have ruminated on the folly of the prodigal son, who spurned his father's household and rushed off to spend his inheritance in the fleshpots. But then "he came to himself." Finally he woke up, as all the slothful and sinful have to do, if they are not to miss God's meaning for them. When the father rushed out of the house and met the boy on the road, when he threw his arms around him and ordered up the party, with rings for the boy's fingers and a fatted calf, one saw vividly how our Father always is, how clearly the initiative always comes from him, how nothing can separate us from his love. Even the grumpy elder brother, resentful that the father's love broke the banks of what he considered justice and flowed out to save a sinner gratis, has taught us a useful lesson. Human beings tend to live comparatively and competitively, ignoring the freedom and cooperation God wishes. We tend to sour at the good fortune of others and so not imitate God, who makes the sun shine and the rain fall on just and unjust alike.

Such lessons come to laser intensity when the Eucharistic celebration moves into the canon of the Mass, where the sacrifice of Christ that showed God's nonpareil love once and for all gathers people into an anamnesis, a recollection that makes the death of Christ contemporary, makes it bore into existence here and now. The Eucharistic prayers rehearse both the need of the human race for this sacrifice of love and the mood of obedience in which Jesus offered it. At the moment of the consecration, when the Holy Spirit both effects and specifies the presence of Jesus in the elements of bread and wine, the second aspect of the sacramental ritual moves to center stage. Christ come as bread and wine manifestly wants to give himself as the nourishment of his followers' deepest selves. He wants to accomplish the abiding that the gospel of John enjoins, to work in the disciples' souls a sharing of divine life. The Father to whom the Eucharistic prayer ascends and the Spirit who moves over the gifts of bread and wind (emblematic of all of human life) are present, as Christ (both priest and victim) makes the Eucharistic prayer and accomplishes the communion with those he has not called servants but friends.

It is all there, the entire drama of salvation, the whole content of the Gloria and Creed. There is the motif of creation, as the water and wine, the bread and oil, the candles and incense communicate God's grace, forward God's plan (mysterion). There is the motif of redemption, as the story of Christ's love, climaxing in the death and Resurrection, occupies the central panel. Divinization comes through people's communing with Christ, and with it comes the

Trinity. Appropriate prayers provide for confession of sin, repentance, and reconversion to the grace of God so lavishly displayed in Christ. The words of scripture, and the sacramental actions of the Eucharistic rite, are all revelatory, tying what people hear and see to the enfleshment of God's Word in Jesus of Nazareth. The social theory of Christianity is concretized in the very assembling of the community, for nowhere is the Church more itself, more the Body of Christ, than at its Eucharistic worship.

Indeed, the word "liturgy" itself means "the work of the people." Above all, the task that one accepts on entering the Church emerges as the obligation to worship God by praying with one's sisters and brothers. And what is to be the primary motif of one's communal, Church-defining worship? The word "Eucharist" itself holds the answer. Eucharist means "thanksgiving." Christians ought first of all to be people whose hearts are full of gratitude to God, whose hearts overflow with thanksgiving for the great things God has done, the nearly incredible love God has shown in Christ Jesus, His Son and their Lord.

Nor are the ethical and missionary motifs lacking. The scriptural readings recall Jesus' teachings, the teachings of Paul, and the teachings of the Old Testament masters. They stipulate both how people are to think and how people are to behave. More holistically, the entire Eucharistic action is a demonstration of how people ought to behave: as though they are members of one another, as though the center of themselves and their time is worship of God, as though the holy love of God circulating in their midst is the realist thing in creation, making sin a chimera, something hardly worth considering.

At the end of the Eucharistic service the people go forth with a blessing. The traditional "Ite, Missa est" (Go, the Mass is ended) has missionary overtones. For Christ sent his disciples forth to spread the word to the ends of the earth and baptize in the name of the Father, the Son, and the Holy Spirit, initiating newcomers into divine life. The Eucharistic assembly, which full Church membership entitles people to share, is both the goal of such activity and its impulse. Thus the Eucharistic assembly tells the Church that whenever its attention wanders from publishing the good news of Christ—by worship, social service, and missionary activity—to self-concern, it is losing its creativity, not listening to the Spirit who came to it in tongues of fire.[1]

Sacraments of Initiation

In the Catholic scheme, baptism and confirmation serve to initiate people into divine life and Church membership. Traditional Catholic teaching, following the views of Augustine on original sin, made the baptism of infants customary, the faith of the parents and assembled community supplying for the incapacity of the little one to fashion a personal act of commitment. Augustine taught that the unbaptized were so separated from God that death would find them unfit for eternal happiness. Baptizing infants therefore seemed both logical and imperative. On the other hand, in the centuries immediately after Augustine, adult converts tended to postpone their reception of baptism, wanting to save the full remission of sins that baptism conferred until they had a life's worth of sins to submit. At the Protestant Reformation the Anabaptists (rebaptizers) argued that only the mature ought to undergo baptism, lest faith be reduced to a cultural convention. The Council of Trent rebutted their views, reaffirming the practice of infant baptism.

More important than this question of when the Church should administer baptism is the symbolism and significance of the rite itself. Building on Jewish precedents (the baptism of Gentile proselytes during Passover), and recalling Jesus' baptism by John, the early Christian communities developed a rite of lustration to signify the candidate's cleansing from sin, entrance upon divine life, and rebirth into total cleanliness. The hold Satan had on the candidate, infant or adult, came free in the solvent waters. The Holy Spirit entered the new Christian, as a new principle of divine life. In Pauline terms, baptism was a descent with Christ to the depths of death and a rising to new godly life. Baptism by immersion made this symbolism plain. The person plunged under the waters and emerged like a new creation. Going down and rising up set a pattern for all subsequent thought about sin and grace. The realm of grace was the above of heaven and the upward thrust of the human spirit toward transcendence. The realm of sin was the stolid, heavy, spirit-binding force-field of the flesh, the whole body-spirit composite resistant to God.

Insofar as the baptismal rite truly communicated the overtones of an initiation, it implied entrance upon a life engaged with the Christian mysteries. Both the mystery religions of the Hellenistic world contemporary with the rise of Christianity and the Gnostic sects emphasized an increasing illumination. Baptism therefore gained the aura of the first stage in an ongoing Christian **gnosis**. The Spirit and trinitarian life come together at baptism brought the soul into an eternal community of light and love. Baptism was a pledge, a down payment, on a life of sanctification that ought more and more to take over the person's being — mind, heart, soul, and strength. The Christian mysteries radiated from Christ, as the celebration of the liturgy dramatized. Yet the triumph of grace over sin and sharing in the divine trinitarian life were equally basic.

One could consider the Church the community of those celebrating the Christian mysteries, riveted to God's plan of salvation. Equally, one could consider the sacraments of the Church rich conduits of further progress in the life that the Christian mysteries entailed. That was a life of faith, hope, and above all love. It was a life that could bless creation, space, and time but still consider heaven its truest citizenship. The little baby squawking as the representative of the community poured water on its forehead and baptized it in the name of the Father, the Son, and the Holy Spirit, became a member of the Body of Christ whose head sat at the right hand of the Father. The Spirit believed to have come into the little one's soul signed it for eternity, making it more precious than anything earthly.

Recently Catholics have tended to confer the sacrament of confirmation as a rite marking a teenager's coming to age, but historically the Church has developed several different theological views and pastoral practices. Confirmation has clear links with baptism and the Eucharist, making the separation of baptism, first Communion, and confirmation somewhat dubious. In this perspective, confirmation merely fortifies the cleansing and divinization accomplished in baptism and so further qualifies the person for participation in the Eucharist, where he or she should find regular nourishment. A second viewpoint has stressed the different stages of the Christian life cycle, with its attendant implications for psychological maturation. In this perspective first Communion appropriately introduces school-age children to the nourishment of their faith, whereas confirmation should consummate their preparation for such adult responsibilities as witness to their faith.

The sacraments of initiation depend for their efficacy on two different accomplishments. What one might call the inner source of their efficacy is the action of God, which makes any sacrament (any official act of the Church designed to communicate divine life) intrinsically effective. Christ, the Spirit, and the Father in concert cannot fail to inform the recipients and strengthen their spirits, regardless of how the ministers of the sacrament, the community assembled, or even the subjects themselves behave. In adults God does not override people's freedom. God does not force people to accept a love they want to reject. But failing explicit rejection, active unbelief, or hatred, the sacrament does good.

However, what one might call the outer source of efficacy is precisely the ministers, community, and recipients involved. What they believe, how they speak, how they pray, the beauty or ugliness of the ritual they create, and the vitality or torpor of the community all leave their mark. The very incarnationalism of Christianity that the sacraments extend requires that this be so. Dealing with embodied spirits, with beings whose psyches are formed by signs and feelings and whose faith is colored by their psychic states, it could not be otherwise. Dealing with social beings, who constantly influence one another toward belief or unbelief, it has to be that the community — parents, friends, neighbors — will have an impact.

One truly can see why sacramental theology frequently fascinates those concerned about the formation of a Christian community (for both worship of God and service of humanity). Sacramental theology often fascinates those who are interested in symbolism, theater, and the communication of insights that can change people's lives. The sacraments carry the potential to make Christianity a thing of neural patterns, active imagination, deep wells of tradition from which people can draw the metaphors with which they make their meaning. When baptism is experienced as credible, moving, and beautiful, it stirs the faith of all involved. If the way the child is handled, loved, and set before the community as a person of infinite worth embarking on the best of destinies makes the Christian conception of divinization persuasive, the community of saints begins to assemble. People remember that they have received their faith from a long line of forebears and pledge themselves to help this little representative of the next generation enter into the rich heritage. The child no longer is simply the son or daughter of Mary and John Doe. The child becomes a blessing and responsibility given by God to all assembled, to the entire community of faith.

When this same child approaches Eucharistic Communion for the first time, or is confirmed, or marries, or receives holy orders, the same rules, emotions, potentialities apply. The sacraments either create a community of faith, a warm circle of common celebration and responsibility, or they miss their mark. Christian faith is all for one and one for all. The one is Christ, the Church, the common life and faith. It brings the many together into something hyperpersonal, into what the fathers of the Church called "the whole Christ." Equally, Christian faith is one for all, making the Body of Christ intent on the flourishing of every member in freedom and love.

Thus the sacramental community is light years away from the Church considered as just another of the world's too many institutions. The sacramental community has no instinct for self-preservation other than what comes from spending itself for the more abundant life of its individual members. Wealth and power are so marginal to the self-conception of the genuine sacramental community that it has to be a Church of the poor in spirit, of those who wait upon the Lord for all their increase. Thus the sacraments point to the political science Christian faith ought to develop, one as far from the *Realpolitik* dominating the world as Jesus was from Pontius Pilate.

Sacraments of Reconciliation

If the Eucharist carries a primary symbolism of nourishing faith, whereas baptism and confirmation carry a primary symbolism of initiation, penance and anointing carry a primary symbolism of reconciling sinners to God, to the Christian community, to the particular people they have offended, and to themselves. The sacrament of anointing also signifies preparation for death and passing into God's keeping, but the weakness afflicting the body of the one anointed necessarily recalls spiritual weaknesses and so the need for reconciliation.

Catholics have long spoken of penance as "confession." It is the sacrament during which one confesses one's sins to a representative of the Church for the mediation of the forgiveness God has promised those who repent and believe afresh. The psychology of confession is remarkable, though often obscured or misunderstood. For penance recognizes that one of the greatest needs that grips fallible, sinful human beings is for ways to make amends, to gain fresh starts, to say "I'm sorry," "I want to do better," "I love you." When it has escaped moralism and legalism, confession has brought immense stores of healing and joy.

Sin imports suffering. The individual sinner is a house divided, as is the community that sin afflicts. Even when sins seem quite private — matters of sexual transgression, dishonesty, or sloth — they retain a communal dimension. At the least, others do not receive the signs of peace and love that a good conscience creates. But frequently sins are palpably social, clearly connecting with such great evils as poverty, sickness, warfare, and despair. The lying, the fraud, the abuse of influence, the slumlording, the malpractice, and the cynicism displayed on the front pages each week suggest the social face of sin.

Repentance and reconciliation therefore enclose a great social potential. When people return to Christ's twofold commandment of love, recommitting themselves to treating their neighbors like other selves, they glimpse the heart of a healthy community and culture. One neither sins nor prays alone. Always the tides of the whole Church, the eddies of the whole culture, are washing around.

Still, Catholic tradition has considered individual sinners the only ones competent to pass judgment on their sins, (some might need help in understanding their consciences). In proper perspective, penance has been less concerned with lists of bad thoughts and spiteful deeds than with what the person has made of the gift of faith, how his or her dialogue with the Spirit has been going. Certainly, the deeds that come to mind in any honest examination of conscience have an objective significance. But the pattern of the deeds, unfolding from week to week, is more significant, because in the pattern lies the person's direction.

The gross sins that penance purges reveal a sorry ignorance of why God has given one time, faith, and spirit. They also reveal the weakness of our sorry flesh, which can fail even a willing spirit. An unwilling, recalcitrant spirit is a more profound problem, as we see when we discuss mortal sin.

For those not enmeshed in gross sins, not committing theft, adultery, genuine blasphemy and the like, penance can assist a move to the illuminative phase of the spiritual life, where the task is making the truths of faith one's own. Then one realizes the toll exacted by inadvertence, by failure to pray, by sloth, by the worldliness gushing from the newspapers and ruling most places of work. But illumination does not come unless one opens to the Spirit, immerses oneself in the Bible and the tradition, feeds regularly at the Eucharistic table. In illumination the mind and heart take center stage. One acknowledges that what one is is more significant than who one knows, what one owns, and the status that others bestow.

What one is certainly shows and is informed by one's actions, especially those through which one takes a stand. But it also shows and is informed by the thoughts one has at daybreak or midnight, when one's spirit is ravenous for meaning, when the bogies of doubt and dread rise up. The illuminative aspects of penance run not merely to the good advice of a wise confessor but more fundamentally to the Spirit's instructing one in the feebleness of self-sufficiency, the vanity of worldliness. For unless Qoheleth's "vanity of vanities" has resonated in one's own soul, one's penance will be superficial, one's need for grace will be more verbal than profound.

We take up the matter of the unitive life, where penance continues to be relevant, when we deal with Catholic mysticism. Here let us attend to what anointing adds to the reconciliation we have been describing. Perhaps the first thing we should say is that anointing makes it clear that the first reconciliation is that of the person to God. As God is the source of our being, the inmost definer of our selves, so our relation to God is the most significant thing about us. The Danish Lutheran religious thinker Søren Kierkegaard put this quite exactly when he defined the self as a relation to the absolute. True, this relation to the absolute never loses its social, communitarian aspects, as we have been at pains to assert. The person suffering what seems mortal illness carries much baggage that only the Church, in the persons of the minister of the sacrament and those attending, can represent. But the great mystery in any individual life is how one stands with God. This is the mystery death spotlights and never removes. We pass out of life hoping, not knowing, that God finds us acceptable. If God should keep offenses, should cling to injuries, who could endure it? All have sinned and fallen short of the glory of God. Few have prayed, helped others, and loved as they might have, as they wished. So all long for a balm that would soothe their guilt and ease their faith. All seek a peaceful ending, reconciled to the death the mystery requires.

The span of human beings is so short, when viewed from near its end, that one boggles that we human beings find it so hard to keep eternity before us. Yet we do. Every day we conspire to blunt the force of death, to deny our mortality and the demand it makes that we not dribble away our little flask. The last sacrament, anointing, would make even our inability to attend, to stay serious, well. Thereby, it would make all manner of thing well, for if we could heal the fears and weaknesses that make death so terrifying, we would feel saved. Then all manner of thing lost could be found, redeemed, woven by God back into the fabric of providence.

The art of dying is the art of commending one's spirit into God's hands. That is what could make dying a homecoming, a retelling of the story of the prodigal son. If one could come to oneself, in a last reflective movement of the spirit where one's whole being came clear and was accomplished, there might be rings and a banquet, a parent with open arms and a warm smile. Amazing grace indeed.

Marriage and Orders

The sacraments of initiation, which on some accountings include the Eucharist, stress a positive view of time. Baptism, confirmation, and the Eucharist all assume that God has anointed human flesh for a shared journey, a marital adventure, in which divinity itself will be the major partner and greatest nurture. The sacraments of reconciliation bring life's negatives into view. Personal sin and mortality raise questions about the justice of God, even about the anger of God, and send all thoughtful people to their knees petitioning God's mercy. The sacraments that deal with the marital and clerical states reassert the Catholic sense that grace perfects nature. By considering the ceremony in which two people pledge themselves to a shared life of love and service, a sacrament, the Catholic community has blessed passion, children, and family life. By considering the ceremony in which men accept Church office (assignment to the ranks of those who formally preach, administer the sacraments, and preside over Church affairs) a sacrament, the Catholic community has blessed the requirements of its corporate life, its inevitable need to distribute authority and regularize key functions.

In the chapter on prayer we consider the contemplative life and the formal regimes that vowed religious have developed to foster it. Here we note that the ceremonies in which religious men and women have taken their vows approximate a sacramental ordination. In the chapter on feminism we consider the question of women's ordination, which recently has caused considerable reexamination of what consecration to Christian ministry ought to entail. We should note here that the great gap in traditional Catholic spirituality has been the neglect of single people. Married people, priests, and religious have fared quite well. They have had sacraments, official ceremonies, and institutional attention that made it clear where they stood in the Body of Christ and how their status might be a pathway to sanctity. But single people, both those never married and those widowed or divorced, have fared less well. No positive ceremonies geared to their situations have helped clarify their religious potential. Little profound elaboration of baptism, confirmation, the Eucharist, penance, and anointing has made these sacraments bear on the prayer or active service single people might develop. Therefore the chapter on personal ethics pays special attention to the spiritual potential of single people.

The Catholic view of marriage has been more ambiguous than one would like. On the one hand, whenever groups arose to denounce the flesh, sexuality, marriage, family life, and the goodness of the world, Catholic tradition rose up to rebut them. In virtue of the Incarnation, the teaching of Jesus, and the practice of the Church from earliest times, all decent employments of human flesh were considered to partake of the goodness Genesis said God had seen in creation. On the other hand, Catholic tradition so praised religious life and celibacy that it made marriage a second-class vocation. Authoritative sources said that consecrated virginity was a higher state than marital commitment, supposedly because it focused more directly on God, actually because in many periods Church leaders took the tainted view that sexuality and women took men away from God. In addition, the Catholic theology of marriage developed the notion that marriage had two principal ends or goals, procreation and the mutual love of the spouses, and that procreation was more primary. Inevitably this biologized marital love, all the more so when Augustinian emphases linked sexual intercourse to original sinfulness. The result was spouses' receiving little official help with their desire to make their lives an erotic adventure in which God would increasingly become the depth and goal of their fire.[3]

Nonetheless, common sense, some theological trends, and pastoral experience have provided elements of a Catholic theology of marriage in which the demands of heterosexual sharing and parenthood have created a great schooling in virtue. Enough lay saints have modeled marital holiness to suggest that prayer, or even willingness to die for the faith, could flourish in a busy family. Enough ordinary married people have shown their love for the Church through constant commitment, financial support, and wise counsel to remind priests and bishops that the clergy ought mainly to facilitate laypeople's growth.

The Catholic conception of orders has kept close ties to Catholic convictions about the Petrine ministry and the structures Christ left his Church. One can argue that these convictions need not have taken the specific historical forms they did. There was no intrinsic reason for the successors of Peter to become Supreme Pontiffs on the order of the high priests of pagan Rome. There was no intrinsic reason for the Church to exclude women and married men from orders or for canon law to make great distinctions between the clerical and lay states. Catholicism could have so stressed the common baptism of all believers that they emerged more alike than different, whatever their functions in the Church. It could have used Pauline imagery (I Corinthians 12) to keep all Church members humble about their need for one another. But it did not, in part because of its rightful preoccupation with those who were to lead the Eucharistic worship and preside over the major decisions facing the local Christian community.

From this concern arose the Catholic stresses on authority, discipline, and obedience. They have contributed to the ability of Roman Catholicism to maintain itself relatively whole and not fly apart into hundreds of different churches, as Protestantism did. But they have exacted a high price from priests and laity alike. Clerical Church leaders could look down on the laity, in the worst case considering them merely a source of money. Higher authorities could neglect ordinary priests, treating them like lackeys far down the chain of command. In the name of hierarchalism and God-given authority, Catholicism could resemble nothing so much as a monarchical realm in which most of the faithful were peasants.

The happier potential in the Catholic understanding of orders, which holy priests and bishops realized in every age, was a ministerial corps free to make service of the faithful its meat and drink. Buoyed by the Spirit given in orders, priests regularly have shared the pains and joys of their people, spending themselves to console myriad ordinary believers, offering kindly wisdom and good example. The Catholic identification of the priest with the sacraments could mystify his humanity and make him too sacral a figure, but it gave him the chance to touch people in their depths, because in hearing their confessions, baptizing their children, anointing them for their final encounter with God, and helping prepare them for marriage, the priest represented Christ, to whom the faithful might open their inmost fears and hopes.

Representative Personality: Kurt Reinhardt

When we authors considered who might personify the patterns of Catholic worship treated in this chapter, a personal acquaintance came to mind. Unlike the saints treated in other chapters, this individual has not been formally canonized. Yet we are certain he is one of the saints, one of the vibrant members of the Body of Christ (as the New Testament thinks about sanctity), and the centrality of the Eucharist in his life makes his story emblematic of Catholic Christianity.

When we first met him, Kurt Reinhardt was a professor emeritus of German at Stanford University. He was then about seventy-five years old, widowed, childless, a prime candidate for loneliness and depression. Yet few people in the Catholic community at Stanford enjoyed richer lives. He had come to the United States from Germany in the 1930s, realizing that Hitler and National

Socialism were making life impossible for him there. He had come to Catholicism from **agnosticism**, having been raised in an unreligious family. His conversion to Catholicism had come while he was recuperating from tuberculosis, and it had inevitably made him a foe of the Nazis.

Kurt had wonderful stories from his university days, when his professors had included Martin Heidegger, the great philosopher, and his fellow students had included Herbert Marcuse, a guru to American Marxists during the late 1960s and early 1970s. Kurt would tell of befriending the son of Thomas Mann and visiting the Mann family in Zürich, seeing where the novelist had composed his masterpieces. He would tell of emigrating to Canada with an idealistic religious group, working on their newspaper, taking home galley sheets to fortify his wife and himself when they huddled in bed against the fierce cold.

But these stories only came later, when we had gotten to know Kurt well enough to be invited regularly to his little studio apartment in a retirement home. Initially we noticed him at daily mass and occasionally visited the courses he gave at the Newman Center. These courses, like his conversations and library, reflected his wide range of interests. He would take up philosophers such as Nietzsche and Kierkegaard, dramatists such as Ibsen and Strindberg, theologians such as Karl Rahner and Edward Schillebeeckx. Inevitably, however, he would also talk about faith, growing old, and what the Church ought to be doing.

Once when Kurt was dealing with the book of Job he got into a painful situation. In the audience was a young father who had lost a child to a congenital disease. The father was willing to bracket the question of God's justice and keep struggling to believe, but Kurt's exegesis of Job, which had stressed Job's "though he slay me, yet will I trust him," put the father off. Out of anger and pain the father attacked Kurt, asking him what he knew about loss, how he dared to try to justify a God who would break parents' hearts. Kurt did not defend himself. He brought forward no mention of his time in the sanitorium, of his flight from Germany, of the loss of his wife. Kurt simply commiserated with the man and then confessed that, no matter what he saw or experienced, he felt obliged to grant God a blank check. His God had to be light in whom there was no darkness at all. His God had to be loving us in all circumstances, even when our pains would not let us suspect this could be so. As bystanders, we saw this conflict as a clash between two good people at different stages of the life cycle. One rightly was immersed in his struggle to build a family; the other was moving away from earthly ties, moving toward eternity.

Kurt's way of preparing himself for eternity was to read, reflect, and above all pray each afternoon at the community mass. Frequently he would read the scriptural lessons, and sometimes at the end of mass he would read a selection from a contemporary theologian, philosopher, or spiritual writer. But nine days out of ten he would make a greater impact by his coming early to pray and the

glow that suffused him when he took the host and cup. After the liturgy, outside
the church, he would joke with the women for a while, then put on his beret and
shuffle home to his apartment, half a mile away. Evenings with his friends were
important to him; he could not have made do without his books and writing; but
the center of his day clearly was the Eucharistic liturgy. The meeting he most
treasured was his tryst with Christ.

This meeting with the sacramental Christ is something distinctively Catholic,
although Eastern Orthodox piety is also deeply sacramental. Just as Roman
Catholics traditionally found it difficult to appreciate why Protestants so treasured the Bible, Protestants traditionally found it difficult to appreciate the
Catholic sense of the Eucharist. For example, there is the Catholic view of
the reserved sacrament. Although this is not as significant theologically as the
sacramental reception of Christ consummated in Communion, the Catholic
conviction that Jesus is present in the Tabernacle has shaped all Catholics'
attitudes toward being in church.

Indeed, the Catholic church on the corner has been not only the place where
one assembled each Sunday to fulfill one's obligation and join with fellow
believers in worship but also the place where one could slip in to visit the Christ
present in the tabernacle on the altar. The vigil light (a candle enclosed by glass)
that burned night and day signaled this presence. It said Jesus was always willing
to listen, encouraging people to pour out their troubles, reorient themselves,
regain possession of a self dispersed through rush and work.

In recognition of Christ's presence in the tabernacle, Catholics would genuflect on entering and leaving the church. To enter a Protestant church and not
do this made them feel out of place, whereas to forget where they were and
genuflect in a Protestant church was embarrassing. Ecumenical sensitivity has to
trade in such little customs as these. It has to ease Christians' way to feeling at
home in one another's churches, probably by mixing accommodation to visitors
on ecumenical occasions with the expectation that visitors will respect the
customs of the host church and try to share them.

Once we entered a Catholic church in Denver, as a break from an academic
visit. The church was typically quiet and cool, with the smell of wax and incense
one associates with Catholic worship. The pale winter light was warmed by its
passage through high stained glass windows. The garish statues on the side altars
called to mind both the problems iconographic religions have with taste and the
need for one generation to be tolerant of the piety of its forebears. We walked to
the center of the church, surveyed the marble altar, looked back to view the rose
window and organ loft, and then made our way out. On the way, we noticed
that a woman had entered after us. She was kneeling with her head bowed and
as we passed we saw tears rolling down her cheeks. Something in her posture
said her tears were expressing troubles no stranger could take away. Something
told us that she was crying from the heart and for the general woe of the world.

In one of his plays the poet T. S. Eliot has a woman confess that what most troubles her is not her own brokenness but a horrible suspicion that the whole world, reality itself, is out of kilter. We have no certainty that the woman crying in the church in Denver was thinking similar thoughts. Trouble with her kids, or losing her job, or having come from visiting a friend in the hospital would have more than sufficed. Catholic churches have served people well simply by being refuges from such daily bruises and worries. But collectively Catholic churches have also served as refuges from the brokenness of reality itself. Their quiet has contested the noise of the city. Their peace has stood against the hectic pace, the constant pressure, the overconcern dominating so many lives. The scenes on their walls, the stations of the cross, and, above all, the crucifix over the altar have said that God has dealt with the brokenness of the world. The flickering vigil lamp, the echoing organ music, and the stained glass have reoriented people's sight and sound.

Thus many Catholics came to love their churches. In a strange city or a foreign country, they would visit a church to enjoy a short stay at home. To kneel and pray, letting the quiet recollect one's spirit, was to take a welcome break. To muse about the confessionals along the side aisles was to recall past sins, guilt, fear, and great relief. Thus Catholic churches could become mystagogic, stirring people's sense of the holy. Thus they drew many men like Kurt Reinhardt, many women like the one we saw weeping, who had deep needs and gifts.

Once Kurt found a faith he could embrace, a home for his large mind and heart, he was nearly bound to become a frequenter of churches. Once he appropriated the Eucharist as the daily form of Catholic piety, he was nearly bound to think of his local church as the center of his religion. Whatever loneliness he experienced seemed to leave him in church. Surely, like most other Christians, he believed God is everywhere, including the human heart. Surely he cherished the trinitarian life coursing within him. But he loved the Christ reserved in church, loved the space containing this Christ, and loved the quiet and the scents that helped him focus. Day by day, Kurt further immersed himself in this atmosphere. Day by day, his participation in communal Catholic worship seemed further to prepare him for eternity.

Glossary

Agnosticism: the position that one does not or cannot know about God, ultimate reality, and other crucial matters. Agnosticism may be a way-station between theism and atheism, but it can become entrenched.

Then people bracket the questions about origin and destiny that give the human spirit its deepest energy. The result tends to be a flattening of their spiritual lives and an entry upon secularism or even cynicism.

Gnosis: knowledge; intimate or even secret understanding. The Gnostics with whom early Christianity fought claimed a better grasp of salvation than what was communicated in the gospel. The mystery religions spoke of illumination that would bring immortality. Thus Christianity sometimes claimed that its saving truths constituted a God-given gnosis. In Pauline interpretation, however, this Christian gnosis boiled down to Christ crucified. The power and wisdom of God to which authentic Christians clung was nothing other than the death and Resurrection of Jesus.

Discussion Questions

1. What were the dangers in adapting the Christian liturgical cycle to the rhythms of nature?
2. What is the difference between Advent and Lent?
3. Why is the Eucharist the foremost Christian sacrament?
4. How does the Eucharistic symbolism of sacrifice relate to the symbolism of nourishment?
5. What do Catholics believe the action of God effects in baptism?
6. Sketch a Christian rite of passage from childhood to adulthood.
7. How should the sacrament of penance reconcile enemies?
8. Should the sacrament of anointing provide for the sick person's forgiving God?
9. How should the sacrament of marriage correlate personal love and procreation?
10. What are the principal qualities the Christian community ought to require of those it ordains to priestly ministry?
11. What qualifications should one put on the description of Catholic churches as refuges or sanctuaries?
12. How can Catholic theology of the reserved sacrament avoid magic?

Notes

[1] On the priorities and models of the Church, see Denise Lardner Carmody and John Tully Carmody, *Bonded in Christ's Love* (New York: Paulist, 1986).

[2] For good brief treatments of the various sacraments, see Joseph A. Komonchak, Mary Collins, and Dermot A. Lane, eds., *The New Dictionary of Theology* (Wilmington, Del.: Michael Glazier, 1987). For book-length treatments, see the series on the sacraments edited by Monika Hellwig and published by Michael Glazier.

[3] For recent Catholic views on marriage, see William P. Roberts, ed., *Commitment to Partnership* (New York: Paulist, 1987).

CHAPTER 11

Private Prayer

The Contemplative Life
Catholic Mysticism
Catholic Devotions
The Cult of the Saints
Representative Personality: Teresa of Avila
Glossary, Discussion Questions, Notes

The Contemplative Life

In a rough and ready description of the spiritual life, one begins by treating contemplation and action. They can be seen as expressions of Jesus' twofold commandment, contemplation directly expressing love of God and action directly expressing love of neighbor as self. On the other hand, reflection makes it clear that Christian actions or works also ought to be expressions of the love of God, whereas Christian contemplation ought to take to God all the neighbors needing God's help. So the single love that is our best index of God's life in us flows back and forth between God and our neighbor, between contemplation and action. Both aspects of the spiritual life finally boil down to trying to serve the mysterious affection God has shown us, the mysterious grace and destiny God has offered us.

We deal with the imperatives of Christian action in the next two chapters. Here the topic is contemplation, the simple regard of God that is the core of Christian prayer. As Catholic spirituality has traditionally understood it, prayer proper differs from meditation. To reflect on the content of faith, the doctrines and truths, or even the sayings of Jesus is merely to prepare oneself for prayer. Prayer proper commences when the focus shifts to God, whom the one praying regards as a personal center of understanding and love, and love flows forth from the heart. Such prayer can be carried by words, whether those of formulas consecrated by long usage or those the person composes spontaneously. Song, gesture, and dance can all convey one's love. But it is enough that the heart, the center of the person, goes out to God, or centers in God, and loves wordlessly, simply, holistically. It is enough that one actualize the "abiding" discussed in the Johannine literature, feeling or relying upon the indwelling of the divine persons.

The contemplative life roots in such experiences of simple prayer. As a term, "the contemplative life" may refer to the vocation of some religious to dedicate much of their time to prayer and live to some degree removed from activities in the world. It may also refer to all the vocations that require inwardness, reflection, and holistic appreciation of the divine mystery: art, writing, perhaps philosophy and theology, and similar callings. Let us consider both connotations of the term, because both have been important in Catholic Christianity.

The monastic impulse to quit the city, move into the desert, and let silence and solitude school one in God's ways was a quite pure expression of contemplative yearning. Granted, some of those who removed themselves into the desert were afraid of the temptations they were experiencing in the world. Rather than risk sin, they sought a simple life free of pleasure, wealth, and honors — free of Satan's snares. But the more powerful motivation, and the one that successful monks had to cultivate, was the beauty of God. Until they fell in love with the divine mystery, which they thought Christ had definitively both clarified and brought into their midst, they were only beginners. Beneath the asceticism, the silence, the apparently banal concern with diet and work, the greatest of the desert fathers and mothers were pursuing a love affair.

When the coenobitic (communal) life developed, contemplation remained the monk's raison d'être. The rules that monks and nuns followed were supposed to free them for intercourse with God. The trade-off made when the focus shifted from the desert solitaries to monastics grouped in communities was between an independence liable to self-deception and a regulated life liable to routinization if not mediocrity. Ideally, one advanced more quickly in a communal setting because the wisdom of the elders saved one from detours. The goal remained the same: holiness, being stripped of selfishness and joined to God. The choice was now between two different means, and for most contemplatives communal living was preferable to complete solitude.

Whether solitary or communal, however, contemplatives have sought a union with God that is more than their own perfecting. As the concern of most monastic communities with the liturgy shows, contemplative prayer has long been regarded as something done for the whole Church. One never ceased to be a member of Christ, a branch of the single vivifying vine. And one's prayer was always supposed to include at least implicit petitions that God would help all God's people, remembering their needs, forgiving their sins, increasing their good measure of grace so that it would become pressed down and overflowing. When theologians and popes spoke of the superiority of virginity and the

contemplative life, they had in mind both the directness with which this life
pursues the love of God and the directness with which it serves the Church's
primary need, access to the Holy Spirit.

Nonetheless, many official views of the contemplative life that the religious
were living gave the impression that life in the world was second-rate or
dangerous. Balanced, cheerful contemplatives themselves might not have
thought this way, but some of the same fear of the body that influenced the
Catholic discipline requiring celibacy of all priests played into the mystique of
consecrated contemplation. When that happened, the incarnate, sacramental
Christ got short shrift. Certainly a healthy contemplation greatly deepened the
Church's appreciation of the Incarnation and the sacraments, but sometimes
removal, distancing oneself from matter and practical affairs, became an end in
itself, dangerously suggesting that holiness meant fleeing the body, human
relations, and even nature.

Contemplative life in the sense of the inwardness required of many creative
vocations needs only a personalizing focus on the divine mystery to make it a life
of prayer. When scientists contemplate the beauty or intelligibility of the physical world as something mysteriously whole, they stand in the vestibule of prayer
proper. When their hearts go out in love of such beauty, in gratitude for their
having been given minds with which to appreciate it, in petition that human
beings not destroy God's creation, they are praying to the one God, however
unawares. One can speak similarly of artists engrossed in their work and sensing
its ties to the mysterious whole of both matter and mind, of philosophers and
theologians who shift from the conceptual categories they have been refining to
let themselves regard God or being in its existential impact, as a primordial
whole. Psychologists reflecting at the end of a hard day, when the pains of their
patients have moved them to wonder about the cracks in reality itself, parents
marveling at the steady breathing of their little child and feeling their hearts
overflow, writers blessed by the muse and then giving her full obeisance, lovers
seeing through shining eyes to souls that seem sparks of infinity also stand at the
threshold of contemplative prayer, if indeed not across it.

One may love God contemplatively in a mental darkness, all images and
thoughts having been stripped away, only a naked, nearly imperceptible dart of
love going forth to penetrate the divine thickness, to cross the apparent void
tempting the lover to despair. One may also love God contemplatively by
dwelling within pictures: murals on church walls, icons, such as the Byzantine
masterpieces dealing with Mary and Jesus, scenes from scripture, such as John
baptizing Jesus, or natural scenes, such as ocean waves dashing against rugged
rocks, sending spray fifty feet into the air. The point in any contemplation of this
sort is simply to engage one's heart, the center of one's self, understanding, and
emotion, with the divine mystery, the whole of God's self hinted by mural, icon,
picture, or natural scene. So sacramental and apophatic (negative, naked) con-

templation are not enemies. The Spirit works in several ways, often leading the same person along now this and now that path.

Catholic Mysticism

In good part because of its corps of religious contemplatives, Catholicism has always respected mystical experience. Although Protestants might stress the dangers of mysticism, or deny that mysticism was compatible with the plain preaching and example of the evangelical Christ, to Catholics, the incontrovertible fact was that a prayer in which God seemed to seize their souls played a huge role in the lives of many of the saints. It was not difficult to make the case that God could seize a person directly, if God wished to do so. It made good sense that one could only deal with the living, true God if one accepted the divine mysteriousness. But for Catholics the most convincing argument was *a posteriori*: after the fact of mystical experience, denials, problems, and interpretations seemed secondary considerations. Virtually by definition, the experience was ineffable. The most one could do in speaking about it was to ward off errors, both speculative and practical.

The speculative errors included the pantheism that identified the core of the personality with God, taking literally figures of speech about divinization and union whose reality never fit into flat, propositional speech. The practical errors included the claim that mystical experience took one outside the realm of ordinary moral restraints, justifying actions that made one prideful, unwilling to serve the whole Church, unconcerned about the poor or life in the world. It was a speculative error to claim that mystical experience removed the need for the mediation of Christ or could not occur through Christ's symbolic representation of the divine mystery. It was a practical error to encourage promiscuous sexual love, or to condemn the flesh, or to follow private inspirations not squaring with long-standing tradition.

Still, the potential for such errors did not vitiate mystical experience itself, and masters spoke about how to dispose oneself for it. If one cultivated the virtues —faith, hope, charity; prudence, justice, fortitude, temperance—and prayed regularly, one might gain the grace of feeling God's touch. If one persevered through the changes in one's interior life, suffering the various weanings away from sensuality and personal gratification, one might advance toward naked contact. The whole enterprise—ascetical, contemplative, mystical—was a work of love. The whole enterprise correlated with the biblical Christ, who had suffered, prayed, felt abandoned, and knew the most intense, habitual union with God.

Insofar as their founders were mystics, the different Catholic religious orders tended to develop distinctive spiritualities that climaxed in distinctive mystical patterns. Thus the Cistercian mysticism of a Bernard of Clairvaux, which built on Benedictine monasticism, differed from the mysticism that Franciscans found in Francis of Assisi. Where Bernard had experienced a nuptial intimacy with God, Francis' union climaxed in the stigmata. Similarly, the Carmelite mysticism so fully and profoundly elaborated by Teresa of Avila and John of the Cross differed from the Jesuit mysticism typified by Ignatius of Loyola. Where the Carmelites had spoken of dark nights and interior mansions, Loyola spoke of being with Christ in his apostolic labors and sensing how all creation communicates heavenly love. It brought no profit to set these different spiritualities against one another, asking which was higher and which lower. Manifestly all shared the effects of a profound union with God, accomplished according to both the idiosyncrasies of the founding figure and the work proper to the particular religious group. It brought great profit to thank God for the rich diversity of grace he had lavished upon his most generous servants and to take home what lessons one could for one's own spiritual life.

Outside of the religious orders, Catholic mysticism was less perceptible, less "organized," but certainly not lacking. God alone knows how many little-noticed individuals, married and single, praying in corners of dark chapels or in the midst of housework, were drawn into the divine beauty and had their souls transformed. God alone knows how much praise, petition, suffering, and joy pulsated in the world because people of little account on the official Church registers kept faith with their devotions, or consecrated their difficult work, or emptied themselves on behalf of their families, neighbors, friends, the poor, and the sickly.

The Eucharist, which holds pride of place in Catholic spirituality, encouraged a sensible mysticism. Those who met Christ regularly in the sacrament nourishing their divine life were bound to believe that the simplest things, rightly contemplated, could reveal God and convey God's love. Bread and wine, even when thinned to the Communion wafer, could change one's sadness into joy. So insubstantial a food as the unleavened wafer could develop robust souls. As influential aids, the prayers of the Eucharistic liturgy, the music, the flowers, the smells all could work on one's spirit until, unpredictably yet frequently, one's cares fell away, one's needs shrank from view, and the only thing that mattered was God himself, present both indubitably and inexpressibly. There were many moments — in the rose garden, in the drafty church at smokefall, after the reception of the host — when time stopped. The Spirit took one outside time. Consolation came without previous cause. The peace and joy in one's heart were unearthly, surpassing the world's understanding.

As those who have not fallen in love cannot understand why lovers behave as they do, so those who have not experienced deep prayer cannot understand why people keep going back to their kneelers, to their solitary walks, to their favorite icons. In their lack of experience, outsiders might overesteem those who are drawn to contemplative prayer, thinking them angels and expecting their human foibles to melt away. Or outsiders might deride the whole venture, saying that plain virtue, solid good works, keeping one's feet on the ground and having a good heart were a better, safer way. The amusing aspect of any discussion of Catholic mysticism was how little anyone could say. As long as people preserved the commonly required faith and morals, great freedom could reign. After all, the Holy Spirit was the only effective teacher of prayer. Direction from those learned and experienced could help, but ultimately each person had to find the peculiar passage the Spirit had in mind. And just as one could only find a writing style by writing or a painting style by painting, so one could only find what prayer the Spirit had in mind by praying — regularly, steadily, in good times and bad.

Perhaps the most helpful advice one could glean from the masters, therefore, was the encouragement to persevere. When a master such as Père de Caussade spoke of holy abandonment, of putting one's whole life and self in God's hands and trusting that one could find no better care, many of those serious about the religious life heaved a sigh of relief and gratitude. When Saint Teresa approximated the same message by saying, "Let nothing disturb you," many others thought of Jesus' discourse about the lilies of the field and resolved to have more faith in God's goodness, God's providence, God's counting of every hair.

Still, serious prayer meant a frightening confrontation with one's own sinfulness. The closer the Spirit took one to Christ, the more one appreciated the abyss caused by Christ's unique sinlessness. Then the mercy of God became all important, nothing superfluous but a strict necessity. Then one saw that none of us is just apart from God's working our justification. Yet when these truths of faith arose in the soul because of the Spirit's direct inspiration at prayer, they bore telltale signs. They were not discouraging. They did not make prayer or morality seem impossible. Rather, they were cause for celebrating the goodness of God, the power of God to work through all human obstacles and weakness, the divine love that had gone out of its eternal self-possession and become the inmost stuff of creation, redemption, and divinization.

Catholic Devotions

As though to balance its high-flying mystical writings, Catholicism developed a wealth of devotions for the simple faithful, primary among which was the Rosary, a practice developed in medieval times by Cistercians and Dominicans.

This devotion, directed toward Mary, the Mother of God, consisted of a series of prayers usually counted on a string of beads. The three prayers involved— "Our Father," "Hail Mary," and "Glory Be"—were the most popular in the Catholic repertoire. Taken independently of the Rosary, they are among the first prayers that have sprung to mind when a Catholic has wanted to use a set formula for speaking to God, or when confessors have wanted to impose a light penance after sacramental confession, stipulating a certain number of prayers.

The "Our Father" is modeled on Jesus' own prayer, as reported in the New Testament (Mt 6:9–13, Lk. 11:2–4). First, it follows Jesus' own intimate diction in referring to God as one's Father. Second, it locates the Father in heaven, the abode of divine purity and fulfillment. Third, it hallows or blesses God's name, which in Jesus' semitic usage meant God's person. By blessing God, the person praying affirms that God, at least, is pure and holy, giving the world an unsullied center. Fourth, in praying that God's Kingdom come, the "Our Father" recalls Jesus' preaching of the Kingdom, which came down to the promise that God was at hand to make a realm of justice and love.

Fifth, in praying that God's will be done on earth as in heaven, the person implicitly submits to God's design for the world, for his or her own life, and for morality—what one is commanded to do and what is forbidden. Sixth, the "Our Father" asks for daily bread, which traditionally has been considered an epitome of all practical needs. Mindful of Jesus' example and promises, believers are to tell God all they need and leave their fate in God's hands. The seventh petition, for forgiveness of trespasses or sins, bears on reconciliation. The prayer sponsored by Jesus himself assumed that people regularly fail, seventy times seven, and so that their regular intercourse with God should include asking forgiveness for their sins and trusting that God will help them make a new start.

Eighth, this forgiveness is a two-way street, not in the sense that people praying are to forgive God any injuries they might lay to God's account, but in the sense that they are to forgive those who sin against them. This part of the Lord's Prayer or *Paternoster*, as the "Our Father" also has been called, recalls Jesus' teachings about love of neighbor and the need to forgive others if one wants to receive forgiveness oneself. Ninth, one prays not to be led into temptation and to be delivered from all evil, recognizing that the faith of a pilgrim is always in peril and always needs God's protection.

Because it is fashioned after Jesus' own prayer, the "Our Father" has had a special dignity in traditional Catholicism, as it has had in traditional Protestantism and Orthodoxy. Spiritual writers frequently offered meditations on its component parts, as they would offer meditations on the Creed. The simplicity of the prayer, its lack of esoteric dogma, its practical slant, and its focus on both trust in God and begging God's forgiveness all have commended it to busy, divided, sinful people, who mainly have thought of God as one sure to find them wanting. The slant of the Lord's Prayer was consoling, because it reminded people from the outset that God was their Father, more interested in their welfare than they were themselves. Today one might fill out the imagery of the Lord's Prayer with reflection on the divine motherhood, but we should note that in Jesus' culture the relation between fathers and sons was warmer, more emotional, than it has been in many other historical periods and cultures.

The prayers to Mary, which in the Rosary outnumbered the "Our Fathers" ten to one, supply a feminine balance to the masculine thrust of the Lord's Prayer. The "Hail Mary" or *Ave Maria* begins with the angel's salutation at the Annunciation, where the history of Christ commenced. One salutes Mary as full of grace and having the Lord with her. One calls her blessed among women and blessed in the fruit of her womb, Jesus. One goes on to praise Mary as holy and the Mother of God, and then asks for her prayers. Specifically one asks her to pray "for us sinners, now and at the hour of our death."

The "Hail Mary" is a brief prayer, therefore, but one full of hope. With Mary as one's intercessor, one could expect defense, help, before the throne of God. Mary was kindly, pure, the Mother that all children desired. Jesus would never deny her requests. Anything that had touched her heart was sure to touch his heart. Women have often identified with Mary as the paragon of their sex, who knows the troubles family life can bring, whose soul was pierced by sorrow, who experienced the depths of desolation at the Cross. Indeed, among Mary's many titles — "Queen of Heaven," "Star of the Sea" — "Sorrowful Mother" has stood out.

Men could think of the girl Mary, so pure God made her the mother of his only begotten Son. Their psyches could place in heaven a feminine grace, understanding, and compassion that made heaven more lovely. The many churches dedicated to Mary testify to the impact the cult of the Virgin has had throughout the Catholic centuries. The popularity of the Madonna in Christian painting offers the same message. Today feminists are reworking the Marian legacy, pointing to Mary's "Magnificat" (Lk 1:47–55), her faith, and other aspects of her strength to make her a herald of liberation and a model for strong Christian women.

The **doxology** "Glory be to the Father, and to the Son, and to the Holy Spirit," which has also figured in the Rosary, has brought an explicitly trinitarian perspective into popular Christian piety. The rest of this prayer, "as it was in the beginning, is now, and ever shall be," associates God with the fullness of time, suggesting that nothing unfolds apart from the divine will and plan. God is the Ancient of Days, from whose unbegotten depths all creation has issued forth. God is the Logos giving nature and history their meaning, and God is the Spirit leading human beings into their future, guiding them to an eschatological climax that can save time from futility, can bring time home for heavenly fulfillment.

These prayers, whether used alone or in concert to make a Rosary, have been the staff of Catholic piety. Imbibed with one's mother's milk, they have served as resources whenever simple people have grappled with the pains and joys of their lives in face of the divine mystery. Like the Creed, the Act of Contrition, and formulas memorized from the Catechism, they have put into the child's memory and imagination, as primal images, pictures that have made God, Christ, and Mary approachable. The many scenes from the gospels read out at Mass each Sunday have only extended and intensified these primal images.

Thus one praying the Rosary could concentrate on joyful, sorrowful, or glorious mysteries that dealt, respectively, with the ministerial life, sufferings, and resurrected life of Christ. People making the stations of the cross—the fourteen commemorations of Jesus' final hours adorning the walls of a Catholic church—have employed a similarly biblical imagination. The point in praying the mysteries of the Rosary or the stations of the cross has been to make oneself contemporary with the scene in question. One could be there in the Garden of Gethsemane, when Christ felt dread at the death he would undergo because of sins such as one's own. One could be there with Mary and the other women at the foot of the cross, when Christ died, or at the tomb when the women first began to suspect the miracle of the Resurrection, or at the Ascension when Christ returned to the Father. As a contemporary, one could tell Christ of one's sorrow, or one's joy, or one's desire to be more worthy of what Christ had done on one's behalf. One could console Mary, beg her help, praise her faith. Through these and many other devotions, traditional Catholics developed a lively religious imagination, filled with scenes on which they could draw as need and the Spirit prompted.

The Cult of the Saints

If orthodox faith has ordained that one is to worship only God, in obedience to the First Commandment, it yet has allowed one to venerate Mary and the saints. The veneration given to Mary has been unique, in recognition of her unique status as the Mother of God, the woman conceived without sin and assumed bodily into heaven. The veneration given the saints has been justified by the holiness of their lives, the way they have pointed beyond themselves to Christ and God. Few Catholics have confused either Mary or the saints with God. However it might have looked to outsiders, or whatever the merits of the view of anthropologists and specialists in the comparative study of religion that Mary has functioned as a goddess, enough of the basic Catechism has seeped into most Catholics' souls to make them well aware of the difference between worshiping God and praising or petitioning Mary.

When it settled the iconoclast controversy in favor of those who supported venerating the saints through icons, the Eastern Church relied on its sense of the Incarnation. Just as the Incarnation justified a sacramental system that would tutor the flesh that Christ had blessed, so the Incarnation justified a modest reliance on other human beings signal for their holiness, when one wanted either to contemplate what a model Christian life was like or to gain intercession before God. In taking flesh from Mary, the Logos had implied that flesh was worthy of God, could be divinized by God, could become a means of God's revelation. Nothing human was foreign to God, so nothing human ought to be foreign to God's children. Moreover, Christ had gathered a people to himself, founding a community that he served as head and spouse. The Spirit of God circulated through the members of Christ's Body, making them mutually dependent, parts of an organic whole.

Thus, the doctrine of the Communion of saints in the Spirit and Body of Christ sanctioned regarding the saints as sisters and brothers bound to feel kindly toward petitioners, anxious to forward the cause of Christ by helping people confess their sins, repair their lives, and grow in the grace God offered. Similarly, the example of the saints helped to explain the possibilities for sanctity that waited in any circumstance. Saints who had been married, or had been nobles, or had been kings showed that any station of life could become transparent to God. Saints who had been pilgrims, beggars, or poor people despised by society, living in rags, testified that God's judgments could differ greatly from the judgments of the world and that the beatitudes preached by Christ (Mt 5, Lk 6) continued in force. Monks in their solitude and deep prayer, teachers in their wisdom, nurses in their service, simple priests in their self-spending— all contributed to a rainbow diversifying the holy light of Christ. Child saints, soldiers dying in battle, martyrs testifying to the faith, mothers winning the souls of their children by their tears, old people dying in fullness of years — together they all consecrated the life cycle.

Admittedly, at times Catholic piety lost perspective and the saints threatened to obscure Jesus and the mysteries of God, whom flesh can never render fully. Admittedly, the development of a bureaucracy of the saints, in which one cared for ills of the eye, another cared for ills of the throat, still another presided over lost articles, and yet another protected wayfarers (updated to include those driving automobiles) threatened to get out of hand. If it was highly significant that St. Jude presided over lost causes and St. Anthony dealt with lost articles (including golf balls), one was verging upon caricature, even cartoon. Nonetheless, rather than relegate God and holiness to an otherworldly beyond, Catholic piety has tolerated a proliferation of holy helpers.

Two New Testament saints who are worth considering are Peter and Mary Magdalene, both of whom proved powerful in Christian history. Peter, the head of the college of the apostles, had an admirable if rash faith. He was the first apostle to call Jesus the Messiah. Peter burst with commitment and love. Yet he also denied Christ and showed himself impetuous, weak, and overconfident. These very human traits made him approachable, one with whom imperfect believers could feel comfortable. Then when the risen Christ told Peter to mind his own business (Jn 21:22), ordinary believers could smile and take a lesson. When Jesus made Peter profess his love three times, as though to blot out Peter's triple denial, ordinary believers could realize that the core of Peter's greatness was his ardent devotion to his Master. The Peter of Acts was a bold, responsible, yet confused figure—a model for those wanting to be both decisive and humble. The Peter whom tradition said had died upside down on a cross in Rome, in a final witness to his Lord, was a martyr who had ended very well.

Mary Magdalene fascinated many ages of Christian art and piety because she so perfectly complemented Mary the Mother of Christ. Where the Mother of Christ seemed serene and composed, though deeply sorrowful, the Magdalene seemed wild with emotion. Thus in the Middle Ages Mary Magdalene frequently appeared in paintings with flaming red hair, posed in postures of ardor or grief. She was the reformed sinner, the woman out of whom Jesus had cast seven devils, the woman who had thrown herself at Jesus' feet, watering them with her tears and drying them with her hair. Because she had loved so much, she had been forgiven much, to the comfort of all later sinners. In her passionate person, Mary Magdalene confuted all legalistic interpretations of following Christ, all efforts at a Christian rectitude like that of the Pharisees.

Indeed, in making Mary Magdalene the apostle to the apostles, the one honored with the task of telling Peter, James, John, and the others about the risen Christ, Jesus had established her as a model of discipleship. Her love had kept her faithful at the cross. Because Jesus was the whole of her life, Mary Magdalene recognized him at his first word. Clinging to his feet, she must have known a joy with few parallels in history. What a wonderful role model this made her. How richly she filled out the profile of feminine discipleship.

At shrines erected to the saints, the most celebrated of which became pilgrimage sites, the ordinary Catholic faithful attempted to translate the teachings of the gospel, and the understanding of faith passed down by tradition, into their own lives and times. During the nineteenth century, apparitions of the Virgin Mary at such sites as Lourdes in France and Fatima in Portugal updated Marian piety and brought to it bear on the threats posed by modern atheism. During the medieval period, pilgrims traveling to Jerusalem, Rome, Canterbury in England, or St. James Compostela in Spain enjoyed a "liminal" zone, a time and space set off from ordinary, secular life and opened onto God's eternity. There the class distinctions usually regulating their interactions fell into abeyance. There their common brotherhood and sisterhood emerged more clearly. All were simply people whose lives were short. None had ever seen God. All had sinned and fallen short of God's glory. All could look upon the saints as needed helpers. All could take the example of the saints as both a rebuke and an encouragement. With the help of the saints, all might amend their sinful lives, might redirect their attention to death, heaven, and hell. All might become serious about what God asked of them. Thus their pilgrimage to the shrines of the saints became a metaphor for life's overall passage. All Christians were on pilgrimage, having here on earth no lasting city. All needed help to make Christ their treasure, and to make heaven their overriding goal, as all the saints had.

Representative Personality: Teresa of Avila

Teresa of Avila (1515–1582) was born of an aristocratic Castilian family. After a childhood punctuated by both dreams of martyrdom and a worldly interest in fashion, she decided to become a nun. While convalescing from illness, she read some of the letters of Jerome. At the age of twenty, Teresa entered the Carmel at Avila. Her early years there were marked by both illness and a frivolous approach to religious life, encouraged by the laxity of her convent's discipline. From the age of forty, however, she became deeply committed to a life of prayer, and soon she began a reform of Carmelite life that returned it to the primitive rule. Eventually she founded sixteen convents where women could live an austere life devoted to prayer and manual labor.

> Teresa's robust common sense, prudence, and trust in providence allied with an extraordinary capacity for work and organization overcame all obstacles. In selecting candidates for this austere way of life, she insisted above all on intelligence and good judgment ("God preserve us from stupid nuns!") because she believed that intelligent people see their faults and allow themselves to be guided, while deficient and narrow-minded people fail to do so, but are pleased with themselves and never learn to do right.[1]

Teresa worked with John of the Cross to reform the men's Carmelite observance. Both saints met with much opposition, but eventually their reforms prevailed. Teresa eventually put her religious experiences onto paper, producing classical works on prayer. She was canonized in 1622, and in 1970 she was declared a doctor (recognized teacher) of the Church, the first woman to be so honored.

In her autobiography, Teresa describes the nearly twenty years during which she was careless about her religious life as a time painful in several ways:

I spent nearly twenty years on this stormy sea, falling and evermore rising again, but to little purpose as afterwards I would fall once more. My life was so far from perfection that I took hardly any notice of venial sins and, though I feared mortal sins, I was not sufficiently afraid to keep myself out of temptations. I must say that this was one of the most painful ways of life that can be imagined. I derived no joy from God and no pleasure from the world. When I was among the pleasures of the world, I was saddened by the memory of what I owed to God, and my worldly affections disturbed me when I was with God. A battle like this is so painful that I do not know how I managed to endure it for a month, still less for so many years. Nevertheless, I can plainly see the great mercy which the Lord did me, in still giving me the courage to pray, while thus consorting with the world. I said "courage" because I do not know anything for which greater courage is needed than for plotting against the King, knowing that He knows it and yet never withdrawing from His presence. For though we are always in the presence of God, it seems to me that those who practise prayer are present in a special way, for they see that He is watching them, while the rest may be in God's presence for several days without remembering that He can see them.[2]

It is characteristic of Teresa to focus on prayer as the epitome of the Christian life. Under her direction, the reformed Carmels became places dedicated to prayer, and through her influence Catholic Christianity has long venerated religious who seek to focus their whole lives on deep contemplation of God. They conceive of this work as something performed not only in the service of their own perfecting but also in the service of the entire Church, for which they pray. Indeed, the ultimate justification of prayer is simply God's own goodness and human beings' constant need. The goodness and beauty of God merit all creatures' raising their voices in praise. The sinfulness of human beings implies that they ought always to be begging God's help.

For the Carmelite school of prayer, contemplation becomes the primary way that God purifies people of sin and leads them to perfection. Perfection entails fulfillment in love, so God has to make people capable of receiving the divine love. Certainly all human beings have some such capacity, because all can receive the divine life at baptism. But contemplative prayer furnishes the Spirit an occasion to bring the requirements and blessings of divine love into people's awareness. Gradually the Spirit would have people experience how completely they depend on God and how completely the love of God surpasses all other blessings. John of the Cross is the Doctor who has most systematically described progress in spiritual cleansing, so that the soul can become a living flame of love, but Teresa's writings overlap with John's on many points.

For example, concerning some of the trials that contemplatives are likely to experience, as they progress in their practice, Teresa has written,

> We very often think that if God abandons us we will soon end in the abyss. We should walk with special care and attention, observing how we are proceeding in the practice of virtue, whether we are getting better or worse in some areas, especially in love for one another, and in the desire to be considered least among others and in the performance of ordinary tasks. We strive always to advance in the love of God. Love can never be idle. . . . There is a loud outcry by individuals with whom one is dealing and even by those one does not deal with and, it seems, never even think of the person. An example? Gossip like the following: "She's trying to make out she's a saint; she goes to extremes to deceive the world and bring others to ruin; there are better Christians who don't put on this outward show."[3]

The last lines of this quotation suggest some of the reasons that Catholics, as well as Protestants, occasionally criticize the contemplative life as tending to preoccupation with self and petty problems. Teresa herself was sufficiently active and down to earth to rebut most such charges. She knew that unless prayer concentrated on God and fostered love of one's neighbors it could be narcissistic. Others have noticed the relatively small place that prayer occupies in the teachings of Jesus and concluded that contemplative removal and mysticism are not necessary for following the evangelical Christ.

They have a good point. Although in the Gospels Jesus manifestly prays to his Father on many occasions, especially whenever he is troubled or needs strength, he does not lead or demand a special way of life set apart from the common people. We know little about Jesus' life prior to his baptism by John, but tradition suggests that he worked as a carpenter and did little that made him seem extraordinary. When Jesus emerged with his message about the Reign of God, the urgency filling him made for a wandering life of preaching, teaching, and healing, but it kept him in close contact with ordinary people and gave him a predilection for sinners, the poor, women, and others on society's margins.

Jesus was enough of a centrist, a middle-of-the-roader, to draw criticism from all sides. Indeed, the Lukan Jesus seems bitter at the criticism he received:

> What description, then, can I find for the men of this generation? What are they like? They are like children shouting to one another while they sit in the market place: "We played the pipes for you and you wouldn't dance; we sang dirges and you wouldn't cry." For John the Baptist comes, not eating bread, not drinking wine, and you say, "He is possessed." The Son of Man comes, eating and drinking, and you say, "Look, a glutton

and a drunkard, a friend of tax collectors and sinners." Yet Wisdom has been proved right by all her children (Lk 7: 31–35).

Teresa of Avila suffered similar criticisms, being buffeted by those who thought she was presumptuous to try to reform the Carmelite tradition and by those who thought she claimed special distinctions at prayer. In fact her absorption in prayer was simply her mode of loving God, as Jesus' mode of loving God had been to preach the news of the Kingdom. As her own example and writings show, contemplative prayer can nurture a great passion for God, purifying those who pursue it. When it does, it suggests the inner mystery of Christ's activity, his union with the Father and so working only to fulfill the Father's will.

Glossary

Doxology: an expression of praise, usually directed to the Trinity. Thus the "Gloria" of the Roman Mass is considered an extended doxology, whereas the common prayer, "Glory be," became the standard expression of praise, both in the Eucharistic liturgy and in private devotions such as the Rosary. Some theoreticians of prayer give praise and doxologies primacy of place, arguing that the praise of God is the most distinctive note of the Psalms, which have long been regarded as the prime models for Christian prayer. This position derives from the view that the purest worship deals with God for God's own sake, apart from the benefits God bestows on human beings. Without denying the legitimacy of petitioning God for help or the importance that human need plays in God's plan of salvation, one can look upon the descriptions of heaven in the Book of Revelation as suggesting that when believers gain definitive union with God, praising the divine splendor becomes their main occupation.

Discussion Questions

1. Why is contemplative prayer often holistic, simple, and wordless?
2. How does contemplative prayer relate to the inwardness of such creative vocations as art and science?

3. What purifications did Catholic mystics say were nearly certain to come through fidelity to contemplative prayer?
4. Why has Catholicism pointed to experience when its support of mysticism has been challenged?
5. How does the "Our Father" summarize Christian faith?
6. What have been the main benefits of praying the Rosary?
7. How have the saints filled out the Catholic instinct for incarnationalism and sacramentality?
8. What advantages and disadvantages likely have accrued to those who prayed to Peter and Mary Magdalene?
9. What sort of role model has the Church offered the faithful in canonizing Teresa of Avila and making her a Doctor?
10. What does Teresa's aversion to stupid nuns suggest about the relation between genuine mysticism and common sense?

Notes

[1] David Hugh Farmer, ed., *The Oxford Dictionary of Saints*, 2d ed. (New York: Oxford University Press, 1987), p. 404.
[2] *The Life of Teresa of Avila by Herself*, trans. J. M. Cohen (Baltimore: Penguin, 1957), p. 61.
[3] Camille Campbell, *Meditations with Teresa of Avila* (Santa Fe, N.M.: Bear, 1985), pp. 76–77.

Social Ethics

Biblical Foundations

At the foundations of most religions, ethics is not an independent aspect of the life that people are trying to live, let alone an academic speciality. Rather, the stories shaping people's imagination, the rituals taking them into the divine mysteries, the doctrines clarifying their core convictions, and their customary judgments about goodness and evil all cohere. In part this coherence stems from the **undifferentiated** state of consciousness that tends to prevail in formative times.

The New Testament recollections of Jesus, for example, precede later clarifications concerning his human and divine natures, what disciples remembered about things he said and did before the Resurrection and what after the Resurrection they read back into his ministry, how Jesus continued to be with his community as a living Spirit and how the Holy Spirit was functioning in his stead. Similarly, there is the Johannine notion (Jn 3 : 21) that those who do the truth come to the light, which suggests the rich, reciprocal relations between action and thought, ethics and doctrine. There is Jesus' ambivalence about the Jewish law, which the New Testament has him sometimes uphold and sometimes disregard. And above all there is the implication that the Kingdom of God entails a new morality of love, which the Resurrection and the sending of the Spirit establish in power.

One looking to the biblical foundations of Christian social ethics therefore has to be content with an overall vision. Few of the particulars, the distinctions, the refinements that Christian ethicists later had to work out appear on Jesus' lips. Jesus never mentions abortion, nuclear weapons, the pollution of nature, the imbalance in the nations' standards of living. We hear nothing about the conflicts between capitalism and communism, nothing about the relative rights of peasants and nobles, nothing about how to correlate guns and butter. The most one can say is that Jesus assumes that those living in the Spirit of the Kingdom will have the proper dispositions to solve the problems that present themselves. Granted docility to the Spirit, intelligence, and hard work, the followers of Jesus should be able to muddle through. Because God has acted to solve the fundamental sources of injustice and immorality, those who take God's solution to heart should be able to make a world fit for human habitation.

In the background of Jesus' ethical orientation lies the Hebrew Bible and the traditions of the Second Temple period. Thus Jesus' contemporaries assumed the Mosaic authorship of the Torah and looked upon their customs about the Sabbath, unclean foods, and the like as expressions of the will of their Lord, who had rescued them from bondage in Egypt and brought them to a land flowing with milk and honey. They assumed the legacy left by the Prophets, who had castigated the people for false cult (running after the fertility gods of their neighbors) and injustice. The Prophets taught that God wanted fidelity from the heart and was more interested in mercy than in sacrifice. To their mind social ruin came from forgetting that only the Lord could be the treasure of Israelite culture and from neglecting the poor, widows, and orphans. The writings that completed the Hebrew Bible included the Psalms, where the praise of God became the nation's foremost anthem. The Book of Job warned that there need be no obvious correlation between living a good life and prospering in worldly terms. In the Song of Songs Israel taught itself that erotic love was a valid analogy for its relation to God. In Proverbs and Qoheleth the people learned that a sober, skeptical, even pessimistic view of human nature had much warrant.

All of this background further complicated the biblical foundations of Christian ethics. Both the Old Testament and the New Testament proved to be variegated works holding in tension many different theologies and estimates of human nature. One could say that murder, adultery, theft, gouging the poor, and neglecting the praise of God continued to be wrong — mortal slashes at the common faith by which the people would stand or fall. People who did not pray, who were not peaceful, or who did not help their neighbors were on a perilous path. But a great deal depended on the inspiration of God. Like Saul, who mysteriously lost the Spirit, and David, whom God never abandoned despite his adultery and murder, individual Christians remained locked in personal dramas that no outside observer ever could plumb. Some people seemed to have more blessings from God than others. For some virtue and wisdom seemed relatively easy, whereas others had to struggle for minimal self-control.

No wonder that Jesus and the Prophets both were more concerned with people's passion than with the particulars of their religious lives. For both these sources of Christian ethics, the great question was whether people were opening themselves to God in faith, were loving the Lord with their whole minds, hearts, souls, and strength. Magdalene, reputedly a great sinner, had become a greater saint when she focused her ardor on Jesus. Peter, manifestly a man of doubtful judgment and impetuous ways, had matured to the measure of the leadership Jesus had thrust upon him, because of his great faith and love. The key to following Jesus was to love him from the heart. The Beloved Disciple (Jn 13:23), who probably inspired the Johannine community, knew that Jesus wanted to call his followers not servants but friends — people to whom he could unburden all the secrets of his heart. Those secrets included the ties to the Father that defined Jesus' inmost identity and knowledge of the darkness of human hearts. Those who do evil hate the light, because it threatens to reveal them as they are. Immorality relates intimately to hard-heartedness, to fearing the light of conscience and God, and to lack of faith. It is from the heart that deeds proceed, whether for evil or for good.

Christian ethics therefore began as an affair of the heart, a matter of religious formation. People would do the deeds reminiscent of Jesus and pleasing to the Father if they lived Jesus' life, loved with Jesus' love. The Spirit sent by Jesus and by the Father had the task of empowering a Christian life from within. Fulfilling Jeremiah's prophecy (Jer 31:33), the Spirit would fashion a new covenant in people's hearts, teaching them at the roots of conscience, anointing them so that they knew instinctively, connaturally, what befit their divine life and what threatened it.

The social aspects of this radical Christian ethics took shape from New Testament convictions about the people of God. In continuity with the Hebrew Bible, the Christian scriptures thought of salvation and the life of faith as communal affairs. People were not saved alone. They prayed, repented, received the sacraments, heard the word of God, and learned about the "Way" (Acts 9:2), as early Christianity called itself, in the assembly of God. Thus brotherly and sisterly love was crucially important, whereas dissension that divided the community was a sure sign that people were not obeying the Spirit. The point to any individual **charismata** was whether they built up the whole Body (I Cor 12). The gift of prophecy was preferable to the gift of tongues, because prophecy did more for the community. But the greatest of all gifts was love, because love was the power by which the community would stand or fall. If outsiders could say, "See how they love one another," the main witness of the Church was accomplished. If people were spending themselves for one another out of love, were bearing one another's burdens, their morality had passed beyond justice to imitate Jesus himself, who so loved his friends he laid down his life on their behalf. The crux of Christian morality had to be love, because Christianity was a life hidden in God, who was love.

Natural Law

One might say that the basic ethical heritage that Catholic Christianity derived from the New Testament was an inclination to shape its moral ideals in terms of the imitation of Christ. The love of God at the core of revelation, salvation, and divinization had been exemplified by Christ to the fullest measure. The Incarnation was a model of what God was like in human terms and what human flesh could become when it gained union with divinity.

A second font from which Roman Catholic ethical theory traditionally has drawn is the natural law that was developed in classical Greece and circulated in the Hellenistic world in which Christianity arose. Platonists, Aristotelians, Stoics, Epicureans, and others who discoursed on ethical matters in the Hellenistic world all assumed that disciplined reflection about both physical nature and human nature could bring people moral guidance. Inasmuch as Christianity decided to enter into a dialogue with Hellenistic culture, trying to accept its best products and give them a new soul, Christian thinkers inevitably came to work with Greek concepts and categories.

One can see this process beginning in the New Testament, for certain Pauline and Johannine reflections betray Hellenistic ideas about light and darkness, about God as the one in whom we live, move, and have our being, about the inferences one can draw from the things that God has made. The apologists and Church fathers continued this dialogue. Such luminaries as Clement of Alexandria, Origen, and Augustine tried to reconcile Athens (the best of pagan thought) and Jerusalem (revealed wisdom). When Catholic thought became more systematic, culminating in the medieval scholastic syntheses, faith and reason were considered partners to a delicate balance. Faith was the foundation, stabilizing reason and opening onto supernatural realms to which reason had no access on its own. But reason could illumine faith, and reason had natural realms in which it was fully competent. Inevitably, therefore, Christian thinkers who were concerned with moral issues assumed that rational reflection had a valid role. This led them to speak about natural law.

In the Christian tradition, the theory of natural law was developed in some detail by Aquinas, along fundamentally Aristotelian lines. It was Aquinas's view that by using our reason to reflect on our human nature, we could discover both the specific ends toward which we naturally tend (such as to live, to reproduce, to acquire knowledge, to have a role in an ordered society, to worship God) and the general end for which God created us, a blessed immortality. When we have discovered these ends, it is then possible for us to determine the means required to achieve them. This understanding of God's plan for us, built into our nature by his act of creation, Aquinas called natural law.

This general approach was taken much further by later Roman Catholic moralists, whose detailed applications of the method illustrate both the approach and its difficulties. They take as their starting point the Aristotelian notion of a natural teleology [finality], the view that the human person as a whole has a function, and that the various human organs and capacities have their functions which subserve the good functioning of the whole. An examination of the proper functioning of each human capability leads to the derivation of moral duties. Thus, one functions best, as a matter of natural necessity, if one has good health, is given an education, is allowed to make free choices, and so on. It is therefore immoral so to act as to damage anyone's health; it is likewise immoral to deprive people of an education, or of their freedom. So far, the approach would be reasonably uncontroversial. However, the same method was used to derive much more specific conclusions. The function of the human reproductive system is to produce children: it is therefore immoral to act in any way that will impede this natural function. Or again, the natural function of sexual organs is reproductive: therefore any use of them for other functions (such as to express homosexual love) is likewise immoral.[1]

This quotation indicates several ethical tendencies that seem characteristically Catholic. First, there is the tendency to trust human reason sufficiently to analyze the ends, the goals, that God has built into human nature. Without denying biblical revelation, Catholic moral theology has tended to think that reason provides a basis for discussing ethical issues with all people of goodwill, many of whom might not accept biblical revelation. Thus, natural law was applicable to all people — Jews, Muslims, pagans, and Christians alike. Human beings were enough alike, in virtue of their reason, will, and embodiment, to share a similar makeup and destiny.

Second, Aristotle had said that the first in the order of causes was finality. In other words, if one was constructing something, or analyzing how others had constructed something, one ought to begin with the goal, the function that the construction intended. Achieving a certain sort of house determined how wise builders selected their materials, composed their blueprints and applied their hammers and saws. In the case of human beings, the first question to ask was for what God had destined them. What were they placed on earth to achieve? As the quotation notes, the general end for which Catholic ethical theory thought God had designed human beings was a blessed immortality — an eternal share of heaven, an eternal enjoyment of the beatific vision.

From this analysis it followed that nothing temporal or limited ought to dominate human consciousness. Only divinity itself could satisfy the desire built into human knowing and loving. To settle for anything less than God was to frustrate one's makeup, use one's freedom to self-destruct. That was the irrationality of sin, the root horror of idolatry. Judaism and Islam agreed: the most basic disorder was putting anything created in place of the sovereign divine mystery. Consequently, all of the prophetic religions limited the claims that temporal institutions could make on human beings. Catholic Christianity not only qualified the claims of Caesar, remembering Jesus' command that one render to God the things that were God's, it also qualified the claims of one's family, teaching that when they conflicted with God's calling (as they might if parents opposed a religious vocation), they had to take second place.

Third, one sees the power of the analysis that the natural law tradition could develop. In contrast to many other ethical systems, which flounder for lack of clarity about what human beings have been set on earth to achieve, the Catholic tradition could discourse lucidly on the rights and obligations that flowed from a teleology (finality) that considered human beings made for heaven. In complementary fashion, Catholic ethics could stress human embodiment to note that social life ought to provide human beings the food, shelter, clothing, education, socialization, culture, defense against enemies, health care, and the like that incarnate spirits required for their flourishing. The social encyclicals of the popes that updated natural law teaching from the end of the nineteenth century focused on the flourishing of the individual person, who had the great dignity of being an image of God destined for heaven. From that focus, they warned about the dangers of both socialistic and capitalistic economic and political systems. Certainly one had to aim at the common good, but narrow, this-worldly views of human destiny threatened to warp perspective on what was truly good.

The author of the article from which the quotation was taken may be optimistic in calling many of the conclusions that Catholic natural law theory drew about the moral duties that were incumbent on communities "reasonably uncontroversial." If you demand the rights that are the obverse of such duties in a totalitarian state, you will soon find yourself silenced. But the author seems on the mark in showing the dangers of overspecifying one's deductions of rights and duties, as in the case of Catholic views of sexuality. Indeed, as we discuss in the next chapter, sexuality has been a Catholic bugaboo in modern times, showing more clearly than most other areas how unhistorical conceptions of natural law, according to which neither temporal change nor cultural diversity makes a significant impact on human nature, have often rendered natural law theory unable to deal with the complexities of modern and postmodern life.

Approaches to War

Perhaps nothing dramatizes the sinful human condition so much as the unremitting history of warfare. When one charts the social history of humankind, the periods of war predominate over the periods of peace. Again and again tribes and nations resort to violence. Whether to gain material advantages or to redress supposed grievances, they paint other people as their mortal enemies and set out to exterminate them. In the Catholic Christian view of reality, such warfare is absurd, testifying to the mystery of iniquity. Supposed "realists" pass by this irrationality too quickly. Making the valid point that one has to deal with people as they in fact are, pragmatic realism is yet unwilling or unable to see that people might be quite different than what they usually choose to be. The limits of our social reality are the limits of our imagination. By offering human beings new images of what they might become, of how they might reconcile their differences, Christianity has greatly enlarged their social reality.

The Bible itself is not blameless on the matter of warfare. Regardless of how one decides the question of whether or not the Old Testament sponsors a doctrine of holy warfare, it is clear that ancient Israel depicted God as its foremost warrior, battling on its behalf. The slaughter of enemies in warfare could be sanctioned as the requirement of a holy God, who wanted no polluted enemies to survive. While admitting that God's ways are not our human ways, present-day theologians seem willing to attribute most of the bloodthirstiness of the Old Testament God to the deficiencies of the biblical writers. In other words, God has suffered from the limitations of narrow, sinful human beings even in the presentation of divine revelation. One has only to read the entire Bible as a whole to sense that a bloodthirsty God, bent on vengeance and destruction, is not at its center.

This is certainly the case in the New Testament. For although the New Testament does not outlaw warfare outright, as it does not outlaw slavery, the demeanor and teaching of Jesus run against justifying war. For example, Jesus does not fight against those who come to destroy him, and he sagely observes that those who live by the sword perish by the sword. The combat that Jesus endorses is spiritual, against the powers of Satan and sin. Paul picks up this tradition in speaking of Christians' warfare as being against principalities and powers. For both Jesus and Paul, those whom one ought to fear are the enemies who can corrupt the spirit and bind it to hell. Enemies who have dominion over one's body certainly can cause much pain, but they cannot diminish one's core freedom.[2]

The basic disposition of Jesus and the New Testament writers is that if people would embrace the grace offered to them in the dawning of the Kingdom, most of the antagonisms that provoke conflict, violence, and warfare would melt away. People looking on others as their equals, as their brothers and sisters, would not be going to battle over territory or possessions. They would not be thinking of politics as a series of power plays bent on domination. They would not consider themselves entitled to lord it over others, by the principle that might makes right, and they would share the goods of the earth rather than competing for them in bloody fashion.

The line of Christian tradition that has kept vivid Christ's way of redeeming the world has tended toward pacifism. Believing that God chose to confront murderous evil with self-sacrificing love, in most generations some Christians have argued that one only contributes to breaking the cycle of hurting by refusing to retaliate. Many questions attend the proposition that one can extend this principle into a political policy, all the more so when politicians are functioning in a pluralistic society whose members disagree about their ultimate destiny. In the sphere of personal life, however, radical Christians make a good case that unless some people say no to the cycles of retaliation that fuel warfare and destruction, the world will not even suspect it has alternatives. Many feminists, religious and nonreligious, agree, arguing that the warfare and violence standard in patriarchal history are products of male dementia.

On the other hand, Christian tradition, which admittedly has been largely a patriarchal preserve, by no means has proposed only a pacificist position about warfare. Indeed, Catholic Christianity is associated with a doctrine delineating the conditions justifying warfare. The doctrine partakes of the natural law mentality outlined in the last section, arguing that social groups have the right, if not the duty, to oppose unjust aggression that seems likely to cause them suffering. This doctrine of a just war coalesced during the Middle Ages, but during the Renaissance and Reformation period it spoke confidently about what a reasonable approach to warfare would entail.

It would, for example, consider force to be a last resort, justifiably entered upon only when negotiation and compromise had completely failed. Any force employed was to be proportionate to the evil it sought to remedy, which ruled out extermination or holocaust. People going to war had to have a reasonable expectation of success, lest their attempts do more harm than good. They had to intend a state of peace and be laboring for an end result that would be a discernible improvement over the state of conflict from which they began. Finally, reflection on the conditions for a just war concluded that there were restrictions on how war could be waged. Warring parties were to distinguish between combatants and noncombatants, sparing civil populations. They were to restrict their weaponry (the means of war) so that it was proportionate to the evils and enemies they were combating. Overall, then, a just war was difficult to find and wage. The most one could say about certain conflicts was that they had had some justification and seemed necessary, lest evils continue that were greater than the sufferings generated by war.

Since the dawn of atomic warfare at the end of World War II, the possibility of waging a just war has greatly diminished. The massive destruction latent in thermonuclear weapons threatens to eliminate not only huge populations but also entire ecosystems, calling into question the survival of the planet. By the principle of proportionality, many Catholic thinkers now are saying that one cannot justify the use of nuclear weapons. Individual liberty is not so ultimate a good that one could rightly risk destroying creation, while defending a high level of material prosperity is an even less acceptable justification.

But if one cannot morally employ nuclear weapons, even in a second, retaliatory strike, can one morally threaten such employment? In answering no, some Catholic ethicists fault both the nuclear arms policies of the superpowers and the recent pastoral letter of the American Catholic bishops. Such ethicists tend to credit the bishops with laying out many of the factors that have to go into any adequate estimate of a modern nation's nuclear arms policy and to praise the bishops' perspicacity in questioning the morality of diverting huge fractions of the resources of many nations into arms production. On the other hand, they argue that the bishops have not been logical or courageous enough to draw the proper conclusion from their own principles. In a time when scientists speak of significant deployments of nuclear arms leading to the phenomenon of nuclear winter (blotting out the sun with clouds of debris and so killing off most earthly life), old principles of just warfare may be outmoded. The quantitative differences between the destructive capacities of medieval and modern weaponry have led to a qualitative difference in what "war" has meant in the two ages.

Approaches to Economic Justice

The Catholic tradition about economic justice, like the Catholic tradition about warfare, is an untidy mixture of biblical idealism and natural law rationalism. From the Bible and the example of Jesus, all Christians have received counsels to mercy rather than legalistic justice, to self-sacrificing love rather than standing on one's supposed rights, to considering other people members of the same Body into which Christian faith had inserted themselves. However seldom it has realized its own ecclesiastical ideals, the Catholic Church in fact has kept alive the idea that people could live as though there were no mine or thine. Similarly, it has supported religious individuals who sought to live stripped lives that freed them for prayer and social service. All of this idealism has attacked the greed and selfishness at the root of most social and economic injustices. Combined with a theology that regarded all people as children and images of God, it has offered those social critics who wished to employ it a devastating critique of acquisitiveness, materialism, disregard of the poor, and Social Darwinism.

How, then, did Catholic Christianity tolerate wealthy popes and bishops, the alliance of the Church with the rich and powerful, and the neglect of the poor? It could do this only by a certain realism that too easily became acquiescence with sin. Jesus did say that we would always have the poor with us. He did not say that this justified complacency about poverty, still less alliance with the wealthy and powerful who benefited from the low estate of the poor.

In traditional perspective, the needs of the many took precedence over the wants of the few. No one had the right to superfluities as long as anyone lacked necessities. The goods of the earth had come from God as a boon to all the inhabitants of the earth, not just a few. Private property was a quite circumscribed right, subordinate to the common good. Because human beings were considered wayfarers, en route to the beatific enjoyment of God, nothing material or economic was to preoccupy them. Certainly they had the right to a decent standard of living, sufficient to let them develop the capacities that would bring them to heaven. The Incarnation justified trying to make communities in which beauty, art, education, and healing all flourished, just as the doctrine of Creation justified considering matter blessed and put into human beings' hands for all decent employments. To say that human beings were wayfarers was not to say that they ought to live in squalor or that their desire to develop creation and live well was not an impetus from God. But it was to say that spiritual development was more important than material or physical development. It was to say that people were more alike in their dignity and so their claims to a fair share of the goods of creation than they were different and entitled to grossly different shares.

How then was one to give differences in talent and industry their due, rewarding those who best developed creation and produced wealth and not rewarding the lazy or unimaginative? Once again, the answers lay in principles of proportionality. As long as their wealth was not purchased at the expense of others' suffering, entrepreneurs who prospered need not feel guilt. They had the obligation, in strict justice, to contribute to the betterment of the poor, and they were wise if they put much of their wealth into charitable alms, but their prosperity itself was not sinful. Only when they paid more attention to their wealth and the creature comforts it could bring them than they did to loving God and their neighbors did their lives fall out of balance.

The social encyclicals of the modern popes have decried great disparities in wealth, whether within individual nations or among the nations as a whole. They have criticized the laissez-faire capitalism that gave free reign to people's greed, warning that God requires special consideration for the poor. If the great dangers in the Communist and Socialist regimes were their neglect of the

dignity of the individual person, which frequently stemmed from their atheistic
suppression of religious liberties, the great dangers in the capitalist regimes were
their fixation with profit and their being driven by greed.

Since their meeting at Medellin, Colombia, in 1968, the Latin American
bishops have explicitly placed themselves on the side of the poor, arguing that
the gospel shows God to prefer the poor and makes him a defender of their
cause. The American Catholic bishops wrote somewhat similarly in their 1986
pastoral letter on economic justice:

> Catholic social teaching does not require absolute equality in the distribu-
> tion of wealth and income. Some degree of inequality not only is accept-
> able, but also may be considered desirable for incentives and the provision
> of greater rewards for greater risks. However, unequal distribution should
> be evaluated in terms of several moral principles we have enunciated: the
> priority of meeting the basic needs of the poor and the importance of
> increasing the level of participation by all members of society in the
> economic life of the nation. These norms establish a strong presumption
> against extreme inequality of income and wealth as long as there are poor,
> hungry, and homeless people in our midst. They also suggest that extreme
> inequalities are detrimental to the development of social solidarity and
> community. In view of these norms we find the disparities of income and
> wealth in the United States to be unacceptable. Justice requires that all
> members of our society work for economic, political, and social reforms
> that will decrease these inequities.[4]

Perhaps this is the place at which to draw some firm conclusions and make it
plain that genuine Catholic Christianity, like genuine Protestant and Orthodox
Christianity, usually runs counter to the culture in which it finds itself. That was
true of the early Christianity that found itself in the Roman Empire and
Hellenistic culture. It was true of Christendom, East and West, when reformers
regularly turned the gospel against the supposedly Christian authorities who
were conniving at luxury and injustice. It has been true in modern times, when
atheistic regimes and industrializations that gave little heed to workers' welfare
flourished. It remains true in our post-modern age, whether one's studies of
economic justice target fairness within a given society, such as the United States,
or fairness around the globe.

Because money can never be high on the list of Christian goals, all sincere
Christians find the money that makes the contemporary world run thoroughly
dubious. Gross disparities in income, gross disparities in the nations' use of raw
materials, and other signs of economic injustice cry out for critique and remedy.
How some Christians attempt to justify a private enterprise or capitalistic system
that produces such economic injustice bewilders the biblical imagination. Until a

system arrives that genuinely seeks the common good, the welfare of all, and actually limits the profits of the talented or monied few to reasonable incentives, we think Christians ought to judge contemporary economics quite negatively and see in it many signs of sin. The point is not to cast blame or engage in discussions of whether capitalism isn't the lesser of several evils. The point is to elucidate the theoretical principles and practical mechanisms that might produce an economic system befitting both the limits of the natural environment and the fundamental equality of all human beings. The limits of the natural environment suggest that only our restraint today will offer posterity a good life tomorrow. The fundamental equality of all human beings suggests that the ratio of the wealth of those on top to that of those on the bottom ought to be modest (perhaps 4:1), and that Christian churchpeople ought to join with others who are convinced of the priority of spiritual attainments in a fully human life to find better incentives for creativity and hard work than money.

Representative Personality: Mother Teresa of Calcutta

Mother Teresa of Calcutta was born Agnes Bojaxhiu in Skopje, Macedonia, in 1910. Her father was an Albanian grocer. At the age of eighteen she went to Ireland to join an institute of religious women, and shortly thereafter she was sent to work in India as a teacher. Later she obtained permission to work with the poor of Calcutta.

To prepare herself for this work, Mother Teresa studied nursing. She moved into the slums of Calcutta and petitioned the municipal authorities for the use of a pilgrim hotel near a temple of the Goddess Kali. In 1948 she founded an order for religious women who wanted to join her work with the poor and dying. Receiving a good response and seeing her group grow, Mother Teresa oversaw the opening of dispensaries and outdoor schools. She and her followers adopted Indian dress and obtained Indian citizenship in order to identify themselves with the people they were serving. Pope Pius XII approved her order in 1950 and in 1965 Pope Paul VI made it a pontifical congregation, subject only to himself. The group continued to expand, opening centers for the blind, the aged, the crippled, lepers, and the dying. The women called themselves Missionaries of Charity and gained considerable notice when they opened a leprosarium called Shanti Nagar (Town of Peace) near Asansol. For this and her other good works, the Indian government awarded Mother Teresa its Padmashri Prize in 1963.

Mother Teresa came to wider international notice in 1964 when Pope Paul

VI included a visit to her on his Indian itinerary. The pope was so moved by her work that he gave her his ceremonial limousine, which she raffled off to raise money for her leper colony. In 1968 Paul VI asked Mother Teresa to open a home for the sick and dying in Rome, and in 1971 he made her the first recipient of the Pope John XXIII Peace Prize. Her order grew along with her fame, attracting not only more than one thousand nuns but also many lay volunteers who would work for temporary periods. By the late 1970s she had opened more than sixty centers in Calcutta and more than 200 centers world-wide, establishing her group in Sri Lanka, Tanzania, Jordan, Venezuela, Great Britain, and Australia. When Mother Teresa won the Nobel Peace Prize in 1979, the entire world learned of her extraordinary devotion to society's most outcast people. Since then she has continued to expand her labors, opening houses for people with AIDS and becoming a symbol of Christian dedication to the sanctity of life.

Mother Teresa appears here as a famous example of Catholic instincts about social justice. Although her own life is extraordinary, and probably we should regard her work as a unique vocation quite explicitly inspired by God (she claims that the idea to found her group came suddenly while she was praying), she nonetheless dramatizes the concern for the dignity of the human person that the modern popes have made the centerpiece of their social teaching.

Whether it be euthanasia or abortion that she is discussing, Mother Teresa avoids politics and focuses directly on the specific human lives in question. She has asked those who want to make the lives of the sick, the newborn, or those carried in the womb disposable to put such lives into her keeping. Often her work with the dying has been impossible, in the sense that there was no hope for a cure and she and her sisters could only ease the dying person's last days. But that has been enough for her. To show someone the love of Christ as he or she prepared to meet God has justified all her hard work and self-sacrifice.

Mother Teresa has written little and both her speech and her writing tend to be simple, clear, and direct. Many people find her a difficult role model, because her estimable love of the poor is tied to very traditional, conservative Catholic views. Thus, in a chapter entitled "I Love Children," Mother Teresa has said:

If we have today so many unhappy and broken families, and if we have in the world so much unhappiness and so much suffering, I think it is because the mother is not in the home! It is very painful to accept what is happening in Western countries: a child is destroyed by the fear of having too many children and having to feed it or to educate it. I think they are the poorest people in the world, who do an act like that. A child is a gift of God. I feel that the poorest country is the country that has to kill the unborn child to be able to have extra things and extra pleasures. They are afraid to have to feed one more child! In Calcutta we are trying to fight abortion by adoption. In India, actually, they may leave the child in the dustbin, they may leave him in a dark door, but they would never kill the child. In Calcutta we have a home for crippled and unwanted children. (In other places we have similar homes too.) Their parents often can't feed them. Sometimes because they are crippled also, because they are blind, because they are diseased, they don't want their children. Often we pick - them up with their own parents, who have to be taken to the Home for the Dying.[5]

Some of Mother Teresa's rationale for serving the poor comes through in a biography by Edward Le Joly, published in 1983, when her coworkers were approaching three thousand. In Le Joly's interpretation, she finds much inspiration in the poor themselves:

The poor, as a group, are closer to God, more detached from human comforts, from material things. Having fewer obstacles on the way, they are generally God-fearing, God-worshipping, and accept what comes to them as the will of God. "The poor show faith and patience in suffering," says Mother, "and we are privileged to serve God in them. We can console Christ in his distress disguised in them, Christ suffering in his brethren." The poor are also challenging to those who wish to help them. "To serve well our poor, we must understand them; to understand their poverty, we must experience it. Working for them, we come to identify ourselves with them. Our sisters must feel as they feel, feel their poverty before God, know what it is to live without security, depending on God for the morrow."

Mother can turn a blind eye to the shortcomings of the poor, at least when she extols their qualities. When an American woman photographer saw her pushing back with extraordinary energy a whole column of destitute women invading the compound to profit by a free distribution, Mother requested, "Don't take this, please, don't show this." That was in 1981. The same scene had taken place several times in earlier years.[6]

Mother Teresa realizes that her clinics are no substitute for widespread reforms that would eliminate much of the poverty and sickness around the globe. But she doesn't trouble herself with the political tasks necessary to effect such reforms. They fall to other people with other vocations. For her it has been enough to help specific people and perhaps give an example of what Christian love can accomplish.

Probably no greater task confronts Christians who are committed to social reform than translating the love displayed by heroes such as Mother Teresa into the economic and political changes that compassion and justice require. If

Mother Teresa shows what a full faith in Christ's living presence can inspire, it falls to theologians and others working in the Church to develop an overall understanding of faith and culture that is persuasive in its claims that economic justice, peace, and compassion would benefit all people and are realistic goals. The major obstacles to converting the nations from their distrust, self-seeking, and abuse of life lodge in the souls of their leaders and average citizens. People who expect little of themselves and their fellow human beings, who have no living sense of a supportive divine mystery and little experience of spiritual fulfillment—such people are bound to be suspicious, cynical, and persuaded that human existence is a survival of the fittest and that each person and country has to grab what it can. Naturally public figures seldom speak so bluntly, but regularly they act from such convictions. Social ethics remain impotent until better images and better examples of how to be fully human arise. One Mother Teresa is worth a thousand books, a dozen ecclesiastical exhortations.

Glossary

Charismata: gifts of the Spirit. All the endowments by which the Church as a whole and individual Christians thrive come from the Spirit. Faith and Church offices, theology and preaching, witness to social justice and work for peace all depend on the support of the Helper Jesus left. Usually, however, discussions of charismata focus on extraordinary gifts of leadership or service. Moreover, usually commentators are interested in the overall effect of the diverse charismata. For example, the gift of contemplative prayer enriches not only the individuals who receive it but also the entire community, which learns about its deeper spiritual possibilities and is supported by the petitions that the contemplatives place before God. Similarly, gifts of social witness and service not only benefit both the people who receive them and the poor, they also remind the entire community of Christ's second commandment and help all Christians do better at serving their neighbors.

Undifferentiated: compact, existing in a state prior to distinctions, refinements, and clarifications. An undifferentiated consciousness perceives the world with relatively few distinctions. Theoretical matters blend with common sense. Imagination overlaps with judgment and will. The aesthetic realm may run into the religious realm. Myth and doctrine fuse. All education and maturation involve differentiating what previously had been compact, in order to give a complicated, rich reality its due. On the other hand, when people get lost in their distinctions, becoming overly analytical, their powers of synthesis can atrophy and they can lose the sense of wholeness necessary for mental and religious health. Thus contemplative prayer and wisdom both take one into a simplicity that finally becomes ineffable, for both suggest how God is one and the same throughout the complex variety of creation.

Discussion Questions

1. What is the overall vision at the New Testament foundations of Christian social ethics?
2. What is the ethical significance of Jesus' having wanted to call his followers not servants but friends?
3. What are the advantages in the conviction of Natural Law theory that God has built a plan into human nature?
4. How does historical development complicate the question of human nature, for example, in the area of sexuality?
5. How central to Christian faith is the law of the cross—the proposition that one only radically defeats evil by suffering it in love?
6. What are the principal causes of war and how adequately do pacifism and the just war theory respond to them?
7. What are the dangers in saying the Church should make a preferential option for the poor?
8. How radical are the propositions that the needs of the many take priority over the wants of the few and that no one has the right to superfluities as long as anyone lacks necessities?
9. What are the problems with Mother Teresa's position on abortion?
10. What is the relation between the example of Mother Teresa and the politics of producing social improvement?

Notes

[1] Gerard J. Hughes, "Natural Law," in *The Westminster Dictionary of Christian Ethics*, ed. James F. Childress and John Macquarrie (Philadelphia: Westminster, 1986), p. 413.
[2] See Heinrich Gross, "War," in *Encyclopedia of Biblical Theology*, ed. J. B. Bauer (New York: Crossroad, 1981), pp. 958–961.

[3] See Philip J. Murnion, ed., *Catholics and Nuclear War* (New York: Crossroad, 1983).

[4] The American Catholic Bishops, "Economic Justice for All," #185, in *Documents of American Catholic History*, vol. 3, ed. John Tracy Ellis (Wilmington, Del.: Michael Glazier, 1987), p. 1081.

[5] Mother Teresa of Calcutta, *My Life for the Poor* (San Francisco: Harper & Row, 1985), p. 61.

[6] Edward Le Joly, S. J., *Mother Teresa of Calcutta: A Biography* (San Francisco: Harper & Row, 1983), p. 221.

CHAPTER 13

Personal Ethics

Mortal Sin
Venial Sin
Sexuality
Poverty and Obedience
Representative Personality: Bernard Lonergan
Glossary, Discussion Questions, Notes

Mortal Sin

When Teresa of Avila contemplated her years of worldy living, before she repented and became wholehearted about prayer and loving God, she noted that although she had paid venial sins little heed, fear had kept her from committing mortal sins. The distinction between venial, or lesser, sins and mortal sins has been important in traditional Catholic moral theology, and in recent years it has emerged as a consolation. Mortal sins are those that sever the connection between the person and God, that slay the divine life communicated by grace. In some periods of Catholic history, theologians and pastors implied that mortal sin was ever at the believer's elbow, waiting to spring.

For example, one school of moral theology taught that all sexual sins were intrinsically serious or mortal. With sexual sins one could never have the "poverty of matter" associated with other sins (for example, thefts in which the value of the goods taken was relatively slight). The only way one could justify considering sexual sins less than mortal sins was to find that the person had been ill-informed or only partially consenting. Thus the school in question considered masturbation, heavy petting, and the other sexual preoccupations to which adolescents, especially, were prone, sins, which, if they were not absolved before death, would cast the person into hell.

227

The problem with focusing personal morality on sin, whether mortal or venial, is that it encourages people to think of their relationship with God defensively. If sin is at the center of consciousness, God can easily seem a stern judge and the life of faith can easily seem an effort to make sure that one does not cross the line into serious offenses that will enrage the judge. Far better would be an approach that focused on the beauty and love of Christ, giving the motive for a life of communion with God in which sin would appear in all its proper ugliness. Indeed, it is not the sovereignty of God, not the exalted divine station, that rules in the best analyses of the tragedies of sin.

For many medievals who were indoctrinated in hierarchical thinking, the dignity of God was a major consideration and sin was the unchivalrous wounding of God's dignity, a magnified *faux pas*. But God put aside the divine dignity in emptying himself to become human and endure crucifixion and death on human beings' behalf. God went out from the self-sufficiency of heaven to become the great lover of humankind, exposing the divine heart, making himself vulnerable. So the tragedy of sin is its disregard of the divine love. Whether through inadvertence, weakness, or cold disdain, sinners turn away from the goodness shown them in creation and redemption, turn in on themselves to pursue their own pleasures or self-promotion. God then is a lover spurned, a benefactor little thanked, a parent ignored. Sinners then above all are ingrates, people too stupid, self-centered, or fearful to live by the simple truth that everything good in their lives is a gracious gift come down from God, the Father of Lights.

The recent shift in Catholic moral theology away from the legalistic categories suggested by medieval theories of the atonement and canon law has spotlighted these interpersonal aspects of grace and sin, which are prominent in the New Testament. Thinking about what constitutes the relationship between the believer and God, about the transactions that go back and forth in the coin of love, theologians have realized that one does not fracture a profound relationship by daydreaming at a traffic light. A surge of desire for an attractive person standing on the corner hardly qualifies as something able to destroy one's being-to-being relationship with God.

Without denying that human beings can say no to God, present-day theologians tend to think that anyone serious about the life of faith is unlikely to deny God casually, through ordinary weakness or distraction. The human personality usually is confused, divided, and possessed of tensions between mind and body, emotions and reason. The purity of heart necessary to will one thing, whether God or sinful pleasure, comes at most rarely, at exceptional moments. So the key to a person's moral state at any given time is not any one particular thought or action. The key is the general direction in which the person is heading, the overall drift. If slowly, steadily, by a rhythm of three steps forward and two steps back, the person is becoming more mature, more realistic, more loving, one can say that the Spirit has him or her well in tow. Despite occasional failures, even misdeeds that on the objective books could be serious, there are reasons for giving the person who prays and really does love God the benefit of the doubt. This is even more so when cultural change has made many of the absolutes that used to dominate Catholic moral theology debatable, not because lax theologians are pandering to the whims of their undisciplined contemporaries, but because it is often not immediately clear what the truly loving, life-giving course of action would be.

Consider, for example, the person who feels alienated from the local parish and stops going to Sunday mass. On the books the obligation to attend mass on Sunday still holds. No one in Rome has announced that this obligation has ceased to bind under pain of serious sin. But many Catholics, theologians and laity alike, have questioned a blanket application of this rule that would leave no room for divergences. The Church itself has acknowledged the need for flexibility, by allowing people to satisfy their Sunday obligation on Saturday evening. This is a tiny concession, to be sure, but it cracks the absolutism of the mentality that sees mortal sin everywhere.

It is possible, though by no means certain, that a given person staying away from the Eucharistic celebrations of the local church is keeping faith with conscience. It is possible for conscience to say that, for the moment, going to church seems to do more harm than good—cause more resentment, create more upset. Certainly there are perspectives from which one might ignore the all-too-human failings of priests who cannot prepare good sermons, of congregations that cannot sing, stop snuffling, or pay more attention to prayer than to what their neighbors are wearing. Certainly there is a valid, traditional sense in which the human side of the Eucharistic exchange matters very little, because God is the main actor, rehearsing the history of salvation, representing the sacrifice on the cross, offering himself under the appearances of bread and wine to nourish his people. But individual, personal faith is a delicate, growing affair. It has its seasons, its wounds, its immaturities, and its hidden battles. Wise observers are thus slow to rush to judgment and are quick to cut people slack in the measure they seem thoughtful, serious, and not simply lazy or self-serving.

The single person frequently suffers questions of conscience more sharply than the married person or the person living in a religious community, because there is more inner solitude and the external supports are more extrinsic. When one sleeps alone and frequently eats alone, both freedom and loneliness can loom larger. The consolation offered by recent treatments of mortal sin is along the line that Paul took in Romans 8: nothing can separate us from the love of God. God is more bent on our flourishing, our salvation, than we ever could be. Most of our problem is that we find it hard to let go, to trust that the silence could be God's eloquent presence, that the loneliness could be a providential purification or release for serving others. None of us ever knows with certitude that we are pleasing God, but it is equally true that none of us can be sure God is not smiling on us, accepting our feeble efforts to love back, even indulging the petty flailings our fear and resentment throw up. We all have to believe that God could be as good as Jesus describes his Father to be. When we do, mortal sin is both more serious and less threatening than it was when our images of God were impersonal, vague, or legalistic.

Venial Sin

The great enemy of personal ethics in the Christian scheme is the sin, the naysaying, that refuses God primacy in one's heart. As causes of such naysaying, the Catholic tradition has spoken of the world, the flesh, and the devil. Alternatively, the tradition has spoken of wealth, honors, and pride as the preoccupations that render people distant from God, embarked on pathways likely to culminate in a profound no to God's program of love. The lesser enemy of personal ethics is the venial sins that whittle away one's resolve to love God with one's whole mind, heart, soul, and strength, the weaknesses and self-indulgences that express one's continued lack of conversion, purification, illumination, and union with God.

Catholic tradition usually has associated such venial sins with human finitude and the effects of original sin, concluding that they are well-nigh inevitable. Relatedly, this tradition usually has considered sins of the flesh, focusing on food, sex, exuberance, and partying, to be less significant than sins of the spirit. Admittedly, habitual excesses regarding food, drink, sex, buying material goods, and the like pose obstacles to spiritual growth. Many people seem mired in sensuality, unable to muster the willpower and imagination necessary to pray, study, and pursue God. But the great evildoers are not the slothful and sensual. The great evildoers are the energetic egomaniacs, the fierce haters of God, and willful perverters of conscience. It would be better for a man to drink too much, eat too much, smoke, and be too friendly with women than to grow so hard, so ambitious, so self-centered that he rides roughshod over others to make a fortune, gain a prominent post, or stand apart in splendid isolation, feeling superior to the common herd. It would be better for a woman to be vain, or unwilling to love herself as she ought, to be timid to the point of cowardice, compulsive about food, or anorexic than to become a calculating manipulator of others, a cruel spirit careless of the toll she exacts as she makes her way to wealth or power. The satanic sins are the variants of Lucifer's "I will not serve." Refusing to bow to the imperatives of God that are lodged in conscience, refusing to admit that their neighbors are other selves, the great sinners grow inured to causing pain and defying God. So they end up alone, not even loving themselves, trying their best to create a genuine hell.

But just as the most useful view of Christian ethics does not pivot on mortal sins, so it does not pay more regard to venial sins than to the positive possibilities for growth that every life holds out. On the job, people who regularly examine their consciences discover that there are many ways in which they might improve how they apply themselves to their work, how they treat customers or fellow workers, how they thank God for the means to earn a living, how they regard each eight-hour performance as an opportunity to serve God, their ultimate employer.

In personal relations, friendships, and love affairs, we always find things we might do better. If we can view them as opportunities to grow in love, as more ground to conquer, they need not be discouraging. On the far side of every venial sin, every discouraging failure, lies the chance to profit from one's mistakes, to learn more about one's own character, and to find how the Holy Spirit would have one grow wiser and stronger. The basic pattern of the wisdom regime encoded in our human makeup is so simple and universal that we tend to overlook it. One need only become reflective, a person who examines her or his conscience each day, to offer the Spirit a regimen, a discipline, through which the Spirit can work considerable enlightenment.

In the past, Catholic moral theology and discourse about the ethical life sometimes discouraged people from experimentation and adventurousness. Theologians who thought that Catholic tradition had mapped out the moral terrain once and for all saw no need to consider trial and error. Their goal was to have the simple faithful, as they tended to think of those listening in the pews, perform and behave as the manuals laid out the ideal. Occasionally they admitted that full moral maturity only came when people had internalized the principles of justice and charity, but it was not clear that they considered the average person capable of such maturity.

A better model would be trying to help people form their consciences so that in freedom, with an increasing share in the liberty of the children of God, they might come more and more to do what the tradition considered virtue as a matter of course, almost unthinkingly, because the vicious alternatives scarcely came to mind. Then virtue would flow in the wake of one's main interest, one's love affair with God. Then vice truly would be perceived as ugly, unattractive, and unreasonable, as all the classical analyses of sin argue it has to be. A person in love with the living divine mystery finds it nearly impossible to blaspheme, no matter what vulgarity of language or gesture high spirits may inspire. A person who is deeply involved with another person, feeling called upon to be honest and loving to a special degree, certainly is venturing into territory that can bring heartbreak and the giving or receiving of deep pain. But seldom will such pain be vicious or express serious sin. Much more often it will come from the temporary weakness, the brief breakdown, of a person trying to bring off something wonderful and not yet able to manage it.

Two examples come to mind at this juncture, one from a direct experience on the lecture circuit and one from a book on women's experiences with institutional religion and God. The direct experience on the lecture circuit came when we were discussing the challenges facing the Catholic Church in the year 2000 with a group of about one hundred college students. The group was assembled for its regular class on interpersonal relations. We were guests, present for twenty-four hours to present a miniconference on contemporary Catholicism. In discussing drugs, crime, and other negatives, we found ourselves saying that the main task of the churches and universities would seem to be to present truly persuasive alternatives. It is not enough to just say no. For the long haul, one has to have things one loves better, things that are more exciting and satisfying. We nominated such foundational educational experiences as becoming passionately involved in scientific research, artistic creativity, religious contemplation, erotic love, or service of the poor, saying that if the churches and universities could bring these experiences alive as modalities of the spiritual life, as involvements that prove in their very experiencing what human beings are made for, then much of the social chaos threatening our country might fade away. When we asked the students how many of them had had experiences with learning, prayer, love, or some other way to ecstasy that was powerful enough to assure them they knew what we were talking about, to our joy perhaps twenty of the students raised their hands. Whatever their weaknesses and problems, those twenty have great potential for developing a personal ethical life most pleasing to God.

Our second example stems from a book we came across that focused on women's difficulties with patriarchal Christianity.[1] Many of the pieces in it report positively on creative alternatives that certain individuals have found in lesbian relationships and the new witchcraft. Overall, the surface of the book represents a consensus that is greatly at odds with either past or present Catholic orthodoxy concerning morals. And yet, under the surface, clearly visible and kicking with life, are people struggling to grow, to be honest, and above all to love. Again and again they speak of having been dead, sinfully down on themselves, cracking up from not being able to fit the official schemes, and finding vitality, joy, and what they could only call pieces of God by taking alternate, officially deviant routes.

Ideally, no such deviance would be necessary. But actually, in fact, the deficiencies in the Church, in Christian tradition, in current culture, and in individuals themselves sometimes combine to make deviance, following an unorthodox drummer, seem necessary and so not only legitimate but inspired. If the reality is that people have come alive, to a love of God, self, other people, and nature that previously was at best merely verbal, then the reality is that the

Holy Spirit has been at work in their souls. Jesus said one could know advisers, leaders, by their fruits. The tradition of discerning the spirits has said that sin, both mortal and venial, and grace can be known by their effects, both personal and social. In the freedom for which Christ has set us free, people who discern the spirits and stake their case on the fruits of their choices deserve more applause than caution. Those who would condemn them should be warned that they may find themselves fighting against the living God.

Sexuality

The popular perception is that Roman Catholic officialdom is preoccupied with sexual issues. Abortion, women's ordination, priestly celibacy, divorce, annulment of marriages, birth control, sterilization, artificial insemination, fornication, adultery, masturbation, homosexuality, AIDS, pedophilia, and no doubt other sex-related issues have claimed large, probably inordinate amounts of the attention that Catholic Christians recently have paid to personal ethics. The Church has not neglected such greater issue as the nuclear arms race, care for the poor, and justice among nations and between social classes. Liberation theology has made a most useful impact. But sexuality often has predominated in discussions of personal morality, receiving far more attention than prayer, work, art, science, play, nature, and the other elements of a holistic spirituality.[2]

One might defend a preoccupation with sexuality, were it consistently merely a means to elucidate the path to passionate love of God, neighbor, and self. Sometimes such a preoccupation has been a good service of such passionate love, but often Catholic discussion has been legalistic, fearful, or so otherworldly that it seemed out of touch with the Incarnation. The fact is that sex is the most profound stimulus to consider the mystery of being human. Men and women meet each other as like and different in so basic, intense, and pervasive a fashion that sex is the first problem both have to solve, more profound than the problems raised by race, age, religious affiliation, ethnic background, or socioeconomic status. When people make their sexuality gracious, complementary, a basis for both fair-sharing and mutual appreciation, they accomplish more than half the task of being human. When they turn sexuality into a battleground or experience it as a burden, they so twist and complicate the task of being human that it seems more a prison sentence than a glorious stimulus to grow.

If children are conceived and raised in a happy love, comfortable with sexuality, they are likely to prevail against all future odds. One wishes them good health, a fine education, and enough income to stave off want. They have rights to decent housing, useful work, just political regimes, and houses of worship that make religion beautiful. But the beginning of human prosperity is the love of two parents whose bodies, minds, hearts, and souls are inextricably entwined. The ideal is an eros that has made sharing bed and board, trying to become one flesh, an image of God's passionate love for his people. The main problem with Roman Catholic approaches to sexuality, both learned and lay, has been their slighting of such eros, their unease with it, their fumbling the issues of how it mediates a God who is light in whom there is no darkness at all, a God who is love, full of desire for all those born of woman.

For want of wisdom about eros, the good advice that Roman Catholicism often offers about abortion, marital relations, homosexuality, and the rest regularly miscarries. The play, pleasure, and intrinsic challenge of what people most crave has not come into focus. Even those who are docile to Roman Catholic teaching have not learned how deep prayer is like deep sexual union. Even those battered by love gone wrong have not been offered God's tenderly romantic embrace.

Not to put too fine a point on it, Roman Catholicism often has seemed to fear sex far more than to bless it as God's closest presence and wryest joke. Others can deal with the knotted question of how Hellenistic dualism and clerical celibacy have conspired to produce this effect. The more useful point here would seem to be trying to redeem the good sense Catholicism has mustered through the ages from the negativism that has turned off so many modern people.

The good sense, a dividend from monasticism and religious life, has been to discern and preach that sex, like everything else created, cannot substitute for God. If the attraction of God or a life of ministerial service should take the form of a desire to bypass family life, one ought to praise such an instinct and help it grow fruits that enable it to pass the evangelical test. When advertising, literature, and the going cultural definitions of pleasure have glorified a sexual hedonism, Catholic common sense has been a champion of sanity, balance, and those victimized by sexual obsession. It has rightly stigmatized pornography, prostitution, and most abortions as closures to God that are bound to warp people's souls.

The negativism has shown in the tardiness with which Roman Catholicism began to work on a theology of marriage that would not subordinate the personal love of the spouses to procreation and in the paucity of Catholic contributions to a spirituality for single laity. Instead of linking marriage and parenthood with the basic sacraments of baptism and the Eucharist, so that the most common vocation in the Church would stand in line with the most important ways of developing divine life, traditional Catholic theologians made marriage something common in the pejorative sense, a lesser way than what appealed to its elite. Similarly, instead of treating baptism and the Eucharist as sacraments that could enable single people to love their bodies, emotions, and erotic minds,

Catholic theologians either paid single people no heed or produced ethical statements that treated them as eunuchs. Instead of showing that the liberty of the children of God applied to how single men and women dated, fell in love, expressed their love, and honored the spark of God in their clod, the tradition usually appeared with fists full of warnings, caveats, prohibitions, making the undeniable fact that marriage is the most appropriate context for sexual intercourse a kind of club.

Someplace there is a more excellent way, a zone of beautiful balance. Someplace sexual attraction comes on the horizon with a fully positive glow, free of the clouds of worry about fornication. In that same place, married people receive trust from their religious leaders that encourages them to plan their families responsibly, lovingly, with spirits unclouded by fine distinctions between natural and artificial contraception. That same place looks upon homosexual love as varied, mysterious, perhaps another gift of God. It cries over the follies of those who want an AIDS policy that would prefer a pure rejection of condoms to the preservation of lives that issued as images of God and were worthy of Christ's blood. It sees the rejection of women's needs and women's gifts as abhorrent to a Spirit who moved over the waters brooding the life of creation, to a God who could no more abandon Israel than a nursing mother could abandon her child. Indeed, it is even willing to imagine the sexuality of Jesus, not simply as an abstract theological deduction from his full humanity, but as a prime determinant of his perception and love. With no prurience, it is willing to think about the married life of Mary and Joseph, the sex life of the bachelor Jesus, not necessarily challenging traditional assumptions and definitions about the virginity of all three, but to make it plain that God might have used sexual intercourse not just in a mode of abnegation but also quite positively. Until Catholic Christianity comes to center its sexual ethnics in that place, it will not convey the healing touch of God's grace to humanity's sorest places, the wounds in all our psyches where we doubt God could find us attractive, God really could fall head over heels for such as we.

Poverty and Obedience

In discussing sexuality, we have followed in the train of the long-standing Catholic interest in the way of perfection. That interest made chastity a matter of solemn religious vows. It did less well with marital and single love, but its nervous interest did help keep romance, fidelity, and procreation properly central in people's estimates of what God asked of them. Poverty and obedience filled out the traditional elitist program. As monks and other religious dealt with their sexuality by consecrating it to God, so they dealt with material goods and their own willfulness by placing them under the discipline of religious vows. The analogies in lay life, both married and single, have lagged behind, as they did with sexuality. What, then, ought one to say to people at large today about their approach to material possessions and independence? How ought poverty and obedience to figure in modern personal ethics or spirituality?

First, the situation seems clearer regarding material possessions and poverty than it is regarding independence and obedience. For impoverished countries, the first order of business obviously is to help people secure the material necessities without which no decent human life can flourish. The poverty that leads to malnourished children, poor education, crime, and hopelessness is a great evil, a major enemy of God. Christian instinct has long been that if one person has two shirts and another has none, the person with two ought to surrender one. Sophisticated economists may mock the attempt to apply this basic instinct to national or international affairs, but Christians will be wise to retain it. Those who really believe in God, for whom God is not simply a safe notion, know that we children of God are much more equal than distinguished into classes such as privileged and poor. The goods of the earth are for all the earth's people. Nature produces a sufficiency of goods and wealth to provide a good living for a reasonable number of earthly inhabitants. If there is starvation and massive underdevelopment in our world, the fault lies with ourselves. It is our sin, our greed, our stupidity and hardheartedness that cause the gross economic and political injustices twisting our world out of shape.

All the religious institutions that trumpet this message, Catholic Christianity included, are great benefactors of humankind and witnesses to God. Individuals who renounce mammon in favor of serving others or witnessing to God are exemplary heroes. Still, the churches could do more with Jesus' saying (Mt 19:24) that it is easier for a camel to pass through the eye of a needle than for rich people to enter the kingdom of God. Without turning into despisers of beauty and God's creation, they could give much sharper, more prophetic critiques showing the dangers of mammon, the intrinsic role mammon plays in the sufferings of our world, and the hypocrisy of those who push away demands for economic reform with a theology of fallen human nature that calls such demands perfectionistic and leaves final justice in God's hands. Matthew 25 is a better indication of the justice God wants, the impatience God has with our self-serving protests of impotence.

Those living today in the affluent nations with a spiritual hunger that makes them stripped and poor, makes them the enemies of consumerism and the neglect of people in want, must be dear to the Jesus of Matthew 25. When they convert their lean existence into works of practical help, they swell the complement of the saints. So do the people who negotiate the difficult terrain of the personal independence, the willfulness, that the traditional vow of obedience treated. On the one hand, our time needs free-spiritedness as much as any other time did, if only because free-spiritedness is the great condition for creativity and passionate love. On the other hand, much modern social chaos stems from the unwillingness of individuals to subordinate their own interests to the common good, and such modern nations as the United States have made a fetish of individual liberties. Insofar as a wrongful individualism has led to a wrongful competitiveness and selfishness, in turn producing economic regimes that are careless of the common good and indifferent to massive suffering, a wrongful individualism has been most useful to Satan.

Insofar as totalitarian regimes, in fact powered by most willful individuals but supposedly by servants of the common good, have crushed creativity and warped passionate love, they have given socialism a very bad name. Socialism probably should be the natural Christian politics. One for all and all for one ought to be the basic instinct of each Christian cell, for Christians are members of one another and branches of a single vine. They are children of God enjoined to love one another as their Master has loved them. Thus destructive competition, selfishness, and neglect of the common good ought to be as foreign to Christians as frequenting prostitutes or polluting themselves with pornography. Their spirits ought to rebel, the way the nose rebels at a noxious smell. On the other hand, Christians ought to honor the individuality of each member, because they see each as a different expression of God. So for Christianity the only proper social existence is one that fulfills individuals in a whole greater than the sum of their parts. This whole is the Christ in whom one day God will be all in all.

Confusing the pilgrim Church with this heavenly entity, many Church leaders thoughout history have arrogated to themselves an authority to direct the consciences of all the faithful. When that has happened, virtue has lain with those who resisted in the name of the liberty of the children of God and the impossibility of distant authority knowing what the Spirit has inspired on the spot. The result has been a healthy tension that has kept both leaders and subordinates on their toes. Good leadership would listen to the consensus of the faithful, honoring the charismata the Spirit dispensed as the Spirit wished. Faithful members of the Church would show themselves docile to the **magisterium** and inclined to give it the benefit of the doubt. When great rifts developed between the theologians and the bishops, or between the leaders in Rome and the people in the pews, as they did following Pope Paul VI's 1968 encyclical on birth control, prudent parties on both sides worked out a tacit accommodation. Church leaders would continue to put forward the theological line they thought necessitated by tradition and fidelity to the gospel. Ordinary members would continue to behave as their **existential** consciences told them they should, listening respectfully to their bishops. And both sides would pray for creative solutions that might heal the rift.

In the more recent Catholic debate about dissent from **noninfallible** magisterial teaching, our sympathies have been with the theologians, such as Charles Curran, who have argued for the rights of conscience and the necessity of a faithful dissent when conscience does not square with Roman edicts.[3] Further questions remain about the wisdom of having such dissenters work in situations that make them seem responsible for presenting official Catholic doctrine. But there can be no doubt that some saints and eminent theologians down through the ages have publicly dissented from papal and curial edicts, whereas the Catholic tradition about the necessity of following one's existential conscience, even if it prove erroneous, makes it clear that all Christians owe their first obedience to the Holy Spirit. Thus the docility one owes Church authorities never overrides the freedom one has under the Holy Spirit, any more than such freedom, when genuine, produces people who despise the authority of those holding office in the Church or expect a perfect realm free of all human foibles. As Catholic tradition has long said, virtue stands in the middle, being a lovely balance that itself testifies to God's grace. Where human conflicts and tensions seem irreconcilable, condemning us as people who will never get along, God remains greater. Whether the issue be sexuality, wealth, or independence, our hearts are not the final words. The final word is the love of the God with whom all things are possible.

Representative Personality: Bernard Lonergan

Bernard Lonergan (1904–1984) was a Canadian Jesuit theologian who was renowned for his work on theological method. The basis of Lonergan's proposed reconstruction of theology was his view of human consciousness. Building on the work of Thomas Aquinas, Lonergan delineated the dynamic structure of human consciousness, paying special attention to the act of understanding. Prior to the act of understanding (insight), Lonergan found a rich collection of experience. Understanding amounted to grasping that which gave such experience its order or form, what made it intelligible. But understanding was hypothetical: what might make sense of one's sensible perception, imagination, and rudiments of knowledge. To gain genuine knowledge one had to pass from understanding to judgment. Judgment involved reflection, going back over one's experience and understanding, and even going to the depths of one's own human constitution, to verify that one was in fact capable of discerning the truth.

The fourth level (after experience, understanding, and judgment) in Lonergan's description of the dynamics of consciousness was decision. It is not enough to know what is so. One has to act in accordance with such knowledge. For example, knowing that smoking is dangerous to one's health, one has to take the cure. Knowing the Christ is a surpassing treasure, one has to repent and believe in the good news. For Lonergan, ethics derives from the imperative claim of human consciousness that we develop a consistency between our knowing and our doing. If we do not perform the truths we have discovered or come to believe, we are hypocrites and suffer terrible self-division.

At the term of the dynamics of human consciousness stands the divine mystery. Once discovered, it reveals that it has been present from the beginning, luring our minds and hearts forward. But the religious dimension that perfects our ethical thrusts first presents God as an unrestricted goodness, as one whom we should love without reserve. The religious life then becomes precisely an unrestricted, ever-transcending life of love. We can put no limits to what God can be for us or can ask of us. We have fallen in love with one of another species, one who exists beyond all species, and we have started to sense that our destiny is what eye has not seen, ear has not heard, it has not entered the human heart to conceive.

For Bernard Lonergan, then, the wellsprings of religion, Christianity included, are the dynamics of human awareness over which the divine mystery presides. All meaning reposes in human awareness. Without it biblical revelation is but squiggles on musty pages and the sacraments are but weird motions performed by people in funny clothing. Lonergan certainly hallowed tradition, Church authority, and the objective social order. He was well aware of how history shapes human consciousness and of the rich variety of the horizons — intellectual, aesthetic, religious, and more — that dictate what consciousness can survey. But he found existential consciousness, and so conscience, to take their final measure from the falling in love and being in love unrestrictedly that make human beings naturally religious.

In correlating religious conversion with moral and intellectual conversion, Lonergan the sober methodologist turned poetic:

Similarly, religious conversion goes beyond moral. Questions for intelligence, for reflection, for deliberation reveal the eros of the human spirit, its capacity and its desire for self-transcendence. But that capacity meets fulfillment, that desire turns to joy, when religious conversion transforms the existential subject into a subject in love, a subject held, grasped, possessed, and owned through a total and so an other-worldly love. Then there is a new basis for all valuing and all doing good. In no way are fruits of intellectual or moral conversion negated or diminished. On the contrary, all human pursuit of the true and the good is included within and furthered by a cosmic context and purpose and, as well, there now accrues to man the power of love to enable him to accept the suffering involved in undoing the defects of decline.

It is not to be thought, however, that religious conversion means no more than a new and more efficacious ground for the pursuit of intellectual and moral ends. Religious loving is without conditions, qualifications, reservations; it is with all one's heart and all one's soul and all one's mind and all one's strength. This lack of limitation, though it corresponds to the unrestricted character of human questioning, does not pertain to this world. Holiness abounds in truth and moral goodness, but it has a distinct dimension of its own. It is other-worldly fulfillment, joy, peace, bliss. In Christian experience these are the fruits of being in love with a mysterious, uncomprehended God.[4]

When Bernard Lonergan reflects on the authentic human existence that such a dynamic consciousness, wedded to the divine mystery, pursues, he in effect shows what the personal ethics of the mature Christian look like. The mature Christian, centered in the love poured forth in our hearts by the Holy Spirit (Rom 5:5), is respectful of tradition and docile to Church authority, but the crux of his or her moral life is what conscience dictates. By an intellectual conversion that equates the real with what has been properly verified, a moral conversion that equates the good with what has proven to be objectively beneficial, and a religious conversion that both establishes one's being in an unrestricted love of God and lets God's grace become the first principle of one's actions, the mature person has left the world of the unconverted, casting off sensuality, selfishness, and idolatry, to follow the lead of the Holy Spirit at the depths of his or her being. There the Spirit is refashioning the image of God, purifying it of sin and luring it toward a marriage with the divine beauty. There the Spirit is encouraging a habit of peace, joy, and freedom that can prevail even in the midst of disappointments and sufferings.

The watchwords indicating the way to such maturity are four, corresponding to the successive stages of the dynamics of personal consciousness. Lonergan named these watchwords the "transcendental precepts," meaning that they apply always and everywhere. They are: Be attentive. Be intelligent. Be reasonable. Be responsible. At the term of consciousness, where religious conversion takes over, one might add a fifth precept: Be loving.

These precepts internalize and personalize the implications of Christian ethics. In the light of the gospel, which says that God offers us the love that can make us whole and redeem us from dehumanizing sin, Catholic Christianity calls people to trust their experience, listen to it, honor it, and believe that it mediates the touches of God. It calls people to use their heads, respect their minds, and believe that God has given creation sufficient intelligibility to make investigating it worthwhile. It asks people to be judicious, reasonable, and sufficiently reflective and disciplined to take reality as it shows itself to be, rather than as what one's egocentricity, extroversion, or superficiality might like it to be.

Fourth, the Catholic tradition calls for responsibility, not because it thinks people are justified by works, but because it trusts the way God has structured human consciousness and knows from experience that knowledge not issuing in love is feckless. Last, Catholic Christianity wants one to let go, drop below the confines of the mind and will, and reach out to the hand the Spirit is offering and make one's loving unrestricted, as high as the heavens and as deep as the oceans, tracking all the places where God has worked beauty and healing. This is the mystical spirit hinted by the Epistle of James in its reference to the Father of lights, and by Ignatius Loyola, the founder of the order to which Lonergan belonged, in his contemplation of God's love playing throughout creation and history. It leads to the holy abandonment praised by the mystics, to Teresa of Avila's marvelous "Let nothing disturb you." Such a vision knows painfully well the ravages of sin, not the least in the self, but it finds God's grace to have abounded much more. It knows the grace that brings the Easter liturgy to sing of a happy fault, a *felix culpa*, and it is in no danger of holding such grace cheap.

In contrast to distinctively Protestant views of conscience, which have their own wisdom, the Catholic slant of a genius such as Lonergan is to find God always implicit in what we human beings are and are called to be. Building on our nature, the grace of God would make us truly free, children feeling so loved by their heavenly parent that they put up with trials and deficiencies almost gladly, knowing that before long they will be home, and knowing as well that even though they are not yet home they never lack the care of God's Spirit, the concern of God's Son, the provident protection of the unbegotten Source of all that is or could be.

Glossary

Existential: concerned with one's here and now, holistic, intensely personal being. Existence is the act by which creatures step forth from nothingness. It is one's inmost identity, where God directly places and keeps one in being. So values, choices, and experiences are existential in the measure that they cut to our center and summon a response in which we give back ourselves. In contrast, values, choices, and experiences remain merely notional or superficial until they engage our centers, our hearts, and so call forth all that we are: emotion, intellect, desire, love. Pascal's famous distinction between the God of Abraham,

Isaac, and Jacob and the God of the philosophers expresses the difference between existential religion and merely conceptual or academic religion. In Pascal's own experience, the living God was like a consuming fire.

Magisterium: the official teaching authority of the Church. One can locate this teaching authority and charism at many different levels of the Church, speaking, for example, of the magisterium accomplished by professional theologians, but the foremost connotation of the term is the office of the bishops and pope as pastors in succession to the apostles. Roman Catholicism grants the bishop of Roman a primacy in this magisterial office, although ideally not one exercised apart from the whole college of bishops. Theologians who focus on the papal form of the magisterium also tend to include the papal curia, according the different congregations and bureaus that serve the pope's teaching office a share in his authority. A sophisticated system of theological "notes" used to indicate the different levels of authority that various vehicles of teaching (encyclicals, statements of curial offices, consensuses of theologians, and so forth) possessed, but this system has broken down in recent times.

Noninfallible: teaching that does not fulfill the restricting conditions associated with formal (*ex cathedra*) pronouncements by the pope or by the bishops in concert. Such teaching can be fully authoritative, but it does not put into play the special charism Catholics (and some others) believe that God has vested in the Church, whereby the Church cannot fail to provide the truth necessary for salvation. For Catholics this charism has a special focus in the Petrine ministry, inasmuch as the Bishop of Rome presides over the entire Church and expresses its unity. Noninfallible teaching does, however, partake of the vicissitudes of history (as infallible teaching may), and liberal Catholic theologians would limit its claims upon the conscience of believers to what its inner intellectual persuasiveness, and the docility due one's ecclesiastical superiors, can produce.

Discussion Questions

1. What are the sins that you think could slay the life of God in a person's soul?
2. What is the significance of the fundamental option, the basic values, that the overall direction of a person's moral life suggests?

3. What are the effects of venial sins of sloth and sensuality?
4. On the analogy of a human love affair, evaluate the effects of distraction, petty lust, greed, and the like on one's relationship with God.
5. What is a balanced view of the relationship between sex and love?
6. What are the advantages, and the disadvantages, in having much of one's moral theology in the hands of celibates?
7. Why is authentic Christianity likely to express a countercultural attitude toward wealth?
8. What is the freedom of conscience, the independence, necessary for creativity and mature love?
9. Why does Bernard Lonergan wax eloquent about religious conversion?
10. Describe the effects that obeying Lonergan's transcendental precepts for ten years might produce.

Notes

[1] See Linda Hurcome, ed., *Sex and God: Some Varieties of Women's Religious Experience* (New York: Routledge & Kegan Paul, 1987).
[2] See John Tully Carmody, *Holistic Spirituality* (New York: Paulist, 1983) and Denise Lardner Carmody, *The Double Cross: Ordination, Abortion, and Catholic Feminism* (New York: Crossroad, 1986).
[3] See Charles E. Curran, *Faithful Dissent* (Kansas City: Sheed and Ward, 1987).
[4] Bernard Lonergan, *Method in Theology* (New York: Herder & Herder, 1972), p. 242.

PART IV

Contemporary Trends

CHAPTER 14

Peace and Justice

Vatican II Statements
Liberation Theology
John Paul II
The American Catholic Bishops' Pastoral Letters
Representative Personality: Mary Harren
Glossary, Discussion Questions, Notes

Vatican II Statements

When one discourses on "contemporary trends" in Catholicism, Vatican II is the obvious watershed, the obvious place from which to start. It divides Catholicism into a past era, in *ancien régime*, stretching back as far as the Council of Trent, and a present era, in which the implications of the Council continue to work themselves out, no doubt more painfully than many of the Council fathers expected. Vatican II treated most of the pressing problems of faith and cultural adaptation that had surfaced by the middle of the twentieth century. It was a pastoral Council, more inclined to speak of what the Church had to do if it were to develop viewpoints that were both faithful to tradition and persuasive to contemporary human beings than to issue dogmatic definitions. Through many of its documents ran a great concern about peace and justice, but nowhere more so than in the document on the Church in the modern world (*Gaudium et Spes*).

Representative statements of this document on peace include the following: "Peace is not merely the absence of war. Nor can it be reduced solely to the maintenance of a balance of power between enemies. Nor is it brought about by dictatorship. Instead, it is rightly and appropriately called 'an enterprise of justice' (Is 32:7). Peace results from that harmony built into human society by its divine Founder, and actualized by men as they thirst after ever greater justice" (#78).[1]

We may note, first, the positive pursuit in which the Council fathers were engaged. Well aware of the destructive potential in modern weaponry, they were not content to think of their Church as merely supporting the standoff between the superpowers. Even less were they willing to support dictatorial regimes claiming that the suppression of human rights was a necessary condition for maintaining military preparedness and keeping deadly enemies at bay.

Second, the peace that the bishops wanted to encourage brought to mind the words of the prophet about a work of justice. Only fair dealing, equity, brought into focus the peace that would gladden their hearts. In the background of their thinking may have been Augustine's classical definition of peace as "the tranquility of order." One cannot have social order without justice. No amount of policing or repression of disaffected citizens can supply for furnishing members of a society the sense that they are sharing burdens and rewards equitably. Order is the result of minds and hearts achieving some harmony, some agreement that the system of rights and duties under which people are living rings true, gives all participants their due, at least in a crude sense. Until a society attains such a justice, persuading its citizens that, on the whole, their social compact is a fair deal, it will know no substantial peace. The same condition holds for the global human community. Until all nations have solid grounds for saying that the pains and joys of life on earth are spread around fairly, one will have no substantial tranquility, because there will be no healthy economic or political order keeping global relations harmonious.

Third, true to their heritage from natural law theory, the bishops think that the harmony proper to the globe is an expression of the order built into human society by God, its founder. The implication is that God has given human beings laws, inbuilt structures and imperatives, that reason can discern and good will can obey. The further implication is that God always provides sufficient grace to enable people to follow such divine intentions. This quotation does not spell out what such ingiven harmony entails, but other parts of the modern Catholic tradition deal with such matters as a proper distribution of wealth, respect for the religious and cultural rights of individuals, the dignity of the human person that forbids the state's using people as means to ends, rights to a decent standard of living (adequate nourishment, housing, health care, education, and the like), protection of citizens against external foes, and much more.

The Council did not focus on many specific constituents of the modern nations' difficulties in attaining peace, but *Gaudium et Spes* did note that "significant differences crop up . . . between international institutions born of the popular desire for peace, and the ambition to propagate one's own ideology, as well as collective greed existing in nations or other groups" (#8).[2] In mentioning ideology, the Council could have had both Marxist and capitalist propaganda in mind, since papal encyclicals prior to the Council had noted the problems with both points of view, as have encyclicals since the Council. Marxism is ever liable to subordinate the dignity of the individual to the needs of the atheistic state, whereas capitalism is reluctant to make economic prosperity the servant of the common good rather than of a relatively few entrepreneurs. Both philosophies are liable to become tools of greed, although the capitalist countries seem more intent on financial or material prosperity whereas the Marxist countries seem more intent on acquiring power.

In its dogmatic constitution on the Church (*Lumen Gentium*), the Council said of justice: "Let the laity also by their combined efforts remedy any institutions and conditions of the world which are customarily an inducement to sin, so that all such things may be conformed to the norms of justice and may favor the practice of virtue rather than hinder it" (#36).[3] The focus on the laity stems from the view, still prevalent in the Council but less prominent in theology since that time, that clergy and laity ought to dwell within two separate spheres and have little overlap. The sphere of the laity was the world, where the practicalities of warfare, economic justice, civil rights, race relations, and all the rest worked themselves out. By vocation, Christian laity had the duty and right to develop competence in all the matters that were necessary for the healthy running of government and culture. Church officials were supposed to encourage such competence, respect it, and listen to it. The tone of the conciliar documents retains something of the pre–Vatican II Roman tendency to lecture the laity from on high, but overall they represent a considerable advance over the monarchical style of the popes and clergy prior to the advent of John XXIII.

The notion that worldly institutions and conditions could be an inducement to sin remains rather abstract, but the general implication is plain. When people are not being treated justly — do not have adequate food, housing, work, and the rest — they are tempted to revolts that can be destructive. When they must live or work in conditions not befitting human dignity, they can feel they have little to lose but their chains. Classical Marxism fed on the resentments of the workers who were victimized by newly industrialized Europe. Socialist revolutions in many lands have been fueled by gross disparities between the wealthy few and the many poor. Perhaps the bishops had in mind the great revolutions produced in the Soviet Union and China, as well as the classical modern revolutions accomplished in America and France, but they may also have had in mind the conditions in Latin America, where traditionally Catholic cultures had done little to keep the rich from gouging the poor.

Virtue only flowers when justice prevails. People can lead saintly lives in conditions of injustice and warfare, but on the whole such condition are no recipe for human prosperity. True to its instincts about grace building on nature, the Catholic tradition expressed in the conciliar documents believed that people need a decent standard of living, pride in their work and family life, and confidence in the fairness of the social arrangements shaping their lives if they are to mirror Christ as God intends.

Liberation Theology

Reflecting on the manifest injustice in many countries of the world, and in the economic and political patterns of the international community, many Catholic theologians have come to interpret the gospel as a call to achieve this-worldly justice. Without denying that the gospel transcends all this-worldly concerns, dealing with a God whom the world can never exhaust, many liberation theologians developing native Catholic theologies in Latin America, Africa, and Asia have rather stressed how the Church ought to be helping people free themselves of poverty, sickness, political oppression, and the other evils that blight their lives.

For liberation theology, the theses of Vatican II about peace and justice have an admirable biblical ancestry. Probably the most important paradigm in the *Tanak*, the Hebrew Bible, is the Exodus from Egypt, and many liberation theologians have joined with traditional Jews and black slaves in regarding the Exodus as God's definitive statement about bondage to oppressive powers. Inasmuch as God led the Hebrews out of slavery in Egypt, fighting on their behalf at the Red Sea, God declared himself the champion of those who wish to escape from vicious overlords and gain a land of their own, flowing with milk and honey. To be sure, the Bible attributes such liberation to the divine initiative, and it is noteworthy that between the Exodus under Moses and the entry upon the promised land under Joshua the covenanted people wandered for a generation, grumbling, growing feeble in faith, and trying God's patience. But the finale of the story remains victory and success. God exalted the lowly and put down the proud of heart. As the song of Moses after the Exodus put it: "I will sing to the Lord, for he has triumphed gloriously; the horse and his rider he has thrown into the sea. The Lord is my strength and my song, and he has become my salvation" (Ex 15 : 1 – 2).

For the New Testament, the Exodus was a type, a prefigurement, of the victory accomplished by Jesus the Christ. In dying and rising, Jesus led an exodus from this world of sin ("Egypt") to God's heaven. In principle, Jesus defeated the worst of enemies, sin, Satan, and death. He liberated people from the fears that had cast a pall over humanity since the dawn of consciousness, making the leitmotiv of Christian existence a great joy.

The liberation theologians take pains to argue that such a victory should enable Christians to labor enthusiastically for a realm of justice on earth. Thus José Miranda, reflecting on the **realized eschatology** of the Johannine literature, thinks that a robust Christian faith would have no doubt that human beings can make a decent, just existence on earth.[4] He therefore criticizes Christians who seem passive in the face of injustice and evil or who paint present existence as simply a vale of tears on the way to heavenly fulfillment.

Gustavo Gutierrez, the Peruvian liberation theologian who has produced some of the most influential writings of the movement, has elaborated not only these biblical themes but also the spirituality that the gospel implies when one gazes unblinkingly at the sufferings of the world's poorest people. For Gutierrez, one cannot be authentically Christian without identifying with such poor people, so that one comes to stand by their side (at least mentally, and ideally physically as well). Jesus' beatitudes and his own example of stripped, free living serve well at this point, as do the prayers of the saints who took upon themselves the burdens of the sick and the dying, who spent themselves to bring the compassion of Christ to the wretched of the earth.

However, Gutierrez and other liberation theologians are equally concerned to elucidate the virtues of the poor, the many ways in which they may understand the gospel better than the wealthy and powerful. Because God is their only recourse, the poor can be more open to the gospel than the wealthy. The world can hold fewer attractions for them, whereas the value of faith and neighborly love can be more plain. The point is that when one really sees how the majority of people must live in today's world, many of the traditional preoccupations of the Church and the theologians seem irrelevant. Until both come to grips with the fact that well over half the more than five billion people now sharing the earth live in considerable deprivation, neither will grasp the true dimensions of Christ's redemptive activity.

Gutierrez has balanced his political accents with fine writings about prayer and the lessons in the great biblical story of Job.[5] Leonardo Boff, a Brazilian liberation theologian, has criticized the institutional Church for being itself an impediment to liberation, insofar as its clericalism has kept the mass of the Christian laity in subservience.[6] Like Miranda (and more than Gutierrez), Boff has accepted certain analytical techniques from Marxist theory, thereby earning great suspicion in Rome.

The Latin American theologians, who have taken the liberationist lead and been imitated by Africans and Asians, usually make it plain that they are not accepting Marxist atheism. The main value they find in Marxism is its analyses of labor relations, ideology, and class conflict. Concerning ideology, for example, Marxists have raised the consciousness of most educated people, so that today most look carefully at the connection between the values a given political regime is professing and where the major profits from that system actually go. The classical Marxist case was the ideology of *laissez-faire* economics that fueled capitalist societies, where the lion's share of the profits went to a few entrepreneurs. Things have become more complicated in later capitalism, as a result of the participation of many ordinary citizens in the ownership of businesses and the emergence of labor as an organized partner. But the liberation theologians still find merit in the Marxist outlook, because it drags into the spotlight the relations between the wealthy nations of the Northern Hemisphere and the poor nations of the Southern Hemisphere. Such relations have tended to make the southern nations warehouses of raw materials and cheap labor for the benefit of northern entrepreneurs. (One could speak of a Christian entrepreneurship, if the goal of its development were the common good or, even better, the benefit of the poor, but most contemporary entrepreneurship does not satisfy that condition.)

The liberation theologians are also interested in how religion has colluded with unjust regimes and favored the wealthy against the poor, finding such a collusion diametrically opposed to the biblical Christ. They examine the combination of economic, political, religious, social, historical, military, sexual, racial, and other factors in Latin America, arguing that the majority of the (dictatorial) regimes are radically opposed to both biblical and Church teaching. Since 1968, when the bishops made a preferential option for the poor, much of the Latin American church has borne prophetic witness against the exploitation, murder, injustice, and other sinful abuse that flourishes in the countries that church serves. As well, the Latin American Church has protested against northern nations such as the United States that support repressive, murderous dictators. The recent controversies centered on Nicaragua merely continue a long-playing dispute that previously centered on El Salvador, Guatemala, and (early in the twentieth century) Mexico.

Because of their opposition to brutality and exploitation, many priests, nuns, and laity alike have lost their lives. The dictatorial regimes have dropped their veneer of Catholic piety and shown what actually drives them: naked ambition for wealth and power. Playing on the obsessive fear of Communism that gripes the Latin American wealthy, right-wing Christians, and many leaders of the United States, those serving the status quo have not scrupled to slay archbishops at the altar, as they did with Oscar Romero of El Salvador. This is the bold, unbridled evil that liberation theologians have to face. This is the reason they insist that Christ takes sides against corrupt power, even when putative Christians abet it. Conservative Catholics rightly criticize any bending toward class warfare, but liberation theology puts on them a burden to follow Jesus in his concern for the poor.

John Paul II

From the beginning of his pontificate, Karol Wojtyla promised to be a striking pope. Polish to the core, he was bound to bring a new style to the heavily Italian Vatican, whereas his personal experience of duress under Nazi and Communist regimes suggested he would offer a unique perspective on oppressive political regimes, especially those of Eastern Europe.

To the surprise of some, John Paul II has shown himself more akin to the liberation theologians on topics of peace and justice than opposed to them. Admittedly, he criticized liberation theology during the first years of his pontificate, denying that priests and nuns ought to get directly involved in political affairs. He also stressed that representatives of Christ must always focus on the supernatural means of redemption and salvation, avoiding any collapse of the gospel into a program of social betterment. His curial commission charged with maintaining doctrinal orthodoxy came close to harassing liberal theologians such as Edward Schillebeeckx, Charles Curran, Gustavo Gutierrez, and Leonardo Boff. One of its main tenets was that one could not accept some parts of the Marxist system and reject others, as the liberation theologians often claimed to do.

But the pope's own statements about peace and justice have agreed more with the main tenets of liberation theology than they opposed them. John Paul II has insisted that all people have basic human rights to a decent standard of living, a fair wage, religious freedom, political participation, and the like. He has positioned the gospel and the Church as champions of the poor and downtrodden. To his mind the Church has to speak out against injustice and corruption. He can no more separate vibrant Catholic faith from labor to build the earth and provide all people a good life than he can separate it from prayer and worship.

John Paul II has placed special emphasis on the dignity of human work. For example, in his commentary on the documents of Vatican II, written before his election to the papacy, he said:

> The fundamental premise of the Church's social doctrine is the primacy of ethics over economics. . . . The Constitution [*Gaudium et Spes*] also recalls "Some Principles Governing Economic and Social Life as a Whole," beginning with human labour. This, it points out, "surpasses in value all other elements of economic life, for the latter are only means to an end" (GS 67).
> . . . Corresponding to this right [to work], society has the duty to provide work and reward it equitably. The Constitution speaks out against the fact that "it frequently happens, even today, that workers are almost enslaved by the work they do." Instead, "the entire process of productive work must be accommodated to the needs of the human person and the nature of his life, with special attention to domestic life and particularly

that of mothers of families, taking sex and age always into account" (GS 67). As well as the right to a fair wage, there is also a right to rest and recreation.[7]

In September 1981 John Paul II issued an encyclical, his third, on work. It commemorated the ninetieth anniversary of Pope Leo XIII's encyclical *Rerum Novarum*, which most analysts consider the first of the great social encyclicals that have highlighted modern papal teaching. John Paul II's encyclical appeared at a time when workers in his native Poland were battling the Communist authorities, trying to establish their union, *Solidarity*, as a counterweight to the state's ruthless control of workers in the interests of what it considered the common good.

Solidarity had become the great symbol of the people's hope for freedom, creativity, consumer goods, and human rights. Thus commentators read with special interest the pope's remark on labor unions:

Catholic social teaching does not hold that unions are no more than a reflection of the "class" structure of society and that they are a mouthpiece for a class struggle which inevitably governs social life. They are indeed a mouthpiece for the struggle for social justice, for the just rights of working people in accordance with their individual professions. However, this struggle should be seen as a normal endeavor "for" the just good: in the present case, for the good which corresponds to the needs and merits of working people associated by profession; but it is not a struggle "against" others: even if in controversial questions the struggle takes on a character of opposition toward others, this is because it aims at the good of social justice, not for the sake of "struggle" or in order to eliminate the opponent. It is characteristic of work that it first and foremost unites people. In this consists its social power: the power to build a community. In the final analysis, both those who work and those who manage the means of production or who own them must in some way be united in this community. In the light of this fundamental structure of all work — in the light of the fact that, in the final analysis, labor and capital are indispensable components in the process of production in any social system — it is clear that, even if it is because of their work needs that people unite to secure their rights, their union remains a constructive factor of social order and solidarity, and it is impossible to ignore it.[8]

The claim that one cannot overlook the solidarity of working people no doubt was a message coded for Poland. Overall, however, this encyclical, like many of John Paul II's others, including the very recent *Sollicitudo Rei Socialis* (On Social Concerns), marks a middle ground between Communist and capitalist attitudes. In denying the Marxist doctrine of class struggle, John Paul II has counterasserted the Christian hope for cooperation among all social classes,

based on brotherly and sisterly love. In making ethics predominate over economics, and defending the rights of workers, the pope has opposed capitalist
regimes that deny workers equal partnership in productive enterprises, as well as
Communist regimes that consider workers, indeed all citizens, pawns whom the
state may move about as it wishes. For John Paul II, a dialectical relationship
between individual citizens, whose human dignity the state ought never to
compromise, and the agencies commissioned to prosecute the common good
ought to keep both poles of the social order properly restrained and cooperative.

The major criticisms of Pope John Paul II's social theory have come along
two lines. Some critics have felt that he does not understand the exigencies of
modern business and so has championed workers at the price of undercutting
capitalist ambition or Communist need for centralized planning. Other critics
have been pleased with his instructions for the outside world but have felt that
the Church's practices toward its own members undercut the efficacy of such
instructions.

Specifically, these latter critics have faulted the Church for being slow to
develop a theory of the rights of those who work for the church, of clergy and
theologians, and especially of women. Catholic hospitals have sometimes
seemed to violate the Church's own teachings about unionization and the rights
of workers. Church banking policies have led to public scandals and raised
questions about how good a steward the Vatican has been of the financial
contributions of the faithful. The Curia's treatment of theologians accused of
deviance has bordered on medieval abuses, falling far below the standards of
legal proceedings in the developed countries. Around ordination to the priesthood, which as been the rite of passage to Church power, Church officials have
hedged many controls (most notably denying orders to women and married
men) that critics charge serve the preservation of the current power blocs more
than the good of the Body of Christ at large (especially its preeminent right to
the ministries of Word and Sacrament). The institutional Church does not exist
for its own sake. It exists for the good of its common membership. It is not clear
that John Paul II accepts the radical implications of this ecclesiology, so it is
questionable that he sees the requirements for justice and peace within the
Catholic community.

The American Catholic Bishops' Pastoral Letters

A remarkable occurrence during the 1980s was the emergence of the American
Catholic bishops as a significant moral voice on the national and international
scenes. For whereas the bishops had long issued pastoral letters outlining the

Catholic position on many matters of public interest, during the past decade they changed their letter-writing process and engaged such major issues as nuclear arms policy, American economic policy, and women's rights in the Church.

The new process that the bishops recently have utilized involves broad consultation with those an intended letter affects and those possessing special expertise. Thus the bishops met with governmental officials and experts on the technical and legal aspects of nuclear armaments, as well as with moral theologians, before issuing their pastoral letter "The Challenge of Peace." They issued several drafts of the letter, encouraged reactions, and refined their statements in light of the reactions. Encouraged by the good reception that both the content of "The Challenge of Peace" and their new process had received, the bishops developed their letters on the American economy and the role of women in the Church in the same way. Thus even those who disagreed with their doctrine tended to applaud their desire to give all parties to an issue a fair hearing. For the first time in generations, American Catholic church leaders had engaged their people in an honest give and take, putting aside the baronial style of their predecessors, who had considered communication within the Church largely a one-way street.

We have seen something of the bishops' views of the American economy, as well as the views of Pope John Paul II. We concentrate here on the bishop's views of nuclear deterrence, which lay at the heart of their pastoral letter on the challenge of peace in the contemporary world. Numbers 173 – 175 of that letter suggest both the style of the pastoral on peace and its overall position:

> Pope John Paul II makes this statement about the morality of deterrence: "In current conditions 'deterrence' based on balance, certainly not as an end in itself but as a step on the way toward a progressive disarmament, may still be judged morally acceptable. Nonetheless in order to ensure peace, it is indispensable not to be satisfied with this minimum which is always susceptible to the real danger of explosion." [77]
>
> In Pope John Paul II's assessment we perceive two dimensions in the contemporary dilemma of deterrence. One dimension is the danger of nuclear war, with its human and moral costs. The possession of nuclear weapons, the continuing quantitative growth of the arms race, and the danger of nuclear proliferation all point to the grave danger of basing "peace of a sort" on deterrence. The other dimension is the independence and freedom of nations and entire peoples, including the need to protect smaller nations from threats to their independence and integrity. Deterrence reflects the radical distrust which marks all international politics, a condition identified as a major problem by Pope John XXIII in *Peace on Earth* and reaffirmed by Pope Paul VI and Pope John Paul II. Thus a

balance of forces, preventing either side from achieving superiority, can be seen as a means of safeguarding both dimensions.

The moral duty today is to prevent nuclear war from ever occurring *and* to protect and preserve those key values of justice, freedom and independence which are necessary for personal dignity and national integrity. In reference to these issues, Pope John Paul II judges that deterrence may still be judged morally acceptable, "certainly not as an end in itself but as a step on the way toward a progressive disarmament."[9]

The bishops note John Paul II's awareness of the fragility of deterrence relationships, and then they take up two of the thorniest policy questions: what uses of deterrents one projects in scenarios where war breaks out, and how deterrence and military capability affect the likelihood of warfare.

We can leave these more debated and technical questions to the experts, noting only that the more detailed the bishops' analyses and suggestions became, the more criticism they generated. The general criticisms offered in response to "The Challenge of Peace" fell into two categories. Conservatives and militarists tended to charge that the bishops were naive about the threats of Communism, the possibility of dialogue with Communists, and the differences between the Communist and "Free World's" ways of life. To the mind of such critics, nuclear might was the only way to keep the Russian bear at bay, while any weakening of the American nuclear arsenal would bring war a step closer.

People from the other end of the political and theological spectrum tended to find the justifications offered for deterrence shaky. Arguing from the most recent predictions of scientists, which tended to see any significant use of nuclear weapons as leading to both massive human fatality rates and a serious danger of destroying all life on earth, leftist critics concluded that nuclear attack would be intrinsically immoral: no supposedly greater good would exist to justify it. But if this were so, how could one maintain deterrence, which boils down to threatening to use one's nuclear weapons, and which to be credible has to convince one's foe that one's threat is real? May one morally threaten to do what is immoral? Isn't such a threat itself immoral, and doesn't it both tend to subvert the judgment that nuclear warfare is unacceptable and to turn international politics toward brinksmanship?

Perhaps it is a sign of the bishops' virtue and wisdom that they so regularly end up in the middle, attacked by both ends of the political spectrum. Still, five years after this pastoral letter the United States and the Soviet Union seemed on the verge of completing an agreement to reduce stockpiles of some nuclear weapons. Even though the number of weapons involved was small, the symbolic value of the agreement was considerable, for it suggested that the two superpowers might be at the threshold of an era in which they would progressively scale down the arms race. If so, then momentum would have shifted to the opinion held by the majority in both countries that nuclear warfare ought to be banned from the realm of serious consideration. According to such an opinion, nothing could justify a significant employment of nuclear arms, and nuclear warfare therefore becomes a negative moral absolute — a course of action never to be initiated.

In delineating mutual distrust as the underlying cause of the arms race, Catholic moral leaders have simply agreed with many other analysts. But in speaking hoepfully about the possibility of breaking down walls of distrust and building channels of peace, Catholic moral leaders have challenged the cynical view of human nature indulged by hawkish militarists around the globe. Much in our political or diplomatic capacity depends on our imagination. How we view ourselves and our opponents, what we make of the human nature we and they hold in common, shapes how we read the data germane to political decisions. The bishops are not willing to agree that either traditional Communist dogma or past Communist practice predetermines American relations with Communist nations to frustration and failure. Presumably the bishops know full well the cynical advice in the Communist repertoire to the effect that the good of the cause justifies using any means, just as they know full well that a cynical pragmatism often controls American politics. But their faith in God requires the bishops to keep the future open. If the Spirit of God is never dead-ended, then achieving peace remains a real challenge — something that human wisdom and goodwill definitely could accomplish.

Representative Personality: Mary Harren

Our exemplar of Catholic concern for peace and justice is a woman we knew in Wichita, Kansas. As Kurt Reinhardt came to mind when we thought of Catholic worship, so Mary Harren came to mind when we thought of peace and justice. She might be amused or embarrassed to find herself being used in this way, but if she protested we would say, "That's the price you have to pay, Mary, for having become such an admirable gadfly."

Mary Harren grew up in traditional Catholic patterns, marrying and raising six children. She undertook various tasks for her local parish and diocese, saw her kids through Catholic schools, and rejoiced when Pope John XXIII opened the windows of the Church to let in some fresh air. Her husband died before the children were completely raised, and although she and he had shared a deep faith and commitment to social causes, her interest in peace and justice became all-absorbing after his death. For example, she spearheaded the formation of a small **Catholic Worker** community in Wichita and became deeply committed to the Catholic peace movement. We have not kept track of her most recent adventures. When last seen she had just returned from a trip to the Soviet Union that had encouraged her to think positively about a Christian socialism. She had also become part of a nationwide network tracking the path of the trains carrying nuclear arms from Pantex in Amarillo, Texas, to the sites where they would be stored.

The Mary Harren in our minds, composed of impressions from a few hours of shared prayer and political discussion, no doubt is only a pale reflection of the actual person. We are not attempting a canonization procedure here, any more than we were in dealing with Kurt Reinhardt. But the saints, with a small *s*, have always functioned beyond their strict biographies. Just as any text escapes the control of its author and is used as those who read it find good, so any striking, admirable person can become symbolic, a metaphor for certain aspects of the common task of growing more human. What stood out in the Mary Harren we knew was her blend of common sense, humor, and idealism. Family life had shown her the challenges of keeping bread on the table, raising children to be happy and productive, getting school and church authorities off their backsides, asking what difference one wanted to make in the world, what legacy one wanted to leave.

When one keeps asking this question, correlating it with both the energy one has developed in mothering a large family and the Catholic faith one has long loved, the great problems of one's time can become personal imperatives. Knowing and loving one's small-scale city, one can realize that a lot of people are suffering more than seems necessary. The political and economic system of any city develops through the self-interest of those bright enough and aggressive enough to try to stamp it with their image. On the margins live poor people, the majority of them women and children, who for various reasons are not equipped to do well in the games that distribute political power. Noticing these things, a person of faith can be stirred to action. An instinct of faith can combine with a maternal instinct to defend those who seem helpless, those whom the system neglects or abuses.

If one takes such instincts to the New Testament, the example of Jesus, and his teaching about the kind of people who populate his Father's Kingdom leap from the pages. With whom did Jesus tend to consort? The average people of his day, or even the riffraff. What was his passionate concern? To bring such people hope, healing, and dignity. How did Jesus do this? By using the supremacy of God to relativize all human power structures and following the Israelite prophets in denouncing injustice, hardheartedness, and neglect of the orphan and widow.

If one then goes to Catholic history and theology, looking for the follow-through on Jesus' beginning, one obtains numerous lessons in ambiguity. On the one hand, a steady stream of saints concerned about the poor witnesses to the perennial impact of Jesus' own example. On the other hand, organized Christianity appears frequently to have wandered from Jesus' prophetic concern for justice. Allying itself with the secular powers, in many periods it made no preferential option for the poor. Relatedly, it did not produce the witness against warfare and power politics that the example of Jesus suggests it should have. Christian theology offers wonderful foundations for a life in God that would spontaneously issue in fair-sharing and neighborly love, but Christian ethics frequently has obscured such a simple, healthy outlook, partly to honor the complexity of human affairs and sinful motivation, partly from a lack of profound faith and a surplus of institutional self-preservation.

A bright yet still ordinary layperson such as Mary Harren learns some of these things by reading books, but she learns more through her experience of how the Church operates in her own town. Regularly she finds herself bonded to the remnant of believers who feel as she does, joining with them in prayer and concerted political action. She is grateful for the portions of Christian tradition that encourage both prayerful union with God and intense commitment to social justice. In such exemplars as Dorothy Day, the co-founder of the Catholic Worker network, she finds that prayer, even mysticism, and work on behalf of the poor show a natural affinity. Similarly, she finds that peacemaking, reconciliation, and defending the earth go hand in hand with the love of God at the center of all authentic Christianity. So she gradually rounds out a full religious program, bit by bit determining what her own role in the ongoing work of the redemptive Christ ought to be.

Wichita is a center of the aviation industry in the United States. In addition to the small planes that its general aviation plants produce, a major Wichita employer is a Boeing plant that does much work on military planes. The aviation industry therefore means a great deal to the local economy. The cycles of Wall Street and the battles over the defense budget are important news. Mary Harren and some like-minded friends decided that Wichita's dependence on businesses doing little for the poor and much to support American militarism was deplorable. As they read and thought about the interconnection of poverty, military budgets, neglect of the feminine side of culture, religion, and mental health, they became radicalized. Compared to the vision of what might be that they found in the New Testament and Christian tradition, the local culture, which they agreed was but a variant of the prevailing national culture, appeared pathological. Mary and her friends did not expect to overturn so massive a condition, but they did feel obliged to mount whatever protests, and sound whatever alarms, they could.

So they began to picket outside the Boeing plant. When the bishops' pastoral letter on nuclear arms came out, they became strong supporters, even though the letter was less decisive than they thought ideal. As they studied the nuclear arms industry in the United States, they realized how much was done secretly, under wraps, with a desire to avoid publicity that might stir people to question the wisdom and morality of producing more and more horribly lethal weapons.

At last report, Mary Harren had settled her life's energy on protesting all that seemed unjust and destructive in American culture, especially its militant anti-Communism. Certainly she knew she would never become expert in the technology of weapons production, or the intricacies of international negotiations, or the ethics of big business, but she realized that did not matter. What mattered was following her conscience, her instincts of faith, which told her that she had to stand up and be counted. That realization is what we find so admirable. In the final analysis, surely God will ask each of us whether we tried to make a difference.

Glossary

Catholic Worker: a movement expressing itself in houses dedicated to helping the poor and unemployed. Peter Maurin and Dorothy Day are the first names associated with this movement, which for the past fifty years has drawn many idealistic youths and given them a taste of Catholic radicalism. The early Catholic Workers were marked by the experience of the Depression and sought to harmonize service of the poor with somewhat utopian notions about living off the land and studying Catholic culture. The movement had natural affinities with pacifist groups and soon spawned nonviolent protests against military actions, racism, and other trends contrary to the love of Christ.

Realized eschatology: the notion that the substance of salvation and final fulfillment is already present in time, as a result of the victory of Christ and the sending of the Spirit. The Johannine writings of the New Testament are a major source of this outlook, and the British scholar C. H. Dodd gave it its name. Scholars have since debated precisely how to qualify the sense in which the "now" of Christian faith predominates over the "not yet," but on the whole many New Testament scholars and theologians agree that realized eschatology offers the Church a healthy counterbalance to its historic tendency to sacrifice this-worldly justice and achievement to a preoccupation with heaven.

Discussion Questions

1. What is implied in calling peace "an enterprise of justice"?
2. How did Vatican II see the relations among peace, ideology, and greed?
3. Why has the Exodus been so important to liberation theologians?
4. How ought religion to balance its prophetic challenges to unjust regimes with its support for decent human culture?
5. What are the implications of Pope John Paul II's saying that "the fundamental premise of the Church's social doctrine is the primacy of ethics over economics"?
6. How does the right of workers to organize themselves into unions epitomize a proper economic order?
7. What legitimates the doctrine of deterrence?
8. How does using nuclear weapons to deter nuclear war tilt the perception of nuclear war?
9. How might raising six children dispose one to becoming a social activist?
10. What are the natural affinities among prayer, work for peace, and identifying oneself with the plight of the poor?

Notes

[1] J. Detetz and A. Nocent, eds., *Dictionary of the Council* (Washington D.C.: Corpus Books, 1968), p. 316.
[2] Ibid., p. 315.
[3] Ibid., p. 229.
[4] José Miranda, *Being and the Messiah* (Maryknoll, N.Y.: Orbis, 1977).
[5] Gustavo Gutierrez, *We Drink from Our Own Well* (Maryknoll, N.Y.: Orbis, 1984) and *On Job* (Maryknoll, N.Y.: Orbis, 1987).
[6] Leonardo Boff, *Church, Charism and Power* (New York: Crossroad, 1985).
[7] Karol Wojtyla, *Sources of Renewal: The Implementation of Vatican II* (San Francisco: Harper & Row, 1980), pp. 302–303.
[8] John Paul II, "Laborem Exercens," #20, *National Catholic Reporter*, September 25, 1981, p. 24.
[9] John Tracy Ellis, ed., *Documents of American Catholic History* (Wilmington, Del.: Michael Glazier, 1987), pp. 839–840.

CHAPTER 15

Women in the Church

Historical Perspectives
Ordination and Abortion
Family Life
Spirituality
Representative Personality: Rosemary Haughton
Glossary, Discussion Questions, Notes

Historical Perspectives

Inasmuch as Roman Catholicism, like all other Christian and world religious groups, has operated in patriarchal cultures, and has itself had a patriarchal institutional structure, present-day **feminists** are bound to have many problems with the treatment women have received from Roman Catholicism down the ages. One has to avoid an anachronism here, and one has, as well, to retain a cross-cultural perspective. Not only should we not expect past ages to have shown the sensibilities toward women that have evolved in post-modernity, we also should not think that Roman Catholicism has been uniquely misogynistic. One can epitomize the first point by suggesting that most medieval women would not have recognized the liberated woman targeted by radical feminists today (though they may well have sympathized with many of the pains and aspirations that have produced such a target). On the second point, it should suffice to point out that Protestantism and Orthodoxy also present many problems to those who are critical of Christian patriarchy, and that Judaism, Islam, the religions of India, and the religions of East Asia have generated at least as many grievances from women.

This said, the fact remains that Catholic Christianity has treated women as the second sex, never escaping the patriarchy of its Jewish and Hellenistic origins. The Torah that had evolved by the time of Jesus certainly gave grounds for respecting women, but it conceived of the covenant between God and Israel as granting men primacy in virtually all matters. The Hebrew Bible presented many valiant women, but in its depiction of creation, its symbolism for evil, and its laws, Eve and her daughters fared less well than Adam and his sons.

Jesus stands apart from the views of women that one finds in both the Hebrew Bible and later rabbinic literature (what rabbis of Jesus' own day were teaching, and how they were treating women, is a matter of some dispute, since our best records about the rabbis come from some generations after Jesus). Without radically overturning the sexual arrangements of his day, Jesus treats women as equally fit for Christian discipleship and he consorts with them freely. He makes close friends with Martha and Mary, the sisters of Lazarus. Women accompany him on his ministerial journeys and are more faithful than his male disciples at the end. His parables use women as readily as men, relating faith and the growth of the Kingdom as much to women's spheres as men's. His teaching about marriage takes away the special privileges of men and holds both sexes to a lofty ideal of fidelity. Jesus does not present women as temptresses; instead he tells men to look to themselves for the roots of lust. He sends Mary Magdalene to the apostles as the herald of his resurrection, and his own mother appears as a paradigm of faith, far more prominent than his earthly father.

Whether this relatively egalitarian treatment of women should lead us to call Jesus a feminist is a matter of semantics. Against the use of the term stand such apparent facts as Jesus' not having made any women members of his inner circle of twelve primary disciples, and his not having championed women's full equality in political, economic, or religious life. In principle Jesus may have considered women the full equals of men, but he did not impress on his community a great need to institutionalize sexual equality.

Feminist scholarship, preeminently that of Elisabeth Schüssler Fiorenza, has found the New Testament to possess several strata of tradition bearing on the conception and treatment of women.[1] In addition to what one can glean from the gospels about Jesus' own attitudes, and what one can infer from Jesus' habitual championing of society's marginal people and reputed sinners, there are indications that women held positions of leadership in many local churches, functioning as the equivalent of what the later Church called bishops. According to *Acts* women participated in the missionary activities of the early Church, and some missionary couples apparently shared an apostolate as full equals.

But the patriarchal structures of their parent Judaism, along with the house codes of the Hellenistic culture to which they were trying to accommodate the gospel, led the second and third generations of Christian believers to shift from a sense of discipleship that might have made women and men full equals in faith (on the model of Gal. 3:28, which says that in Christ there is neither male nor female) to what Schüssler Fiorenza calls "love patriarchy." By that she means a hierarchical system, with men at the top, that would show the outside world the structures of subordination predominating in Hellenistic culture but would remove much of their sting by stressing Christian love. So the husband would be the "head" of the wife, as Christ was the head of the Church, but the love between the two would obviate competition, antagonism, manipulation, or abuse.

From this mixed heritage the patristic Church tended to extract more patriarchy than love. The very term *patristic* Church is an indication that by the fourth century men were not only ensconced as the natural officials of the Christian community but were using biblical imagery, especially that of the fall, to warn against the weaknesses of female nature. Monasticism exacerbated this tendency, making women temptations the ascetic had to avoid, and such influential Church fathers as Jerome, Tertullian, Augustine, and Chrysostom all wrote passages that can only be called misogynistic.[2] Female martyrs won much praise, and the same Augustine who bemoaned his years of enslavement to women's beauty spoke movingly of the virtues of his mother Monica. Virgins and female monastics also drew much admiration. But a telltale motif in the accounts of female saints' heroic deeds was that they had become as virile in their faith as any man, casting off feminine weakness.

This pattern held throughout the medieval, Counter-Reformational, and modern periods. Female saints gave wonderful examples of prayer and care for the sick. Abbesses occasionally ruled over not only nuns but also monks. Mystics such as Hildegard of Bingen and Teresa of Avila took a feminine sensibility to the heavenly heights. The Virgin exerted great influence in popular piety and put a feminine softness, approachableness, and maternity close to the Godhead. Many sisters, daughters, wives, and mothers shaped the joys of family life, bore a large share of the sorrows, and exemplified wholehearted faith. Yet the institutions of first Christendom and then the nationalistic modern Western cultures gave women little access to official power. The Church excluded women from priestly orders, thereby closing them out of ecclesiastical power, and by shifting to a celibate clergy it tended to separate sexuality and femininity from the administration of the sacraments, suggesting that femaleness did not correlate well with the divine holiness. Inasmuch as it took over Roman notions of priestly office, and took in Hellenistic notions about the relation between matter and spirit, Roman Catholicism made women alien to its hierarchical conception of leadership.[3]

Only with the rise of recent liberation movements has a feminist consciousness taken hold in the developed Western nations (with many third-world women now taking notice). A few women in many past ages argued for greater sexual equality, but women's advance toward full political and cultural enfranchisement is a very new phenomenon. On the whole, Roman Catholic authorities have reacted conservatively, if not defensively, worrying about the impact that radical changes might have on family life and social stability. On the other hand, their defensiveness about closing ordination to women and treating women as less than men's equals in many areas of theology and Church life have left them vulnerable to the charge of not being willing to own up to sexist bias and clinging to male supremacy for the sake of the advantages, power, and self-image it offers. (Church leaders may also be leery of the many cultures in which machismo makes women's ordination problematic.) The American Catholic bishops' proposed pastoral letter on the life of women in the Church, which as we write has been issued in first draft, goes a long way toward accepting a moderate feminist critique of the past treatment of women in the Church, though it does not challenge the policy of denying women priestly ordination.

Ordination and Abortion

The two issues that have bulked largest in recent Catholic feminist discussion are women's rights to ordination and abortion. Both issues would have been considered outside the pale of reputable discussion in virtually all past eras, but today they symbolize the journey Catholicism has to make if it is to deal fairly with women's rising desire to be accounted fully human and fully Christian.

We favor opening priestly ordination to qualified women, and on the whole we support the opposition of the Roman Catholic hierarchy to abortion.[4] We also think that honest, charitable discussion of what is involved in both these questions will go a long way toward developing a proper Roman Catholic sponsorship of women's flourishing in faith.

Ordination has both symbolic and strictly theological aspects. Because leadership and power in the Church have come to be associated with orders, any qualifications on the pool of talent eligible for orders have greatly shaped Church leadership and life. People who are convinced that many women have superb gifts that would make them excellent priestly ministers are liable to think that the Catholic Church has sadly limited its resources by refusing ordination to women. (The same holds for the Church's refusal, by and large, to sponsor a married priesthood.) People who are further convinced that feminist insights in philosophy, theology, and cultural history offer many of the antidotes to pathologies in modern culture, both secular and religious, lament the loss of women's specific points of view. The Church's claims to appreciate women, its honest admission that women are a majority in the pews and on the rolls of parish workers, and its attempts to champion women's place in contemporary culture all ring hollow to those who think that a full confession of women's equality with men in basic humanity ought to translate into full access to Church leadership.

The point is not that anyone has a claim to office in the Church, apart from the community's commission and approval. Similarly, the point is not that past ages have managed with an all-male, celibate clergy. The point is not even that there are no New Testament indications that women could not preside at the liturgy, or be authoritative missionaries, or (conversely) that the then contemporary patriarchy was incompatible with Christian faith. The point is that nothing in past tradition (by what is not a unanimous opinion of present-day professional theologians but probably is a majority consensus) seems to forbid the Church to change its institutional policies and respond to both the desire of many of its members and the pastoral needs of present times (especially the growing scarcity of priests in many areas) by increasing its pool of ministerial talent. The ordination of women would be no panacea, solving all pastoral problems. It would be a good practical response to both a movement that is arguably inspired by the Spirit (because producing many good fruits of increased faith) and the difficulties Catholicism increasingly faces in providing its people the essentials of Christian nourishment: Word and Sacrament.

Abortion is a more complex question, and probably one with more resonances outside the Church, in the world of secular feminism and liberalism, than inside the Church. For although there is a contingent of Catholics speaking out for free choice, along with much sympathy for women who are forced to face the dilemmas of a decision about abortion, most opinion polls show a strong consensus among Roman Catholics supporting their Church's official position that abortion is wrong, highly undesirable, and tragic. Depending on how one asks further questions about abortion, more or less nuance appears. Questions of rape, incest, and defective fetuses all complicate responses of an absolute prohibition against abortion, so it is safer to say that the lay Catholic instinct still is that abortion is abhorrent than it is to say that most Catholics reject abortion in all circumstances. When abortion is used as a contraceptive, or when the fetus is considered so nonhuman that it should receive no rights at law, or when abortion is justified in terms of economic hardship, Catholic sympathy for abortion seems very low. In the other, harder cases, including abortions that result from attempts to save the life of the mother, many Catholics would grant some leeway.

Abortion does not stand on its own, however. It is not simply a medical procedure with stark ethical implications. It relates to women's rights to shape their own fertility, to fathers' rights to have their 50 percent of each child's genetic endowment honored, and to matters of sex education, contraception, adoption, child rearing, education, and much more. Insofar as Roman Catholicism has forbidden artificial contraception, it has weakened its moral authority with many who otherwise would applaud its stand against abortion. If the topic is family life in American ghettoes, or the ties between poverty and the population explosion worldwide, birth control strikes many as being necessary on a variety of counts. One can admire Catholic efforts to promote so-called natural methods of birth control, and one can agree that chemical birth controls have dangers that render them undesirable. But until Catholic policy seems to respect the right of marital partners to determine in good conscience what shape their family life ought to take, Catholic policy is unlikely to receive the full support of even the Catholic laity and lower priesthood, let alone of outsiders. Most opinion polls put the number of American Catholics who approve of birth control at above 80 percent and show little significant difference between Catholic and non-Catholic rates of usage. One cannot immediately infer faith convictions from statistics about moral practice, but obviously there often is a rough correlation between them.

The questions put by both the ordination of women and abortion are not easy, even when one feels that one's basic opinions are clear. For the long haul, the most important consideration would seem to be keeping faith with a Lord and gospel that consider women at least as good candidates for the Kingdom as men. Because of its historical patriarchalism, Roman Catholicism carries a burden of proving that it is willing to befriend women and support their struggles to contribute their talents to humanity's most pressing problems. Recent statements of Pope John Paul II, the American Catholic bishops, and Catholic theologians (including liberation theologians from such previously macho cultural groups as Latin America and black America) suggest that this will is growing stronger.

Such change as seems to be afoot would not have come about if many women had not risked a great deal in criticizing past Church policies and refusing to let the emperor continue to wear no clothes. Much more remains to be done. Opening the question of women's ordination would, in our opinion, remove the last great barrier to believing that Roman Catholicism is not irredeemably sexist and does want to honor women's strict equality with men not only on its own terms (prejudicial against women in the past) but also on the new terms disclosed by feminist scholarship and theory as necessary for the future.

The relations between the sexes are always going to be a primary zone that any generation has to negotiate. They present the most basic antagonisms and complements of our species. Unless Catholic faith can bless them, in all their eros and daily sweat, it will not deliver the full grace postulated by the Incarnate Word. Be it a matter of how one ought to symbolize God, or how one ought to speak about marriage, or about ordination, abortion, lesbianism, or divorce, women cannot be the second sex, the tagalong, the daughters of Eve who are more dangerous than the sons of Adam. Neither can they be the exalted madonnas, the virgins removed from the grit of the real world, the overly wise and underemployed "others." They have to become just what presumably they are in God's sight: as needy and holy as men.

Family Life

In many feminist discussions, those of Catholics included, women's rights to self-determination, especially in the areas of work and sexuality, predominate. The discussants sometimes forget that the majority of women aspire to motherhood and family life, even when they want career opportunities and control of their own fertility. Only when the women's movement began to attend to the hopes and problems of this majority did it come in sight of being a populist movement. For Catholics, the women's movement has meant a new look at the theology of marriage, with generally positive consequences.

For example, those stepping back to survey just what sexual love entails have found themselves reconfronted with procreation and parenting. Whereas many no longer find the traditional priority given to procreation over the personal love of the spouses persuasive, many do find the past tradition wise in its concern for the dignity and sanctity of new life. Indeed, one could pass beyond the usual language of the tradition to speak in more personal accents about the significance of parenthood. If, as we implied in the last chapter, Judgment Day will find us being asked what difference we tried to make, having begotten and raised new life may become a prime ticket to paradise. That would reverse the sentence of Genesis (3:16) that makes childbearing women's punishment for the disobedience of Eve. It would also invite men to consider parenthood as much their vocation as that of women.

The Catholic Church has a history of defending family life by protecting individuals' right to marry whom they wish, to beget children as they see fit (even in the face of governmental opposition, though in accordance with Church teaching on birth control), and to pass on their faith to their children. On the other hand, the Church has honored Jesus' sayings that subordinated familial loyalty to Christian discipleship, and the respect it has paid virginity and religious life has sometimes depreciated marriage. So there is room for a renewed theology of marriage that focuses on the bond between the romantic love that brings people to join their lives and the children that love tends to create. If Catholic theology would pay more attention to its biblical authorities, taking to heart the Johannine dictum that God is love (and those who abide in love abide in God and God in them), it could clarify both the personal and the procreative sides of this central human institution. Indeed, it could clarify precisely what the sacrament of matrimony ought to stress.

In many religious traditions, marriage is not a sacrament. In most Protestant churches, only baptism and the Eucharist qualify as unfailing signs and means of grace. To make marriage a sacrament therefore is to imply that something intrinsic to the wedding of two people serves God's intent to reveal the divine love. One would have to make the same case in defending the sacramental status of penance, confirmation, orders, and anointing, and such an effort no doubt would suggest how forgiveness, taking on adult responsibilities, being commissioned for ecclesiastical service, and healing the body and soul for their last encounter with God all can mediate the heart of the Christian matter. But perhaps it would remain signally appropriate to call matrimony a sacrament, because matrimony so directly focuses love and life, two of the three great Johannine watchwords (the third is light). For women, such a deepening of the Church's appreciation of marriage might show how personal autonomy and equality with men is a necessary condition for the flourishing of family life, as well as for Church membership and personal spirituality.

The argument would be that romantic love only matures in fully personal freedom between two equal partners. Differences in disposition, talent, education, social conditioning, and the like will often lead the partners to divide the tasks of marriage. But the freedom and equality at the heart of their mutual self-giving should guarantee that they make such a division of tasks not according to social stereotypes or Church dicta about the preeminent authority of the husband and father but only as their unique situation suggests. Fundamentalist Christian churches are more liable to patriarchal power plays than recent Catholic marital teaching has been, but the temptation is always present to read the differences between men and women as aspects of a natural law or a hierarchy that God expects to obtain everywhere. Thus Catholic interest in protecting mothers and safeguarding the rights of women, like Mother Teresa's view that the root of most modern problems is women's not being in the home, could combine to predetermine Catholic family life in favor of traditional patterns that many spouses now find stifling. If a couple freely chooses such patterns, that is well and good. What eventuates should be the result of their joint consultation, however, and it should express the desire to make a flourishing common life that both joined them in the first place and ought to have been sacramentalized in their wedding ceremony.

Granted this, one can agree with Lisa Sowle Cahill's recent effort to locate family life within a series of further connections:

> Most Western Christians take it for granted today that the individuality of neither wife nor husband, nor their intimate relationship, ought to be subordinated almost entirely to the interests of family, tribe, or nation. What is not so clearly a part of the Western consciousness is the degree to which a "marriage" is a nexus of interdependent relations among couple,

family, and larger social arrangements. We tend to idealize and isolate the couple in their love, their freedom, and their responsibility, and so to arrive at an unrealistic or simplistic view of the many elements which constitute a marriage, contributing to its success or failure.[5]

In sacramental terms, this truth would relate to the presence of the couple's friends and Christian community at their wedding, and it would suggest clarifying the function of these witnesses in the whole shared life the couple are initiating.

Working with homeless people in Gloucester, Massachusetts, Rosemary Haughton has had occasion to reflect on the changes in the traditional image of family life that divorce, abandonment, widowhood, and other disruptions have brought into the lives of millions of present-day Westerners:

"Alternative" households are actually quite common; in fact among the women with whom I work the choice to share home and child care with another woman is often the obvious way to afford the rent and achieve some independence as well as companionship. These unquestioned demographics and social facts demonstrate from another point of view the need to reevaluate the theology of sexual relationships. The alternative is to label all these households deviant in some way, and attempt to persuade, exhort or blackmail them into returning to more acceptable situations, or consenting to live the rest of their lives regarding themselves as inevitably bad in some way. But they are not obviously different from traditional households in quality of life and relationships. Wounded they may be, often permanently scarred by their experiences, but if we are honest we can see that they are no more (and no less) struggling, loving, failing and succeeding, despairing and hoping, living and partly living than traditional households. We can see these things, and we have to draw conclusions from them, and the conclusions do not support the theology of marriage as we have inherited it.[6]

From the underside of marital history, then, women's presently raised consciousness is demanding that we roll up the shutters that have kept us from seeing how much struggle goes on in most households and open our thought, our lives, to the redeeming action of the Spirit. The allusion to T. S. Eliot ("living and partly living") puts the issue on dead center: only God can transform our partiality, can straighten our bentness, and the way that God tends to work such salvation is by bringing us to realize that divinity alone is a love stronger than death.

Spirituality

The recent interest in women's status within the Church has dovetailed with an equal if not stronger interest in women's spirituality. "Spirituality" is not the most precise term, but by consensus it recently has come to stand for the existential aspects of faith, where the individual and the community alike struggle with the divine mystery, pray, try to express the love of neighbor central to the gospel, and in general emphasize the experiential aspects of faith. Opposed to spirituality, in this sense, is faith that is mainly notional, conceptual, or legal. Useful as work on such other aspects of Christian faith may be, those who are more interested in spirituality tend to account them extrinsic, not at the heart of the Christian matter.

When they survey the history of Christian spirituality,[7] many feminists note both that women have played a stronger role there than they have in doctrinal theology or institutional Church history and that much of what women have been taught has not served them well. In her introduction to a collection of essays on women's spirituality, Joann Wolski Conn has recently summarized the main difficulties in the spiritual traditions to which most women have been exposed:

> For women the possibilities for mature humanity/spirituality are restricted. Models of human development universally recognize that movement away from conformity and predetermined role expectations and toward greater autonomy (i.e., self-direction, self-affirmation, self-reliance) is necessary for maturity. Yet women's experience shows that most women are socialized into conformity to subordinate roles or are arrested at the threshold of autonomy. To make matters worse, the most prevalent psychological models of human development stop at autonomy, at a notion of maturity as differentiation from others, as independence, as taking control of one's life. Yet women's experience convinces them that maturity must include not only autonomy but also relationship. It must value not only independence but also belonging. That is, women's experience makes them suspicious of autonomy as the goal of human maturity, while it makes them struggle against social pressures even to reach as far as that ambiguous goal.
>
> Christian teaching and practice, instead of promoting women's maturity, has significantly contributed to its restriction. Women have consistently been taught to value only one type of religious development — self-denial and sacrifice of one's own needs for the sake of others. Whereas men have been taught to couple self-denial with prophetic courage to resist unjust authority, women have been taught to see all male authority

as God-given and to judge that assertion of their own desires was a sign of selfishness and pride. The problem lies not so much with the model of religious development as with its application. For example, to encourage self-denial without attention to the way women are prevented from having a self (i.e., sufficient self-direction, autonomy) is, in effect, simply to promote conformity to a male-approved role.[8]

If one wants to move to autonomy and relationship, the model of Jesus is encouraging. For Jesus appears on the scene as self-possessed. Nothing **heteronomous** drives him from without. He is his own person, so much so that many onlookers marvel at the personal authority with which he speaks and acts. Watching Jesus, one sees realized the authenticity that Lonergan sought from the transcendental precepts. Jesus is willing to override the letter of the Torah, when human need requires him to heal on the Sabbath or consort with those who are legally accounted sinners. He will take no guff from the official teachers sitting on the chair of Moses, though he upholds their claims to authority. In every way Jesus is a free spirit, seldom more so than in his appreciation of tradition and his concern that his miracles might lead people to look in the wrong direction.

For Jesus the right direction was the Spirit and Father within him. His autonomy, that is, is connected with his relationship to the trinitarian godhead. The will that Jesus was fulfilling reposed in his heavenly Father. The power that went out from him, and the inspiration that drove him to the desert, came from the Spirit who had annointed him at his baptism, as though to commission him for ministry. So Jesus' independence was not a splendid isolation, and his strength of will was not arrogant. Yet he enjoyed a unique confidence and trust, which may well have been the reason he had so few fears of failure, so few worries about what others thought.

Jesus also established close relations with his followers, including close friends with families such as Martha, Mary, and Lazarus. His maturity or autonomy did not make him antisocial. He thought of his disciples as both a new family and a transfamilial community. He thought of his own ministerial desire as like that of a mother longing to gather her chicks under her wing. But the chicks would not come to him; Jerusalem stayed away. The pain this brought Jesus suggests the intensity of his desire to establish close ties with Jerusalem, with all of his fellow Jews.

The Catholic Church has presented Jesus as the great model of Christian life, and imitating Jesus has been the hallmark of mainstream Catholic spirituality. Yet a tacit ambivalence about Jesus has complicated Catholic spirituality, because the Church has been slow to grant its members freedom on the model of Jesus' own. Sometimes theologians have offered the rationale that Jesus alone was sinless and divine, a potent argument, but one that applies to Church officials as much as to ordinary Church members. At that point the staple theological move is to tie the authority of the Church to that of the sinless, divine Jesus, so that human beings who, on their own, have no authority to ask of others an obedience that could create heteronomy gain such an authority by standing in for Jesus. Protestant theology is useful at this point, because Protestant theology was born in pangs of conviction that the Church is always sinful and that individual conscience, despite its similar sinfulness, always has rights that precede those of Church authorities. But such Protestant truths have gotten at best a lukewarm reception from Catholic officials, whose gamble has been that heteronomy is better than autonomy gone astray into individualism or idiosyncrasy.

What has tended to be lost is precisely what present-day Catholic feminists are seeking: the maturity found in relations among autonomous, self-possessed individuals. Only when people are treated as adults, encouraged or even forced to be responsible for their own lives, will mature communities develop. Amusingly enough, only when such maturity obtains will adolescent fits of rebellion decrease and genuine dialogue between charismatic individuals and officials who have overarching responsibility for the Church prosper. By not respecting the call of the Spirit to grow to the measure of the free-spirited Christ, many Church authorities have obstructed their own best interests.

As Wolski Conn suggests, women have suffered special debilities from this Catholic hesitancy to promote models of self-reliance and relationship that might have translated the imitation of Christ for each new age. Only a few heroines—Catherine of Siena, Joan of Arc, Teresa of Avila—imitated the decisiveness of Christ. The feminine majority learned to hear and obey. The recent Catholic interest in spirituality has forced many people to rethink their responsibilities to God, themselves, and the Church. It has suggested to many that only a loyal opposition, a refusal of obedience to inauthentic traditions, squares with either the example of Jesus or the inspiration of the Spirit.

Representative Personality: Rosemary Haughton

The impact of feminist thought on Catholicism has developed an impressive group of theologians. Rosemary Ruether and Elisabeth Schüssler Fiorenza deserve special mention. Ruether was the pioneer, associating concern for the history and marginal status of women with Christian socialism, ecology, and a generally prophetic desire to help Church life better measure up to the gospel.

Tirelessly, she has spurred a generation of feminist scholars to see the plight of women as part of an overall mentality that has caused Christians to abuse Jews, the earth, and the poor. One might call this mentality a desire to dominate, and one might associate it with the hierarchical thinking that is typical of both classical Catholic theology and the stereotypically male mind. In contrast, Jesus represented and called for a mentality of service, reconciliation, and concern for those most in need.

Elisabeth Schüssler Fiorenza has made her mark in New Testament studies, proposing a feminist **hermeneutics** and showing that women fared better in the first Christian generations than they did in later Christian history. Like Ruether, she has applied her findings to the reforms that present-day Christianity needs and has offered suggestions for how feminist insights might help Christianity become more egalitarian, more associated with the forces of life against the forces of death, and a better champion of the suffering against the forces of injustice and oppression.

Rosemary Haughton has been relatively slow to come to feminist issues, but for twenty years she has been offering Catholics solid books of spirituality. Indeed, her literary gifts, combined with her background as an English convert, mother of ten, and member of a utopian Christian community, have made such of her books as *The Catholic Thing* and *The Passionate God* virtual classics.[9] Recently Haughton has turned to biblical stories about women, offering original interpretations of familiar gospel scenes that vividly show the strength women can find in Christian faith.[10] Nonetheless, *The Passionate God* remains Houghton's most profound expression of her theological vision, so it is from it that we shall draw.

Haughton's usual style is to probe what actually happens to human beings, their experience, and insist that theology make sense of it. A theology detached from experience, not conceived as the dialogical partner of people's joys and pains, interests her not at all. Indeed, she describes theology as reflection on experience in the light of faith. In her own reflections, Haughton seldom wanders far from the sufferings of the majority of the world's masses, the sufferings that seem inescapable from being human. Thus her work in Gloucester with the homeless and her move to reflect on what women, the neglected half of the race, have suffered and are now trying to bring to consciousness are of a piece with her earlier concerns.

The thesis of *The Passionate God* is that God pursues us like an ardent lover, wanting our full flowering in vibrant life, and that God is not beyond using our weaknesses and sufferings to accomplish his ends. Suffering, defeat, and diminishment therefore can serve what Bernard Lonergan has called "the law of the cross," which is the intelligibility of redemption. God redeems us, buys us back from sin and meaninglessness, by breaking throughout both our resistance and our weakness, as spring breaks through the cold and apparent death of winter.

Haughton writes poetically, and frequently she draws on poets and novelists, avoiding the jargon that is characteristic of professional theologians. But her poetry is no prettification of the Christian message. If anything, her imagery is stark, bruised, and marked through and through by contemplations of what ordinary people undergo when they try to keep faith with the mysterious God, who seems to ask them to put up with pain, injustice, and ample grounds for doubting whether their lives in fact make sense.

The following paragraph from the introduction of *The Passionate God* is vintage Haughton:

Like spring, this breakthrough of newness is violent. We are sentimental about spring. We concentrate on fluffy birds, the chubby pinkness of apple-blossom, the reassuring soft green of new grass. But spring is not gentle or cosy. It is an eruption of life so strong it can push bricks apart and make houses fall down. It thrusts through, and because of, layers of rotten past. The diamond brilliance of the cuckoo's note is the result of many fledglings shouldered out of the nest to their deaths, as all new life thrusts aside whatever impedes it. Even in the sheer perfection of each growing thing there is an integrity which is painful in its accuracy. The scent of lilacs in the dawn cuts through fuzziness of disordered desire, the etched whiteness of lily of the valley against dark leaves sears the imagination. These are not soft things; they have a tenderness ascetically fined down to an essential longing. This is the violence of absolute love, which takes the Kingdom of Heaven by storm in a silence of total concentration on the one thing necessary.[11]

"A tenderness fined down to an essential longing"—that might describe Haughton's own spirit. The tender instincts that moved her to live and work with the homeless in a foreign country have kept her eye alerted to the varieties of human growth and need, so that she can write as movingly of people as of flowers erupting in spring. Yet this tenderness has been hammered down, made fine to the point of quintessence, by her willingness to take the blows that come when one goes apart from the crowd and identifies with the suffering Christ. The essential longing can only be for God, the one who alone can fulfill the human heart, alone can make right the pervasive wrongness that twists so many lives out of joint. Like Sebastian Moore, who has written some of the best religious psychology focused on redemption,[12] Haughton finally joins such human longing to the longing of divinity itself. Her God is best disclosed through the analogy of the romantic love that began in the medieval Provençal and brought into human history the new thing of a Christian eros.

It may be accidental that Rosemary Haughton, rather than a male Catholic theologian, has best made the connections among romantic love, passion, the law of the cross, and the other ingredients of God's movement through our dying and rising. It seems fated, though, that she would apply this constellation of factors to women's recently raised consciousness and finally emerge as a champion of women's spiritual strength. Indeed, the movement from *The Passionate God* to *The Recreation of Eve* has the logic of a preordained inevitability. Nonetheless, it is interesting that this movement was mediated by two other factors. One was Haughton's work with the homeless, which brought her face to face with the dark side of American family life. The other was a sustained meditation on the experience of the women who appear in the New Testament.

Such women had the privilege and challenge of knowing Christ in the flesh. In Haughton's exegesis of the texts, what the New Testament women learned got bred into their bones as strength to be their own people. That would have been impressive in any time, but it was doubly impressive in the patriarchal culture of Jesus' day. Thus Mary, the mother of Jesus, probably was not the mild, even saccharine figure of traditional Marian piety, but rather a strong young woman taking on considerable social disapproval and having to struggle mightily to understand the mission of the son she had raised. One could speak similarly of Mary Magdalene and many of the other women who figure in the gospel stories.

Ultimately, the crux of the breakthroughs that Haughton finds constituting redemption are exchanges of love between human beings and God that regularly work through human brokenness. Like Christ on the cross, those who suffer in faith become transparent to spiritual transformation. Then the Spirit of Wisdom may take over their hearts and use them for God's greater purposes. At the end of *The Passionate God*, Rosemary Haughton perorates about this Wisdom as follows:

> At this point in the history of the world and of the Church, which is the point where "Spirit knows it knows" and is aware of Wisdom at work in all creation, there is a great deal to do in very particular ways, but if the practical choices are to be rightly made they must be of the kind that Wisdom inspires. They will not be discovered by "think-tanks" and teams of experts (though these may come in at some stage) but only discerned by minds and hearts open to the exchange of love. There is a need to be "wise as serpents and simple as doves", to try to think with the ruthlessly honest intelligence of Jesus and love with the terrible folly of Jesus. We are always glad to be thought wise, but an older meaning of the world "simple" was less complimentary than our modern one, which implies a certain admirable and elegant spareness. "Simple" meant foolish, even half-witted, and certainly poor. In the end, that is the kind of poverty which is required of the companion of Jesus; for Wisdom herself puts on

the fool's gear and in that guise can only be recognized by those who are themselves fools. "For since, in the Wisdom of God, the world did not know God through Wisdom, it pleased God through the folly of what we preach to save those who believe. For Jews demand signs and Greeks seek wisdom, but we preach Christ crucified, a stumbling block to Jews and folly to Gentiles, but to those who are called, both Jews and Gentiles, Christ the power of God and the Wisdom of God" (I Cor. 1:41-4).[13]

Glossary

Feminists: those who advocate the strict equality of women with men in basic human potential and aptness for Christian maturation. The term has acquired a pejorative connotation in conservative circles, conjuring up strident advocates of revolutionary new social arrangements that would throw out the past and grant women's every whim. That is clever propaganda, but it has produced the anomalous situation of asking many women, and men, to deny what they know in their bones are real injustices women have suffered in the past and real liabilities women suffer in the present when they seek to develop their talents or offer their gifts. In our usage, a feminist is simply one who takes women as seriously as men and wants women to have as full a measure of the liberty of the children of God.

Hermeneutics: the science of interpretation. Usually the term applies to textual interpretation, but it can have the wider connotation of discerning meaning in any cultural artifact. In focusing on hermeneutics, many of the humanities and humanistic sciences recently have drawn attention to such significant shapers of human meaning as social consensus, paradigmatic symbols, the byplay between classical texts and innovative applications, and the evolutionary need of our species to furnish whys sufficiently persuasive to enable us to put up with demanding hows. The benefit for theology and faith in hermeneutical studies is that they can make plain the orientation of consciousness toward ultimate meaning and its ineluctable immersion in mystery, both of which can make God a constant partner of human existence.

Heteronomous: concerning subjection to an alien law, a set of controls imposed from without. In strictly political terms, heteronomy implies the existence of a slave living at the behest of foreigners. In psychological terms, it implies childhood or underdevelopment, when one lives by reacting to outside pressures, rather than from personal values freely chosen. In theological terms, the question is what sort of maturation the Spirit works to develop and how such maturation squares with the spiritual authority of the institutional Church. For the Protestant theologian Paul Tillich, the ideal was neither heteronomy nor autonomy but theonomy—a subjection to the living God that would harmonize the freedom of the mature self with the good of the whole community.

Discussion Questions

1. What are the grounds for calling Jesus a feminist?
2. How did women lose ground during the patristic age?
3. How would you argue the case that one need not be of the same sex as Jesus to represent him as a Catholic priest?
4. What should be the relation between the right of a fetus to live and the right of a mature woman to control her own fertility?
5. What sort of love ought the sacrament of matrimony to bring into symbolic clarity?
6. How seriously should theologians of family life take what Rosemary Haughton has called "alternative households?"
7. Why do many feminists interested in spirituality stress autonomy?
8. What are the theological implications of women's regular interest in relationships?
9. How can suffering and diminishment serve the purposes of the God passionate to redeem human beings?
10. Why is Christian wisdom likely to strike many as foolishness?

Notes

[1] See Elisabeth Schüssler Fiorenza, *In Memory of Her* (New York: Crossroad, 1983).
[2] See Elizabeth A. Clark, *Women in the Early Church* (Wilmington, Del.: Michael Glazier, 1983).
[3] See Mary Collins, "The Refusal of Women in Clerical Circles," in *Women in the Church*, I, ed. Madonna Kolbenschlag (Washington, D.C.: Pastoral Press, 1987), pp. 51–63.

4 See Denise Lardner Carmody, *The Double Cross: Ordination, Abortion, and Catholic Feminism* (New York: Crossroad, 1986).

5 Lisa Sowle Cahill, "Community and Couple: Parameters of Marital Commitment in Catholic Tradition," in *Commitment to Partnership*, ed. William P. Roberts (New York: Paulist, 1987), pp. 85–86.

6 Rosemary Haughton, "The Meaning of Marriage in Women's New Consciousness," Ibid., pp. 150–151.

7 See Cheslyn Jones, Geoffrey Wainwright, and Edward Yarnold, eds., *The Study of Spirituality* (New York: Oxford University Press, 1986).

8 Joann Wolski Conn, "Introduction," in *Women's Spirituality: Resources for Christian Development*, ed. Joann Wolski Conn (New York: Paulist, 1986), pp. 3–4.

9 Rosemary Haughton, *The Catholic Thing* (Springfield, Ill.: Templegate, 1979) and *The Passionate God* (New York: Paulist, 1981).

10 Rosemary Haughton, *The Re-Creation of Eve* (Springfield, Ill.: Templegate, 1985).

11 Haughton, *The Passionate God*, p. 17.

12 See Sebastian Moore, *Let This Mind Be in You* (Minneapolis: Winston, 1985).

13 Haughton, *The Passionate God*, pp. 334–335.

CHAPTER 16

Internationalism

The Church in the Third World
World Religions
International Conflict
World Hunger
Representative Personality: Karl Rahner
Glossary, Discussion Questions, Notes

The Church in the Third World

No responsible theologian would say that demographics are everything, but most theologians today are impressed by the figures on Catholic church membership. By the year 2000 more than half of the the Roman Catholics in the world will be living in third world countries. A huge number of these will reside in Latin America, but gains in Africa, India, and East Asia will also swell the rolls of the church. By comparison, Catholic membership in Europe and North America, the traditional powerhouses of Catholic thought and finance, appears stagnant. Both areas are suffering significant declines in vocations to the priesthood and to the religious life. A majority of Europeans now consider themselves religiously unaffiliated if not outright unbelievers. The robust numbers of the Catholic population in the United States continue to be impressive, but many American Catholics preserve more independence from traditional Catholic doctrine and culture than the Roman authorities would like. Thus Rome can find it appealing to consider the third world as so many fields ripe for the harvest and plan for them a Catholicism that would be more faithful than what one finds among critical first-worlders.

The likelihood, however, is that Latin American, African, Indian, and Chinese Christians are not going to accept a Christianity that is frozen into European or North American forms. One can see this in the liberation theologies emanating from the third world, and also in the turn that missionary theology has taken. Thus Latin America has pioneered the development of "base communities" (comunidades de base) — small-scale groups in which people can come to know one another well, share their faith by reflecting together on scripture and celebrating the Eucharistic liturgy, and planning political responses that might carry their faith forth into the unjust, impoverished societies in which they live. Relatedly, the Latin Americans have been working to develop lay ministries that might supply for the shortage of priests that many areas suffer. There, catechists and ministers of the Word probably will play important roles in the Latin American future.

For African Christians, a major question has been how to correlate Christian notions with native beliefs about healing, communication with ancestors in dreams, and convictions about the priority of song and dance in religious celebrations. Authorities in Rome who are concerned about uniform liturgical rites have worried about the Africanization of traditional Catholic ceremonies, even as they have accepted the fact that Africans will only feel comfortable with Catholic Christianity in the measure that they can worship through forms with which they are familiar. A further problem has been clerical celibacy, which jars with traditional African notions about manhood and maturity. Not to establish a family has meant being considered less than a full man in African cultures. Even more challenging to the European-based expectations of Roman Catholic leaders has been the petition of Africans for the approval of polygamy. Sociological, economic, and other factors have conspired through African history to make polygamy acceptable, even desirable, in some areas.

For Catholics to demand monogamy of their lay African members and celibacy of their African candidates to the priesthood has been a major hindrance to Catholic missionary efforts. How much adaptation to local customs is possible without losing things essential to Catholic identity, or things proven wise through long experience, is hard to say. Much pastoral wisdom will be required to make the adaptations in liturgical, doctrinal, and moral theology that are necessary to develop a faith both authentically African and authentically Catholic. It seems certain, however, that unless Church authorities in Rome discuss these matters with people on the spot in Africa, trusting that the Spirit will show local bishops, missionaries, and lay leaders where the way to a vital African Catholic church lies, the harvest actually reaped will be much less than what might have been.

The situation is different in both India and China. In fact, "Latin America" and "Africa" are both only concepts of convenience, best discarded when it comes to the practical tasks of dealing with the people of Honduras in contrast to the people of Chile, the people of Zaire in contrast to the people of Nigeria. But

India presents a very different cultural climate than that of Africa, as does China. Catholic numbers in India continue to be small, yet vocations to the priesthood and religious life have been impressive. For example, presently there are more Indian Jesuits than Jesuits from any geographical area other than North America. Much of the spiritual interest among Catholics working in India has focused on correlating Christian and native Indian traditions about meditation, holiness, and imagery for God. With Hindu, Buddhist, Jain, Muslim, and Sikh religious treasuries upon which to draw, Indians have offered Christians very impressive partners for religious dialogue. The tradition of adapting Christianity to native Indian ways goes back to Roberto Di Nobili, a seventeenth-century missionary who lived like an Indian sannyasi, if not to the apostle Thomas, whom Indians claim as the founder of their church. Catholic attitudes toward caste, transmigration, **bhakti**, and much more will have a great say in whatever flourishing the Indian church will enjoy.

Different, though analogous, problems face Catholic efforts in China, where a thaw in previously frozen relations with the Communist government seems under way. From the time of Matteo Ricci, Christian missionary activity has had a model of acculturating Catholic faith to Chinese traditions. But Ricci's methods ran afoul of the Chinese Rites Controversy of the seventeenth and eighteenth centuries, the upshot of which was an imposition of European forms (Latin for the liturgy) and a rejection of Chinese customs (veneration of ancestors) that condemned Christianity to being a foreign, alien religion. In addition to negotiating the present form of the European-Chinese cultural divide, Catholic missionaries will also have to deal with the Communist ideology now ruling China, along with the history of brutal repression of religious groups under Mao Zedong.

The common denominator in surveys of the major third-world areas to which Roman Catholicism can look for future growth is the clamor for sufficient local autonomy to adapt essential Catholic faith to native cultural traditions. Whereas the distance of native African, Indian, and East Asian cultures from that of Europe obviously is greater than what Latin Americans experience, even in Latin America (and North America) the local cry is for freedom to work out a truly indigenous Catholicism. Many in all areas recognize the need for a unifying center, such as the papacy, that can keep the various national churches parts of a greater whole. But virtually everywhere missionary theology turns over the questions of adaptation, cultural pluralism, freedom to experiment, and the right to develop a native clergy, theology, and liturgical life.

Still, at the end of his pioneering study of the implications of the shift of Christian membership toward the third world, the missiologist Walbert Bühlmann chose to reflect on hope.

This theological hope can be verified in history—not, of course, with mathematical certainty. Compare the workings of evolution attaining its ends with incredible precision from primitive beginnings. Then take a quick glance at the history of the missions, how the initial impulse through Jesus Christ was carried on by apostles, bishops, and monks, how the Franciscans and Dominicans broke through the barrier of Islam during the middle ages and penetrated Asia, how in the 16th century, after the upheaval of the Reformation, the Jesuits moved out into the newly discovered worlds, how in the 17th century a new impulse came from the founding of *Propaganda Fidei*, how in the 19th century, after the French Revolution had destroyed the home base, many new missionary institutes arose and missionary activity truly attained its high point of achievement. Whenever the Church seemed on the point of death, there came a renewal movement, and even while the tide was ebbing the signs of new forward movement were apparent. . . . So we have only to make our way with confidence and remain open to new situations. We are at the end of one world, not at the end of *the* world. Life goes on. Forms may change, more than we would like, but the realities remain. Nothing damages the Church and her mission more than the desire to cling to historically conditioned forms. If we have the courage to let go of structures that are out of date, God will enable us to find new structures through observing the signs of the times. In doing this, we have to allow for a certain insecurity. It is not necessary to have a map of the Promised Land before we leave Egypt.[1]

World Religions

Traditional cultures make little separation among religion, ethics, and aesthetics. All three feed into the self-definition that makes people members of their particular tribe, so all three can generate chauvinism. On the international scene today, the traditional world religions continue to play powerful roles. One has only to mention fundamentalist Islam to summon forth a dozen images, all too vivid and negative, that suggest how forcefully religious passions can impact upon political policies, even to the point of inciting wars. Israel, with its conflicts between secular and fundamentalist Jews; Northern Ireland, with its endless enmity between Catholics and Protestants; and India, with its tensions between Muslims and Hindus, all show the need for dialogue, mutual understanding, and tolerance. In today's global culture, the traditional religions now face the obligation to become promoters of peace, through mutual understanding, and it becomes incumbent on irenicists within each major religious tradition to ride herd on those stirring up hatred and violence.

As Catholics interested in both the political and the religious sides of the interactions between Catholicism and non-Christian religious traditions have thought about these matters, they have naturally reflected on what adaptations of traditional Christian doctrine might facilitate both the missionary advance of Catholic Christianity and a transdenominational progress toward mutual understanding, appreciation, and peace. This has raised considerable Catholic interest in the world religions, and one can now speak of ongoing dialogue between Catholics (and Protestants) and representatives of Buddhism, Hinduism, Judaism, and Islam. Prominent Catholic theologians such as Karl Rahner and Hans Küng have addressed the matter of interreligious dialogue, generally speaking from within Roman Catholicism about the evidences of grace in other religions.[2] More ambitious or radical theologians have started to question traditional Catholic Christology, asking whether the unique claims made for Jesus Christ stand up in light of world religious dialogue or, on the contrary, should be changed to reduce the differences between Christians and other of God's people.

In introducing a collection of essays on this topic, Paul F. Knitter has explained the provocative title of the collection (*The Myth of Christian Uniqueness*) as follows:

Insofar as it might be misleading, the title of this book makes its point. We are calling "Christian uniqueness" a "myth" not because we think that talk of the uniqueness of Christianity is purely and simply false, and so to be discarded. Rather, we feel that such talk, like all mythic language, must be understood carefully; it must be interpreted; its 'truth' lies not on its literal surface but within its ever-changing historical and personal meaning. This book, then, rather than intending to deny Christian uniqueness, wants to interpret it anew. In fact, we suggest, from various perspectives, that the myth of Christian uniqueness requires a genuinely new interpretation—one so different that, perhaps, some will say the word "uniqueness" is no longer appropriate.

Christianity, of course, is unique in the precise and literal sense in which every religious tradition is unique—namely that there is only one of it and that there is therefore nothing else exactly like it. But in much Christian discourse, "the uniqueness of Christianity" has taken on a larger mythological meaning. It has come to signify the unique definitiveness, absoluteness, normativeness, superiority of Christianity in comparison with other religions of the world. It is this mythological sense of the phrase, with all that goes with it, that we are criticizing in this book.[3]

The question for people of Knitter's bent is not whether Christians should consider the pathways of other religious people salvific. Vatican II, in its Declaration on the relation of the Church to non-Christians (*Nostra Aetate*), had already affirmed such a positive view of non-Christian pathways, putting to rest past imagery that portrayed all the unbaptized as headed for hell. The question is whether the traditional Christian understanding of Jesus as the unique incarnation of the divine Logos and so the unique Savior of humankind from sin should retain its force today.

To answer that question, one would have to work through many terminological issues. One would also want to raise queries about the practical implications of either affirming the traditional Christological faith or changing it significantly. Is it possible to update the classical formulations of Christology worked out at Nicaea and Chalcedon, so that one may communicate their substance in new terminology that would carry fewer mythological overtones and be less offensive to non-Christians? Can a Catholic Christian find some points of view from which the Buddha or Muhammad could stand on the same level as Jesus? The problem is the natural multiplication of questions such as these, because of the centrality of the doctrinal matters at issue.

Without prejudging the results of praiseworthy reflection and research such as that presented in *The Myth of Christian Uniqueness*, our own instinct is that Christological accommodation has significant limits. We have worked with the world religions sufficiently to have no doubt that all the major traditions harbor sufficient wisdom and beauty to open people's hearts to God and to assist God's desire to bring all people to salvation.[4] When faced with narrow-minded Christians, we gladly stress the wit of a Chuang Tzu, the holiness of a Gandhi, the monotheism of the Qur'an, the joy of Hasidic Judaism, the sophistication of Hindu yoga, and the detachment of Buddhist wisdom, as evidence that divinity indeed has not left itself without trace anywhere. To put it in the words of Peter in Acts: "Truly I perceive that God shows no partiality, but in every nation any one who fears him and does what is right is acceptable to him" (Acts 10: 34).

On the other hand, from the time of Peter, Paul, John, and the other founders of New Testament faith, Christian conviction has been strong that no one ever spoke as Jesus had, manifestly possessing the words of eternal life, and that what had happened in the incarnation of the Logos and his death and resurrection had brought forth a new creation, once and for all fulfilling God's desire to rework the human condition.

Can one keep faith with traditional Catholic Christianity and not espouse a high Christology such as this? We think not, though naturally we want to remain open to arguments of our betters that might put matters differently. We are confident, however, that it is more important for Christians to be modest about their own ethical performance, theological sophistication, impact on world history, degree of sanctity, and the like than for them to be modest about the

Christ blazing from the pages of the New Testament, romancing their high mystics, and challenging all cultures to a radical honesty and love. If they cannot say that Jesus is the decisive expression of God's love, they will be hard-pressed to prove that their faith is the treasure handed down through the Christian centuries.

International Conflict

Dialogue among the world religions has a value in its own right, inasmuch as it advances people's understanding of both divinity and human nature. It relates to the prime international task of securing peace and justice, however, because the world religions retain considerable ethical influence. Moreover, unless reasonable, moderate people in all the major religious traditions — Christianity, Judaism, Islam, Buddhism, and Hinduism — exert a restraining influence on the fanatics in their midst, religion will continue to be a major goad to violence and warfare. The religious leaders who work for peace rightly receive such worldwide recognition as the Nobel Prize for Peace. Elie Wiesel, the Jewish novelist, Desmond Tutu, the Anglican prelate from South Africa, and Mother Teresa have all been honored for calling humankind to pause, rethink its solidarity, and find alternatives to injustice, discrimination, and warfare.

Catholic authorities have often been moderating forces on the international scene, though perhaps no Catholic agency so stands out for clearly making reconciliation its goal as does the American Friends' Service Committee. Similarly, Amnesty International receives more notice for its work documenting violations of human rights than does any Catholic agency. On the other hand, Catholic individuals and groups have worked with these two agencies and many others all over the globe, and the international character of Roman Catholicism, as recently symbolized in its peripatetic pope, makes it a natural resource when people think of the impartiality and long-range perspective needed in arbiters of international disputes. Thus the papacy has assisted in settling Latin American conflicts, and its steady call for peacemaking and establishing international justice has given it considerable moral authority around the globe. Indeed, the papacy itself does not always realize how much people expect of it, for when it seemed to conduct business as usual with Kurt Waldheim, the Austrian leader accused of Nazi war crimes against Jews and others, it seemed surprised at the outcry.

Let us consider the utilities of a moral authority that is not wedded to the interests of any particular nations, for such a consideration should help to clarify the unity that Catholicism needs if it is to offer various third world churches the freedom essential to their developing a strong indigenous faith. First, there is the mechanism of the papal encyclicals, whose significance is hinted at by their publication in such major secular news outlets as the *New York Times*. The encyclicals increasingly have addressed the whole world, all people of goodwill, and frequently they have received a good reception. Thus Pope John XXIII's *Pacem in Terris* became a well-respected resource for discussions of international cooperation, whereas Pope John Paul II's *Laborem Exercens* stimulated considerable reflection among those open to a middle way between Marxism and capitalism.

Second, there is the international character of both the papacy and Catholicism, which ought to keep some tension in the political loyalties of Catholics. In most eras the papacy has been closely tied with the Italian church, and in the past the Papal States and papal claims to a civil realm clouded the distance the papacy ought to have had from any particular set of national interests. The principally religious nature of the recent Vatican and the election of a non-Italian pope have reminded those with eyes to see that the Catholic Church ought to be above the politics that transpire on the level of state-to-state interactions. Insofar as the popes have kept a good balance between seeking what appeared good for their Catholic people in such areas as Eastern Europe and what served the overall, common good of a world always needing progress toward justice and peace, they have succeeded in what could be a delicate task. It has not always been clear that the papal rejection of political roles for priests and nuns has squared with the pope's own relations with secular powers, but on the whole papal internationalism has made it plausible that representatives of Christ must be careful about choosing sides in military or political conflicts.

The liberation theologians, as we have seen, teach that there are times when loyalty to Christ forces one to take political sides, and Pope John Paul II's siding with the Polish workers against the Communist Polish authorities may well illustrate the correctness of what the liberation theologians have taught. On the other hand, any agency wanting to represent God rather than the special interests of particular human groups has to make it clearer than either the liberation theologians or the popes frequently have done that the Catholic Church wants to be with any people who are truly honest and loving, who are truly seeking justice and peace by legitimate means, and that it is bound to be against any people who are dishonest and hateful, and are not seeking justice and peace or are doing so by morally dubious means.

The usual tack of popes such as John Paul II appears in an allocution he delivered to the South African Catholic bishops in November 1987. Four paragraphs from that address suggest the pope's efforts to strike a balance between advocating fighting for justice and avoiding the sort of partisanship that sparks violence:

To all who have some understanding of the complex reality of Southern Africa, it is obvious that this aspect of your mission is extremely important: proclaiming, guaranteeing and bearing witness to a hope that "does not disappoint us, because God's love has been poured into our hearts through the Holy Spirit." And today I express my full solidarity with you in that hope which springs from the victory of the crucified and risen Christ — that hope which is invincible.

During the past years you have borne witness to hope in many ways, thus showing your people the relevance of Christ's Paschal Mystery for their lives. Year in, year out, you have stood with your people, and at the same time you have withstood such unjust criticism in transmitting to them the uplifting message of the Gospel. In statements that have spanned decades, you have insisted on justice and the need for true reconciliation, proclaimed the commandment of love, and invited your people to prayer and to universal fraternal solidarity. In particular, you have raised your voices on human rights, the fundamental equality of all persons, the defense of the oppressed, and the concrete exigencies of justice throughout our [sic] region.

For its part, the Holy See has been firm in its own proclamation of human dignity. Eighteen years ago, in Africa itself, Paul VI stated: "We deplore the fact that . . . there persist social situations based upon racial discrimination and often willed and sustained by systems of thought; such situations constitute a manifest and inadmissible affront to the fundamental rights of the human person . . ." In 1974, in his address to the United Nations Special Committee on Apartheid, Paul VI appealed once again for the banishment of systematic discrimination. In so doing, he expressed his conviction that "the cause is urgent and the hour is late."

Since then the events of history have confirmed this judgment. At the same time, reason itself pleads that violence not be accepted as the solution to violence, but that it "must give way to reason, mutual trust, sincere negotiations and fraternal love." In the present context of apartheid, a call to conversion becomes ever more relevant and necessary for your people. The only adequate solution to the problem is the conversion of hearts.[5]

John Paul II makes it plain that apartheid, the great symbol of problems between the races in South Africa, is morally unacceptable. He also makes it plain that the root of the solution is conversion to reason and love, so that the primary witness asked of Christians is to such reason and love and against political violence. The pope leaves unanswered the question of a Christian political involvement that would go beyond simply witnessing to reason and love and yet would avoid violence. One can sympathize with any public leaders who have to grapple with so vicious a warping of social life as apartheid, yet one can also suspect that Catholicism will not make its full contribution to lessening conflict around the globe until it incarnates its spiritual wisdom into effective agencies of political change, as the Mahatma Gandhi did for the liberation of India.[6]

World Hunger

Just as world peace would seem to be a cause taking people beyond nationalistic boundaries in defense of the earth itself, so world hunger would seem to be a problem that any internationalist organization would feel required to address. Thus one has found various Catholic relief agencies working in East Africa and the other areas afflicted with famine. *Bread for the World*, an ecumenical group with broad Catholic support, has labored to spotlight the problem of world hunger, make clear its causes, and create effective ways of improving the situation in critical areas.

Writing some years ago, Arthur Simon, the executive director of *Bread for the World*, expressed the difficulty many Westerners have in appreciating the significance or the dimensions of world hunger:

We will not deal effectively with hunger through private acts of charity alone. It is possible for us to feed a hungry family or two — an action not to be despised — without disturbing the conditions that brought about their hunger. In order to make lasting gains against hunger, the concern from which charity flows must also give rise to justice.

Put another way, we should care enough about hungry people to ask *why* they are hungry. And if we ask that question, the answer is as simple as it is complex. People are hungry because they are poor. . . . Poverty in most countries defies the imagination. Peter Drucker has said, "What impresses the outside world about the United States today is not how our rich men live [but] . . . how the poor of this country live" . . . Where in our own cities do you see — as you can in India — people carrying buckets of water from or bathing at public water taps, emaciated cattle wandering in the streets, women scooping up dung for use as fuel, children picking out undigested grains from the dung for food, people sleeping in the streets, urinating in the streets, begging in the streets, and dying in the streets?

. . . In ordinary times really poor people go hungry. When the price

of food goes up, their ranks swell and death increases. The list below
shows the average percentage of disposable income that people from
various countries paid for food in the early 1970s:

United States	17%	Indonesia	50%
Great Britain	22%	Peru	52%
Japan	23%	Zaire	62%
Soviet Union	38%	India	67%

More is at stake than percentages. 17% of $10,000 is one thing; but 60% of
$300 is quite another.[7]

Figures change with the years, and scientists make breakthroughs that suggest
the end of famine. Yet population growth, natural disaster (drought, flood), and
political corruption contribute to keeping billions poor and hungry. Using the
years 1976–1978 as a control group, to produce an average per annum world
agricultural and food production rated at 100, one can take heart from the fact
that in 1986 world agricultural production stood at 119 and world food production stood at 120. However, per-capital food production for the world stood at
only 103, because population virtually kept pace with increased food production. Indeed, in sub-Sahara Africa per capita food production stood at 93 in
1986, although total food production stood at 120. In Bangladesh per capita
food produced was only 96, although total food production was 125.[8]

One could investigate the statistics on housing, land use, fuels, education, and
other indices of the general state of the world[9] and come to conclusions
converging toward what we have suggested about food. The countries that were
poor in 1976–1978 have made only marginal progress in the past decade, when
one considers their situations on a per-capita basis, and in some areas they have
lost ground. The gap between the rich nations and the poor nations has not
closed, although shifts in the international economy and the emergence of the
United States as a great debtor nation have muddied the definition of "poverty"
and "affluence." The fact remains, however, that people in the first and second
worlds can barely imagine conditions in the third and fourth worlds. Any church
claiming an international membership and responsibility has to be haunted by
these figures, and even more by the faces that give the figures flesh.

In addressing members of the Food and Agricultural Organization of the
United Nations assembled in Rome in November 1987, Pope John Paul II
stressed both the global, international overtones of the problem of hunger and
the dangers to the environment posed by the technologies associated with the
developed countries (and so often assumed part of what developing countries
need to escape poverty):

In considering the present state of the food situation in the world, one is
impressed by the contrast between the existence in some areas of large

surpluses, especially of cereals, and the present state of crisis in other areas because people lack sufficient food, to the point that there exists a real danger of death through starvation. In responding to this tragic situation there is an urgent and inescapable need for international solidarity. There exists a duty, now and in the future, to make resources available to those whose lives and welfare are most threatened. This is particularly true insofar as world food production exceeds the needs of the present world population. . . . Above all, a new mentality is required, directed at achieving a genuine form of justice in international relations, in which the interests of the less powerful will be proportionately better defended and the excessive protection of particular interests will be replaced by a sincere pursuit of the true common good of the human family as a whole. . . . Another serious question affecting food and agriculture which must be faced from a global perspective is the urgent matter of the protection of the environment. . . . In developing countries — which are generally characterized by a hostile climate and adverse weather conditions — there is the acute problem of the destruction of the forests in the wet tropics and of desertification in the dry tropics, problems that threaten the feeding of the population. The findings of science must be put to use in order to ensure a high productivity of land in such a way that local population can secure food and sustenance without destroying nature.[10]

Ecological sensitivity is a relatively new note in papal theology, and one should give the papacy credit for expanding its sense of international justice and needs to include physical nature. Indeed, one should give the papacy great credit, overall, for its labor to keep abreast of global problems and suggest what Christian faith says about the technological, political, and economic means proposed to solve them. Catholicism at its international best is a combination of a central authority truly engaged with the problems of the planet as a whole, appreciating their crisscrossings and mutual influences, and myriad believers laboring on the spot in troubled areas, trying to succor the hungry, defend the oppressed, and generally contribute to a more just international order. One can quarrel with particular aspects of the papal or overall Catholic system of strategies, but often that would cause one to lose the forest among the trees. The fact is that the Roman Catholic Church, The World Council of Churches, and the United Nations are probably the most prominent of the relatively few international agencies on whose sense of global requirements and priorities the fate of the human race now rests. As such, these agencies deserve the support of all thinking people, despite the many flaws for which they can be justly criticized. Without their steady concern for reconciling enemies, promoting peace, advancing justice, and aiding the world's worst sufferers, the planet would have little hope for a decent year 2100.

Representative Personality:
Karl Rahner

Karl Rahner (1904–1984) was the most influential Catholic theologian of his age. He appears here as a forerunner of the global thinking that recently has been forced upon Catholicism. Rahner's essay interpreting Vatican II as the first expression of an existentially global Church is the clearest expression of such thinking,[11] but one can find the foundations of Rahner's ability to move beyond a Eurocentered Church in his basic theology, including his famous thesis about "anonymous Christians." It is this thesis that seems most relevant here, for in elaborating it one finds Rahner's foremost achievement: locating the presence of God in the dynamics of human consciousness.

For Karl Rahner (a student of both Thomas Aquinas and Martin Heidegger, the leading German philosopher of the middle years of the twentieth century), human consciousness has a distinct **intentionality**. It is an awareness structured by a natural desire for the beatific vision of the divine essence. Creating and elevating this natural desire, God makes divinity itself the horizon of human awareness. In one of the many lapidary phrases for which his students blessed him, Rahner spoke of God as "the beckoning whither of our now." His students were grateful for such epitomizing summaries because Rahnerian prose typically ran to considerable complexity. Now and then, however, Rahner would say things simply and cogently. For example, another of his best summaries was, "God gives himself."

To call God "the beckoning whither of our now" is to say that God lures us forward. Our existence in time (which fascinated the early Heidegger) is a movement toward we know not what end. We are beings directed toward death, but what does death signify? For Christian faith, it must signify a passover, an opportunity to give oneself to God definitively. Inasmuch as the human heart is always restless, never finding complete fulfillment in anything created, the beckoning of God makes us all pilgrims, possessing no lasting city on earth. Rahner's own theology offers ways of balancing this viatorian quality of human existence, so that a properly incarnational theology would help us feel enough at home in the world to make beautiful sacraments, but restlessness always remained characteristic of both the man and his thought.

This restlessness implied that the second Rahnerian dictum we mentioned, "God gives himself," understood grace as something fully dynamic. Even when God makes divinity the horizon of human awareness, so that the mystery we perceive at the beginning, the depth, the height, and the end of our situation and lives can be called the presence of the trinitarian God, believers have to grope their way through faith and suffering. Rahnerian "realized eschatology" therefore produces a rather sober estimate of human nature and human prospects. Human nature is not corrupt and Christian salvation is not something extrinsic. But the difference between now and not yet remains very significant. While we endure the trials of time, we do well to keep the suffering Christ clearly in our focus. The divine life poured forth in our hearts by the Holy Spirit is a treasure far surpassing all the trials of time, but people of flesh and blood do not appreciate this treasure without considerable chastening. Until they have plumbed their own hearts and come to appreciate the waywardness with which they are shot through and through, they will not understand the utter gratuity of God's best gift: when we were sinners, God loved us.

All this relates to internationalism by the most direct route. What Karl Rahner found in Christian existence he applied to people everywhere. The explicit, "categorical" revelation of human destiny shining from the face of Christ, God's Yes, was implicit in every human situation, even those of people who had never heard of Christ. By the mercy of God, being human and becoming a child of God, a partaker of the divine life, had been made to coincide. All who achieved human authenticity were (with God's help) saying yes to the self-gift God had made clear in Christ. To stake one's time on justice and love was to vote, however inchoately, for Christ's way.

Naturally, Rahner did not wish to deprecate the benefits of the explicit revelation carried by Jesus of Nazareth, the Bible, and the sacramental life of the Church. Naturally, he admitted that he could only defend his view of human destiny on the basis of what he had already accepted in faith. Rahner's was not a **natural theology** trying to operate apart from Christian revelation. But it was a universal theology, applied to all of God's images. It was an interpretation of faith that eschewed any Christian provincialism or egocentricity. The center of Rahner's theology was what God had done in Christ. What God had done in Christ was to make a new creation. After Christ (or from the first existence of human beings, in virtue of Christ), the desires of the human heart were taken up into God's mercy and made requests for a share in the divine deathlessness. After Christ, or in virtue of Christ, the inarticulate groaning of human beings for fulfillment became the Holy Spirit's making a saving prayer.

Since Karl Rahner accepted the full historicity of human existence, he factored into his universalist understanding of grace the social conditioning that all human beings undergo. Much of this conditioning, down the ages, has occurred through religious symbols, categories, rituals, and forms. Thus Rahner thought that one had to infer a positive role for Hinduism and Buddhism, Islam and Confucianism, in the grace-lured lives of the people of India, Arabia, and China. One had to look positively on whatever inclined people to say yes to the hands they had been dealt (without accepting injustice or becoming fatalistic), to whatever spurred them to fidelity in love, honesty at work, and self-sacrifice on behalf of others. The beauty of Rahner's theology is its depth and simplicity. His God is nothing absent, missing, or removed. In all its incomprehensible fullness, its ineluctable mystery, and its demanding opacity, the Rahnerian divinity is the obverse of the challenge of being human — of keeping faith with conscience and finding a way to bless the time one has been given, even when one's life has been sorely trying.

On every continent, in every historical period, the Church has existed only to promote the good living of a faith that would dramatize this radical, universal presence and offer of God's love. The cardinal mysteries of Christian faith — Trinity, Grace, and Incarnation — ought so to predominate over the lesser doctrines in the hierarchy of truths that missionaries, Church leaders, and laity alike would be free to praise and serve God in the myriad divine guises. However anonymously, Christ really is playing in 10,000 limbs and faces only apparently not his own.

Toward the end of an extended interview given not long before his death, Karl Rahner offered opinions about the future of Catholic theology that reflected both his staple convictions about grace and his awareness of the Church's new internationalist situation:

> Previously, with the evangelization that the Church was required to carry on throughout the world, European theology likewise had to be exported. Even today, most of the bishops in the world — in Africa, in Asia, in Latin America — mainly studied in Rome. But if the Church really is or must become an actual World Church, not only in theory but in concrete life and practice as well, then clearly there will also have to be theologies in all the world that differ from specifically European theology.
>
> In time, an African, an Asian, and a South American theology must arise. These will be theologies of the one and same faith. They will also understand themselves as always being under the Roman teaching office. But they will differ from the Western European theology that was, more or less, the only one in the Church, North America notwithstanding, until now. A certain pluralism in theology must exist simply because we are multidimensional human beings, and because the historical and cultural situations in individual countries are not the same. Nevertheless, theology must adapt to these culturally, historically, and even ethnographically different situations.[12]

Glossary

Bhakti: an Indian term for devotional love, passionate emotion directed toward God. The *Bhagavad Gita* legitimizes bhakti and speaks of the believer's being dear to Krishna (the relevant form of God). Thus

Hinduism has thought long and hard about the permutations of devotional love, developing rituals that might import it into every corner of village life, the life cycle, and the individual psyche. Bhakti is a good example of the data that a positive, benign Christian theology of the world religions does well to investigate as a presence of divine grace. However much Christian faith may want to clarify or purify such a phenomenon, by referring it to the death and resurrection of Christ, it misses God's providence if it cannot accept much of what bhakti has meant on Hinduism's own terms and find that salvific.

Intentionality: the directedness of human consciousness, its pursuit of ends or goals. The fact that human thought intends answers, clarifications, truths, goods, meaning, and the like distinguishes it from animal consciousness. True intentionality depends on the ability of human beings to reflect, so that they are both subjects and objects of thought, but for religious analysts intentionality breaks out of the reflective circle, which could be a prison, in acts of transcendence toward an unlimited, divine mystery. Thus Karl Rahner made God the One beckoning from beyond and luring our now toward his heavenly always.

Natural theology: discourse about God that purports to prescind from revelation and deal only with what reason on its own can infer. The praiseworthy effort in much natural theology has been to find bases for speaking with all people of goodwill, many of whom do not accept biblical revelation or Christian tradition. The danger it has always run is of falsifying Christian existence, by pretending that the theologian's own worldview isn't in fact shaped by his or her relation to God in faith.

Discussion Questions

1. What should the shift of the center of the Catholic population toward the third world imply for Catholic ecclesiology?
2. What are the trade-offs that reformers have to make in trying to move from a European theological outlook toward a pluralism of theologies rooted in other cultures?
3. What part does religion now play in global conflict?
4. What do you think makes Jesus Christ unique?
5. How might Roman Catholicism promote a transcendence of nationalism?

6. How does Catholic opposition to South African apartheid epitomize the Church's bind in fighting injustice?
7. How does Christ's gospel suggest one ought to view statistics on world hunger?
8. What is the new mentality that Pope John Paul II would have people bring to bear on international problems such as world hunger?
9. How might God be "the beckoning whither" of your now?
10. What are the advantages and the drawbacks in speaking of good Hindus or humanists as anonymous Christians?

Notes

[1] Walbert Bühlmann, *The Coming of the Third Church* (Maryknoll, N.Y.: Orbis, 1978), pp. 406–407.

[2] See Karl Rahner, "Basic Theological Interpretation of the Second Vatican Council," in his *Theological Investigations*, vol. XX (New York: Crossroad, 1981), pp. 77–89; Hans Küng, *Christianity and the World Religions* (Garden City, N.Y.: Doubleday, 1986).

[3] Paul F. Knitter, "Preface," in *The Myth of Christian Uniqueness*, ed. John Hick and Paul F. Knitter (Maryknoll, N.Y.: Orbis, 1987), p. vii.

[4] See Denise L. Carmody and John T. Carmody, *Ways to the Center*, 3rd ed. (Belmont, Calif.: Wadsworth, 1989), *The Story of World Religions* (Mountain View, Calif.: Mayfield, 1988), and *Interpreting the Religious Experience: A Worldview* (Englewood Cliffs, N.J.: Prentice-Hall, 1987).

[5] Pope John Paul II, ""Violence Breeds Violence," *The Pope Speaks*, vol. 33, no. 1 (Spring 1988), pp. 74–75.

[6] For a poetic entry into the consciousness of third-world peoples, see Margaret B. White and Robert N. Quigley, eds., *How the Other Third Lives* (Maryknoll, N.Y.: Orbis, 1977).

[7] Arthur Simon, *Bread for the World* (New York: Paulist, 1975), pp. 39–40.

[8] *1988 Britannica Book of the Year* (Chicago, Encyclopaedia Britannica, 1988), p. 113.

[9] See the annual reports issued by the Worldwatch Institute entitled *State of the World*. They are edited by Lester R. Brown and published by W. W. Norton in New York.

[10] Pope John Paul II, "Feeding the World," *The Pope Speaks*, vol. 33, no. 1 (Spring 1988), pp. 61–63.

[11] See Rahner, "Basic Theological Interpretation of the Second Vatican Council."

[12] Karl Rahner, *I Remember* (New York: Crossroad, 1985), pp. 91–92.

CHAPTER 17

Tensions in the Church

Catholics Fallen Away
Progressives and Conservatives
Blacks and Hispanics
Ecumenism
Representative Personality: Edward Schillebeeckx
Glossary, Discussion Questions, Notes

Catholics Fallen Away

The "fallen away" Catholic is a stock figure in both literary and academic life, as he or she is in many other places. When novelists want a policeman or private detective who once had an intense religious formation but now has been beaten into agnosticism by the corruption of society, they regularly give him a Catholic background. Mystery writer Robert Parker's central character, the private detective Spenser, is a good example. On the academic circuit, it is commonplace to meet people of good mind and heart who once had close ties to Catholicism but since have drifted into secularism, often because of marital difficulties that Catholic teaching seemed to exacerbate. Perhaps 50 percent of American Catholics now attend Sunday Mass regularly, down significantly from the 1960s, but sociologist Andrew Greeley thinks that a single event explains the drop. His figures suggest, as well, that since the effects of that single event worked themselves out, attendance at Mass has continued to hold steady, though along a lower plateau.

Here is Greeley's summary of what happened:

There was a sudden and sharp decline in church attendance among American Catholics after the birth control encyclical [1968] so that between 1969 and 1975, the proportion of Catholics going to Mass almost every week fell from two-thirds to one-half. The entire change could be accounted for by a simultaneous change in attitudes towards some of the

298

church's sexual ethic — most notably those parts of the church's sexual teachings which dealt with birth control and premarital sex. This decline in church attendance stopped in 1975 and has not resumed, in part because there has been a 'bottoming out' effect with regard to sexual teaching. The percentages accepting the church's doctrine are now so low that it would be difficult to go much lower.[1]

To be sure, many Catholics who do not accept the Church's position against artificial birth control and premarital sex still attend Mass. But the trauma experienced after the birth control encyclical has left a permanent impression. The laity felt betrayed when Pope Paul VI reaffirmed the traditional prohibitions, because they knew that Vatican II had taken up the matter and produced many statements by both bishops and theologians that urged a change in the Church's position. Well-informed laity knew, as well, that a majority of the advisory panel that Paul VI had convened prior to the encyclical had judged that Catholics ought to be free to compose their own consciences on the matter. So the decision expressed in the encyclical suggested that Rome was out of touch with the circumstances of most Catholics' lives and had little regard for the judgment of the laity.

One would not want to hang the entire disaffection of many Catholics from the Church simply on Paul VI's decision about birth control. Greeley himself points out that Catholics regularly express disappointment at the poor quality of the sermons they hear in church, whereas his own analysis of the root difficulties of contemporary American Catholicism is that it has yet to articulate a Church practice (ethical, liturgical, doctrinal) expressing the symbolic changes unleashed by Vatican II. Prior to Vatican II, most Catholics had thought of God as rather stern, a Judge whom one did not want to offend. The return to biblical imagery and a pastoral tone offered an alternative model: a God who was full of love and kindly concern. Responding to this alternative model, the post–Vatican II generations have felt liberated from the legalism and guilt that had predominated in many pre–Vatican II minds. This in turn gave them the confidence to make up their own minds about birth control, premarital sex, divorce, social injustice, and other matters in which they could easily come into conflict with official Church teaching.

Greeley's personal prescription for winning back those Catholics still open to their tradition has been to write novels stressing the problems of passion, love, and faith. The characters in Greeley's novels are all too human, but they discover in their pains and searches that God may still be with them, repeating the patterns of Christ's cross. Greeley's novels have been great commercial successes, riding atop the best-seller lists, but they have been ravaged by the critics. Still, one has to give Greeley credit for trying to carry out the program his sociological analyses have suggested is necessary. He has given up on the

American Catholic bishops, thinking that they simply have written off the sociological data and analyses that he and his colleagues have generated. But Greeley has not given up on Catholics themselves, finding that despite their newly won affluence and lower attendance at Mass, the great majority retain "Catholic" in their sense of identity. For better or worse, they accept the often intense formation they received (especially those who attended parochial schools) and at least occasionally wish they could feel more comfortable in the official institution of the Church. In terms of self-identity, Greeley finds them nearly as Catholic as their Irish or Italian ancestors a century ago.

The population figures on Catholics worldwide show considerable growth, as has been mentioned previously. Most of this growth is in the third world, which has brought the problems of adaptation discussed in the last chapter. In Europe and North America, however, secularization has taken a considerable toll on the Church. Even people still on the Catholic membership lists frequently live most of their lives outside the traditional parish circle. They work and socialize not on the basis of a common religious allegiance but on the basis of whatever bonds they can fashion with the people who drift into their orbit or appeal to them. Thus the statistically serious but not crucial question of fallen away Catholics is perhaps most interesting for what it suggests about the pastoral theology necessary in the first world. Can a deep understanding of faith such as Karl Rahner's illumine what pastoral practice ought to stress? We believe it can, and we believe that the upshot is a series of suggestions akin to Greeley's stress on the religious imagination but worked out with clearer ties to well-defined and thought out theses about the nature and function of the institutional Church.

The Rahnerian equation of being human and prospering by the grace definitively clarified in Jesus Christ suggests that how people are developing, what is happening to their consciousness and conscience, ought to be the crux of pastoral concern. Ideally, people are becoming more honest and loving. Ideally, their prayer and action, in a rhythmic cooperation, are making them more joyous and peaceful. If their Christian faith is clarifying the trials they experience at work, in personal life, when they engage in politics, and when they confront the systematic sources of poverty and injustice in the world, then their faith is doing precisely what it should. Christians get no exemption from the law of progress toward wisdom that rules in all people's lives. One has to be attentive, intelligent, reasonable, responsible, and loving. One has to move from experience, to reflection about what one's experience likely signified, back to what one hopes will be a better next experience.

In the past, Catholic ethics and spirituality suffered from a view of sin that inhibited people's freedom to pursue the experiences that intrigued them. Especially in the area of sexuality, signs labeled "forbidden" shot up as soon as one got a fancy notion, casting a pall on the experiences that are most crucial in adolescence and early adulthood. The Church viewed itself as the guardian of timeless truths, the perfect society reflecting on earth the wisdom and holiness of heaven. It was not a pilgrim Church, all of whose members were simply sinful people condemned and blessed to have to hack their way through. In the measure that future ecclesiology makes the Church more a sacrament of the humanity that people are seeking everywhere, so that it better blesses all honest efforts people make to become more loving, it should throw up many fewer barriers to enthusiastic membership.[2]

Progressives and Conservatives

To the mind of many Catholics, however, accommodation has gone overboard and Vatican II has left much debris in its wake. Pope John Paul II has taken a centrist position about Vatican II, developing many of the social implications of documents such as *Gaudium et Spes* (on the Church in the modern world). On doctrinal and ethical matters, however, he has been slow to sanction developments that would give individual conscience more leeway. Through the Congregation for the Doctrine of the Faith and its head, Cardinal Ratzinger, John Paul II has cracked down on doctrinal and moral theologians who teach that individual conscience may faithfully dissent from official Church positions. Before dealing with the theological problems this has raised, let us try to appreciate what may have been its motivation. As we do, recall that "orthodoxy" means not just "right doctrine" but also "right praise."

Prior to Vatican II, Roman Catholicism had developed a liturgical mystique that offset much of the legalism in its moral theology. This mystique came back to us recently, when we attended an ecumenical service for Ash Wednesday, the beginning of Lent. The preacher was Father Walter Burghardt, one of the leading Catholic preachers in the United States. In keeping with his appearance, the college choir had prepared selections from a Mozart Mass: the Kyrie and the Gloria. The choir did a fine job, and with the outpouring of Mozart's nonpareil melodies came a nostalgia for the beauty Catholic faith once nourished. Here was the highest human art wedded to the most profound Christian sentiments. Here was praise and petition truly befitting a Lord who might give the mercy the human heart so desperately seeks, a Christ who had forgiven sinners, a Lord one desperately wanted to trust would go kindly with one's sinful soul and murky destiny. When it came to the Gloria, the thrill moved down the back of the neck to the base of the spine. Old theses about human beings having been made above all for worship, pure praise of God, rushed back into awareness. It was a proud thing to be a Roman Catholic, a latter-day heir to the tradition that had filled the marvelous European cathedrals with music angels might envy. It was joyous to bow one's head and let the tears flow.

We have experienced similar fits of nostalgia, perhaps sentimentality, in such unlikely places as movie theaters, when, for example, the fare was Robert Redford's *The Milagro Beanfield War* and the focus was traditional Hispanic treatment of the saints. For centuries, poor people, not knowing where to turn, offering the little icon in their shabby home light and food, have beaten back depression and despair. Sophisticates might laugh at their anthropomorphizing of faith, whereas Protestants might think the Reformers' critique of the cult of the saints well founded. Much magic and superstition probably did enter in. But the Catholic "little tradition" so humanized faith and conveyed consolation that the Church now seems wise to have indulged people's recourse to St. Jude, the Virgin, and the rest.

The significance we see in these recollections of times past is the rightness of the conservative's wish to preserve past treasures and not surrender what had been gorgeous art and consoling religious practice to minds shaped by rock music and advertising. The traditional Catholic world had a wholeness and sanity whose loss would be tragic. When conservatives fight to preserve such wholeness and sanity, they fight the good fight.

On the other hand, much in traditional Catholic Christianity was inimical to historical development and kept people from personalizing their faith through free choice. To gain maturity, people have to strike out on their own, listen to their own voices of conscience, and challenge traditions that no longer seem vital and may even be distorting. People may legitimately debate about where to draw the line in such matters, about what traditions still are vital and what have begun to distort genuine discipleship. But the search for a personal, free way is as old as the New Testament and as legitimate as Paul's clarion call, "for freedom Christ has set us free" (Gal. 5:1). The Holy Spirit may smooth away many conflicts, but fidelity to the Holy Spirit does not assure one a rose garden. The example of Jesus proves that.

So, the conservative spokespersons who would veto all protests against Church teaching about birth control or other matters affecting personal life coming within the competence of lay people or professional theologians have a difficult row to hoe. They are bound to seem either ignorant of Church history, which shows in that age after age Christians have sought reforms and new developments, or insensitive to the dynamics of conscience, which is bound to feel the lure of God toward an honesty and love not guaranteed by fidelity to doctrinal formulas. They are also likely to seem like frightened parents who do not trust their offspring to use their heads, learn from their mistakes, and do the best they can before God and their own consciences. Sometimes the conservative position on these matters seeks support from a view of human sinfulness that is dubiously Catholic (since Catholicism does not accept the depravity of human nature taught by Luther and Calvin). Sometimes it calls on an image of papal authority that is hard to square with either tradition or the theology of recent giants such as Rahner, Lonergan, and Schillebeeckx. In such cases, the conservatives' praiseworthy desire to preserve the heritage represented by Mozart masses, a moving cult of the saints, and wise counsel about the relative value of all worldly endeavors, sexual love included, is badly served. Onlookers see mainly a desire to stop history and muffle honest experimentation, which naturally, necessarily, they reject or even despise.

In a balanced view of the ideal attitude toward Vatican II, Cardinal Ratzinger has said,

> It is impossible ("for a catholic") to take a position *for* or *against* Trent or Vatican I. Whoever accepts Vatican II, as it has clearly expressed and understood itself, at the same time accepts the whole binding tradition of the Catholic Church, particularly also the two previous councils. And that also applies to the so called "progressivism," at least in its extreme forms. . . . It is likewise impossible to decide in favor of Trent and Vatican I, but *against* Vatican II. Whoever denies Vatican II denies the authority that upholds the other two councils and thereby detaches them from their foundations. And this applies to the so-called "traditionalism," also in its extreme forms.[3]

One may question the Cardinal's fuller interpretation of the key terms in his statement, as well as his sense of what was implied and licensed by Vatican II. But the balance he would strike between respect for the past and not letting the past become a stranglehold on the present is admirable. Trent and Vatican I were of a piece with Mozart and the cult of the saints. They had much to recommend them in their own day, and they remain part of a patrimony that Catholics of any religious cultivation will want to respect. But Vatican II arose from the same need to discern the signs of the times that had prompted Trent and Vatican I. Its authority is as directly related to the Holy Spirit and mission of the Church as was the authority of its predecessors. The further implication, which we perhaps draw out more boldly than the Cardinal would, is that ongoing interpretation of Trent, Vatican I, and Vatican II is as legitimate as the original convocation and work of those councils was. History never takes a rest. The Spirit is always laboring to help us discover what Christ means here and now. So built into the structures of Church life is the inevitability of doctrinal development, experimentation, failure, controversy, and the other ingredients of a human, struggling Body of Christ. Otherwise Catholicism would not be a sacrament of an incarnate Logos. Otherwise it would be an ahistorical, rather Docetistic entity. In the measure that one keeps a full humanity in tension with the divinity of the Logos, one legitimizes most of what loyal (not extreme) progressives desire and realize is necessary.

Blacks and Hispanics

In this section we consider black and Hispanic Catholics. Black Catholics are a small fraction of the American Catholic population, though in Africa and Latin America black traditions obviously are crucial. In the United States, the accident of being in Catholic rather than Protestant colonial areas accounts for the faith of the long-standing black Catholic families. Both Catholics and Protestants held slaves, and Catholics did not distinguish themselves as emancipationists. Thea Bowman, a dynamic black nun now working in Mississippi and New Orleans, is a descendant of slave grandparents. Her work, which has been featured on the television program "Sixty Minutes," focuses on teaching black children, and other minority children, the reasons for pride in their heritage. With music, dance, and other artworks, Bowman impresses upon her audiences the vitality that Christian worship gains when people express their emotions and celebrate the goodness God has both showered on them and put into their hearts.

In 1984 the American Catholic black bishops issued a pastoral letter on evangelization. Introducing the letter in his collection of documents on American Catholicism, John Tracy Ellis quoted from the letter and wrote:

> "From the earliest period of the church's history in our land, we have been the hands and arms that helped build the church from Baltimore to Bardstown, from New Orleans to Los Angeles, from St. Augustine to St. Louis." Rarely has an official pronouncement of American Catholic churchmen been more suffused with historical memories than is true of this pastoral letter. Moreover, with the exception of the native American Indians, never has the history of a segment of the Catholic community of the United States contained a sadder story than that of the black Catholics. The neglect, the discrimination, and the indifference with which they have been treated account in good measure for the fact that today of the more than 28,000,000 American blacks only about 1,300,000 are Catholics. Yet the black bishops do not dwell here on the negative aspects of their racial history. Instead they acknowledge the improved situation of their people, outline in detail the principal instruments for their evangelization, while candidly admitting the distance that has yet to be traversed before blacks in general, and black Catholics in particular, may be said to have achieved true justice and their rightful recognition within the national community.[4]

The only word fitting the treatment of blacks in the United States is "racist." Simply because of their color, millions of blacks have been treated as inhuman. Slavery and racism remain great expressions of historical evil in the United

States, great signs of what would have to change for the United States to accept the conditions of salvation. In principle, both the Bible and Catholic tradition have allowed plenty of scope to attack slavery and racism. The Pauline notion that in Christ there is neither Jew nor Gentile, slave nor free, male nor female could have sponsored a strict egalitarianism. But the white population would not take this message to heart, and white religious leaders were slow to compel them. Only when Martin Luther King, Jr., consummated the drive of black Americans to gain equality under the law did significant numbers of Catholics join in the change of heart that equality implied.

As Christians have yet to come to terms with the fact that Jesus was a Jew, so they have yet to come to terms with a salvation that ought to render color, sex, and ethnic origin secondary. This applies to Hispanic and Asian-American Catholics as much as to blacks. How Vietnamese Americans, for example, are to fit into the typical Catholic parish remains challenging. How Hispanic traditions, which have always predominated in the Southwest, ought to fit into the overall planning of the American bishops is similarly challenging.

The Hispanic bishops issued their own pastoral message in 1982. In one moving section, their reflections assume the style of a prayer to the Mother of God:

Madrecita, our history is filled with men and women who have been a great inspiration for us. They have struggled and have given their lives that we might have a better life. We give you thanks: for the Indians who suffered the pain of the conquest and who fought for the good of their people; for the Africans, victims of slavery and humiliation; for the missionaries you brought from Spain, men of apostolic vision filled with courage, love and compassion; for our forgotten heroes, who have remained hidden in obscurity; for the saints who blossomed in our lands like the roses of Tepeyac. What joy we feel, *Madrecita*, seeing so many who have brought beauty to our people with the gifts your Son has given to them: the artists, writers, singers and poets who dream; the educators, the learned and the technicians; the businessmen, farmers, professionals and shop owners; domestic and farm workers; migrant workers and labor unions who give strength to the voice of the worker; politicians who truly represent the people; soldiers who have fought to defend freedom. *Madrecita*, a very special thanks for the priests and religious, our co-workers in the vineyard of the Lord, who have given themselves to our people and who have truly loved them. Without the wealth of their talents and the totality of their commitment, the Gospel of your Son would not be proclaimed in all its fullness. We give thanks to God, *Madrecita*, for having called us to be the apostles of your Son in our day. We ask you to walk with us still.[5]

The whole letter is a moving expression of Hispanic faith, wanting only more attention to the accomplishments and needs of Hispanic women.

Black, Hispanic, and Asian-American Catholics bring home to the American church the problems of pluralism we have treated on the international scale. In the history of American Catholicism, differences in ethnic background have caused numerous tensions among the immigrant groups. Nonetheless, despite the difficulties of Poles or Italians living under Irish or German bishops, as white people from the same continent the European immigrants shared much.

In the nineteenth and early twentieth centuries, the desire of the papacy to centralize Church authority tended to sweep aside the special needs of individual countries. Thus Rome was suspicious of the adaptations American Catholics had made to their religiously and ethnically pluralistic situation. Analogously, the white leaders of American Catholicism have been slow to appreciate the special needs of Catholics not fitted into the American mainstream. Local churches have done great service in helping minorities and immigrants adjust to American life, but the precisely religious accommodations necessary to establish a pluralistic American church have only begun to be broached. No doubt pain will attend creating the proper balance between freedom and submission to patterns thought good for the entire American church, but one may hope for greater clarity about the freedom that can flow when all groups profess the same central tenets of faith.

Language perhaps excepted, nothing is more significant than the fact that white, Hispanic, black, and Asian Catholics all are trying to shape their lives to the model of Jesus Christ. Similarly, nothing is more significant than the life of God all Christians share in virtue of their faith and worship. "Practical" people tend to brush aside claims such as these, doubting that creedal agreement could prove more powerful than political interests or cultural forms. Such people forget, however, that creedal words are only faltering expressions of the prior presence and mystery of God. In the measure that their faith is alive, all Christians treasure divinity itself, proclaiming God the center of their lives. Can any Christian say that God cannot be the bedrock foundation of a unity freeing people to be their distinctive selves and ethnic groups?

Ecumenism

The tensions suggested by the lapsing of significant numbers of Catholics, the disagreements between conservatives and progressives, and the efforts of minorities to win their rightful place in the American church certainly relate to social trends in the culture at large, but we have been able to treat them as largely infra-Catholic matters. By definition, ecumenism entails relations with other Christians—mainstream Protestants, Orthodox, and Evangelicals. Vatican II occurred in a climate of optimism about ecumenical relations between Roman Catholics and these other groups. Influenced by the formation of the World Council of Churches in 1948, many Catholics and Protestants alike looked toward the reunion of all the major churches, thinking it a feasible goal.

The twenty-five years since the opening of the Council have produced significant advances toward that goal, especially on the level of theological understanding, but many ecumenists have become discouraged by the lack of progress toward structural unification. Soberly, they have come to realize that all the churches have a great deal invested in their separateness, because for 450 years it has entered into their self-definitions. Thus Catholics have defined themselves in contrast to Protestants and Protestants have defined themselves in contrast to Catholics. Eastern Orthodox have looked on both groups as Western Christians who are significantly out of touch with primitive traditions articulated at the first seven ecumenical councils. At the top, among the leaders of the various churches, words about reunion have far outpaced deeds. Under Pope John Paul II and Cardinal Ratzinger, rising Catholic concern about doctrinal purity and fidelity to the magisterium has further complicated the work of Catholic theologians trying to reach agreements with their Protestant counterparts.

A noteworthy exception to the pessimistic assessment of ecumenical possibilities that has prevailed in the past decade is a work published in 1983 by Heinrich Fries and Karl Rahner, *Unity of the Churches: An Actual Possibility*. Early in this work the authors preview their positions by facing the question of unity and advancing eight theses. Their orientational remarks and first two theses represent some of the most creative ecumenical thinking to have come from Roman Catholic theologians in some time:

What short answer can we give when we are asked whether a unity of faith and church could be achieved in the foreseeable future among the large Christian churches? A difficult question, which most Christians probably answer with no. But we say yes, under the following conditions—which seem to us to be realizable in a relatively short time, if one perceives that this unity is such a radical obligation coming from Jesus that one has the courage to postpone a number of rather insignificant scruples. These, then, are the conditions we mean, although it may be that we have forgotten a few. I. The fundamental truths of Christianity, as they are expressed in the Holy Scripture, in the Apostles' Creed, and in that of Nicaea and Constantinople are binding on all partner churches of the one Church to be. II. Beyond that, a realistic principle of faith should apply: Nothing may be rejected decisively and confessionally in one partner church which is binding dogma in another partner church. Furthermore, beyond Thesis I no explicit and positive confession in one partner church is imposed as dogma obligatory for another partner church. This is left to a broader consensus in the future. This applies especially to the authentic but undefined doctrinal decrees of the Roman church, particularly with regard to ethical questions. According to this principle only that would be done which is already in practice in every church today.[6]

Fries and Rahner go on to consider the further conditions for a real but conscientious union among the major Christian churches, but these first two theses are the foundation of their enterprise. By giving some definite content to Christian faith, and linking it with the earliest expressions of allegiance to Jesus, they assure that the ecumenical Church they envisage will in fact be the Church of Christ, of the apostles, and of the early councils. By developing a second, complementary thesis that allows each of the historically different major Christian communions to retain its own peculiar understandings and expressions of faith, they cut the gordian knot of past ecumenical stalemates. In effect, they claim that most Christian communities already have sufficient unity to justify confessing both their togetherness and their need to do better.

It is no accident that the same Karl Rahner who envisioned a world Church emerging for the first time from the experience of Vatican II participated with Heinrich Fries in working out the conditions for a real ecumenical reunion of the major Christian churches. Relatedly, Rahner had previously clarified the special status of the cardinal mysteries of Christian faith (Trinity, Grace, and Incarnation), developing the notion of Vatican II, expressed in its Decree on Ecumenism (#11), that there is a hierarchy of truths (which implies that not all Church teachings are equally crucial). In all this work, Karl Rahner was attacking the great bugaboo of modern Christian theology, its inability to express the heart of the Christian matter in terse statements that people could correlate with both their own experience and Christian history.

The correlative of Rahner's grasp of the heart of the Christian matter is an unusual degree of flexibility about doctrinal and ethical expressions. Rahner himself remained a European Catholic intellectual, elaborating his theology in dialogue with modern philosophy in the wake of Kant and Hegel. But Rahner saw that the historicity of human nature means constant change and diversity. The more such diversity abounded (as, for example, African and Asians entered the Church), the greater the need for deep, persuasive treatments of the few things that are truly necessary.

The difficulties that Roman Catholic leaders have experienced with proposals for uniting the churches have reflected the leaders' reluctance to accept a view of unity and diversity as radical as Rahner's. Most Catholic officials have considered the Petrine ministry, the role of bishops, and other institutional aspects of Church life closer to the creedal core. At the time of the Protestant Reformation, Roman Catholicism thought of itself as a mother church suffering the rebellion of willful children. Reunion had to be on Rome's terms, which amounted to recanting the convictions that had led to revolt and returning to the fold. Even in the twentieth century the Roman Catholic Church did not join the World Council of Churches, fearing that to do so would compromise its claim to be the one true Church. Roman Catholics have cooperated with many agencies of the World Council, and Vatican II's understanding of the Church gives non-Catholic bodies a high ecclesial status. But questions of authority, power, and Church order have continued to bedevil ecumenical progress, despite the increasing accord that mainstream theologians have achieved on such previously divisive issues as justification, the relation of scripture and tradition, and the sacraments.

Perhaps the key insight remains what Fries and Rahner stress in their beginning: ecumenical union is a radical obligation coming from Jesus (see Jn 17). Most ecumenical meetings nod to this obligation, but then they pass on to questions of doctrinal fidelity or divinely constituted Church authority. Thus many interchurch groups postpone intercommunion (receiving the Eucharist together), understanding their abstinence as both a painful sign of the separations their sins have caused and a stimulus to further work. If such groups could accept the Rahnerian theses, they might find sufficient union in their present existences to justify making intercommunion a sign of both how much they already share and how much the priority remains with the divine grace symbolized in the Eucharistic food.

Representative Personality: Edward Schillebeeckx

Edward Schillebeeckx (1914–   ), a Belgian-born Dominican theologian who has done most of his teaching in Holland, is widely regarded as the Roman Catholic theologian who has done the most to correlate biblical, historical, and doctrinal theology, above all in his two large volumes *Jesus* and *Christ*.[7] Schillebeeckx has encountered difficulties with the Congregation for the Doctrine of the Faith, as a result of his efforts to spotlight the humanity of Jesus and rethink traditional views of Jesus' divinity in light of current hermeneutics and philosophical anthropology. Like many others associated with the Dutch church, he has been more "progressive" than curial theologians have found suitable. For our purposes, the strong links Schillebeeckx forges between faith and social justice are especially relevant. Indeed, when one looks for a Catholic commitment that would both love the Church wholeheartedly and criticize everything in society that falls short of the gospel, including the Church, that of Edward Schillebeeckx quickly comes to mind.

In 1982, after the announcement that Schillebeeckx had won the Erasmus Prize for theology awarded by the Dutch government, Huub Oosterhuis, a well-known Dutch religious poet and journalist, interviewed Schillebeeckx on a variety of topics. The resulting book, *God Is New Each Moment*, amounts to a digest of the main concerns and convictions of Schillebeeckx's work. For this chapter on tensions in the Church, perhaps some exchanges bearing on the prophetic side of Church office are most relevant. Some may find what follows inflammatory. We ask them to remember that Schillebeeckx has few peers when it comes to historical perspectives on doctrinal matters.

O. [Oosterhuis] This book containing our conversations may perhaps be bought by people who no longer feel at home in the Church and who have no possibility of criticizing or accusing that power that you have mentioned. The only way they may have of protesting is just to stay away—the silent "lapsing" that has taken place during the past thirty years or more in the Netherlands and elsewhere. And hardly anyone comes forward now as a candidate for the priesthood! But the bishops are still asking us to pray for new vocations. What do you think ought to be done about this?

S. [Schillebeeckx] On the one hand, our bishops are making it impossible for people to come forward as priests, but on the other hand we are asked to pray for priests. That is a falsification—a falsification of what prayer really is as well. Thomas Aquinas had a relevant comment to make here. In one text he said: There are certain matters in which man has such control of himself that he may act completely on his own account, even if this goes against a possible prohibition issued by the pope. In such a case, a papal commandment or prohibition must be seen as wrong. It has *ipso facto* no validity or power. Then in another text, Thomas says: It is sometimes necessary to oppose a papal commandment, even at the risk of being excommunicated. Thomas is clearly relativizing the Church's hierarchy! For him, the highest authorities are the gospel and the human conscience. If the system is functioning properly, the Church acts as a mediator between the two.

The centralization of the Church's power in the Roman structures began in the eleventh century. Luther's and Calvin's criticism of the Church—and the criticism of the whole of the Reformation—didn't just come down from heaven! The Church had identified itself so completely with a Christ it had made into an absolute ruler—a misrepresentation of

Christ, in other words — that it had in fact become a power structure, an institution that was removed from the criticism of the gospel. Those encyclicals written during the nineteenth century, for example, transferring the power of Christ directly and almost unreflectingly to the pope — they were terribly mistaken. And the same thing is happening again under the present pope![8]

Several contextual remarks may be necessary. First, the Dutch church, from whose midst Schillebeeckx and Oosterhuis were speaking in 1982, was feisty indeed, having established "criticism" as a prevailing mindset. At its best, this mindset was neither completely negative nor destructive. At its best, it was simply the reaction of people who deeply loved the gospel and the Church and so wanted to make them harmonize more beautifully. Second, since 1982 the Roman authorities have demoralized the progressives in the Dutch church, mainly by appointing conservatives to all vacant bishoprics and key posts. The Dutch have been told to toe the line, and because most of the progressives have not wanted to create an outright schism from Rome, most have reluctantly obeyed.

Third, the "lapsing" Oosterhuis mentions has affected all of Northern Europe, as secularism has taken hold. One of the main stimuli to the progressive movement was the sense that only a retrieval of the radical good news of Christ, if need be in opposition to established societal and ecclesiastical policies, might make Christianity attractive again. Since the nineteenth century, many Catholics had found the Church simply another building block in a bourgeois society they considered lifeless and unjust. By the postwar years they were voting with their feet, leaving the Church in droves. The Second Vatican Council, at which the Dutch bishops and theologians (including Schillebeeckx) distinguished themselves, had raised hopes that new life would surge through the Church. The Dutch hoped for reform on such matters as birth control and priestly celibacy that would help them connect local parishes to the family and political lives of the ordinary laity. But such was not to be, for from the time of Paul VI's encyclical on birth control (1968), the papacy grew more adamantly opposed to the Dutch progressives, with the result that some of the best talent left the ministry (Oosterhuis had been a Jesuit priest, poet, and university chaplain).

Fourth, since 1982 Pope John Paul II has taken a fairly radical political line, speaking out sharply against economic injustice, the arms race, and political oppression. No doubt this has pleased Dutch progressives such as Schillebeeckx and Oosterhuis. However, John Paul II has not applied the same mentality to self-criticism within the Church. He has remained committed to the models of papal power Schillebeeckx disparaged, brooking little criticism. The American Catholic bishops recently have done better, turning the spotlight on the Church's own sinful treatment of women. If such self-criticism should spread throughout the Catholic hierarchy, much of what Schillebeeckx has championed might come to pass.

For the goal that makes Schillebeeckx so admirable is simply a responsible freedom. He wants people to be taken over by the good news of Christ, by the person of Christ, and to show the effects of such a takeover by their free-spirited love. Indeed, he thinks that those in love with God ought to mature to a freedom that will demand more of itself than anything strictly legal or official ever can. It will, as well, be confident enough to criticize religious authorities, when they seem to be stifling the gospel or obscuring the radical demands and consolations of Christ's love. In our view, this is precisely the goal that both progressives and conservatives ought to seek. For both, the aim of pastoral practices and doctrines ought to be mature Catholic Christians who deal with one another and the society around them in complete candor, fearless because the Spirit within them molds them in the image of their Master.

Glossary

Docetistic: pertaining to an early heresy that denied the full humanity of
     Jesus, saying that he only seemed to be a normal man but in fact was
     not (was only divine). The term applies, by extension, to all tendencies
     to detract from the fullness of the Incarnation or to deny the
     enfleshment that Christian life ought to achieve. Opposed to Docetism
     is the Catholic instinct that human flesh itself is the prime sacrament
     and revelation of divine grace. Indeed, Catholic instinct ought to be
     that people draw closer to God in the measure that they become more
     human—more honest, loving, creative, and free.

Discussion Questions

1. Why is sexual ethics so prominent among the reasons Andrew Greeley
   offers for the decline in American Catholics' attendance at Mass?
2. How might viewing the Christian community as a sacrament of the
   humanity that God is working to develop everywhere reinvigorate the
   allegiance of Roman Catholics?
3. What was the liturgical mystique developed in traditional Catholicism?

4. Evaluate Cardinal Ratzinger's statement about the councils of Trent, Vatican I, and Vatican II.
5. What is the significance of American Catholics' having been no less racist than other American church groups?
6. What is the significance of the American Hispanic bishops' litany making small mention of women?
7. Why is the separation of the Christian churches a great scandal?
8. What is the main proposal enshrined in the two theses of Fries and Rahner?
9. How does Schillebeeckx's criticism of the Catholic Church reflect the contacts between Dutch Catholics and Protestants?
10. Why should the gospel produce the freedom implied in Aquinas' views of Church authority?

Notes

[1] Andrew M. Greeley, *American Catholics Since the Council: An Unauthorized Report* (Chicago: Thomas More, 1985), pp. 208–209.
[2] See Denise Lardner Carmody and John Tully Carmody, *Bonded in Christ's Love: An Introduction to Ecclesiology* (New York: Paulist, 1986).
[3] Joseph Cardinal Ratzinger (with Vittorio Messori), *The Ratzinger Report* (San Francisco: Ignatius Press, 1985, pp. 28–29).
[4] American Black Bishops, "What We Have Seen and Heard: Black Bishops' Pastoral Letter on Evangelization," in *Documents of American Catholic History*, vol. 3, ed. John Tracy Ellis (Wilmington, Del.: Michael Glazier, 1987), p. 895.
[5] American Hispanic Bishops, "Pastoral Message," ibid., pp. 768–769.
[6] Heinrich Fries and Karl Rahner, *Unity of the Churches: An Actual Possibility* (New York: Paulist, 1985), p. 7.
[7] See Edward Schillebeeckx, *Jesus* (New York: Seabury, 1979) and *Christ* (New York: Seabury, 1980).
[8] Edward Schillebeeckx, *God Is New Each Moment* (New York: Seabury, 1983), pp. 80–81.

CHAPTER 18

Conclusion

The Heart of the Catholic Matter
The Future Crux
Discussion Questions, Notes

The Heart of the Catholic Matter

Catholic Christianity is not, and should not aspire to be, different in substance from Protestant or Orthodox Christianity. The center of all Christianity has to be Jesus Christ, and no church in its right mind either claims a monopoly on the representation of the inexhaustible riches of the Logos Incarnate or wants to battle others whose representations might be complementary to its own. As exposed by the Bible, the early creeds, and the conciliar statements, the meaning of faith in Jesus Christ is a patrimony all Christians share. The wonder is that Christians have so often failed to appreciate this common patrimony and so have reckoned one another enemies. The wonder is that the difference between mainstream and fundamentalist Christians is making enemies today.

Still, there are legitimate differences in style, sentiment, and even theology. Such differences ought to be nowhere near as important as the common substance all Christian traditions share, but in fact they have made a considerable impact on how various Christians have viewed God, themselves, and the world. The heart of the Catholic tradition probably is expressed in the sacramentality it shares with the Orthodox (somewhat in contrast to the Protestant stress on Scripture) and the Roman mentality separating it from the Orthodox. This sacramentality inculcates the notion that God still comes through space and time, flesh and imagery, as God came definitively in Jesus of Nazareth. It reaches out to be catholic, with a small c: concerned with all decent manifestations of divine grace. Thus it embraces politics, sex, food, art, sport—nothing human ought to be alien to Catholicism. To be sure, in many periods Catholics were not faithful to this tradition, being led by Augustinianism or Jansenism or some other tic of the moment to suspect the flesh, look dourly at history, and wish that God had not linked life to sex. And, to be fair, one must note that monasticism, asceticism, negative theology, and other staples of the Catholic tradition always kept front and center how divinity transcends the best of sacraments, how God is never contained by the world and so may reside in the heart like an unquenchable thirst, a restlessness nothing earthly will ever quiet.

Because of this openness to the transcendence of God, Catholicism became a tradition of both/and. The spirit expressed in Søren Kierkegaard's either/or is foreign to most Catholicism. One can always speak of the imperatives of the gospel, the conflict between God and mammon, the hours of decision when two roads diverge. But leaning on this imperative dimension of the gospel has been more characteristically Protestant than Catholic. To the great enrichment of modern biblical studies, Protestants such as Barth, Bultmann, and Tillich stressed the existential cut of the gospel, its demand for personal decisions. The better Catholic scholars recognized the truth in such modern work, without letting it become the entirety of the gospel.

For there is realized eschatology, making all time potentially meaningful, as well as eschatology postponed or imminent or deflected into apocalyptic. There is incarnation as well as death and resurrection. In sending the Spirit, Christ gave the world what it needed to endure history, occasionally even to make history beautiful—relatively worthy of the Lamb that was slain. There are the grace notes attending human mortality, sexuality, parenting, and eating and drinking. The inner melody coming out in such grace notes is the divine life itself, though Eastern Orthodoxy has better plumbed the riches of this life than Roman Catholicism. But the Catholic interest in action and morality, as well as mysticism, did elaborate the work of God in people's hearts, the operative and cooperative grace that supplied the mechanics of purification, illumination, and sanctifying union with God. At its best, then, Catholicism has stood directly on center, beautifully mediating between time and eternity, the rights of both now and then.

Insofar as its relations with Rome have stamped its sensibility, Catholicism is more hierarchical, orderly, legalistic, institution-minded, and perhaps clerical than either Orthodoxy or Protestantism. The Roman genius was for military affairs, imperial administration: serried ranks of cohorts, peerless roads and aqueducts, crisp legal traditions. Trying to baptize the culture tossed into its lap by Constantine, the Church soon established itself as the successor to the pagan religion, utilizing many of its priestly forms. This did not immediately produce the grandiose ideology of the bishop of Rome as the *Pontifex Magnus*, the great high priest, but it sowed the seeds of the regalia and sense of power that later emerged when the papacy saw medieval Europeans looking like sheep without a shepherd.

Catholics are bound to feel ambivalent about this Roman legacy, since the medieval period (considered on all sides distinctively Catholic) had many glories but for centuries now has seemed alien, whereas the modern period revealed the many unattractive aspects of a church preoccupied with its institutional power and forms. The peaking of papal claims at the First Vatican Council one hundred twenty years ago left Catholicism looking hopelessly anachronistic. History was moving away from kings and hierarchies, while Roman Catholicism was solidifying its monarchical imagery. Catholic doctrine, liturgy, and managerial style all reflected the monarchical impulse. The Church presented itself as a pyramid, the laity constituting a broad base far from the peak of power and supposed closeness to God. The laity were to hear, obey, and provide financial support. They were to watch the divine liturgy, as participants in spirit but spectators in fact. Clergy separated from the laity in dress, family life, and training supposedly mediated the otherness of divine things, but often at the price of the graciousness of the God who had pitched his tent in human beings' midst, wore no special garb, consorted with the most needy of his day, and died as a common criminal, the epitome of spirit brought down to dust and blood.

Catholic Christianity is a long tradition, however, and the history of it is consoling as well as disedifying. It has known periods of beauty and periods of grime, times when spirituality reached wonderful heights and times when the Spirit seemed barely flickering. This could make cultured Catholics cynical, or wise, or wondering how to keep their balance on the razor's edge between the two. It could liberate free spirits into even greater freedom, as it seems to have done for Edward Schillebeeckx and Karl Rahner. To know the history of Catholic Christianity is to have antidotes to most excessive reactions to present trends. Neither euphoria nor depression befits. As Ignatius Loyola counseled regarding the emotional ups and down of the interior life, in times of consolation one ought to keep a sober check on tendencies toward enthusiasm, remembering that when the current overflowing of the Spirit's impetus recedes one may well be brought low. Conversely, in times of desolation one ought to recall past consolations, drawing the always relevant lesson that nothing is impossible to God. So an even keel, neither mania nor depression, is the upshot of both Catholic history and Catholic spirituality. All things exit into mystery, as all remain in God's hands. Like Saint Teresa saying, "Let nothing disturb you," the best Catholic theology turns unknowing, the need to go by faith, into strong effort to trust that God will be God, as good as Jesus promised.

Does this mean no passion for justice, no prophetic anger and will to make a better world? At times it has seemed to work such effects at the top of the Catholic pyramid, but through the ranks and along the bottom the Spirit has always raised up critics, naysayers, people determined that the beatitudes still ring out. Thus the works of education and art were not the whole story. Alongside stood the hospitals, the hostels for the poor, and the political movements groping after an effective Christian socialism. The same pope speaking in imagery so remote it might have come from Shangrila could write crisp denunciations of brutality, warfare, and economic injustice. The same tradition that could treat its priests and women like chattel could muster magnificent gestures of humanity and tender love. Catholicism is always both/and. It is never simplistic, naive, purely otherworldly, or purely pragmatic. To the amusement of its adherents and the irritation of its foes, it has been as wise as serpents and as simple as doves. Insiders and outsiders alike might blaze with fury at its arrogance or stupidity, but fair-minded people within and without have had finally to smile at what a piece of work God had made it.[1]

The Future Crux

Moving from description to prescription, let us use the framework suggested by a venerable Catholic dictum resurrected by Pope John XXIII: in necessary things, unity; in doubtful things, liberty; in all things, charity.

The things necessary for Catholic Christian identity clearly lie on the consciences of all Catholics as obligations in faith. To our mind these necessary things include the basic tenets of the classical creeds: the humanity and divinity of Christ, the understanding of divinity as trinitarian, the conviction that God accomplished the definitive essentials of salvation once and for all in Christ, the nature and work of the Church that represents Christ in history and mediates salvation, the forgiveness of sins, the resurrection of the body, and the life of the world to come. There are also the essentials of Christian history: achievements of glory and infamous moral failures, teachings shown to be wise and teachings too quietly discarded, tensions between allegiance to earth and allegiance to heaven, indications of the unearthly holiness of the inspiring Spirit and indications of bestial human sinfulness, seasons when the sacraments were lustrous signs of a truly mysterious God and seasons when magic or credulity reigned, a Bible either ignored or read flatly, two-dimensionally and a Bible speaking words of everlasting life.

It is necessary to affirm the essentials (including the hierarchical constitution of Roman Catholicism), but above all the primacy of the love of Christ, and to brook no diminishment of their crucial importance. It is necessary to preach, teach, and live the astounding message of God's gratuitous love, God's finding a foolishness wiser than human wisdom, a way to redeem suffering and sin through painful yet glorious love. Unity on these necessities or essentials is nonnegotiable. Without them, Christianity could not be, Catholicism would shrivel into antiquedom.

But how does one distinguish between the necessities, requiring unity, and the doubtful things, allowing liberty? Only with the wisdom of Solomon and the help of the Spirit. More practically, by taking the creeds, the gospel, the magisterial statements, the history of Christian faith to heart and, by study and prayer, gaining a Catholic instinct. Instinct of this sort is the result of long living, like the sureness spouses have about the mind of one another, the confidence the masterly scholar has of how a new piece of evidence fits in, the feel by which the skilled craftsperson or athlete solves the new problem. Following Karl Rahner, we have favored a wide interpretation of liberty, correlated with an equally wide field of dubious things, things that can vary with geography, history, and special circumstances. If the necessary things, the cardinal mysteries, the core tenets of faith are plumbed deeply, they free up the intermediate and peripheral things, giving one wide discretion, ample range for negotiation.

Historically, anything that has varied significantly through the ages clearly cannot be substantial in the sense of inert or unchangeable. Doctrinally, anything that has been seriously contested within the orthodox camp should be held lightly. Distinctions are necessary here, of course. The divinity of Christ has been contested, but one should not hold the traditional statements about it lightly (though one should take seriously faithful efforts to translate the tradition for contemporary times, which in turn may create a species of "lightness," at least concerning language and symbols). The law of celibacy clearly is a much lighter, more dubious matter than are the propositions of Chalcedon or the New Testament about the divinity and humanity of Christ. The obligation to confess one's sinfulness, pray, and celebrate the good news of Christ's resurrection obviously is imperative, whereas the obligation to accept the current curial position on the participation of priests and nuns in politics, or on the use married people may make of new medical technology,[2] probably is relative.

"Relative" does not mean nonexistent. It simply means accepting the fact that specifics of behavior are not subject to the same certitudes and cannot command the same importance as general imperatives of Christian existence. It further means enjoying the freedom this realism carries in its train and not letting anyone convince one, against history, common sense, and excellent theology, that there are authorities higher than the gospel and personal conscience.

Third, and most important, in all things charity and warm love, should prevail. This may be read as a platitude, or it may be intuited to be the most important sentence in this or any other book about Catholicism, Christianity, religion, or human nature. When the Johannine theologians wrote that God is love, and that those who abide in love abide in God and God in them, they put their finger on the most helpful and dangerous of the Christian counsels to wisdom. Augustine did the same when he told people to love and do what they would. Love covers a multitude of sins, because love is the presence of God in our midst cleansing our hearts, quickening our faith and hope, making us members of one another, offering us the peace that surpasses understanding.

These phrases, sometimes lyrical and sometimes flat, have echoed down the Catholic tradition, like Gregorian chants bouncing off the stiff, cold walls of medieval cathedrals. When the cathedrals were filled with such glorious sounds, their coldness vanished, they became houses of the living God, than whom there was nothing more supple and lovely. The same with love welling up in the human heart. No excess, wrongheadedness, or danger of overenthusiasm ever led the canonical theologians and saints to back away from the primacy of love in either Christ's life or the existence of Christ's followers. In Catholic tradition, love is the friend of reason, not the enemy, and reason serves love well, defending it against itself when it would turn purely sensual, or so otherworldly its feet left the ground, or in any way divorced from the limits consequent on the Incarnation. But love remains the crux, whereas reason is best honored when it most enables love, supports love, and clears love's way.

So in all things one must love; one is privileged to try to love. In all things one has to hope and pray that the love of God is developing a rationale, a usefulness, that will be redemptive. Take the worst case of recent memory, the Nazi Holocaust of 6 million Jews, as focused recently in a review by Cynthia Ozick of a book by Primo Levi, a survivor of Auschwitz: "What we learn overwhelmingly from Levi is this: If there is redemption in it, it cannot be Auschwitz; and if it is Auschwitz, it is nothing if not unholy."[3] Ozick herself provides some nuances and implies some qualifications, and there is a sense in which Catholic theology could accept her sentence. Limiting oneself to what the mind could find or the senses might feel in Auschwitz, the healthy, proper, required response would be utter hatred of Auschwitz, utter abhorrence and rejection of what the Nazis meant Auschwitz to be and accomplished there.

But what the mind can find or the senses may feel is never the last word in any theology, Christian or Jewish. And whereas Christian theology can agree with Jewish theology about the presumption of speaking about the mind of God (and whereas it should leave to Jewish theology whether Ozick's sentence squares with Jewish orthodoxy), Christian theology has to say that nothing, not even Auschwitz, can separate people from the love of God, whether or not they can feel such love, find it credible, or keep themselves from giving up all hope. God is not defeated by the Auschwitzes of life, anymore than God is defeated by the trash of all the cultures that have rushed to forget Auschwitz, the cross of Christ, the resurrection of Christ, or other calls to be serious.

God had a presence in Auschwitz, if only usually in the mode of missingness. And God had victories in Auschwitz, times when the evil was not allowed its full way, times when people revolted and did not give in. So even in hateful, crushing, apparently defeating circumstances, charity applies. On the cross, Christ had no victory, no glory, nothing comely about him. All seemed and in some ways was emptied, sullied, fractured. Yet Christians have made the cross their foremost symbol of God's love and triumph, because they have intuited how the cross was fulfilled in the resurrection. Charity is as paradoxical, as profound, as that: love stronger than evil and death, love showing itself to be not just alpha and omega but also the ink of all the useful letters in between.

Discussion Questions

1. Sketch the Catholic essentials in terms of the doctrines of God, salvation, the Church, and eschatology.
2. Why is historical study necessary for discerning the heart of the Christian matter?
3. How is Christ the one thing necessary for Christian unity?
4. Describe the love of God: what it looks like, how it feels, the first and main thoughts and emotions it creates.

Notes

[1] See two works by Lawrence S. Cunningham, The Catholic Heritage (New York: Crossroad, 1983) and The Catholic Experience (New York: Crossroad, 1985).

[2] See Edward V. Vacek, S.J., "Vatican Instruction on Reproductive Technology," Theological Studies, vol. 49, no. 1 (March 1988), pp. 111–131.

[3] Cynthia Ozick, "The Suicide Note," The New Republic, March 21, 1988, p. 35, in review of Primo Levi, The Drowned and the Saved (New York: Summit Books, 1988). We owe this reference to our friend and colleague Grace Mojtabai.

Bibliography

HISTORY

BUCKLEY, MICHAEL J. *At the Origins of Modern Atheism.* New Haven: Yale University Press, 1987.

CHADWICK, HENRY, AND OWEN CHADWICK, EDS. *Oxford History of the Christian Church.* Oxford, England: Oxford University Press, 1977 ff.

CHADWICK, OWEN, ED. *The Pelican History of the Church.* Hammondsworth, England: Pelican, 1960 ff.

CUNLIFFE-JONES, HUBERT, ED. *A History of Christian Doctrine.* Philadelphia: Fortress, 1980.

DOLAN, JAY P. *The American Catholic Experience.* Garden City, N.Y.: Doubleday, 1985.

ELLIS, JOHN TRACY, ED. *Documents of American Catholic History.* Wilmington, Del.: Michael Glazier, 1987.

FREND, W. H. C. *The Rise of Christianity.* Philadelphia: Fortress, 1984.

HENNESSEY, JAMES. *American Catholics.* New York: Oxford University Press, 1981.

JEDIN, HERBERT, ED. *History of the Church.* New York: Crossroad, 1980 ff.

MCGINN, BERNARD ET AL., ED. *Christian Spirituality: Origins to the Twelfth Century.* New York: Crossroad, 1985.

PELIKAN, JAROSLAV ET AL. "Christianity," in *The Encyclopedia of Religion,* ed. Mircea Eliade. New York: Macmillan, 1987, vol. 3, pp. 348–431.

PELIKAN, JAROSLAV. *The Christian Tradition.* Chicago: University of Chicago Press, 1971 ff.

RAITT, JILL, ED. *Christian Spirituality: High Middle Ages and Reformation.* New York: Crossroad, 1987.

WORLD VIEW

BROWN, RAYMOND ET AL., ED. *The Jerome Biblical Commentary.* Englewood Cliffs, N.J.: Prentice-Hall, 1989.

COOKE, BERNARD. *Ministry to Word and Sacraments.* Philadelphia: Fortress, 1976.

CORIDEN, JAMES ET AL., ED. *The Code of Canon Law.* New York: Paulist, 1985.

CUNNINGHAM, LAWRENCE S. *The Catholic Experience.* New York: Crossroad, 1985.

CUNNINGHAM, LAWRENCE S. *The Catholic Heritage.* New York: Crossroad, 1983.

HAUGHTON, ROSEMARY. *The Passionate God.* New York: Paulist, 1981.

KOMONCHAK, JOSEPH ET AL., ED. *The New Dictionary of Theology.* Wilmington, Del.: Michael Glazier, 1987.

LONERGAN, BERNARD. *Method in Theology.* New York: Herder & Herder, 1972.
MCBRIEN, RICHARD P. *Catholicism.* Minneapolis: Winston, 1980.
MCDONAGH, SEAN. *To Care for the Earth.* London: Chapman, 1986.
NEUNER, JOSEF, AND HEINRICH ROOS. *The Teaching of the Catholic Church.* Staten
    Island, N.Y.: Alba House, 1967.
RAHNER, KARL. *Foundations of Christian Faith.* New York: Seabury, 1978.
SCHILLEBEECKX, EDWARD. *Christ.* New York: Seabury, 1980.
SCHILLEBEECKX, EDWARD. *Jesus.* New York: Seabury, 1979.

RITUAL AND ETHICS

ANONYMOUS. *Meditations on the Tarot.* Amity, N.Y.: Amity House, 1985.
CAHILL, LISA SOWLE. *Between the Sexes.* New York: Paulist, 1985.
CONN, JOANN WOLSKI, ED. *Women's Spirituality: Resources for Christian
    Development.* New York: Paulist, 1986.
CURREN, CHARLES, AND RICHARD MCCORMICK. *Readings in Moral Theology.* New
    York: Paulist, 1979 ff.
FARMER, DAVID HUGH, ED. *The Oxford Dictionary of the Saints,* 2d ed. New York:
    Oxford University Press, 1987.
GREMILLION, JOSEPH, ED. *The Gospel of Peace and Justice.* Maryknoll, N.Y.: Orbis,
    1976.
HOLLENBACH, DAVID. *Claims in Conflict.* New York: Paulist, 1979.
JONES, CHESLYN ET AL., ED. *The Study of Liturgy.* New York: Oxford University
    Press, 1978.
JONES, CHESLYN ET AL., ED. *The Study of Spirituality.* New York: Oxford University
    Press, 1986.
JUNGMANN, JOSEPH. *The Mass of the Roman Rite.* New York: Benziger, 1951.
MAGUIRE, DANIEL. *A New American Justice.* New York: Winston, 1980.
MCNAMARA, VINCENT. *Faith and Ethics.* Washington, D.C.: Georgetown University
    Press, 1985.
O'CARROLL, MICHAEL. *Theotokos.* Wilmington, Del.: Michael Glazier, 1985.
POWER, DAVID. *Unsearchable Riches.* New York: Pueblo, 1984.

CONTEMPORARY TRENDS

BARRETT, DAVID B., ED. *World Christian Encyclopedia.* New York: Oxford
    University Press, 1982.
CARMODY, DENISE LARDNER. *The Double Cross: Ordination, Abortion, and Catholic
    Feminism.* New York: Crossroad, 1986.
CONGAR, YVES. *Diversity and Communion.* Mystic, Conn.: Twenty-Third
    Publications, 1985.
DULLES, AVERY. *A Church to Believe in.* New York: Crossroad, 1983.
FRIES, HEINRICH, AND KARL RAHNER. *Unity of the Churches.* New York: Paulist, 1985.
GREELEY, ANDREW M. *American Catholics Since the Council.* Chicago: Thomas
    More, 1985.
GUTIERREZ, GUSTAVO. *On Job.* Maryknoll, N.Y.: Orbis, 1987.
HICK, JOHN, AND PAUL KNITTER, EDS. *The Myth of Christian Uniqueness.* Maryknoll,
    N.Y.: Orbis, 1987.

KÜNG, HANS. *Christianity and the World Religions.* Garden City, N.Y.: Doubleday, 1986.
MURNION, PHILIP J., ED. *Catholics and Nuclear War.* New York: Crossroad, 1983.
RICHARD, LUCIEN, ED. *Vatican II: The Unfinished Agenda.* New York: Paulist, 1987.
SWIDLER, LEONARD, AND HERBERT O'BRIEN, EDS. *A Catholic Bill of Rights.* Kansas City, Mo.: Sheed & Ward, 1988.
WEAVER, MARY JO. *New Catholic Women.* San Francisco: Harper & Row, 1985.

Index

Birth control, 268
  and decline of church attendance, 298–299
  Vatican II, 95–96
Bishops (American) pastoral letters, 255–258
Black Catholics, 304–306
Boethius, 49
Boff, Leonardo, liberation theology, 251
Book of Revelation, 31, 38
  teachings of, 32–33
Bowman, Thea, 304
Bread for the World, 290
Brebeuf, Jean de, 90
Brownson, Orestes, 91
Burghardt, Father Walter, 301

C

Calvert, Cecil, 88
Calvin, John, 62–63
  and Protestantism, 62–63
Camus, Albert, 162
Canisius, James, 71
Carmelites, 198
  Teresa of Avila and, 205–206
Carroll, Charles, 90
Carroll, John, 90
Cathari, 116
Catherine of Siena, 57, 153
  as early reformer, 58–59
Catholic, use of term, 2
Catholic Counter-Reformation, 64, 69
Catholic Things, The (Haughton), 275
Catholic views
  Creation, 105–108
  ecology, 111–114
  eschatology, 156–171
  history, 114–116
  Incarnation, 122–134
  redemption, 140–154
  Revelation, 108–111
Catholic Worker, 259, 261
Catholic worship
  Eucharist, 178–180
  liturgical cycle, 175–178
  sacraments, 179–188
Caussade, Père de, 199
Celasius, Pope, 45
Celibacy, monks, 39
Cerularius, Michael, 47
"Challenge of Peace," 256–257
Chardin, Teilhard de, 111, 115
Charismata, 129, 212
  definition of, 224
Charlemagne, 46
China, Church and, 283
Chinese Rites Controversy, 67, 283
Christmas, characteristics of, 176–177
Christogenesis, 115
Christology, 122–125
  basis of, 122–123
  definition of, 8
  God the Father in, 124–125

  high Christology, 132, 137
  humanity/divinity of Jesus in, 124
Christ (Schillebeeckx), 309
Church attendance, decline, 298–299
Cistercians, 198, 199
City of God, The (Augustine), 53–54
Clergy, holy orders, sacrament of, 187–188
Cloud of Unknowing, The, 116
Coenobitic life, 195
College of cardinals, 47
Colloquy of Marburg, 62
Colossians, 17, 31
Communion, sacrament of, 183
Communion of saints, 38, 161, 164
  definition of, 54
Confessions (Augustine), 52
Confirmation, sacrament of, 182
Congregation for the Doctrine of the Faith, 301
Congregation for the Propagation of the Faith, 67
Conn, Joann Wolski, 272
Conservatism, and Church, 301–303
Constantine, 39, 40, 41, 43
Constantinople, First Council, 42
Constitution of United States, 91, 94
Constitutions (Loyola), 69
Contemplative life, 194–197
  in communal setting, 195
  compared to creative process, 196
  criticism of, 207
  solitary life, 195
  trials of, 207
  use of term, 195
Copernicus, 77
Council of Chalcedon, 42–43
Council of Constance, 58, 59
Council of Ephesus, 42
Councils of Nicaea, 41–43, 124
Council of Orange, Second, 53
Council of Trent, 65–66, 181
Counter-Reformation period, 21
Covenant Law, 14
Cranmer, Thomas, 77
Creation
  beginning of world, 106–107, 112
  Catholic views, 105–108
  creation of man, 107
  disobedience of man, 107
  Genesis, 106–107
  priestly source, 107
  Yahwist, 107
Cromwell, Oliver, 116
Curran, Charles, 238

D

Dark Ages, 46
Darwin, Charles, scientific contributions of, 78–79
Day, Dorothy, 260, 261
Death
  Christ's death, view of, 147
  life in view of death, 148

Declaration of Independence, 82, 90
Decree on Religious Liberty, 95
Deism, 81, 82
Descartes, René, philosophy of, 80
Deterrence, 256-258
  dimensions of, 256-257
  John Paul II on, 256-257
"Devotio Moderna," 59
Devotions
  doxology, 201
  Hail Mary, 201
  Our Father, 200-201
  rosary, 200, 202
Diatribe about Free Will (Erasmus), 60
Diderot, 80
Divine Comedy (Dante Alighieri), 168-170
Divinization, 13, 51
  definition of, 34
Docetistic, 303
  definition of, 312
Dodd, C.H., 261
Dominic, Saint, 20
Dominicans, 199
Donation of Constantine, 45-46
Doxology, 201
  definition of, 208

E
Eastern Christianity, schism of 1054, 43, 46
Eastern Europeans, immigration to America,
    92-93
Easter Sunday, characteristics of, 177-178
Ecclesiology, 128-131
  distinctive/characteristic nature of
      Catholicism, 129-130
  hierarchial structure of Christianity and, 129
Eckhart, Meister, 50, 51
Ecology, Catholic view, 111-114
Economic justice, Catholic view, 219-220
Ecumenical councils, 40-44
  Council of Chalcedon, 42-43
  Council of Ephesus, 42
  First Council of Constantinople, 42
  Nicaea II, 43
  Nicaea, 41-42
  Sixth, 47
Ecumenism
  goal of, 2
  theses on unity, 307-308
Edict of Milan (313), 38
Ellis, John Tracy, 304
Enlightenment, 80-82
  approach to Jesus, 81
  and Catholicism, 81-82
Epistles, Pastoral Epistles, 25-29
Erasmus, Desiderius, 57
  as early reformer, 59-60
Eschatology
  common understanding of, 158, 161
  heaven, 162-164
  hell, 165-167
  judgment, 159-162

pilgrimage, 156-159
realized eschatology, 261
Ethics. *See* Personal ethics; Social ethics
Eucharist, 133, 151
  Mass and, 178-180
Evil, examples of, 140-142
Existential, 237
  definition of, 241-242
Exodus, 14, 250
Extreme unction, 66

F
Faith, nature of, 142-143
False Decretals, 45
Family life, Church and, 269-271
Feminists, 263
  definition of, 278
Filioque, 47
Finitude, Catholic view, 140-143
Fiorenza, Elisabeth Schüssler, 264, 275
Franciscan Tertiaries, 152
Francis of Assisi, 20, 51, 111, 198
  Franciscans, founding of, 151-152
  mysticism of, 152-153
French Revolution, concern to Catholicism,
    83-84
Freud, Sigmund, scientific contributions of, 79
Fries, Heinrich, 307-309

G
Galatians, 30
Galileo, scientific contributions of, 77-78
Gaudium et Spes, 301
General resurrection, 151
  definition of, 154
Genesis, Creation, 106-107
Germans, immigration to America, 91, 92
Gnosis, 181
  definition of, 192
Gnostics, 18, 41, 192
God
  the Father, and Jesus, 124-125
  See also Holy Spirit; Jesus; Trinity
God Is New Each Moment (Oosterhuis), 310
Good Friday, 177
Grace of God, 20
  Augustine on, 52, 53
Grand Inquisitor, 73
Great Schism, 58, 59
Greek roots of Catholicism, 16-19
Greeley, Andrew, 298
Gregorian Reform, 47
Gregory I, Pope, 46
Gregory VII, Pope, 47
Gregory IX, Pope, 73, 152
Gregory XI, Pope, 58
Gregory XV, Pope, 67
Gutierrez, Gustavo, liberation theology, 251

H
Hail Mary, 201
Harren, Mary, 258-261

K

Kant, Immanuel, philosophy of, 80
Kataphatic theology, 132
Kempis, Thomas à, 51, 59, 115
Kenosis, 128
Kierkegaard, Soren, 185, 315
Kingdom of God, 20, 157
Knitter, Paul F., 285
Know-Nothings, 91
Ku Klux Klan, 94

L

Lainez, James, 71
Lalamant, Jerome, 90
Last anointing, sacrament of, 185–186
Latin America, liberation theology, 250–252
Lent, characteristics of, 177
Leo, Pope, 43
Leo the Great, 45
Leo III, Pope, 47
Leo IX, Pope, 47
Leo XIII, Pope, 94, 254
Liberation theology, 20, 288
    Biblical roots, 250–251
    Marxist analysis in, 251–252
    proponents of, 251
Limbo, 161
    definition of, 170
Little Flowers of St. Francis, The, 152–153
Liturgical cycle, 175–178
    Advent, 176
    Ascension Thursday, 178
    Christmas, 176–177
    Easter Sunday, 177–178
    Holy Week, 177
    Lent, 177
    Pentecost Sunday, 178
Locke, John, 79
Logos, 22, 41–42, 124
Lollards, 58
Lonergan, Bernard, 238–241
    theological method, 238–239
Love, John's gospel, 31
Loyola, Ignatius, 67, 113
    Society of Jesus, 69–71
    writings of, 69–72
Luke, theology of, 24–25
Luther, Martin, and Protestantism, 60–62

M

McBrien, Richard P., 129–130
Maccabees, 15
Magisterium, 237
    definition of, 242
Magnificats, 116
    definition of, 120
Magnus, Albertus, 134
Manicheanism, 72
Manual of a Christian Soldier (Erasmus), 60
Mark, theology of, 22–23
Marriage, Catholic view, 186–187
Martyrdom, 38, 90

Marxism
    concern to Catholicism, 84
    liberation theology and, 252
Mary (mother of Jesus), 42, 51–52
    Annunciation, 115
    Hail Mary, 201
    as intercessor, 161
    magnificats, 120
    Marian piety, 85
Maryland Colony, as Catholic colony, 88–90
Mary Magdelene, as saint, 204, 212
Mass, 178–180
    Eucharist and, 179–180
Matrimony, sacrament of, 186–187
Matthew, 21
    theology of, 24
Maurin, Peter, 261
Mechtilde of Magdeburg, 50
Melanchthon, Philipp, 62
Merit, 65
Messiasgeheimnic, 23
Mill, John Stuart, 84
Miranda, José, liberation theology, 251
Missionary work, 66–69, 90
    America, pre-Civil War, 90
    early Church and, 67
    Jesuits, 71
    modern era, 69
    sixteenth century, 67–69
Missions, 161
    definition of, 170–171
Modern period, 76–99
    American Catholicism, 88–96
    Enlightenment, 79–82
    industrialization, 86–88
    political development, 82–85
    Pope John XXIII, 96–99
    science, 76–79
Monasticism, 39–40
Moore, Sebastian, Christology, 123
More, Thomas, 59, 81
Mortal sin
    as rejection of divine love, 228, 230–231
    sexual sins as, 227
Moses, 114, 250
Mother Teresa of Calcutta, accomplishments/
    work of, 221–224
Mystagogy, definition of, 55
Mysticism, 50–52
    errors in understanding related to, 197, 199
    Eucharist as sensible mysticism, 198
    German mystics, 50–51
    Julian of Norwich, 116–119
    major influences, 50
    orders founded on, 198
    perseverance and, 199
Myth of Christian Uniqueness, The (Knitter),
    285–286

N

Natural laws, 98
    in Christian tradition, 213–214